SPINE SL FADED

C8920

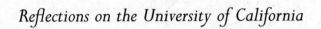
Reflections on the University of California

Reflections on the University of California

FROM THE FREE SPEECH MOVEMENT TO
THE GLOBAL UNIVERSITY

Neil J. Smelser

UNIVERSITY OF CALIFORNIA PRESS
BERKELEY LOS ANGELES LONDON

University of California Press, one of the most
distinguished university presses in the United States,
enriches lives around the world by advancing scholarship
in the humanities, social sciences, and natural sciences.
Its activities are supported by the UC Press Foundation
and by philanthropic contributions from individuals
and institutions. For more information, visit
www.ucpress.edu.

University of California Press
Berkeley and Los Angeles, California

University of California Press, Ltd.
London, England

Library of Congress Cataloging-in-Publication Data

Smelser, Neil J.
    Reflections on the University of California : from
the free speech movement to the global university /
Neil J. Smelser.
        p.   cm.
    Includes bibliographical references and index.
    ISBN 978-0-520-26096-2 (cloth : alk. paper)
    1. University of California, Berkeley—History.
I. Title.
    LD758.S64   2010
    378.794'67—dc22

                                2009033297

Manufactured in the United States of America
19   18   17   16   15   14   13   12   11   10
10   9   8   7   6   5   4   3   2   1

This book is printed on Cascades Enviro 100, a 100%
post consumer waste, recycled, de-inked fiber. FSC
recycled certified and processed chlorine free. It is acid
free, Ecologo certified, and manufactured by BioGas
energy.

CONTENTS

Introduction

UNLIKE MOST ACADEMICS AT MAJOR research universities in the United States, I spent most of my professional career at one institution. I joined the Berkeley faculty as an assistant professor of sociology in Fall 1958 at the age of twenty-eight, just after receiving my PhD from Harvard. I remained at Berkeley for thirty-six years, retiring formally in 1994 at the age of sixty-four, at the time of the third VERIP—the incentive scheme put forward by the University of California in the early 1990s to induce high-salaried senior faculty to retire early. At that time, however, I assumed another position, director of the Center for Advanced Study in the Behavioral Sciences at Stanford, where I served until 2001. I then returned to Berkeley; I have taught a course almost every year in the School of Public Health, taught at other universities on several occasions, taken on miscellaneous assignments as a Berkeley emeritus, continued my research and writing, and maintained contacts in the university community.

In my eventful years at the University of California, I had occasion to touch many parts of that special elephant, thereby gaining perspectives and knowledge from different points of view. My involvements were the following:

The academic faculty. I not only taught in my department, but in my capacity as University Professor of Sociology (1972–94) I also gave courses of instruction on five other campuses: Davis, Irvine, San Diego, San Francisco, and Santa Cruz.

The department. I served two terms as chair of the Berkeley sociology department, 1975–77 and 1991–92.

Committee life. I served on and chaired numerous committees at the department, Academic Senate, Berkeley administration, and systemwide administration levels.

Student services. I was a practicing therapist and member of the psychiatry department, Cowell Hospital, Berkeley campus, 1966–72 and 1981–82.

Organized research units. On the Berkeley campus I was affiliated with the Institute of Industrial Relations in the 1960s; associate director of the Institute of International Studies, 1969–70, 1972–73, 1981–89; and acting director of the Center for Studies in Higher Education, 1987–89.

The education abroad program. I served as director of the UC Education Abroad Program for the United Kingdom/Ireland, 1977–79.

The Academic Senate. I chaired the Policy Committee of the Berkeley Division, 1971–72; chaired the Committee on Educational Policy, 1979–80; chaired the Berkeley Division, 1982–84, and chaired the Systemwide Academic Council and Assembly, 1985–87.

The chancellor's office. In 1965 I was assistant to the chancellor for student political activity (see chapter 1), assistant chancellor for educational development, 1966–68, and was called in as an informal advisor on subsequent occasions.

The office of the president. In 1993–94 I served as special advisor on long-term planning to President Jack Peltason and Vice-President and Provost Walter Massey. In addition, I worked as critic and advisor to both Clark Kerr and David Gardner, past presidents of the university, as they prepared their respective memoirs.

The board of regents. I was a nonvoting but regularly attending and participating faculty representative on the board, 1985–87.

The national laboratories. During my period as faculty representative to the regents I became acquainted with many issues facing the Los

Alamos, Livermore, and Lawrence Berkeley laboratories. Subsequently, between 1989 and 1997, I was a member of the laboratory advisory committees appointed by the office of the president and visited and participated in reviewing each laboratory once a year, sometimes more often.

Out of these involvements emerged a great deal of knowledge and writing about the university. At the end of my service in the office of the president, 1993–94, I took it upon myself to write a long advisory memo on governing the university (chapter 7). In serving on a special chancellor's committee in 2003 that occupied itself with how to predict and deal with political surprises affecting the Berkeley campus, I wrote an analytic and historical memorandum on the topic (chapter 3). In addition, during my last fifteen years on the Berkeley campus, I chaired three important committees and commissions, one reviewing Berkeley's Graduate School of Education (chapter 8), one for the office of the president on the lower division education in the entire UC system (chapter 9), and one on intercollegiate athletics at Berkeley (chapter 10). Out of each of these committees came a document known as a "Smelser report." I justify their inclusion in this volume on several grounds: (a) even though each was the product of a working group, I took full responsibility for writing each report; the prose is mine, with input from members of the committee or commission; (b) each of the documents contains substantial scholarship and analysis; (c) although each was available to relevant audiences in the university community, none was actually published; (d) all three reports caught wide attention and none passed from the scene without having some impact; and (e) the issues raised on each topic have remained alive in the university up to the present. I conclude the volume with a spoof on academic reports—a saga of hosting nearly a hundred education-abroad students for Thanksgiving dinner in London (chapter 11).

A final feature of my career is that the sociology of higher education has been among my research interests. As an expression of that interest I co-edited and wrote half a book on the history of conflict and change in the University of California between 1950 and 1970 (Smelser, 1973a); coauthored a book on the academic job market, including a case study of hiring at Berkeley in the mid-1970s (Smelser and Content, 1980); wrote an epilogue on conflict in American higher education in the 1960s (Smelser, 1973b); and wrote the essays that appear as chapters 2, 4, 5, and 6 of this volume.

Such are the diverse historical circumstances that have precipitated and produced this book of essays. At the beginning of each chapter I include a background statement explaining the context for writing it. To conclude this introduction I will add two general points about my experience in the university and writing about it.

The first point is personal. As my circle of involvements in the university continued to expand, so did my commitment to and affection for the institution. The most decisive transition was in 1965, when I moved from a faculty member in a single department, with little involvement outside it, into a campuswide role in the chancellor's office (chapter 1). My contacts with faculty, administrators, alumni, students, and staff multiplied, and one of the consequences of that year was that I came to appreciate their diverse points of view, though never without a certain critical distance that has seemed to be an enduring feature of my personal history. More important, I switched from a situation of somewhat splendid personal isolation to occupying a central role in an institution that was fighting for its life and under constant bombardment from all sides. I will not claim that this kind of crisis is necessary for creating loyalty to and love for an institution, but it certainly accelerated and cemented those feelings. That cycle of immersion, understanding, and appreciation repeated itself in less dramatic form as I subsequently expanded the number and kinds of involvements in university life.

The second point concerns the issues of freedom and constraint in my history with—and writing about—different facets of the university's organizational and institutional life. In preparing each of the essays in this volume I operated within some kind of constraint—I was commissioned to write an essay by an editor of a volume, I was member or chair of a committee or commission with a definite charge, or I was a staff member in a certain office. Yet within those constraints, when it came to the actual writing I experienced a maximum amount of freedom. I should say, more accurately, that superiors and colleagues *granted* me the freedom to proceed and write in ways I felt were the best. That gift has always endowed me with the feeling that I was trusted in the university, and that trust translated itself further into the sense that I had—through its agents—the university's institutional, intellectual, and personal confidence. That quality translated further into a feeling that I could be both frank and honest in what I was doing and saying. To generalize this point, I think that a mark of a great institution is that, within its commitment to excellence and greatness, it reaches toward those ends not so much by monitoring and direct supervision but by extending trust to those whom it has invited, after scrupulous assessment, to be its citizens. That kind of freedom breeds loyalty. To make that point does not deny the need for organizational direction and accountability, but it certainly reduces the need for continuous and detailed preoccupation with them.

A final note on exposition. In several places in this book the same paragraph appears in two different chapters. In one case an entire page reappears. Normally one handles this by omitting one of the two passages and instructing the reader to "see above" or "see below." In this book I have followed the strategy of permitting minor repetitions, because in all cases the passage in question is essential for the continuity of that chapter and to remove it or to refer the reader elsewhere would break that continuity.

REFERENCES

Smelser, Neil J. 1973a. "Growth, Structural Change, and Conflict in California Public Higher Education, 1950–1970." In *Public Higher Education in California,* edited by Neil J. Smelser and Gabriel Almond, 9–142. Berkeley: University of California Press.
Smelser, Neil J. 1973b. "Epilogue: Social-Structural Dimensions of Higher Education." In *The American University,* by Talcott Parsons and Gerald M. Platt, 389–422. Cambridge: Harvard University Press.
Smelser, Neil J., and Robin Content. 1980. *The Changing Academic Market: Institutional Context and a Case Study.* Berkeley: University of California Press.

PART ONE

Conflict and Adaptation

ONE

Spring 1965

An Analytic and Autobiographical Account (2008)

IN JANUARY 1965, in the wake of the turbulent Free Speech Movement on the Berkeley campus and the demise of its chancellor, Edward Strong, the new acting chancellor, Martin Meyerson, asked me to join his staff as a special assistant in the area of student political activity. This was the hottest seat in the chancellor's office at that moment, given the political fragility of the campus. I served eight months in that capacity until a new chancellor, Roger Heyns, was appointed and I took a scheduled sabbatical leave. Those months were a tense and uncertain period that resulted in an unsteady but palpable restoration of authority on the Berkeley campus and a few steps toward campus "normalcy." They also constituted a period of rapid and mandatory political learning on my part and one of the most demanding seasons of my life.

Over the years many colleagues have asked me to write about this important transitional period, both because it has received less attention than the historic Free Speech Movement days of late 1964 and because I had an "insider's" point of view; now, in 2008, I have finally acceded to those requests. I have returned to the archives of the chancellor's office, to accounts of the events in the press, and to my personal recollections.

The staff of the Bancroft Library were very helpful in supplying materials relevant to the Meyerson administration from the files of the chancellor's office. I also benefited from the research assistance of Ziza Delgado and Catherine Shepard-Haier.

I have decided, for better or worse, to make the account both institutional/political and autobiographical, with the thought that my story will provide a more vivid account of those heady days.

On Sunday, January 3, 1965, I was in Washington, D.C., attending a meeting of the Council of the American Sociological Association. About 5 P.M. I was pulled out of the meeting for an urgent phone call. It was from Erving Goffman, my colleague and friend in sociology at Berkeley. He told me that my two children, a son, six, and a daughter, four, had been dramatically rescued from a fire that raged through their apartment in San Francisco the night before, but he assured me that they were unhurt and safe.

It was beginning to snow in Washington, so I dashed to the airport and was able catch a plane to the West Coast that night. I contacted my estranged wife and my children early the next morning and arranged for the children to stay with me in Berkeley until new lodgings could be found in San Francisco. A picture of them appeared that morning on the front page of the *San Francisco Chronicle.* That unusual publicity resulted from the fact that one of the firemen, during his heroic rescue work, fell backward from a ladder, broke his neck, and died.

As I was making arrangements to cope with this near-tragedy, my home telephone rang. It was Martin Meyerson, the new acting chancellor of the Berkeley campus, asking to see me that day. I arrived at his office a few hours later. Though he was a colleague on the Berkeley campus (dean of environmental design), I did not really know him. When we met, he offered condolences and best wishes for my children. Then he went straight to the point. He asked me to join his staff right away and become assistant to the chancellor for student political activities. I was blown away by the request, but within a matter of moments I accepted.

THE INSTITUTIONAL CONTEXT OF MY APPOINTMENT

As of the beginning of January 1965, the Berkeley campus was in an institutional shambles. In September 1964, the Berkeley administration invoked a rule prohibiting political advertising and soliciting on a thin strip of land at Telegraph and Bancroft Avenues. Students had enjoyed informal use of this strip for years. The action occurred in the context of a history of extensive political activism during the preceding years (Heirich and Kaplan 1965) and in the context of the heated 1964 presidential campaign. The revocation triggered the Free Speech Movement, which involved massive rule violations, demonstrations, vacillating and ultimately unsuccessful efforts to discipline students, a giant rally and sit-in in Sproul Hall on December 2, and a decisive faculty resolution on December 8 that rebuked Chancellor Edward Strong and called for granting some of the students' demands. (A detailed history is given in Heirich [1968]). The protesters and many others regarded December 8 as a decisive and heroic victory. Discredited, Strong was excused from office on January 2, and Meyerson was named acting chancellor for an indefinite period. A side issue was the presence of Alex Sherriffs, vice-chancellor for student affairs, who had been stridently anti-activist during the previous months and had been, like Strong, largely discredited; however, Sheriffs did not leave that office when Strong resigned, and was still formally in charge of student affairs. Kitty Malloy, a steadfast supporter of both Strong and Sherriffs, also remained in a key position on the chancellor's staff.

At the moment he took office, Meyerson faced a situation in which campus authority was more or less nonexistent; the protesting students were exuberant and hopeful, although without a unified program; the faculty was divided and confused; and nobody really knew what to do. That was the situation Meyerson faced in early January and the situation into which he brought me.

MY PERSONAL CIRCUMSTANCES AT THE TIME

The year 1964–65 was my seventh year at Berkeley. I was in good academic and professional standing, having been promoted rapidly up through the ranks to full professor in 1962, mainly in response to several attractive offers from other major universities. My main points of professional reference in those years were my department and the national community of sociologists. I could not really have been described as a citizen of the campus, even though I had been a member of a chancellor's committee on campus discrimination and had kept abreast of campus affairs.

My professional life in spring 1965 was, if anything, overloaded. I was scheduled to teach large required courses in social theory at both the undergraduate and graduate levels. I was in my third and last year as editor-in-chief of the *American Sociological Review*, a very demanding enterprise, and was active nationally in the American Sociological Association. I was also in the early phases of a research training candidacy at the San Francisco Psychoanalytic Institute, where I was undergoing analysis and preparing to begin courses at the institute. The only relief I got for taking the position in the chancellor's office was from the graduate course in theory. There was no supplementary stipend for my new duties.

My personal life was emerging from chaos. I had separated from my first wife in bitterness, conflict, and unhappiness about a year earlier (an event that triggered my entry into the Psychoanalytic Institute), and I was beginning the painful path toward divorce. My children lived in San Francisco with their mother, but I cared for them in Berkeley on Wednesdays and weekends. As I sketch these details of my professional and personal situation at the time, I return to a question I have never been able to answer: why did I say yes to Meyerson? All my efforts to address the question have resulted only in what I regard as superficial and post facto half-truths: this was my first taste of real institutional power; my home institution, which I liked but had not yet come to love, was in deep trouble and needed any help it could get; and the assignment promised to be a thrilling if difficult one. Oddly—especially in retrospect—I do not remember experiencing any fear that accepting his invitation to step into the political cauldron might damage my career. This was odd, because I had seen numerous administrators and faculty colleagues scalded for their past politics—for taking the wrong stand at the wrong moment, for making the wrong decision, for being in the wrong group. Why should I have been immune? In all events, failing to ask that question meant that I approached the assignment with few apprehensions and with a quiet but false confidence that, in the end, probably served me well in the job.

The other question was: why did Meyerson ask me? I have not been able to answer that question either. I had not been active during the Free Speech Movement, beyond sporadically joining temporary groups of faculty members who were seeking ways to ease the campus situation. Certainly I had not taken any public political stands in the months of conflict. I heard later (but never verified) that Meyerson contacted me on the suggestion of Marty Lipset, a colleague and friend in sociology and a confidant of both Meyerson and Clark Kerr (the president of the entire University of California system and former Berkeley chancellor). Perhaps the fact that I was not publicly identified with any faction (and thereby labeled) in the past few months was also a consideration. Perhaps it made some difference that I had recently written a treatise on collective behavior (Smelser 1962) that included the analysis of riots, protests, and social movements. But these reasons, too, have always been speculations on my part.

THE EARLY DAYS

I had almost no time to prepare for the position. Within a matter of days I had moved into an office near the chancellor's in Dwinelle Hall; was assigned a secretary/assistant from the chancellor's staff; was introduced as Meyerson's assistant at a January 12 meeting of the Berkeley Division of the Academic Senate; held a press conference; and, with Meyerson, met with most of the members of the Steering Committee of the Free Speech Movement.

The introduction at the senate meeting seemed almost incidental. I merely rose when introduced, and sat down again. At the beginning of his brief remarks Martin Meyerson quipped that I was a student of riots, panics, and social movements. A notable feature of the introduction was that the name of Alex Sherriffs, who was still vice-chancellor but whom I was in effect replacing, did not come up either in the introduction or in the question period that followed. That omission was a symptom of the pretence that Sherriffs did not really exist in spring 1965, even though he formally remained in office. I had an early, civil but cool meeting with Sheriffs, and almost immediately established cordial working relations with Katherine Towle, dean of students, and Arleigh Williams, dean of men, both of whom were probably glad to see anyone other than Sherriffs in the chancellor's office, because they had had such strained relations with him during the FSM months.

The news conference was well attended and reported in the Bay Area newspapers, although the appointment of a new assistant did not make front-page news. I also remember that Richard Hafner, public affairs officer, and Ray Colvig, public information officer, were present, probably because they did not trust me yet and were uncertain about what I would say. That distrust was justified, because I didn't know what I was going to say either.

Several items in the coverage of my appointment and news conference were noteworthy.

First, all the reports mentioned that I had been a Rhodes Scholar and some mentioned my Harvard background as well. All mentioned my age, thirty-four. (In announcing my appointment before the Academic Senate Meyerson had also quipped that I was "almost under thirty," a reference

Figure 1. Neil Smelser in 1966.
Photograph by Dennis Galloway.
Courtesy of the Bancroft Library,
University of California, Berkeley.

to the slogan "Don't trust anyone over thirty" that had become a kind of mantra among student activists at the time.)

Second, the press coverage was generally benign. The newspapers described me as being a new man on the job, unaffiliated with factions, open to communication with students rather than a rule-enforcer, helpful and cooperative rather than punitive, open-door in attitude and respectful of students. In a "Profile of UC Peacemaker" (*San Francisco Examiner,* January 17), Fred Allgood included a flattering vignette:

> At thirty-four he is young enough to win the respect of student groups and to convince them he is sympathetic to their needs and problems. And he is mature enough for Meyerson to accept his advice on how student activity can and should be controlled.
>
> With a donnish uniform of bow tie, casual clothes, leather elbow pads, and heavy glasses, a habit of answering questions with honesty, vigor, seriousness and humor, and an athletic appearance that suggests the necessary stamina for long conferences, he has the ideal presence for the role of mediator on the campus.

Allgood went on to characterize me as "[standing] alone in the no-man's-land of the University of California politics battle." That phrase often came vividly to mind during the darker moments of those months.

Third, much was made of my research on collective behavior. Meyerson drew laughs when he mentioned it in introducing me to the Academic Senate. He also jested that my course on collective behavior had even been rated highly in the *SLATE Supplement,* a course evaluation pamphlet published periodically. The headline on my appointment in the *San Francisco Examiner* on January 13 was "Meyerson Picks Expert on Mobs." The other news accounts all stressed this background item. The two evident implications of such publicity were that the chancellor's office was mainly interested in "handling" and "controlling" the dissidents, and that I was brought in to apply my expert knowledge. Both implications made good news for the press in the context of the times, but both were misleading. Neither Meyerson nor I—and nobody in the chancellor's office at the time—had an articulated philosophy of manipulating the movement or the dissidents; we were living day by day without much time to reflect or plan and were most often forced by events to be reactive. I frequently joked that our lead time for decision making was five minutes.

By no stretch of the imagination could it be said that what we did or intended to do was "applied social science." To imply anything like that was to endow us with a rationality we did not have. Yet there were several conclusions that I had reached in my comparative study of collective behavior (including riots) and social movements that informed my thinking in a general way and served me well: (a) I had asked the question of what happens after social movements score a dramatic success and had concluded that success generally creates a psychological letdown, generates internal divisions about what to do next, and leaves the movement floundering and seeking for new agendas and justifications. This conclusion was consistent with what I saw happening with the Free Speech Movement that spring. (b) I had also concluded that among the most incendiary influences on a social movement is authorities' vacillation between punitiveness and weakness, which serves simultaneously to victimize and embolden the movement. I had also seen this principle in action during the late months of 1964 on the Berkeley campus. (c) A closely related conclusion was that it seemed the most legitimate policy on the part of authorities not to engage in direct, partisan ways with activists and antagonists, but to stick, as steadfastly as possible, to a posture of neutrality. In retrospect these lessons seemed to inform my outlook, but only as general orientations and never as fixed principles to be trotted out as specific rules to be applied.

The second noteworthy feature of the news conference was that I framed some of my responses with reference to the issue of free speech. These remarks seemed innocuous enough, and even into February I was quoted in the *Daily Californian* (February 17, 1965) as saying "already we've seen some helpful reformulations of the free speech issue and many reforms are on the way." Meyerson had also been making conciliatory and liberal statements that were respectful of students and sympathetically echoed their preoccupations (*Daily Californian,* January 4, 1965). The atmosphere of those first days was such that Mario Savio, the FSM leader, could warn at a rally that students could be deluded by a false sense of security brought on by the university's present attitude. He said, "They could kill us with kindness" (*Daily Californian,* January 7, 1965). Within a week or so after the press conference, however, I received an invitation (along with Meyerson) to come to dinner at the home of Regent Donald McLaughlin, a leader of the conservative wing of the board. I had known McLaughlin independently, mainly because I was a friend of his son during my graduate school years at Harvard and afterward. I had taken advantage of my acquaintance to pay a visit or two with McLaughlin during Fall 1964, mainly to talk with him about what I saw as the failures of the Strong administration in dealing with the Free Speech Movement. The other guest at dinner was John Lawrence, a noted Berkeley physicist, an outspoken conservative critic of the student movement and the faculty's December 8 resolution, and a member of the small "Truth Squad" of right-wing faculty (Heirich 1968: 358–59) who were active on the campus, with the board of regents, and in Sacramento. After dinner the four of us—McLaughlin, Lawrence, Meyerson, and I—went to a separate room, and the true purpose of the meeting became clear: an occasion for Lawrence and McLaughlin to impose their views on Meyerson and me. In particular, Lawrence gave me a long, vigorous tongue-lashing for even *using* the term "free speech" in my press conference, because that endowed the movement with an undeserved legitimacy. I remember being very unsettled by this attack, but tended to listen rather than argue back, largely, I suppose, because I sensed that Lawrence was more interested in lecturing than in discussing or arguing. To my knowledge, that episode did not influence either Meyerson or me one way or the other. I did experience a certain muffled resentment toward McLaughlin for arranging the occasion—I suspect that Lawrence put him up to it—though that did not disrupt my friendship with him and his wife, Sylvia.

The initial meeting with the FSM Steering Committee was a generally cordial one. Martin advertised it as a friendly effort on our part to get to know those present and to learn things that might be useful and helpful to us. The students did not speak with one voice, though several messages came through: they were glad to be rid of Strong; they were flush with victory and did not want the new administration to "roll back" any of their gains; they wanted full freedom to do what they wanted by way of political activity on campus; and they exuded hope that the Meyerson administration would be receptive to furthering the objectives of the student movement, although these objectives were not very well articulated. John Searle, the Berkeley philosopher and faculty friend and confidante of the FSM at that time, was also present at the meeting, along with one or two other sympathetic faculty.

The meeting proceeded and ended without consequence, although I must report one very instructive incident. At the beginning of the meeting Meyerson said, quite ingenuously, that he would like to acquaint himself better with those present and proceeded to ask them, in a kind of go-around-the-table exercise, to say something about when and why they came to Berkeley, what they were majoring in, and what they planned to do after leaving college. The questions had a disastrous effect; almost all the students gave brief, muffled, and inarticulate answers and seemed to resent the questions. There was a good reason for these reactions. Meyerson had jolted them by making things mundane and profane whereas most of the students still regarded themselves on a sacred, quasi-religious mission that dwarfed anything personal in their lives. To bring up the personal was to trivialize everything and to insult the movement; but Meyerson couldn't be openly accused of that because the questions he asked were evidently friendly, innocent, and legitimate.

Later in 1965 John Searle joined the administration of Chancellor Roger Heyns, in a vague way as my replacement. He had in the meantime turned against the movement when he came to resent what he regarded as its subsequent corruption and excesses. In a letter written to Carey McWilliams of *The Nation* later in 1965 Searle gave a revealing account of the frame of mind of the FSM and its "new radicalism":

Clark Kerr is a labor-management negotiator and also a famous liberal. In labor-management negotiations both sides want something and if they can't get all they want, they will try to get as much as they can: if not fifty cents, then maybe twenty-five cents. All such negotiations presuppose such a system of interests. Now in FSM style radicalism such compromises are absolutely out of the question. Total defeat is much preferable to partial victory, both morally and tactically. Morally, because there is absolutely no selling out in being totally defeated; tactically, because total defeat increases the polarization of the issues, thus recruiting new radical adherents and increasing the bitterness and militancy of the existing adherents. In fact, the only victory worth having is a resounding symbolic victory [letter retrieved from chancellor's files].

Searle was on target with these words. Furthermore, though framed in political language, they are consistent with my interpretation of Meyerson's mischievous questions: those on a sacred mission despise the secular, whether framed in terms of political "interests" or personal concerns, because both corrupt the purity of the sacred.

I report one other notable feature of those early days. After the announcement of my appointment, I learned that some of the student activists had snooped around, asking other faculty about me and what my political "line" was—a perfectly comprehensible kind of inquiry about a new, unknown person in a position of unknown power. One thing they learned was that I was in psychoanalytic training. This was a hot item for student activists already carrying an attitude of distrust of the campus administration. My psychoanalytic connection, like my "expertise" in riot control, apparently raised some suspicions that I might possess some manipulative powers of which they were unaware. The presence of Dr. Saxon Pope, former director of psychiatric services at Cowell Hospital on campus, on the chancellor's advisory staff may have added to these suspicions.

Actually, at the end of Meyerson's and my first meeting with the activist core, one student pulled me aside and asked, in a hostile tone, "Are you going to be psychoanalyzing us away?"—to which I responded in true psychoanalytic fashion by saying nothing. Years later, in the 1980s, I had a chance meeting in the Strawberry Recreation Area with Michael Lerner, a conspicuous campus activist in the turbulent years of the 1960s, later a defendant in the Seattle Seven trial, and even later a rabbi and communitarian spokesman. In a kind of mock-congratulation, Lerner told me what a genius I had been in psychological manipulation, that I had given students genuine hope while in reality there was no such hope, and had guided them into fruitless and self-defeating behavior. Such perceptions were, in my estimation, completely unrealistic and tapped into the latent paranoid fantasies that often reside in the ideologies of extreme social movements (Smelser 2007). They also tapped into threatening undertones that perhaps the motivations for participating in the movement might be psychopathological in nature. Such fears were made manifest in the May 17, 1965 issue of the *San Francisco Chronicle* in a news report entitled "FSM Byproduct—Group Therapy." In that article David H. Powelson, chief psychiatrist at Cowell Hospital, reported a 20 percent drop in student admissions to the psychiatry department between October 1964 and January 1965. Powelson explained the drop as follows: "Many persons tend to go into a group for therapy. . . . Where they might have gone to a psychiatrist, they [found another] way to work out their problems."

I do not wish to magnify the significance of either the hostile reaction to Meyerson's questions that treated students as ordinary students or to the riot-control and psychoanalytic-manipulation fantasies, because in the end they were such minor aspects of the larger scene. But they do reveal the social-psychological complexities of the situation that we were dealing with in those unsteady days.

At this point I should mention a final, strange feature of my situation in the chancellor's office. I learned only after several months in the office that my secretary/assistant was having a love affair with Alex Sherriffs, himself divorced earlier. Such a scene was right out of early Florentine politics. Sherriffs had been cast as my significant but unseen arch-enemy because I had displaced him and because we were poles apart politically on issues of student political activity. When I heard about the affair, I became unglued, for it meant that any semblance of confidentiality of office was a phantom, and that any and every thing I did or said was available to Sherriffs during after-work hours of the same day. I never asked her about this liaison during my stay in the chancellor's office and in fact maintained a cordial though more guarded working relationship with her until I departed. She and Sherriffs subsequently married. Approximately fifteen years later I met them both at a meeting in Asilomar and in a private moment asked her how she had coped with that anomalous situation years ago. She responded with something vague, referring to keeping her two lives separate. As far as I know, this bizarre situation neither generated any specific mischief nor affected the course of campus history, but it did lend an element of spice to my story.

Of all the concerns of student activists in the months following their victory symbolized by the vote of the faculty on December 8, 1964, three stand out: (a) to safeguard the political gains made with respect to political activity on campus; on that date the faculty had voted that only the time, place, and manner of such activity should be regulated, and the activists pressed for minimal definitions of these aspects; (b) to minimize if not eliminate discipline for violation of these minimal rules; and (c) to gain amnesty or acquittal in the courts for those arrested in the sit-in at Sproul Hall on December 2, 1964. I will cover the issue of rules in a later section and discuss discipline mainly under the heading of the obscenity crisis.

With respect to the sit-ins, some eight hundred students were escorted or dragged from Sproul Hall on December 2, and approximately six hundred of these were arrested for trespassing and resisting arrest. The charges were brought by the Alameda County District Attorney, and the trial, heard by Judge Rupert Critttenden, ultimately began on April 1, 1965. In the months preceding the trial, the press covered every aspect of it. Bail funds were raised by sympathetic faculty and others for most of those charged (*Daily Californian,* Feb. 12, 1965). Of special interest to the chancellor's office was a petition to dismiss all charges, submitted to Judge Crittenden and signed by 245 Berkeley faculty members, headed by Professor Jacobus ten Broek. Around mid-January the chancellor's office received a number of visitations and appeals for the campus officially to request dismissal. Among these was a telegram from the "Parents Defense Committee for Berkeley Students." Judge Crittenden dismissed the faculty petition on January 27, explaining that dropping the charges would not serve the interests of justice.

On January 7 Savio had appealed to students not to desert those arrested. Two days earlier students had announced the launching of a national defense fund, claiming that they had the support of Paul Goodman, Lawrence Ferlinghetti, James Farmer, Bertrand Russell, James Baldwin, Norman Mailer, and Jessica Mitford (*Daily Californian,* Feb. 4, 1965, no contributions specified). The press (*San Francisco Examiner,* Jan. 15) also reported an effort to raise a $50,000 defense fund by mail solicitation. Later in March defendants filed an unsuccessful suit for $45 million against the State, Alameda County, and the board of regents for police brutality, deprivation of the right to legal counsel, and illegal booking procedures (*Daily Californian,* March 12, 1965).

As a final strategy the activists decided to approach the chancellor's office to persuade it to intervene directly. The decisive meeting with me as chancellor's representative took place on January 15, at the request of two attorneys, Malcolm Burnstein and Alex Hoffman, representing the students. Because the meeting involved attorneys I arranged that Professor Arthur Sherry of the Boalt Law School (and member of the senate's Emergency Executive Committee) be present. Three members of the FSM Steering Committee—Mario Savio, Jack Weinberg, and Suzanne Goldberg—were there, along with three other students active in the legal defense effort. I should mention that this meeting occurred only ten days after I joined Meyerson's staff, so I approached it with some anxiety. I did decide in advance, however, that the best stance would be that of a listener and that I would neither make promises nor reject any demand outright.

The first part of the meeting was dominated by the attorneys, who explained in detail why the students would not plead either guilty or *nolo contendere,* but would enter a not-guilty plea. They argued that the university should influence the court by requesting the district attorney to dismiss or by persuading Judge Crittenden informally. Sherry and I said almost nothing during this presentation.

At its midway point the meeting turned ugly and brought on several abusive harangues, mainly by Savio. I summarized the proceedings in a memo to Meyerson:

> The rest of the conversation consisted in the attorneys' and students' predictions and speculations of unwanted consequences if the university failed to intervene in some way on behalf of those arrested. The discussion was discursive, but it is possible to summarize the kinds of consequences that the students predicted and threatened:
>
> 1. That court action against the students would create great hostility among the students, and this would spill over against the university, thus raising once again the conflict that raged from September through December.
> 2. That court action against the students would, as in the case of the Sheraton Palace convictions, make the defendants less respectful of law and order.
> 3. That, particularly if a constitutional defense were chosen, many facts harmful to the reputation of the university would be revealed in testimony.

4. That the solidarity of the student movement would be augmented by their defensive battle against court action, and that the student movement would emerge stronger than if no court action were taken. Predictions were made that student organizations would be organized nationally and internationally.

5. That the defendants would, in unspecified ways, take offensive legal action against the university.

After presenting these ideas, and after discussing various aspects of the students' outlook and activities, the attorneys and students pressed to know what the university was going to do about these demands for action on the arrestees' behalf. I responded to this pressure by assuring that I would report faithfully and accurately their representations to the chancellor. It was further agreed that if I had any communications relating to the conversations of this meeting, I would convey them to Burnstein.

At the end of my memo I summarized my impressions and gave my recommendations to Meyerson:

My own response to the meetings of January 15 is that while the morale of the defendants is still fairly high, desperation is growing among them, and that their delegation to request university action marked a kind of last-minute effort to head off trials and legal convictions. My assessment of their predictions and threats is that they are quite vague and general, and should not influence the university in any way.

It is my unequivocal conviction that the university should take no action in response to these or any other demands for intervention. I am less certain on the question of how the university should communicate its position to the larger public and to the defendants themselves. My present feeling is that no public statement of any sort should be issued by the university, and that it should simply allow justice to take its course. My own position vis-à-vis the defendants and attorneys who approached me is a bit difficult, since I shall no doubt be pressed for some indication as to the university's disposition. Simply to ignore this pressure would, I feel, be untenable. I would like to be able to indicate to Burnstein that the chancellor, while giving the defendants' demands and arguments due consideration, contemplates no action.

That effectively ended the issue of campus intervention. Meyerson accepted my memo, and I was confident that Sherry and the rest of the

Emergency Executive Committee were in agreement. Neither the attor-neys nor the activists attempted to influence the campus administration further on the matter. In another related action, however, the campus was more conciliatory. On December 23, 1964 the district attorney had requested student records from the campus. This set off internal discussions on the issue. Judge Thomas J. Cunningham, the regents' counsel, had advised us to release records only after written authorization from the students. On February 25 I wrote to Meyerson, "it seemed a good time to begin the firm policy of releasing records only if the student gives consent," and he agreed. We also advised the dean of students not to enter into any agreements about disciplining students in lieu of charges to be pressed by the civil authorities. On February 18 I received a phone call from Burnstein on the issue, and a few days later I informed him of the university's position. That phone call effectively closed the "release of records" issue as well.

Reflecting on our decisions regarding trial of the sit-ins and the release of records, it seems to me that the campus administration set the right tone, one consistent with the "lessons" of patient listening, neutrality, noncontestation, and distance. I can testify honestly, however, that our reactions were completely ad hoc and situational, and in no way self-conscious "applications" of general knowledge.

A RARE LOOK FORWARD

After only three weeks in office, I decided, quite on my own, to send an orienting memorandum to Meyerson, setting down my own anticipations of issues and situations that we might confront during the coming months. I reproduce that memo here:

> I thought I would take the opportunity to note down for your consideration a number of possible issues which I think may arise during the coming semester. You are aware of some of these issues yourself. I do not exactly predict that they will happen, but they are issues for which I think the university should be prepared and should know where they stand in advance, rather than having to be hurried into precipitous action.
>
> 1. *The enrollment of Mario Savio.* I note that as of January 19 Mario Savio has not applied for re-admission, though the deadline was January 15. It would not surprise me to see Savio turn up for

registration, be refused, and then begin to complain loudly that he is being discriminated against. It is very important that the university not be caught napping on this one.

2. *The problem of a fund-raising for legal defense* in Pauley Ballroom or some other University Building. It is essential that the university know what it intends to do, or else it is likely to be caught in that spiral of vacillation and changes of decision and apparent weakness.

3. *The trials.* I think the university's posture is absolutely clear. It can do nothing officially or unofficially to influence the court or the district attorney. I feel it is most important to adhere to this policy. Certainly it will sustain some criticism because of the action of the Ten Broek group, but there is nothing it can do about this criticism. I envision one possibility—that a group of faculty members might very well attempt to pass some senate resolution on behalf of the defendants, perhaps at a sparsely attended senate meeting. I have had no word that this is likely to happen, but I think we should keep our ears to the ground.

4. *Demonstrations over the new rules.* I do not really anticipate any widespread student response to the new rules, since hopefully they will be liberal enough, but if the regents introduce some more stringent elements or if one part of the rules appears to be too strict, we may expect at least modest student demonstrations. For this reason I think it is most important that some kind of machinery . . . be set up after the new rules are announced. This will provide an immediate channel for examining the rules, hearing grievances, etc. In the event that a tri-partite committee is set up, I would anticipate that a demand will be made that that committee be established on a troika principle, rather than on the deliberative committee principle with one vote for one person.

5. *Massive violations of the new rules.*

6. *Student attempts to test the advocacy principles. . . .* This kind of activity would be to dare the university to re-create the September situation which gave the impetus to the whole series of disturbances last fall.

7. *Attacks by civil rights groups on university hiring practices. . . .*

8. *Widespread criticism of curricula, course offerings, etc.,* and demands that they be given a more direct voice in planning and executing the academic affairs of the university. Frankly, I do not think that this kind of activity on the part of the students will make much headway, because I think basically that the faculty will resent

intrusions on its academic freedom from below as much as it resents them from above.

9. *Sale of materials on campus . . .*

Again, be assured that I venture these possibilities not in the spirit of paranoia, but in the spirit of being as prepared and as flexible as possible in the event of possibly difficult situations that may arise.

Many of the issues did not arise. The university was not the object of attack on its hiring practices. Student fund-raising for the sit-in trials never really got off the ground, so we had no requests to use facilities for that purpose. Faculty members made no effort to get the senate involved in dismissing charges against students. We did not have massive violation of the new time-place-manner rules, although there were many incidents of probing and testing. Savio did not attempt to re-enroll, but the salience of the issue was confirmed in a telephone call to me from a former vice-president of the university. He had heard (or been pressured by someone who had heard) that Savio was going to be taken on as an employee at the Student Union bookstore, and that we should forbid this. I told him that we had no basis for preventing his employment. Nothing further was heard on this issue, which I assume was based on rumor. However, Savio was hired as a part-time reader for the philosophy department after he dropped out of the university, and that drew the public ire of State Senator McAteer (*San Francisco Chronicle,* March 12, 1965).

Nonetheless, some of the points I mentioned materialized as themes as the semester proceeded. The "sale of materials on campus" point foreshadowed the *Spider* magazine episode; the "test of advocacy" issue was central in different ways in the obscenity crisis and the Vietnam Day events; and educational reform emerged, though in large part through administrative initiative. All these are covered below.

My memo specified only points of anticipation and a few guidelines for strategies; it certainly did not serve as any kind of handbook for planning. It was probably read only by Meyerson. But in my mind it stands out as a rare exception to the fundamentally reactive mode that dominated our responses during Spring 1965.

TIME, PLACE, AND MANNER RULES

Campus regulation of political activity was what the FSM was all about, so it stands to reason that a carry-over issue facing Meyerson was what if any limits would emerge from the shambles of rule-violation, attempts at discipline, and the collapse of those attempts in the FSM period. Almost everybody, including activists, acknowledged the need for time-place-manner (but not content) limits in the faculty's December 8 resolution. One of Meyerson's first acts was to issue "interim" rules on January 4, limiting location and time of sound amplification, specifying where tables and posters could be placed and requiring official registration with the campus as a student organization to hold rallies and man tables, as well as advance notification of speakers.

Some staff and advisors to the chancellor argued for the prohibition of noontime rallies with sound amplification on the Sproul Hall steps and upper plaza. I dreaded such a prospect, regarding it as a likely recapitulation of the revocation of political activity on the Bancroft strip at the beginning of the Fall semester, 1964. Activists had come to regard the use of the steps almost as a sacred entitlement and even made an effort to name them "Alexander Meicklejohn steps." On February 2, I wrote to Meyerson: "I think that any attempt to convince the students that they should give up Sproul Hall steps is . . . fruitless, because many students will feel that is an arbitrary act. I would predict that it might be unnecessarily inflammatory."

The issuance of the January 4 specifications drew no mass reactions from student activists, but members of the FSM Steering Committee (Mayra Jellen and Martin Roysher) attacked them as unnecessary and restrictive of advocacy (*Daily California,* January 4, 1965). I scheduled a meeting with leaders in order "to find out what kinds of concerns they have" (memo to files). Again on January 22, I entertained a delegation of students headed by Martin Roysher and Suzanne Goldberg, during which they first complained about not being consulted before the interim regulations were promulgated. The remainder of the meeting concerned specifics: that the lead time for announcing off-campus speakers was too long; that the sound amplification regulations were unnecessary because the loudspeakers did not disturb office-workers in Sproul Hall if extended beyond 1 P.M.; that the rules on placement of tables were too restrictive, as was the limit on hours of manning tables between 7 A.M. and 6 P.M.; that it was unfair to restrict sales of materials to those relevant to the student organizations' purposes; and that it was unfair to require student organizations to pay for the presence of police. I listened patiently to these complaints, but we responded to none of them.

There were no mass protests against the January 4 regulations but there were a few mischievous probes. On February 11 I got a call from a Student Union official reporting that, when presented with a bill for $20 for amplification equipment, Steve Weissman of the Graduate Coordinating Committee gave it back and said "send it to Neil Smelser." From time to time organizers of rallies nibbled away at the 1 P.M. deadline for ending amplification. On March 21 Meyerson issued some alterations of the interim rules, and these became the subject of daily rallies protesting them, as well as a "counter-rally" on the part of some faculty supporters of the December 8 resolution, at which they called the students "moral spastics" for protesting anything and everything and urged them to "cool it." On April 1 Meyerson issued a new set of interim rules, and on April 15 the Berkeley Division commended these changes by a 198 to 7 vote.

With respect to the time-place-manner rules, I was evolving toward a policy of enforcing them but not taking the bait and going after minor provocations and thereby generating major provocations. On April 23 there was a special meeting in the chancellor's office attended by campus deans, the public information officer (Hafner), and other members of the chancellor's staff (including Alex Sherriffs in one of his rare appearances). I reported that yesterday's rally went after 1 P.M. and hence was a violation, but no police action was taken, which I thought was a wise non-action. Names of speakers were taken and sent to the Faculty Committee on Student Political Activity. I explained that this was my favored mode of dealing with violations. The minutes of the meeting went on: "Smelser . . . asked the group to make suggestions on how future episodes should be handled. It was agreed that every effort should be made to avoid provocation, to stay with the procedures by taking names." I pointed out that this was consistent with procedures set up by the Academic Senate to deal with time-place-manner issues. In the same spirit, those at the meeting confirmed that no effort should be made by police to seize illegal sound equipment before it came onto campus, and that we would not hold officers of student organizations responsible for the illegal use of equipment. This evolving outlook was the opposite of that which Vice-Chancellor Earl Cheit jokingly advanced a couple of years later: "Let's go out and see what's happening on Sproul Plaza and tell them to stop it."

Another feature of my evolving outlook concerned how to respond to daily events on the plaza, to pamphlets, and to items in the daily press.

In the chancellor's staff and among other groups there was always a person or group that became agitated when an item seeming to be embarrassing to the university appeared and, consistent with that reaction, demanded that "this must be set straight." As daily events came and went, I gradually became convinced of exactly how short public memory is and came to believe that denials, corrections, and counter-statements as often as not prolonged the significance of the embarrassing event and did nothing to improve the image or status of the campus. My view came to be that very few things should be officially "answered" or "refuted" because that usually conveyed a certain nervousness or defensiveness on the part of the campus administration. Moreover, declining to respond tended to shorten the life of the incident. Correspondingly, I believed that only very few and very serious events should be "corrected" by issuing statements and calling news conferences. I am not certain that my view was the right one, but I think that following it during this period contributed a certain steadiness.

In the meantime Meyerson and I were working toward speeding up the disciplinary process (an obvious reaction to the impatience we experienced in the obscenity disciplinary hearings, which had just concluded—see below). On April 23 Meyerson proposed an administrative committee to replace the unwieldy faculty committees, and the Emergency Executive Committee backed up the proposal. The idea of a hearing officer was also floated. Nothing came of these suggestions in the short run.

As might be expected, the board of regents continued their interest in the issue of regulating student political activity. In response to the FSM drama, they had formed a Meyer Committee (named after its chair, Regent Theodore Meyer) on student political activity. After a sustained period of hearings, interviews, and meetings, the committee submitted its report to the regents in May. It was more far-reaching and restrictive than existing practices on any of the campuses. Activists sent an abusive letter to the chairman of the board of regents complaining that they were not involved in the process. The regents ignored the letter. The board did not act directly on the Meyer report but referred it to the office of the president on May 21 for implementation. After several weeks of work the president's office sent out its adaptations to all the campuses, considerably watered down from the Meyer Committee recommendations. Meyerson announced immediately that the new campus rules, effective July 1, "conform in general" with the existing interim rules on the campus.

In the meantime, on June 30, I had written a 13-page, single-spaced memo to Meyerson analyzing the document from the office of the president, noting both vagueness and nonapplicability of some of its provisions to the Berkeley campus and the unenforceability of some provisions (for example, requiring a moderator and question-and-answer components at meetings). In that memo I also argued against a recommendation that would deny facilities if words were spoken that indicated that some illegal action was being contemplated. I gave reasons for this: something illegal is mentioned and discussed but does not occur; or the illegal act may occur but not as mentioned. I concluded, "I find it impossible and possibly threatening to the rights of individuals to prevent meetings at which illegal action is being contemplated. The only exception to this policy that I would suggest is when the advocacy of illegal action itself constitutes illegal action—for example the advocacy of the assassination of a public official."

As far as I could determine, the new July 1 rules provoked no reaction among activists, but after all it was in the middle of summer vacation, when mobilization was virtually impossible. The new rules worked their way into the campus structure. The time-place-manner issues, however, would dog the succeeding administration of Roger Heyns in its trouble-ridden years.

A NOTE ON STUDENT GOVERNMENT

One line of student activity had to do with the constitution and politics of student government. Most of this concerned the issue of graduate student membership in the Associated Students of the University of California (ASUC). Graduate students voted to join in an election on February 24, and in a March 2 election undergraduates expressed their preference for graduate students to participate. The issue of graduate student membership was a genuine constitutional one involving the enfranchisement of a class of students, but it also was on the agenda because it was felt by some that graduate student membership would mean a more influential and perhaps more radical ASUC. On March 22 the regents declared the elections void on grounds that too few students voted and that a minority could not oblige the majority of graduate students to pay fees. The ASUC attempted another election in defiance of the regents, but this was aborted by rulings of the Student Judicial Committee. Nevertheless an unofficial "freedom ballot" election was held on April 5, 6, and 7, but the numbers voting again fell short of the 50 percent required by the regents. An equally abortive attempt to seat "graduate senators" was also made. This drawn-out drama excited new tensions and conflicts between more moderate student factions and the more radical SLATE party.

I report these developments as one subdrama of conflict during my period in the chancellor's office. I also have to report, however, that I was little involved, and not very interested, in any of it. The reason for the former was that the ASUC did not interact much with the chancellor's office; rather, they proceeded on their own with the elections, and the point of conflict was with the board of regents, which meant by-passing our office. The reason for the latter was that, although the ASUC had had an important history in campus conflict and SLATE in particular had exercised considerable influence and power through it, I simply felt that the other lines of ongoing conflict were more important and threatening to the campus. There were bigger fish to fry.

THE OBSCENITY CRISIS

My two most trying months in the chancellor's office were March and May 1965. The first was the month that gripped the campus in conflict about the expression of obscenity and the second was the campus chaos associated with the Vietnam Day Committee and the huge anti-war protest on May 21–22. The story of the second comes later in the chapter.

The most general feature of the early months of 1965 was the fragmentation of the energy mobilized during the FSM crisis into multiple directions—protecting those arrested on December 2, resisting any restoration of rules limiting political activity, reforming student government, enacting educational reform, and establishing a Free University on the campus that would give "socially relevant" courses separate from the official university curriculum. Another manifestation was pressing the limits of expression of speech and behavior into the politically and legally sensitive area of obscenity. This went in several directions and culminated in the "Filthy Speech Movement" and its ramifications during March. Before entering that drama, I note a few elements of context.

The Ugly Man Contest

In late February the annual Ugly Man contest, a charity event for the World University Service and Cal Camp, was held. It consisted of a competition among fraternities and other campus organizations. After a ribald campaign, the contest was won by Miss Pussy Galore (after the character in the James Bond movie) sponsored by Alpha Epsilon Pi. Noticed by few but regarded as traditional student high jinx by most of those who did notice, the event became an important reference point for protesters after John Thomson, a young nonstudent protester from New York, was arrested on March 2 for displaying a sign reading "Fuck" on the Student Union steps in Sproul Plaza. Why should fraternities go unpunished for obscenity when he was arrested? (This was one of the few manifestations of social class antagonism among students in the student politics of the period.) On March 3, the day after the arrest, a protester named Robert Hurwitt complained that the amplification from the Ugly Man contest in Lower Sproul Plaza was interfering with the SLATE rally on the upper plaza. I requested that the amplification be turned down.

Lenny Bruce

On February 10 an undergraduate student, Laura Mura, came to my office and asked about bringing the comedian Lenny Bruce on campus for a show. (Bruce was a charismatic and controversial figure and was at the time in the legal "soup," with several obscenity suits against him pending.) She wondered whether we had any objections. I was inwardly alarmed but played it cool, saying that there would be no objection if procedures of advance notification and organizational sponsorship were followed. I heard no more about this, but on March 2, the day of Thomson's arrest, I had a meeting with Mario Savio and a few others who pressed me for permission to bring Lenny Bruce to campus. On the day before they had requested to use the Greek Theater (with a capacity for thousands) for his show, with a lecture hall in the Life Sciences Building as backup, and now they wanted Harmon Gymnasium (capacity six thousand). I was noncommittal but did ask a member of the chancellor's staff to work up a background statement on Bruce.

Two weeks later, at the very height of the obscenity crisis, the subject of Lenny Bruce arose in a meeting with Mario Savio, Steve Weissman, Laura Mura, and Robert Hurwitt. I raised the suggestion, diplomatically I thought, that at the current moment it might not be in their best interests to aggravate the obscenity issue by inviting Bruce and even suggested they withdraw the request. The students, especially Savio, became abusive at this suggestion. I asked that we not publicize this conversation (realizing the hopelessness of such a suggestion) but Steve Weissman agreed, saying that they themselves had some things they did not want to publicize, including a scheme for some students to engage in a "puff-in" (public marijuana smoking) at an upcoming meeting of the Academic Senate.

Nothing happened in the wake of this March 15 meeting, and I even heard a rumor that the request was going to be called off. Nevertheless, I contacted two faculty members, Karl Schorske of the history department and William Kornhauser of the sociology department, both with ties to the activist students, and asked them to persuade the students to call off the invitation. I tried to get John Searle involved as well. In the meantime, my colleague in the sociology department, Philip Selznick, relayed a message to me that Bruce's attorneys were pressing him not to make an appearance on campus because it might be damaging to him in the upcoming obscenity trials. In the meantime the chairman of the board of regents had been hammering daily on both Kerr and Meyerson to ban Bruce's appearance; Martin resisted this pressure, explaining that he could not precensor, and that Bruce might conceivably appear and read out pages from the telephone book.

On March 18 I entered a memo into the files that I had received a telephone call from Alex Hoffman, the Berkeley attorney, saying that Lenny Bruce definitely was *not* coming to campus. My memo was terse and straight-faced, but it reeked with feelings of relief. We had heard independently that Bruce had fallen and broken his leg a few days earlier and that that was the occasion for the cancellation. To this day I do not know whether the request was called of by Bruce (either voluntarily or on account of his incapacitation), by his attorneys, or by the interested students. I know even less about any influence I might have had on events.

The Word, the Rallies, and the Immediate Aftermath

I did not learn of the arrest of John Thomson until the evening of March 2, when a campus police officer telephoned me at home and informed me. I received the news without comment. Inwardly, however, my heart sank. Why had they arrested him? Why hadn't they apprehended the young man, escorted him from the campus, and threatened that if he returned to repeat the action or one like it he would be arrested? The logic that informed my reaction, of course, was that by now I was, like most of my colleagues in the chancellor's office, eager to avoid the negative publicity for the campus that I knew this event would create. How wrong my first reaction was in the light of the events that unfolded over the next month. I could not have guessed that some ill-advised FSM activists would embrace Thomson's action as a free-speech issue and thereby initiate the process of discrediting and ultimately killing the movement; that the campus would be able to discipline those charged and thereby regain some of its authority and legitimacy; or that the events would provoke a noisy counterrevolution from the right that would fail in the short run.

I did not have much time to reflect on this new event, because the next day Art Goldberg (FSM Steering Committee member) and a few others stormed into my office, loudly and abusively demanding that we drop charges against Thomson. Goldberg called his arrest a "crackdown" on our part, rambled on about the violation of free speech (the next day he said before a rally, "A guy has the right to express himself like he wants"; *Daily Californian*, March 4, 1965), and issued threat after threat. As I recall, I remained calm and did not argue, although I did ask him whether he could envision any possible limits on public behavior. At one point Goldberg demanded to know what the university would do tomorrow when there would be a parade of a thousand students carrying signs with the offensive word through Sproul Plaza. I remember saying that I could not know, but there might be a thousand arrests. (Dean Arleigh Williams had heard the same threat and telephoned me on March 4, asking what to do if such a parade occurred, and I advised him to treat offenders in the same way as Thomson was treated.) I also remember cautioning Goldberg that any further displays would be likely to set off a major political reaction in the state—probably a futile warning, because that is no doubt part of what Goldberg and his friends wanted.

There was no parade, but on March 4 there was an "obscenity rally" on the steps of Sproul Hall at which the letters of the word "Fuck" were shouted out as if at a football rally. Others shouted or displayed the word, for example on a sign reading "Student Committee for a Good Fuck." Another student publicly read the juiciest passages from D. H. Lawrence's *Lady Chatterley's Lover.* The police arrested several students and nonstudents. All this was raw meat for the local press, who reported the events with a combination of shock, bemusement, ridicule, and barely-beneath-the-surface glee over great university's new troubles.

The events set off a flurry of frantic meetings among the chancellor's staff, some faculty, representatives from the Office of the Dean of Students, and police about what to do if these displays continued and whether and in what ways to discipline the students. I was in the middle of most of these meetings. There was a consensus that the students ought to be charged by the university (no matter what the civil authorities decided to do). That consensus was bred, I think, both by outrage at the protesters' behavior and by a more or less unspoken sense that the political consequences for the campus would be disastrous if we did not do so.

Our efforts ran into a major snag immediately. There were two student disciplinary committees through which we might have proceeded: the Faculty Committee on Student Conduct, long established but handling mainly "beer and sex" offenses; and a newer Faculty Committee on Student Political Activity, established in early January in response to prodding from the regents and intended to the correct the inadequacies of disciplinary machinery made evident during the FSM period. When approached, both committees declined to hear the case on grounds that it was not in their jurisdiction. At this news I remember cursing my faculty colleagues under my breath for fiddling while Rome was burning or, perhaps more apt, lecturing on principles of navigation as the ship was sinking. (Kerr also criticized the committees for their reluctance; *San Francisco Chronicle*, March 11, 1965.) Meyerson responded to what he called the "difficult questions of jurisdiction" by forming a new ad hoc committee consisting of two members from each of the two disciplinary committees and a new chairman, Professor John Whinnery from the School of Engineering. The choice of Whinnery was a brilliant one. His academic and professional credentials were the highest. He was a supremely unflappable man, utterly committed to due process. He displayed the greatest patience in the face of pressures to turn the proceedings into a public trial and accusations that the committee was railroading the students. The committee carried on through all the legalisms, challenges, and criticisms, and on April 20 all four students were suspended, Goldberg indefinitely. The work of the committee was flawless, and on July 19 Meyerson could respond honestly to a request for review from Clark Kerr that the students were "granted procedural safeguards for a fair and informed decision."

During March and early April my life was made chaotic by dozens of questions and complaints from faculty, students, and outsiders, including the parents of one of the defendants who begged that the chancellor intervene on behalf of their son, who, they argued, was basically a "good boy." We also received a communication from the regents' counsel informing us that board members were interested in speedy discipline. For a period of approximately one month I was telephoned every three or four days by a highly placed staff member in the office of Governor Pat Brown. Every call was identical. The official did not press for a specific outcome but would ask only how the hearings were going, informing me how interested the governor was in their expeditious conclusion. I concluded the governor surely wanted discipline as an outcome but in the interest of self-protection advised his staff member not to press openly for it. I surmised further that Brown, a steadfast friend of the university and strong defender of Kerr and Meyerson (*San Francisco Chronicle*, March 13, 1965), was anxious for discipline because that would help insulate the campus from the ongoing savage attacks from the right. In response to the calls I adopted a reassuring stance but gave no guarantees. I also kept in constant touch with Whinnery, informing him of the interest of the governor's office, and Whinnery kept me posted in detail about the committee's work. I thus found myself exerting a double if not contradictory set of pressures on the committee: to observe the fairest procedures and due process while making haste. Otherwise the chancellor's office did not communicate with the Whinnery committee during its work; we were concerned mainly with the timeliness and steadiness of its work and with its scrupulous observance of due process.

In the meantime the obscenity crisis escalated to the highest levels of the university and state government. On March 9, when it became public that neither disciplinary committee on the campus would take on the obscenity case, conservative members of the board of regents, led by its chair, Edwin Carter, handed down an ultimatum to Clark Kerr to expel the students immediately. For Kerr this raised a constitutional issue of interference in the affairs of the campus. Accordingly, he took the occasion to tender his resignation and persuaded Meyerson (apparently without difficulty) to join him in resigning. (My own feeling at the time was that at some level Meyerson's heart was not fully in this decision because of his own ambitions to be made permanent chancellor, although I never discussed this with him.) Immediately thereafter the right-wing critics of Kerr and Meyerson launched a savage attack in the pages of the *Oakland Tribune* and called for a reinstatement of Edward Strong to the chancellorship. On the personal level, I should add that I was not at all involved in this higher-level drama, which extended beyond the campus, except for being in close and continuous conversation with Meyerson.

The drama continued in full heat during the next few days. On March 11 Meyerson announced the appointment of the ad hoc committee (thus giving evidence that the campus was behaving responsibly in the matter of discipline). Two days earlier both the ASUC senate and the editorial board of the *Daily Californian* made statements commending Kerr and Meyerson (*Daily Californian,* March 10, 1965). On March 12 the Berkeley division of the Academic Senate held a massive meeting (more than 1,100 faculty in attendance) at which, almost unanimously, the faculty condemned the "flaunting of obscenity" by a few students, endorsed the administration's initiation of efforts to discipline them, called for the withdrawal of the resignations of Kerr and Meyerson and for making Meyerson full, not acting, chancellor; and produced a token vote of esteem for Chancellor Strong. On the following day, at a meeting of the board of regents, Meyerson and Kerr withdrew their resignation threats and Chancellor Strong submitted his written resignation (he had not resigned, only taken leave, on January 2). In the meantime, the FSM Steering Committee, in somewhat defensive news releases, simultaneously denied that it initiated or supported the obscenity episodes, assaulted the regents for unconstitutional meddling, and attacked Kerr for using the obscenity issue as an excuse for a power grab and for continuing his assault on student freedoms. In a rally on March 11 Savio attacked Kerr as a "two-faced hypocrite" and hotly denied that the Free Speech Movement was associated with "the unfortunate free sexual intercourse movement" (*San Francisco Chronicle,* March 12, 1965).

The larger political implications of these few days cannot be overestimated. Though threatened, the campus administration held its own with respect to managing its daily affairs. The administration and faculty were fully unified in opposition to the conservative wing of the regents and to the activist student movement—at least the few who had perpetrated the excesses. The Free Speech Movement, unable to dissociate itself from the excesses of the obscenity incidents, was decisively weakened and sent into a downward spiral toward morbidity. Furthermore, Kerr and the campus were able temporarily to stave off the mounting counter-revolution from the right, although attacks continued to be heard, and the counter-revolution reemerged in full force during Reagan's gubernatorial campaign of 1966 and in the firing of Clark Kerr in 1967.

A final factor connected with the obscenity crisis further accelerated the decline of the Free Speech Movement and its leadership. Despite the embarrassment that the obscenity demonstrations carried for the steering committee, they continued to be active in resisting and complaining about the discipline of the four students—indeed, it was their main preoccupation during March and April. Activists immediately condemned the arrest of Thomson and demanded that charges be dropped. Only a few days after the obscenity rallies, Savio argued that the students should not be disciplined, and if they were, the board of regents could expect trouble (*Daily Californian,* March 10, 1965). FSM speakers repeatedly and publicly advocated no discipline for the students who were charged and attempted to discredit or alter the hearings. A group called the "Physics Department Graduate Students' Association" attacked John Whinnery for unfairness when he said that those involved in the obscenity rally would be "disciplined expeditiously." Mario Savio came to my office on March 23 and demanded that the hearings be open as a matter of due process (and, I might add but Savio did not, subject to heckling and disruption.) Student activists and the attorney representing those charged, Peter Franck, demanded that the hearings be public and that the proceedings be released. At the time of the suspensions—April 20—Goldberg promised a challenge in the courts (*Daily Californian,* April 22, 1965), which never materialized. Even after the suspensions were imposed, a group of students demanded that the Emergency Executive Committee create yet another committee to open new hearings on the obscenity cases, on grounds that the previous ones were biased; the EEC rejected the request.

In response to the news of the suspensions, activists staged a "sit-on" on the steps of Sproul Hall steps to protest. Between six hundred and a thousand students were estimated to have attended. Students threatened to use amplification equipment after it was officially shut down. I said that that was a violation, and if the dean recommended disciplinary action the cases would be sent to the Faculty Committee on Student Political Activity. I was quoted as saying that any new violations would be "an unfortunate retrogression in the progress we had made" and that in any event alternative facilities had been made available in Lower Sproul Plaza for continuing the meeting. At the rally Michael Lerner boldly announced that "this is the beginning of a new and larger student protest that will overshadow the events of last semester" (*San Francisco Chronicle,* April 23, 1965) and Savio announced that "the honeymoon with Marty [Meyerson] is over."

The same day the activists sent a telegram to the regents, signed by Savio, Suzanne Goldberg, and other students (calling themselves the "Provisional Committee to Protect Student Rights"). The telegram proclaimed the continuing crisis of the university and demanded reinstatement of the suspended students and appointment of a new committee by the Berkeley division. Regents ridiculed the telegram (*Daily Californian,* April 26, 1965). Savio, who had been criticized by members of his Steering Committee for having nothing to back up the threats in the telegram, then resigned from the movement. That event made page one headlines in every San Francisco Bay Area newspaper.

Savio's resignation was merely the final flutter of a movement that was already nearly dead. (At the end of March, the Steering Committee had been formally "dissolved" into a "list of representatives" from other organizations; *Daily Californian,* March 30, 1965). On the day of Savio's resignation the *San Francisco Chronicle* reported that five other members of the Steering Committee had already left town or had quietly withdrawn from the movement. Art Goldberg was suspended and facing criminal charges for obscenity. Herb Caen of the *Chronicle* wrote that Savio resigned because the regents had rebuffed the ultimatum and because he had lost the confidence of much of his student following after the Berkeley faculty had declared that obscenity was "not a free speech issue" and called for disciplining the students.

Spider Magazine: A Subdrama within the Obscenity Crisis

Early in the term a little magazine named *Spider,* obviously amateur and low-cost, was started by a number of students who had been active in the Free Speech Movement. Its editors explained that its purpose was to reflect the concerns of contemporary students: "sex, politics, international communism, drugs, extremism, and rock and roll" (Heirich 1968: 158). Some of the language and illustrations were evidently obscene. My own private reaction to the publication was that it was a low-quality, tasteless, irritating, but basically harmless rag. In mid-March, however, the magazine became the focus of a crisis—superimposing itself on the obscenity storm—and a source of embarrassment and urgency for the campus administration. As such, the tempest over the magazine is an example of a minor item that becomes elevated to a major item because of a change in its context. Here is an account of some particulars, including my role in the events.

At the obscenity rally on March 4 a great image of a spider was displayed, obviously to call attention to the magazine (*San Francisco Chronicle,* March 5, 1965). In the subsequent few days sales apparently thrived, both because attention had been brought to it by the obscenity rallies and because its publishers surely realized that the little magazine had suddenly assumed a new and more provocative significance. We also heard an increasing number of complaints about the publication and its sales, which were said to be offensive to some passers-by. Finally, because the chancellor's office, especially Meyerson, was by early March under intense outside pressure to discipline offenders at the obscenity rallies, the problem of *Spider* also became urgent.

The administration dealt with the problem initially by sending a complaint about the magazine submitted by Dean Arleigh Williams to the Faculty Committee on Student Political Activity. That committee recommended banning the magazine from the campus, along with a shady play called "For Unlawful Carnal Knowledge." Accordingly, on March 18, Meyerson issued a ban on both, which was to be in effect until the committee made a final decision. The ban cast the administration into the always difficult role of moral censor. The news made front-page headlines in the *Berkeley Daily Gazette* (March 19, 1965). The next day a rally attended by an estimated 1,200 protested the ban and, predictably in retrospect, various groups proceeded to defy it and sell the magazine on campus. The embarrassment thus continued.

On March 18 a group of chancellor's staff held a strategy meeting on what to do about sales of *Spider*, especially by nonstudents. Meyerson had extended the ban until the end of the month. At the end of that meeting Martin asked me to go onto Sproul Plaza and try to persuade a group of people selling the magazine to stop the sales and leave the campus. Inwardly I balked at doing this, but in the heat of the whole obscenity tempest, and out of loyalty to Meyerson, I agreed to do so and ventured on to the Plaza with Arleigh Williams.

My effort failed completely. I should have remembered Williams' admonition that the main effect when an administrator confronted a defiant group on the plaza was to attract a throng of a hundred shouting, taunting students and nonstudents. That is exactly what happened. Furthermore, partly because my heart was not in this little expedition, I remember being especially inarticulate, not knowing what arguments to make beyond telling the group that they should leave because the chancellor wanted them to and mentioning the possibility of discipline if they didn't. I left after a while, but the sellers did not. The *Daily Californian* reported continuing sales. On the next day several dozen graduate students from the sociology department signed a letter to the *Daily Californian*. The letter was addressed to me. It began by complimenting me for "being one of the most conscientious and dedicated teachers and scholars in the university community" and for "maintaining the highest intellectual standards in the classroom." It went on to say, however, that I had affiliated myself with an administration that was violating the December 8 faculty resolutions, disregarding due process, and engaging in "arbitrary Administrative power." I had disappointed them, they concluded, and they "respectfully" urged me to resign (*Daily Californian*, March 19, 1965).

To this day I rue that whole episode. I know that is an irrational feeling, because the event soon faded from the scene, did not impair my ongoing activity in the chancellor's office, and left no mark on my later reputation, and nobody but a handful of old-timers can now dredge up any memory of it. It was the only moment in my time in the chancellor's office that I was publicly criticized (and this only in an obscure letter in the campus newspaper). I suppose that might be regarded as a sign of success—that I maneuvered my way through those months so unscathed—but my foray onto the plaza was out of keeping with my evolving philosophy of how to deal with protest (in this case, letting it die a natural death) and damaging to my only partially conscious self-image as a quiet hero helping the cause of the campus but basically operating behind the scenes. I also think Meyerson should not have asked me to undertake that fruitless expedition, though I fully appreciate the magnitude of the pressures on him at the moment.

The *Spider* issue gradually faded as the obscenity crisis worked its way toward resolution through the disciplining of the students. There was a flurry of activity around March 23 and 24 when Meyerson upheld the ban, with heated arguments over whether *Spider* should be regarded primarily as a political publication or an obscene magazine, and whether it might be sold in the ASUC bookstore but not on the plaza. Outside sales continued in defiance of the ban. Meyerson lifted the ban at the end of March, with a face-saving but unenforceable proviso that students could sell it only if it could be shown to serve the purposes of their student organization. SLATE continued to sell the magazine, and on April 2 the *Oakland Tribune* reported "brisk sales." As the weeks passed, however, the excitement over the magazine flagged, and it passed from the scene like so many of the experimental forays in that Spring.

A Post-mortem Gasp: The Free Student Union

Almost immediately after Savio's departure, members of the executive committee of the FSM, after an all day meeting, determined to form a separate new organization, pressed by Jack Weinberg and Bettina Aptheker. She called for a labor-union type organization that would use the student strike as its principal weapon. Weinberg said the time was ripe for such an organization, because "all across the country people are looking to Berkeley and following our activities" (*Daily Californian,* April 29, 1965). An organizational meeting was held in Harmon Gymnasium with Aptheker, Weinberg, and Michael Lerner speaking. The leaders reported that two thousand had joined by paying 25-cent membership dues; they had announced a goal of five thousand members.

The new Free Student Union (FSU) generated a small squall on May 4 by setting up and manning tables in Sproul Plaza. Police hauled away several FSU tables as directed by the dean's office on grounds that the Union was not registered. I recommended that we deal with the "illegality" issue by persuading the organization to register as a student organization. We gave the FSU a week of grace to comply, and I invited representatives of the group to meet with me and some faculty members to discuss the interim rules (*Berkeley Daily Gazette,* May 5, 1965). They refused the invitation, but on the next day the FSU voted to comply with the interim rules requiring application for table permits. About the same time a member of the fledgling organization came to me to recommend a working group made up of regents, administrators, faculty, and students to work out a "more workable" set of rules for campus political activity; I said I would take the idea under consideration. They tried to be heard at a regents' meeting on May 21 but were denied. On May 29 the organization attempted again to test the rules by demanding an extension of amplification on Sproul Plaza beyond the deadline. Finally, they agitated unsuccessfully for office space in the Student Union.

The press paid little attention to the FSU. I also felt at the time that it could not be taken seriously and regarded it as part search for a new model for activists, part fantasy, part bluster, and part face-saving in the face of the ignominious collapse of the FSM a few days earlier. We played it straight with the new organization, however, and within a short time it seemed to melt away.

EDUCATIONAL REFORM

The issue of student-oriented educational reform had been in the air for some time but was not the most salient item on the activists' agenda. Part of the concern had to do with accusation that faculty were in bed with the national power establishment, helping its war designs and weapons-making, and sucking research funds to their own coffers to the neglect of their proper mission of dedication to students. The pamphlets and the public rallies made frequent references to depersonalization, lack of "relevant" education, the university as factory, and large courses not taught or graded by instructors. The slogan, "I am a student; do not fold, staple, or mutilate" became a kind of hostile mantra in student protestors' rhetoric. Bill Trombley wrote an article entitled "Knowledge Factory" in *the Los Angeles Times* (Jan. 20, 1965), quoting FSM leaders to the effect that Berkeley is a place where "human nerves and flesh are transformed under the pressures and stress of the university routine."

The campus extended an early, small peacemaking gesture by permitting the granting of "E" grades (incomplete), rather than F, for work the preceding semester so students could make up the work. Predictably, the decision was welcomed by the students and sniped at by Regent Cannaday, who charged we had "capitulated to pressure" (*San Francisco Chronicle*, January 23, 1965). More generally, however, Meyerson was beginning to speak in terms of educational reform. He took a keen interest in the upcoming Proposed Experimental Program (the Tusssman Program) and announced that an administrator ought to extend beyond the caretaker aspects of his office and "sponsor new experimental programs outside the existing units which sometimes find it difficult to initiate because of traditional commitments." I can report independently that his sentiment was a genuine one, because from time to time in our private conversations he would bring up points of educational inadequacy in mass research universities and seek my reaction to possible lines of reform. However, although educational reform was part of the rhetoric of the student activist movement, I had not heard much student talk about it during the Spring semester of 1965.

On March 2 Meyerson made a major move, delivering a long, somewhat pedagogical and philosophy-of-education message to the Academic Senate. He mentioned educational models such as St. John's at Annapolis, as well as Oxford and Cambridge, and advocated different kinds of general education. At the end he called for a kind of "commission on the state of education at Berkeley." He asked the Emergency Executive Committee to consult widely in the senate about the best ways to deal with the intellectual ferment about education on the campus. Conspicuous faculty members (including its chair, Charles Muscatine, Department of English) were appointed to an education commission. Meyerson called on the faculty to make definite and practical proposals. A modest amount of hopeful commentary in the press was stirred by Meyerson's initiative.

Momentum continued on March 23 when Martin and I met with a steering committee to set up the machinery for reforms. The preliminary report issued by the Muscatine committee was, in my estimation, a quite bold one, calling for changes in instructional offerings, praising student idealism, assailing admission standards for being too dependent on grades, augmenting general education, and improving advising. It incorporated a great deal of the student rhetoric of the day. In a predictable move, Savio found fault with its timidity, scolded the faculty for its lack of courage, and declared that "students would have true independence and excellence in education only after they had organized themselves into trade unions" (*Harper's Magazine*, October, 1966).

In the end these educational efforts drew significant attention and initiated a number of changes, notably a faculty board of educational development and an assistant chancellor for educational development on the Berkeley campus, which were established in Fall 1968. The specific charge to the BED was to entertain, foster, develop, and put into place experimental programs. As the first assistant chancellor for educational development (1966–68), I steered the ship of educational innovation over stormy seas for two years, but that is another story to be related at another time. Suffice it to say that the issue of educational reform through the 1964–68 period was unique in that it occupied a place but not high salience in the reformers' agenda, was taken up with more initiative by administrators than either students or faculty, and in the end made only a modest scratch on the furniture of the campus at that time (see chapter 2 for a more extended account).

THE VIETNAM DAY EVENTS AND THEIR AFTERMATH

At the time, and even in retrospect, the collapse of the FSM and the sputtering of the FSU seemed to me to mark the effective demise of the student movement that had gained such potency and achieved such results in the second half of 1964. I have also spoken from time to time of an imaginary experiment to the effect that if the Vietnam War had not escalated, the American student protest movement would have fizzled in 1965. (I am less confident in saying this about Europe's student activism, however, because I regarded the structural problems facing the European systems of higher education as much more profound than those in American universities and colleges, and the European systems were no doubt going to be experiencing their own independent troubles. Nevertheless, the Vietnam War and its accompanying anti-Americanism was a primary component of student protest in Europe as well.)

That mental experiment is, of course, an idle one, because the Vietnam War did escalate, and it dominated campus protests for the remainder of the decade and indeed until the effective end of the war. I was in on the first phases of the massive anti-war activity during Spring 1965, and here is an account of that drama from my perspective.

Expression of opposition to the Vietnam War became evident early in the semester and built up gradually, reflecting, more or less, the increasing aggressiveness of the Johnson administration. An escalation of the war occurred dramatically on January 31, 1965 with the transfer of a fighter squadron from Okinawa to Danang Air Force Base. Bombings of targets in North Vietnam began almost immediately. In early March 3,500 U.S. Marines were dispatched to South Vietnam, a figure that increased to nearly 200,000 troops by the following December. The incidence of military conflict increased correspondingly.

An article in the *Daily Californian* on February 3 called for protesting America's involvement in Vietnam to congressmen. A week later a rally on Sproul Hall steps featured speakers from the War Resisters League and other organizations, who appealed to young men to refuse to join the armed services until the United States was out of Vietnam (*Daily Californian*, February 9, 1965). At a public meeting two days later a former Vietnamese diplomat called for a pullout of American troops (*Daily Californian*. February 11, 1965). A few days after that the Berkeley University Teacher's Union condemned the bombing of North Vietnam (*Daily Californian*, February 17, 1965). Of special interest was the anti-war rally on February 18, sponsored by SLATE, Campus Women for Peace, and the Committee for Non-Violent Action, indicating, as it did, increased interest by student activists in the war (*Daily Californian*, February 19, 1965).

Anti-war activity on the campus continued through March and April, much of it led by the Berkeley University Teachers' Union. Eighty Berkeley professors signed a letter protesting the war that was published by the local press on March 1. A number of Berkeley faculty traveled to Michigan for the giant anti-war "teach-in" held on March 24. (That event became a kind of model for the subsequent anti-war meetings on October

15–16, overseen by the new chancellor, Roger Heynes, who came to Berkeley from Michigan). Large anti-war meetings were held on March 25 and 26, with Berkeley faculty as the main speakers. A week-long fast to be held at the Oakland Army Terminal was initiated at a Sproul Steps rally on March 26. Campus peace groups also participated in the mass march on San Francisco to protest the war on April 9. About that time anti-war activists began serious planning for a massive event in late May (*Daily Californian*, May 7, 1965).

Jerry Rubin was a key leader in organizing the May 21–22 demonstrations. This was the Jerry Rubin who was later (1967) to become co-leader (with Abbie Hoffman) of the Yippies (Youth International Party), a far-left protest organization emerging from the Students for a Democratic Society. He was also to be a leader of the massive demonstrations at the Democratic National Convention in Chicago in 1968 and a defendant in the famous Chicago Eight (or Seven) trial in 1969. Rubin was admitted to Berkeley as a "limited student" (non-degree) in February 1964 and withdrew in May, 1964. Somebody told me he had audited my undergraduate social theory course, mainly to hear my lectures on Karl Marx's *Das Kapital*, but became bored after those lectures and left. (The class had more than 300 students in attendance, with no roll taken, so I could know nothing about the truth or falsity of that story.) Rubin helped create and operated through the Vietnam Day Committee, said to have one hundred members, with the conspicuous presence of faculty members, led by Stephen Smale, Morris Hirsch, and John Lewis. Rubin and Smale were its cochairs and real leaders, and they were the ones who negotiated with me about upcoming events. Other familiar names of activists also appeared (for example, Betina Aptheker and Jack Kurzweil). Because of the presence of many faculty members on the committee, we were inclined to negotiate more seriously and in better faith than if it had been the usual mix of student and nonstudent activists; that proved to be a misguided understanding on our part because the presence of faculty members did little to temper the actions of the protesters.

On May 11 Rubin and Smale submitted a written statement asking for various arrangements and the use of facilities on May 21–22. Several campus spaces were requested, as well as a suspension of "all the usual regulations regarding limitations on the distribution of literature, fund raising, speakers approval, and other political activity" for the period of the demonstrations (*Daily Californian*, May 12, 1965). Over the next few days I met with them several times and worked out agreements. On May

18 I explained to Meyerson that I had reached the following understandings with the VDC: on-campus parking would not be permitted; dining facilities would not remain open beyond normal hours; the Terrace (a restaurant on Sproul Plaza) would remain open all day Saturday, sandwich distribution permitted; the Student Union would remain open only during regular hours; no sleeping quarters permitted. I also gave permission to use the Lower Sproul Plaza for the whole time but restricted the use of the Upper Plaza, and denied permission to use the West Gate area. Smale asked that the campus pick up part of the financial cost, and I said no. In response to a further request from Meyerson, I explained that the only "rule" that was relaxed was that the office of the dean would grant additional space for tables if requested. Earlier, on May 14, Meyerson had ruled that no classes would be cancelled. In the meantime, Rubin was quoted by the *Daily Californian* (May 14, 1965) as saying that the chancellor's office had granted the use of certain athletic fields for Vietnam Day "because we were afraid of a confrontation." When I confronted Smale and Rubin on this item, they ingratiatingly explained that they were misquoted, and would write a retraction in the newspaper. They did so a few days later, writing in a letter to the editor that the chancellor's office had been "very cooperative."

Other developments did not bode well. Certain speakers from the moderate "right," such as Robert Scalapino and Eugene Burdick, had withdrawn, calling the upcoming events a "circus" (*Berkeley Daily Gazette,* May 20). An editorial in the *San Francisco Examiner* (May 18, 1965) called the occasion "rigged" and imbalanced, and the State Department, after promising to send representatives, withdrew from participating a week in advance because the program was "not balanced." McGeorge Bundy, President Johnson's assistant for national security affairs, withdrew at the last moment on account of "prior commitments." These withdrawals simply augmented the sense that the events were going to be a massive anti-war exhortation. They also assured that the tone of the days was not going to be in the nature of an "educational protest" (Smale in the *Daily Californian,* May 3, 1965) or an academically oriented "teach-in," as some advertised it.

The events on May 24–25 were indeed something like a circus, even though it was attended by 5,000–7,000 people rather than the advance estimations of 25,000–50,000 predicted by the event's leaders. The organizers and participants basically threw our advance agreements to the wind, as they themselves unilaterally "suspended" the rules governing political activity. In the days following we heard many complaints from students and others regarding the size of signs, manning of tables by off-campus groups, tables larger than permitted, huge banners, commercial food concessions, unauthorized signs, a "circus" atmosphere, and assertions that the university had been "taken in." The press coverage was heavy, dominated by headlines such as "Thousands Mob UC Teach-in" and "U.S. Vietnam Policy Blasted at Teach-in"—headlines not upstaged by the story on "Matrimony for Savio" (with fellow-activist Suzanne Goldberg). Whatever the success of the event in mobilizing protest against the war, I felt the campus administration had been damaged by appearing to compromise its high-road stance of political neutrality. After the event we had to hassle the VDC for expenses incurred, and in the end we were only partially compensated.

I remember being very upset at the outcome of the Vietnam Day protests. This was based on the facts that (a) I had lost control of May 21–22, even though I had made every effort to negotiate the conditions under which activities were to take place; (b) many complaints came in after the events, both about the violations of understandings with the organizers and about the "biased" and "propagandistic" character of the days' activities. My unhappiness had nothing to do with any feelings I might have had about the rightness or wrongness of the war; it was based on my chagrin that the campus (and by implication, I) had been embarrassed.

By July, Rubin and his associates were already planning for even greater demonstrations on October 15–16, which were designated "Days of International Protest." A planning meeting was held in Dwinelle Hall on July 7. Even though I knew I was going to leave the chancellor's office in the Fall and wasn't going to be around for the October days, at the end of July I decided to write a memorandum to Lincoln Constance (who had taken over as acting chancellor from Meyerson late in the Summer). The memo read as follows:

[Matters of legality] remain in the hands of the legal authorities. Nevertheless, the University has every obligation to protect its own financial interests, and to see it that its regulations are adhered to during any protest or other political activity. In this connection, I would suggest that the University adopt the following policies if the Vietnam Day Committee requests the use of facilities on October 15 and 16:

(1) To determine whether a massive protest on campus would interfere with other University activities, such as class day meetings, Family

Day festivities, and so on. If so, the request should be either declined, limited to non-disruptive times, or shifted to another date.

(2) Facilities should not be granted until full payment for last spring's Vietnam Day is given to the University, and until advance payment for any University outlays is provided by the sponsoring group. Furthermore, the sponsoring group or groups should be required to sign a statement for financial responsibility for any damage that might be done to University buildings or landscaping.

(3) The sponsoring group for any demonstrations should be required to agree in writing to certain procedures that will help to insure that University regulations will not be violated. For example, they should agree that, in advertising the event, no non-authorized organizations are invited to participate (this will allow the University better to assure the regulation prohibiting non-students from circulating material and setting up tables will be observed). For another example, the sponsoring group or groups should agree in advance that certain kinds of displays will not be made. For a third example, the sponsoring groups should agree in advance to abide by any request by an authorized University official to lower the sound level or otherwise moderate the proceedings. The sponsoring groups should be notified that if they do not adhere to these pledges, they are endangering their future access to the facilities.

These agreements between the University and the sponsoring organization should be drawn up in a fairly formal way, and the University should have the advice of legal counsel in drawing them up. These relatively formal agreements will avoid a sort of *ad hoc* verbal agreement between individuals and University representatives that last Spring proved to be a quite unsatisfactory means of making arrangements for such a massive and complex event as Vietnam Day.

Incidentally, I do not mean these procedures only to apply to anti-war activities; they should perhaps be common policy for any costly large-scale event that takes place on campus and makes use of campus facilities.

I make these suggestions in no spirit of wishing to harass any organization, but rather to prevent, in a fairly careful way, the development of the completely unrestrained and disruptive features that characterized the Vietnam Day events last May.

I regard that memo as simultaneously an effort to shape future policy; as a commentary on the unworkability of informal, ad hoc agreements between a single university representative (as I had been) and individuals and organizations determined to do anything they want to do; and as an expression of my personal regret about our being overwhelmed the previous May. The chancellor's files indicate that my memo was forwarded to Chancellor Heyns in anticipation of the October 15–16 demonstrations, but since I had departed well before the planning to deal with these events took place, I cannot assess what effect, if any, it had on the Heyns administration's thinking and preparations. I do know that the chancellor's office was more systematic in its approach to that event and demanded a written memorandum, signed on October 12 by Smale and John Searle of the chancellor's office, regarding facilities to be used, reimbursement of the campus, and other matters. At that time, too, the administration took greater care to coordinate with the police, to use neutral parties (such as members of the campus ministries) as "monitors," and to achieve better political "balance." The events in October were conducted in such a way that William Trombley could write that "to date Heyns has avoided confrontation with the Vietnam Day committee by a process of constant conversation and persuasion" (*Los Angeles Times,* November 2, 1965).

In retrospect I regard the sequence of events from early May to late October as an important episode in the learning process that universities and colleges were evolving to face situations of unprecedented political protest and group conflict that had descended upon them and for which they were ill-equipped to manage. The nature of this evolution was from ad hoc, naïve, and amateur coping toward a more prepared and professional stance.

AUTHORITY BY DEFAULT

As can be seem from the narratives in this chapter, the Berkeley campus faced a situation in Spring 1965 that had two special features: (a) many political and organizational situations that it had not experienced before; (b) a campus authority system that was reevolving slowly and irregularly toward restoring normalcy, but along a path that was tentative and fraught with ambiguity and uncertainty. Under these circumstances all kinds of requests and situations come up the line of authority for handling, because those down the line don't know what to do or are afraid of doing anything. I certainly experienced that situation in my period in the chancellor's office, and I give a few examples of how this process of "authority by default" worked out.

- On February 15 a student came to me, protesting a grade change from E (incomplete) to F in a course he had taken, with the result that he could not drop the course retrospectively. He obviously did not want the F on his transcript. I informed him of his right to appeal after consultation with the dean, and to have a conversation with the chair of the Committee on Courses.

- On February 21 I was approached by a group of Interfaith Workers to use campus facilities for their work. I recommended that the dean's office take up regular negotiations with the group, adding in a memo to the files "I don't think I am the person to be doing this [negotiation] because the thing is not really a political matter."

- On April 26 Donald Coney, the campus librarian, apprehensive of a threatened sit-in, asked me what he should do. I told him I thought the sit-in was only a remote possibility and that he should keep the library open but report to the police any damage in the event that a sit-in occurred.

- On May 21, at the beginning of the Vietnam Day events, I received a call from a local clergyman, Keith Chamberlain, asking whether clergymen could attend as witnesses, because participating students were "afraid that the fraternity crowd will come and make trouble." I said that the clergy should feel free to do so.

- Mario Savio came to me, unannounced, on March 2, complaining about the university's taping of rallies; he also demanded to know what kinds of dossiers were being kept on students. I recommended to Meyerson that we stop taping the rallies and also that we should keep only minimal, factually established materials in the student files.

- On June 29 representatives from the Graduate Coordinating Committee (FSM), the Free Student Union, and the American Federation of Teachers came to me to demand space in the Student Union. I turned this down after talking with Student Union officials.

· On May 5, I received a call from the campus accounting office, in which an officer, N. M. Mundell, said he was under pressure to mail fellowship payments directly to students (to avoid the inconvenience that students experienced in having to pick them up). Mundell was worried about this, and believed that direct mail would entail mailing checks to students who had dropped out. I supported Mundell in this matter.

As far as I could or can determine, I was not really authorized to deal with or make decisions with respect to any of these matters, with the exception of Savio's request. But in the absence of clear understandings people came to me, and I sometimes responded to their visits with some kind of decision, which almost immediately became official, even though I had no formal power in the matter. From these kinds of episodes I concluded that a great deal of "authority by default" accrues under conditions of ambiguity.

IMPRESSIONS OF A FEW CHARACTERS IN THE DRAMA

During my time in the chancellor's office I interacted with scores of others on campus—colleagues on the chancellor's staff and the dean's office; faculty, both through the Academic Senate channels and individually; student and nonstudent activists; and miscellaneous individual persons who contacted me as representatives of interested organizations or on their own. I would like to record a few memories.

Despite my sensitive position in the Berkeley campus, I almost never communicated with Clark Kerr or any of the members of the board of regents. My friendship with Kerr developed only later. Kerr's formal communications were mainly with Meyerson; I know he also interacted informally with known faculty colleagues on the Berkeley campus. But as Martin's assistant I did not communicate with the president's office, and I went to only one meeting of the board, and that was to make a presentation on academic policy. I did receive phone calls from members of the board of regents occasionally when they were concerned or irate about some campus situation. Because of the basically local (campus) reference of my work, I am not able to comment on such interesting "higher-level" questions such as why Meyerson was not appointed as full chancellor, though I, like others, heard all the rumors—that he was too liberal for many regents, that he hurt his chances by pretending to the regents to be

·more hard-line than he really was, and that there was a residue of sentiment among some regents that a Jew should not be chancellor. I am not,
however, in a position to verify any of these assertions.

Martin Meyerson

During the months I worked with Martin I developed the deepest respect
and affection for him. He was a committed academic and intellectual.
Some might have considered him too much so, because he was sometimes
thought to intellectualize unduly about the demanding practical conditions around him. I never found that a fault. I found him an extremely
intelligent and sensitive man with full commitment to the highest values
of the academy. His bent was to take the high academic road, although
he had a realistic political sense as well. His leadership skills were impressive, and I have always marveled how he held the loyalty of so many
different groups in the faculty. In general he respected others, and the
two of us developed a relationship of the greatest mutual respect. We
interacted easily and had very few disagreements. He was free in his
expressions of gratitude for my service. He brought me easily and frequently into his family. He had two other special assistants, Robert
O'Neill from Boalt Law School on legal matters and Dale Jorgenson of
the economics department on issues of educational reform. But because
almost everything was fraught with politics in those months, Martin and
I developed the closest and most intimate relationship. I felt that we were
a very close two-person group under constant threat.

Under such circumstances, those under fire often develop an attitude
that has been called "groupthink," a bunker mentality that identifies who
are one's friends and who are one's enemies, rigidifies that outlook, shuts
out information that is inconsistent or unfriendly, and rejects others who
do not appear to be fully on board (see chapter 3). Although Martin and
I shared likes and dislikes, we never fell into such an attitude. It was almost
as though we didn't have time to do so. That mentality certainly developed in the last crisis months of the Strong administration, and I saw
evidence of it in the beleaguered inner circle of the Heyns administration
(of which I was not a member, even though I was in his administration
for two years.)

Martin had a keen sense of humor and a playful side. We could always
joke about the grimmest moments and situations. At one moment in the
spring he asked me to head a little committee of three, which he called
the Committee on Pieces of Paper. We gathered all the communications

that go out to students each year from the library, the registrar's office, the Office of the Dean of Students, the financial aid office, and the housing office. He asked us to analyze their content and tone. In doing that we concluded that these messages revealed a preoccupation with rules and sanctions if rules were broken (you cannot graduate if you haven't paid your library fines), which together made an unfriendly, nonsupportive, distrustful impression. As chair of this little group I wrote up some recommendations for making these communications more humane and submitted them to Martin. As far as I know the report disappeared almost immediately and has never been heard of since.

Martin could also be teased. I would sometimes tell him that he would go down in history as a great Puritan moral guardian, à la Oliver Cromwell, for his accomplishments in rooting out obscenity on the campus. Then I would say, no, that's wrong, you will be regarded more like Pierre Mèndes-France, who did the right, necessary, and dirty work of extracting France from Algeria during his brief premiership in 1954–55, then was crucified for his good deed. I saw Martin's humor fail him only once, on April Fools Day, 1965, when I wrote him a spoof memo reporting an unbelievably hostile phone call from a feared member of the board of regents. Martin took it literally and became very alarmed. I had to spend some time apologizing for the tasteless jest.

About a year after he left the chancellor's office Martin was appointed president of the State University New York at Buffalo and later took on the presidency of the University of Pennsylvania in 1971. We lost close touch with one another, though he did attempt unsuccessfully too hire me at Penn at one point, and our paths crossed from time to time in the American Academy of Arts and Sciences and elsewhere. When we did meet we always fell into the warmest of reminiscences. When he died in June 2007, I was greatly saddened.

Arthur Ross

As chair of the Emergency Executive Committee, Ross was a source of bedrock support for the Meyerson administration and managed to engineer the same support from the rest of the committee and to a large degree from the remainder of the faculty. He and I had a very good and cordial working relationship, marred only by Ross's occasional outbursts of hostility and punitiveness toward the student activists that I believed to be excessive and unhelpful. I frequently described him to Martin as "our Irish cop."

Richard Hafner

As public affairs officer, Richard Hafner was the steadiest, most sensitive, most dedicated to and protective of the campus of anyone I knew. We came to like one another immediately and discovered how many outlooks we shared in common. Because I so often felt that the chancellor's office resembled a military high command post, I dubbed him "General Hafner," and the label has stuck ever since. I also teased him for being the only public relations officer in the country whose primary interest was to keep the university's name out of the news. For years afterward I would drift into his office to take the pulse of the campus, especially when it was in trouble. Like war veterans, we have remained steadfast friends ever since. Later I also became good friends with Ray Colvig, the public information officer, who also helped see me through the crises.

Mario Savio and Other Activists

I had every reason to dislike Savio because he was the perceived and, in many respects, the actual leader of the group that was a constant thorn in our side, and because he broke into abusive tirades at me on many occasions. Despite this, he would let down his guard from time to time and reveal a sensitive and humane side. He was the only one of the lot whom I liked personally, though I never showed those feelings to him. The man experienced great unhappiness subsequently—an autistic child, a divorce, bouts of mental illness, a history of heart problems. He died in 1996 at the age of fifty-five. At the news of his death I experienced some quiet remorse.

I came to regard Art Goldberg as abusive, though I was able to have some feeling of sympathy for him when he led a small minority of the FSM Steering Committee into the morass of the obscenity situation and thereby did so much to destroy the movement. Steve Weissman was the smartest of the activists, capable of some objectification of the political situation, but partly because he was so smart I did not trust him at all. Martin Roysher was a kind of courier of the Steering Committee who frequently brought messages, reports, and demands to me and felt me out on one issue or another; he had a demeanor that was so polite and ingratiating that I couldn't trust him, either. For reasons revealed above, I regarded Jerry Rubin as thoroughly opportunistic and manipulative. As for the remainder of the activists with whom I came into contact, it was difficult to get to know, much less develop any kind of relationship with, any of them, because they were always in an official protesting posture, and, as representative of the chancellor's office, I had assume a posture, too.

THE DAILY ROUND

It is difficult to characterize a "typical day" in my life during my months in the chancellor's office, because each day brought unanticipated events, situations, or concerns that had to be dealt with by a phone call, a personal meeting, a letter, or a consultation with the chancellor or others on the campus. Those alone were usually enough to occupy all my time. In addition, I also had to lecture three times a week and meet students in office hours for my theory course; meet with individual graduate students whom I was supervising; dart off for a psychoanalytic hour four times a week; tend to the editorial duties of the *American Sociological Review* (mostly after hours); and pick up my children every Wednesday afternoon and every weekend. Needless to say, my ongoing scholarly research ground to a complete halt during these months. I was under great stress the whole time, but the pace of events was so rapid-fire that I didn't have much time to indulge myself in responses to stress. Nevertheless, over the years I have paused and wondered occasionally not only why I took on this assignment but also how I was able to do it. I have no definitive answers for that final question either. What comes to mind, however, is Martin's comment at the moment of his announced resignation in March 1965: "Whatever these last months have been, they have not been boring" (*San Francisco Chronicle*, March 11, 1965). I also know that those months were the most educational and exciting of my life.

REFERENCES

Heirich, Max. 1968. *The Spiral of Conflict: Berkeley 1964*. New York: Columbia University Press.

Heirich, Max, and Sam Kaplan. 1965. Yesterday's discord. *California Monthly* 75 (Feb.): 20–32.

Smelser, Neil J. 1962. *Theory of Collective Behavior*. New York: Free Press of Glencoe.

Smelser, Neil J. 2007. *The Faces of Terrorism*. Princeton, NJ: Princeton University Press.

TWO

Berkeley in Crisis and Change (1973)

IN THE PERIOD AFTER HE was discharged as president of the University of California in 1967, Clark Kerr established the Carnegie Commission on Higher Education, which, mainly through its research and publications, exercised a decisive influence on American higher education for decades. As part of that operation, Kerr created the Technical Advisory Committee (TAC) as sounding board for ideas and projects and for reviewing items to be brought before the commission. Situated in Berkeley, the TAC was composed of scholars and others knowledgeable about higher education. I served on the TAC for five years (1968–73) and spent another three years on the Carnegie Council's Project on Undergraduate Education in the late 1970s.

As one of its scores of projects, the commission sponsored a special study of colleges and universities under stress in the 1960s and 1970s. David Riesman and Verne Stadtman, both active on the Carnegie Commission, edited the book. They asked me to write on Berkeley largely, I suppose, because I had been in the center of things during the years 1965–72, serving in the chancellor's office for three years and on the Policy Committee of the Berkeley Division of the Academic Senate. I had

First published in *Academic Transformation: Seventeen Institutions under Pressure,* ed. David Riesman and Verne A. Stadtman, 51–79 (New York: McGraw Hill Book Company, 1973).

also just finished my book on conflict and change in California higher education between 1950 and 1970. They asked me to step back and reflect on the dynamics and the consequences of the near-decade of turmoil beginning with the Free Speech Movement of 1964. This essay reflects the fruits of my efforts.

During the past eight years, the name of the University of California at Berkeley has become synonymous with crisis and change. Though its episodes of political turmoil have been surpassed in size and dramatic effect—at Columbia, Harvard, the Sorbonne, the Free University of Berlin, and Tokyo University, perhaps—Berkeley can nevertheless lay claim to number one ranking in crisis creation in the 1960s. The Berkeley campus electrified the academic world with the Free Speech Movement in 1964. Since that time it has witnessed the so-called Filthy Speech Movement in Spring 1965; the Oakland Army Terminal protest in Fall 1965; the Navy Table incident and strike in Winter 1966; an attempt to close the Oakland Induction Center in Fall 1967; the controversy over Social Analysis 139X, the course taught in part by Eldridge Cleaver, in Fall 1968; the Third World Liberation Front strike over ethnic studies in the first months of 1969; the People's Park controversy in Spring 1969; the anti-ROTC agitation and the "trashing" in Spring 1970; and the attempt to "reconstitute" the campus in a political direction in the wake of the American intervention in Cambodia in Spring 1970.

These and innumerable other minor crises and "near misses" have involved the university in months of intense and bitter controversy; days of physical confrontation between protestors and the police and military; thousands of arrests; many injuries and a fatality; hundreds of thousands of man-hours in crisis-related meetings; and hundreds of altered collegial and personal relations. While the scene has cooled noticeably—and, to many, somewhat mysteriously—few predict confidently that crisis and confrontation have ended in Berkeley.

Why did these episodes erupt first at Berkeley? Why have controversies arisen over certain issues and not others? Why have the controversies been so continuous and of such great magnitude? How has the campus been changed by the turmoil? In this essay I shall reflect on these questions. Even though I have personally been in the eye of the hurricane on many occasions, and even though, like everyone else, I have seen the years of turmoil from a particular vantage point that influences my reflections, I shall attempt to be as dispassionate as possible.

My interpretative framework is fairly simple: A number of changes were occurring in the larger society and at Berkeley itself prior to the period of turmoil. These changes modified the campus social organization and its pattern of social groups. The new social organization made previously latent issues more meaningful to more people, and the new groups more likely than before to define these issues as controversial. From these prior changes we can understand much about the content and magnitude of the issues that gripped the campus in the 1960s. In addition, once controversy broke out, it developed a dynamic of its own, which superimposed new bases for conflict on the original issues. Finally, the political turmoil itself initiated pressures for further change; but the precise effects of the turmoil are difficult to ascertain because they are intermingled with the effects of other, possibly independent processes of change.

PRIOR CONDITIONS AND DEVELOPMENTS

The first background development, by no means specific to Berkeley, was the emergence of American society from the quiescent Eisenhower era into a period of more intense political involvement. The civil rights struggle became more intense, direct action emerged as a common political strategy, and the peace movement became stronger. The latter was augmented substantially by subsequent American involvement in a war regarded by many as illegitimate. Society as a whole was headed toward a period of political ferment.

That colleges and universities mirror and sometimes magnify the social and political conditions of the larger society is a general principle. For this reason alone we would expect an increasing preoccupation with political activity on the Berkeley campus in the 1960s. But distinctive characteristics of that campus made the principle especially applicable there. Along with institutions like Wisconsin and City College of New York, Berkeley had long been recognized as a center of student political activity. In addition, it had recently witnessed a number of episodes that had increased political consciousness on the campus—the formation, in 1957, of SLATE, a student political party composed of a number of liberal and radical political groups; protest against capital punishment, particularly against the execution of Caryl Chessman, in 1959–60; demonstrations against the House Un-American Activities Committee in 1960; and a variety of civil rights agitations directed against Bay Area restaurants, retail outlets, automobile companies, and other establishments in the early

1960s. Relations between the political activists and the campus administration were uneasy at best and sometimes broke into open conflict, as in the controversy over directives limiting off-campus political stands and the demonstrations against compulsory ROTC in 1960–61. A SLATE manifesto in the summer of 1964 indicated that some of the politically active students had developed an openly hostile and even revolutionary attitude toward the Berkeley administration.

Ecologically, the Berkeley campus is conducive to the mobilization of mass protest. The south campus area has a population of indeterminate size, consisting of a shifting mixture of culturally alienated (bohemians, beatniks, hippies), politically active, and transient youthful people. Readily mobilizable by pamphlet and word of mouth, this population has moved in and out of the alliance with student activists depending on the issue at hand. Also available in times of crisis was a "floating" group of easily mobilized people around the Bay Area, most from other campuses in the urban area, some from San Francisco's enclaves of cultural and political alienation, and some from the student bodies of local high schools. Furthermore, both student and south campus life had come to be concentrated in Sproul Plaza, an open area flanked by the student union and the main administration building and, at the northern end of Telegraph Avenue, connecting the south campus residential area with the main campus, especially the buildings housing the social sciences and the humanities. In the natural rhythms of campus and Telegraph Avenue life, large groups of potentially mobilizable people thronged through Sproul Plaza.

The decade before 1964 also witnessed significant changes in the size and composition of the diverse groups, or "estates," constituting the university population. The campus enrollment grew from 14,927 students in 1953 to 26,939 in 1964, a growth of about 80 percent. At the same time, trends leading to, and culminating in, the California Master Plan for Higher Education of 1960 changed the internal composition of the student body. In keeping with the trend to increase the standards for admission to the university, the Master Plan fixed the percentage to be admitted as the top 12½ percent of graduating high school seniors and to divert lower division students to community colleges and state colleges, the number of lower division students increased from 5,494 in 1953 to 7,232 in 1964, a growth of only 32 percent. In keeping with the trend to transfer highly qualified students from other sectors of California's higher education system to the universities later in their college careers, the number of upper-division students grew from 5,739 in 1953 to 10,145 in 1964, an increase of 76 percent. And in keeping with the emphasis on the University of California's role as the exclusive public grantor of doctoral degrees in the state, the number of graduate students grew from 3,796 in 1953 to 9,562 in 1964, an increase of 152 percent. The composition of the student body changed as follows:

	Percentage in 1953	Percentage in 1964
Lower division	37	27
Upper division	38	38
Graduate	25	35
	100	100

For the faculty, the late 1950s and the early 1960s were a kind of golden age. Leading universities were bidding aggressively with one another for top talent, and the coffers of the private foundations and the federal government were opening. Leading universities drove one another's rank and salary schedules upward; they reduced teaching loads to make their faculty positions more attractive; and they became increasingly generous in granting time to faculty to conduct research and head research institutes. Yet the need for teaching increasing numbers of undergraduates persisted. How did the Berkeley campus respond?

Between 1953 and 1964 the number of full professors at Berkeley increased from 460 to 612, reflecting in part the campus's need to promote in order and retain qualified faculty. The number of associate professors grew only slightly, from 225 to 247. The assistant professors increased from 270 to 383. The total growth in the regular faculty in this period, however, was only 18 percent, in contrast to a growth of 80 percent for the student body. In the meantime, non-faculty research personnel, many of whom were supervised by faculty members in research institutes, increased almost eightfold, from 186 in 1953 to 1,424 in 1964.

The gap between the rate of regular faculty growth and the rate of student growth was filled by appointments to non-regular faculty positions. Whereas increases in the "instructor" and "teaching associate" categories were negligible, the number of "lecturers" (mainly visitors and temporary appointments) grew from 198 in 1953 to 279 in 1964, and the number of teaching assistants (graduate students on temporary teaching appointments) almost tripled, growing from 565 in 1953 to 1,430 in 1964. The teaching assistants' duties, moreover, were concentrated in the large undergraduate courses, especially in the lower division.

Thus Berkeley, already a prestigious university in the eyes of incoming students, appeared to be upgrading itself in several ways. The university reduced the percentage of admissible California high school students from the top 15 to the top 12½ percent of the graduating class; it was taking the cream of community college and state college students as transfers, and it was becoming increasingly professionalized as a leading national center of graduate education. Yet when undergraduates arrived, they often found themselves remote from the most senior faculty—who were teaching undergraduates less, teaching graduates more, and were more involved in research—and found themselves being serviced more by junior faculty, temporary faculty, and semi-faculty. Students might well have perceived that they were being invited to an elite institution only to be educated mainly by its second-class teachers in a large, impersonal setting.

In short, under great pressures to grow and upgrade, the campus had partially fragmented its functions. It had grown at the top, but the senior professors were decreasingly involved in one of the major activities of the university, undergraduate teaching. It had also expanded greatly at the side with the addition of non-faculty research personnel, who were involved in one of the major activities of the campus (the generation of knowledge through research) but who did not enjoy the faculty's privileges of tenure, membership in the Academic Senate, or on-campus parking. It had grown rapidly at the bottom with teaching assistants, whose roles are marginal in the sense that they are one-third faculty, one-third student, and one-third employee. By growing at the side and at the bottom, it had multiplied the number of its second-class citizens, who were, to be sure, involved in some of the central functions of the campus, but who did not receive rewards commensurate with full citizenship and whose investment in and loyalty to the institution was understandably less.

The first-class citizens may have experienced great gratifications from their work, but some also experienced a vague sense of accumulated guilt for neglecting their students. (Some of the political crises of the 1960s provided an opportunity for faculty and students to become momentarily very close to one another.) Many of the non-faculty research personnel experienced feelings of exclusion and perhaps exploitation. (During the 1960s some of the non-faculty research personnel exerted a low-key but persistent drive to secure privileges that would bring them closer to faculty status). Many of the teaching assistants—and perhaps some junior faculty—felt unjustly treated and had conflicting loyalties toward the different constituencies of which they were partial members. (Teaching assistants played an important mobilizing role in many of the crises of the 1960s. In general they split into several subgroups—those who were active in campus political issues, those interested in their "employee" status, those identified with the faculty, and those who were undecided or indifferent.) All these psychological consequences suggest that when conflicts among different constituencies arose, each constituency experienced deep internal divisions and unexpected and volatile factions were likely to form.

One final background factor must be mentioned: the administration of Chancellor Edward W. Strong during the several years prior to 1964. From the beginning, this administration had been perceived by many faculty members as an ineffective one. Regard for Strong was not high, and some faculty members preferred to deal directly with President Clark Kerr. This, combined with the fact that Kerr had been chancellor of the Berkeley campus previously, created a certain jurisdictional ambiguity between president and chancellor with respect to the administration of the Berkeley campus. Faculty dissatisfaction was further crystallized around the transition from the semester system to the quarter system, which many faculty members felt was "shoved down their throats" by the university administration against their preferences, and by the refusal of Strong to rehire Eli Katz—a young faculty member in the German department—on grounds of his refusal to answer questions about his alleged Communist party connections. Many faculty members regarded the Katz case as an important academic freedom matter, and in Fall 1964 the Berkeley Division of the Academic Senate condemned the administration for its handling of it. In sum, many members of the Berkeley faculty appeared dissatisfied with the administration in 1964 and were predisposed to join in opposition to it.

These background considerations offer some clues as to why the issue of the use of university facilities for political activity was such a lively one in 1964, and why politically active students, teaching assistants, and faculty members coalesced in numbers sufficient ultimately, in December of that year, to depose the chancellor and shatter the campus administration's authority. The conflict was magnified by two additional circumstances. (a) At the very outset of the crisis of Fall 1964 the administration came to be regarded as repressive, because the act that triggered the Free Speech Movement (FSM) was the administration's decision to revoke certain privileges of student groups that had been informally granted for some time. (b) Once the confrontation began, the administration seemed to alternate between a position of capitulation and a posture of retaliation with harsh discipline. These circumstances mobilized many who reacted against the administration not as much in terms of the substantive issues of the conflict as in response to the apparently authoritarian behavior of the administration.

The revolution of December 1964 was superficially a temporary one, in the sense that *formal* authority was quickly restored by the law-enforcement agencies and by the regents, who appointed a new acting chancellor. Crises, however, are not terminated merely by formally reestablishing authority. The very fact that a crisis of authority occurs creates new issues and escalates the bases of conflict. New groups form in the crisis period, groups that are prepared to raise previously unraised questions about the legitimizing values and goals of the institution as a whole, and to rewrite history from their own perspectives. Moreover, when authority is challenged openly, groups that previously were not visibly dissatisfied may generate new expectations about their place in the institution and about their share in its authority system.

One issue—the viability of the campus administration's authority—seemed to dominate the Berkeley campus immediately after December 1964. Under stable conditions the main question about an authority system is *how* authority is exercised—effectively, benevolently, repressively, or whatever. Once the legitimacy of authority has been successfully challenged, however, the issue becomes one of *whether* authority can be exercised at all. Under these circumstances the person who holds authority struggles to rebuild and maintain the support of the constituencies who can bolster his claims to authority, and those who have successfully challenged it continue to deny it, partly by attacking the values by which it is legitimized and partly by prodding it and testing its viability. For almost a year after December 1964 the main issue on the Berkeley campus was whether authority could be exercised. Both Martin Meyerson in his brief eight-month administration as acting chancellor and Roger Heyns in the early months of his administration fought to retain this capacity. In was of great symbolic importance that Meyerson was able to "get away with" disciplining four of those involved in the obscenity crisis without stirring a massive campus reaction. It was also significant that this discipline was exercised shortly after an enormous show of support by the faculty. It was of great symbolic importance that Heyns was able to prevent the unauthorized placing of political signs on campus in the fall of 1965 without triggering a serious challenge to his authority. In that year after the FSM many of the issues appeared to be small—how many minutes after 1 P.M. could noontime political rallies continue? How large could political posters be? In reality they were very large issues, because they tested the legitimacy of the administration's authority.

After a crisis the struggle to reestablish authority is often hindered by the fact that many previously quiescent constituencies have become activated and attempt to exert influence. The students, the faculty, the alumni, the board of regents, the press, the law-enforcement agencies, the legislature, and the governor—all these, often themselves split into contending groups—emerged as political influences to be contended with on a day-to-day basis after the crisis of 1964. This activation of interests constricted the maneuverability of the chancellor, threatened to weaken his tenuous control of the campus situation, and forced him to devote more of his energy to pacifying or holding angry constituents at arm's length than to ameliorating the problems that gave rise to the crisis in the first place.

Some of these constituencies, such as the faculty and alumni, are significant primarily as political groups without whose support the campus administrator's position might be untenable. Other constituencies, such as the board of regents and law-enforcement officials, are significant both politically and legally. Various types of ultimate authority reside in them, and they have the legal right to intervene in campus affairs. When the authority of the campus administration was under fire in crisis, these constituencies rushed on the scene, sometimes on their own, sometimes in response to public pressure. As often as not this intervention, while perhaps necessary and justified by the logic of maintaining order, fanned the flames of crisis and intensified the political divisions on the campus. For example, the calling of police or military forces in November 1968, during the Third World Liberation Front strike in the early months of 1969, and during the People's Park crisis in May 1969 immediately heated up these situations and precipitated new mobilization and new actions by different campus groups. Also, the regents' threat to intervene in the obscenity crisis, precipitating statements by Kerr and Meyerson that they intended to resign, produced an enormous mobilization of the faculty in their support. And while the board requested that the two continue, the entire incident revealed exactly how fragile the authority of the statewide and campus administrations was at the time. Again, the regents' intervention in denying academic credit for the Eldridge Cleaver course—which had been approved by the appropriate faculty committees—raised the whole issue of the faculty's delegated authority, inflamed many faculty members and students, and deepened the division between those who did and those who did not approve of the course. Finally, at another level, budgetary intervention by the legislature and governor, motivated in part by political, interventionist considerations, has had a persisting and corrosive effect on faculty morale.

One of the immediate effects of a large campus conflict is that various constituencies of the campus (students, faculty, teaching assistants, etc.) take sides and declare their loyalties. Yet as I noted earlier, the lines of polarization at Berkeley after December 1964 never followed the lines of constituency membership exactly. In fact, because the constituencies were either heterogeneous or marginal—and therefore ambivalent in their loyalties—polarized political conflict tended to split each constituency. Thus the campus was faced with a kind of "multiplier effect" whereby any serious conflict *between* constituencies (typically, between students and administration) led to the intensification of conflict *within* the various constituencies (for example, faculty members favoring the administration versus faculty members favoring the students). Needless to say, this effect seriously undermined the system of collegial consensus on the basis of which the campus has traditionally been governed.

Finally, reflecting the positions taken in conflict, just as the loyalty oath of the early 1950s effected a lasting realignment of loyalties and antagonisms, so the crises of the 1960s left a number of layers of scar tissue that are ready to reopen with the appearance of any new crisis.

Given this general diagnosis of the genesis and dynamics of conflict, what can be said most generally about the issues that have gripped Berkeley in the past eight years? Every issue seems traceable to the fact that the campus has been subject to enormous political pressures—agitation from the left, intervention from the right, and, and mouse-trapping by both at once—and that these political pressures have posed a continuing crisis of legitimacy for the Berkeley administration. Thus every one of the following interrelated issues has ultimately concerned the relations between campus authority and political activity:

1. What kinds of political activity are to be authorized on campus? (FSM, Oakland Induction Center march, Navy table incident)

2. What political uses of the campus facilities are to be authorized? (Vietnam Day Committee, Vietnam moratorium, reconstitution)

3. Should the campus become directly and officially involved in political activity—or, depending on one's point of view, become involved in different ways than it is now? (Vietnam moratorium, protest against CIA and Dow Chemical interviews on campus)

4. To what degree should delegated campus authority—of administration, faculty, and students—be protected from intervention by the board of regents, the legislature and the governor? (an explicit or implicit issue in almost every crisis)

5. To what degree should others than the campus administration (faculty, students, employees) have authority on the campus? (Social Analysis 139X, Third World Liberation Front strike)

6. What are the relations between campus authority and civil authority? (FSM, Oakland Induction Center crisis, the presence of police on campus during many crises)

7. What is the status of the university's authority with respect to the use, control, and disposal of legally defined property and facilities? (People's Park issue)

EFFECTS OF THE YEARS OF TURMOIL

Because of the dramatic quality of the political controversies that have occurred at Berkeley, it is tempting to overemphasize their impact by attributing all subsequent changes to political conflict. The actual causal role played by crises, however, is subtler. Several changes of the past few years were under way in any case, and campus crises played a minor if any role in them. I refer to the development of the new School of Journalism, the new School of Public Affairs, and the new Program of Religious Studies. In other cases the changes were perhaps imminent, but the crises played a catalytic role, as in the liberalization of undergraduate course requirements, the modification of the grading system, and the modest efforts to break from the traditional lecture and discussion-section method of teaching. In still other cases, changes can be attributed more directly to political ferment, as with the creation of a new Department of Ethnic Studies and the increased level of student participation in affairs formerly reserved for administration and faculty. As might be said of all social change, however, no one factor, such as political turmoil, can be assigned an exclusive role; it combines and recombines in complex ways with other forces.

In many respects Berkeley in Spring 1972 has changed very little from Berkeley in Spring 1964. The architectural face of the campus is not dramatically different, except for some new facilities, most of which are "expected" additions to a university—a new auditorium, a new undergraduate library, and a new art museum. The campus's "table of organization" of colleges, schools, departments, research units, and service units is virtually unchanged. The course catalogs of 1964 and 1972 are very similar in content. The same research institutes pursue the same general types of research they did several years ago. The calendar of campus events reveals a similar array of scholarly and cultural activities as before. The size and composition of the student body have not changed much, with the exception that there are many more minority faces now than there were then; the proportion of graduate students has not changed radically; and though this is difficult to document, there are probably larger proportions of students who are politically radical, who are interested in social and political issues in general, and who are involved in the "action" of hip culture. Yet the vast majority of students come to the campus to pursue a course in academic studies, graduate, and proceed to some line of occupational endeavor.

How then have things changed? As might be expected, the most immediate impact of the political crises has been political. The controversies have been given heavy exposure by the mass media and have aroused widespread concern and outrage among the public and the state government. The political repercussions of the crises on the Berkeley campus played a direct role in the demise of Strong; in the threatened resignations of Meyerson and Kerr; in the firing of Kerr in January 1967; in keeping the political position of Heyns frequently in jeopardy; and in precipitating his resignation. The disturbances have also produced direct countermeasures such as more careful surveillance of student and non-student behavior by the campus administration, an increase in the number of disciplinary actions, and more police on the campus more often. Issues generated by events on the Berkeley campus were foremost in the political backlash that swept Ronald Reagan into office in 1966. The most direct effect of this backlash on the Berkeley campus has been on its budget—the most convenient and effective weapon available to the governor and the legislature. In addition, the legislature has passed a few pieces of hostile legislation and initiated a few investigations, and the governor has issued menacing statements periodically that call for "political balance" and "political tests" in recruiting faculty. It is difficult to be certain, but some evidence, mainly from the election results of 1970, indicates that the political mileage to be gained by using higher education as a whipping boy may be decreasing slightly.

The board of regents has intervened in the campus mainly in three ways. First, it has responded to crisis by passing general regulations and resolutions (for example, new disciplinary regulations designed to prevent specific actions that occurred in the crisis immediately before). Second, it has withdrawn previously delegated power from the campuses and occasionally attempted to use that power (for example, in the areas of appointment and tenure, as in the cases of Herbert Marcuse, Angela Davis, and two Berkeley faculty members whose promotions were delayed in Summer 1970). And third, it has attempted to strengthen the campus administrators' authority and disciplinary power over students and faculty. By and large, the regents have much more direct short-run control over the behavior of campus administrators who are directly accountable to them than they do over the behavior of faculty members and students. When regents have become alarmed over situations on campus, they have attempted to strengthen the hands of those campus authorities to whom they have the most direct access. Whether this strategy has been effective is questionable, however, because regental efforts to strengthen the chancellors' authority and to induce them to exercise it strictly are likely to engender further faculty and student distrust of and opposition to the administration.

Faculty response to each crisis has followed a typical pattern. When a crisis breaks, faculty caucuses begin to meet and hammer out positions;

numerous individuals and groups spring into action like so many Lone Rangers or posses, each trying to ease the situation by persuading warring factions to talk with one another. Gradually faculty sentiment coalesces, usually through the mediating efforts of the Policy Committee of the Berkeley Division of the Academic Senate. Some resolution acceptable to most of the major faculty factions is drawn up and put to a vote at a mass meeting of the division. In crises primarily affecting relations among the campus constituencies (FSM, the strike of December 1966, and the Third World Liberation strike), the voice of the faculty has had an important effect in calming the situation and pointing toward at least a temporary resolution. In crises when the campus was overwhelmed by external political conflicts (People's Park, reconstitution), the effect of formal faculty action has been negligible.

Through the years of crisis faculty factions have shifted continuously. At present faculty opinion appears to be broken mainly into four groups: (1) a small conservative group whose sympathies lie with the governor and the majority of the board of regents; (2) the majority of the faculty, who are moderate or indifferent to the political goals of the interventionist right and the radical left; active members in this group have formed the Council for an Academic Community, a sizable and well-organized faculty lobby; (3) a minority of liberal or radical faculty, whose sympathies lie closer to the goals of the left student movement of the 1960s; (4) a group—overlapping with the liberals and radicals—working for the unionization of the faculty; a small but fairly active chapter of the American Federation of Teachers has formed on the campus.

It is my impression that the majority of the faculty—the moderates—are caught in a dilemma. Traditionally their enemy has been the interventionist right; their struggle has been to resist intrusions on academic freedom from above and their natural allies have been on the left. One result of the crises of the 1960s is that many faculty members find themselves also threatened by the student left and sense incursions on their traditional academic freedoms from that quarter as well. Yet they are uncomfortable fighting against the left, and especially uncomfortable when they find themselves agreeing with sentiments of the interventionist right. This dilemma goes far in indicating why many faculty members tend toward vacillation, paralysis, or withdrawal in matters of campus politics (see chapter 4 for an elaboration of this principle).

As indicated earlier, these divisions run deep, and have, to a degree, undermined faculty consensus on such fundamental issues as the idea of a university, appropriate authority relations within it, and appropriate conduct for a faculty member both in out of the classroom. A few departments in the social sciences and humanities and a few professional schools are badly split, difficult to govern, and plagued by frequent, interminable, and bitter meetings. Morale has sagged in these departments, and energy for research and teaching has been drained correspondingly. The sciences and some professional schools, such as engineering, appear to have suffered much less from these effects. Faculty distrust of other faculty members is also reflected in two episodes in the Berkeley Division of the Academic Senate. First, the creation of a Representative Assembly to replace partially the town-meeting forum of the entire division was motivated in part by the desire of moderate faculty members to prevent "irresponsible" resolutions from being passed at ill-attended faculty meetings dominated by extremists. Second, the recent adoption of a code of conduct for faculty—including the specification of obligations as well as the rights and the specification of sanctions and disciplinary procedures—was motivated in part by the desire of moderate faculty members to curb what they regarded as unethical behavior on the part of some of their colleagues during the reconstitution crisis, when some classes were converted into political action groups or discontinued meetings as classes. Of course, many other considerations went into the formation of the Representative Assembly and the formulation of the faculty code of conduct, but the distrust of faculty was one important ingredient.

With respect to faculty governance and academic affairs, faculty responses have been conservative. The Berkeley Division of the Academic Senate established a special student-faculty commission on governance (the Foote Commission) in the wake of the strike in December 1966, but its report, which contained numerous recommendations for campus reorganization and decentralization, went largely unheeded by both administration and faculty. Earlier, immediately after the FSM crisis, Meyerson had established a select committee on education (the Muscatine committee), and its report, *Education at Berkeley*, issued in 1966, was a notable faculty response to both long-term curricular concerns and short-term student pressures for change. The Berkeley Division adopted many of the committee's recommendations, and the Berkeley campus was one of the first to establish a major administrative-faculty unit (the Board of Educational Development [BED]). For several years this agency sponsored programs in group tutorials, combinations of academic work and fieldwork, interdisciplinary studies, and the like. These efforts were curtailed and deflected in other directions in 1968 for a number of reasons. First, the combination of only limited faculty interest in innovation and the onset of budgetary stringency imposed inherent limitations on the magnitude of experimental programs. Also, the political crisis around Eldridge Cleaver and Social Analysis 139X discredited the BED to some extent and led to more stringent administrative controls over faculty appointments in experimental courses. Around that time, experimentation seemed to degenerate in a political tug-of-war between a group of liberal and radical students on the one hand, who pressed for courses, some of which were potentially explosive politically and questionable by traditional academic standards, and faculty and administrators on the other hand, who insisted on the maintenance of standards. Also about that time the all-student Committee on Participant Education, which had been working cooperatively with the BED, broke off and proceeded independently, mainly in initiating non-credit courses and in working with individual faculty members. Finally, many departments began to incorporate experimental courses, thus further decentralizing the work of the BED. The movement for educational innovation must therefore be regarded as a victim of politicization in large part; its impact on the entire campus was modest, though a few valuable traces of the movement—group tutorial programs, undergraduate seminars, field study courses, and the like—can be observed from place to place.

Two main academic units that can be said to have emerged directly from the campus turmoil are the Experimental College ("the Tussman Program") and the Department of Ethnic Studies. The former, a vigorous effort to expose students in their first two years to an intensive interdisciplinary education, generated considerable enthusiasm among many of the students and faculty involved but foundered after several years for lack of faculty interest. The Department of Ethnic Studies, now apparently a permanent fixture on the campus, has enjoyed considerable popularity among minority students. During 1969–70 more than four thousand course enrollments were counted, mainly among minority students, in the courses in the history, socioeconomic conditions, and culture of several ethnic groups.

Despite this favorable start, the department faces serious ambiguities. The first has to do with the goals of the department. The administration's policy has been to regard the department as a normal academic unit whose business it is to conduct courses of instruction; many in the department prefer a more free-wheeling arrangement, with greater emphasis on serving the needs and activities of the constituent groups themselves. Thus far the administration and the department have maintained a kind of standoffish relationship with respect to this fundamental ambiguity. Second, the department faces an uncertain budgetary future. Third, the academic relations between the department and other academic units—in terms of transferability of courses to major programs in other departments, for example—are not entirely clear. In general, the department has thus far existed more or less in isolation from the mainstream of faculty and administrative activities on the campus. And finally, it is not certain whether the department can sustain sufficient interest on the part of its faculty and students to succeed in the long run.

Despite the frequent turmoil, the low morale of many faculty members, and the budgetary squeeze, Berkeley has managed to survive as a high-quality academic institution. The rate of resignation of tenured faculty since the Free Speech Movement has been about 2 percent per year, and in 1969–70 only seventeen tenured members (of a total of 2,079) resigned, the lowest number in six years. I suspect that the uncertain political and economic future for the campus has presented a more severe problem for recruitment than for resignation, however, particularly among young potential recruits without the security of tenure. In the 1970 version of the American Council of Education's survey of the prestige of graduate institutions, Berkeley repeated as most distinguished in quality of graduate faculty and effectiveness of graduate programs. The same kind of standing could not be claimed for the undergraduate program, however, since it still suffers a deficit of faculty involvement. To improve undergraduate education at Berkeley significantly—as President Hitch has asked—would require, at a minimum, the input of substantial new resources to increase the faculty-student ratio and to recruit faculty committed to the development of new programs.

How does Berkeley look to students in 1972? Typical undergraduates still have most of their fare in large lecture courses and discussions led by teaching assistants. They find, however, that "the requirements"—language requirements, breadth requirements—have been liberalized and that some major programs demand fewer required courses. They also find that in some quarters of the campus the classroom is somewhat more open with respect to the degree to which students may influence classroom activity. Discussions in many social science and humanities courses are more heated politically than before, and most faculty in those areas would probably agree that the level of what they used to call student manners and respect for academic authority has declined. A few classes of professors who have conducted research or taken political stands unpopular with the radical left have been disrupted by groups of intruders. In these instances most other students have shown indifference or quiet resentment toward the intrusion. The faculty Committee on Academic Freedom has condemned faculty intimidation and classroom disruption and the administration has taken disciplinary action against those who indulge in it.

Undergraduates participate little in departmental governance and in the machinery of the Berkeley Division. Their opportunities for participation in administrative committees are somewhat greater. Graduate students find their academic programs still primarily professional in character, though some departments have liberalized the number and kinds of requirements along the road to the PhD. Graduate students participate more than undergraduates in departmental affairs, and student participation in some of the professional schools is even more extensive. The success of this participation is mixed; sometimes it has increased student-faculty cooperation and led to a productive student input, and in other cases it has simply moved the adversary student-faculty stance into committees and department meetings. And despite the increase in participation, discontent about the rate of progress is voiced by some faculty and students.

Informally, student life continues to combine the principles of anomie and social pluralism. On the one hand, the student body is heterogeneous, large, and individuated by diversified housing arrangements and casual student contact in the classroom. On the other hand, the student finds a fantastic array of opportunities for developing social ties—in departmental clubs, in political groups, in the drug culture, in encounter groups, and in volunteer activities in the community. Political consciousness is still high among many students and much political activity may be observed in different corners of the campus. Except for the massive attempt to "reconstitute" the campus politically after the Cambodian invasion, however, no episode of mass student political action has occurred on the campus for the past three academic years.

The campus student government, the Associated Students of the University of California (ASUC) was, like so much else at Berkeley, politicized in the Free Speech Movement and subsequent crises. It has experienced a shift from being a relatively quiescent agency concerned with student activities and services toward being a body more aggressively concerned with political issues. The student radical movement, however, has itself been divided on the issue of whether to work through ASUC channels. Some have felt it a promising avenue, largely because of the substantial financial resources of the ASUC; others have felt it useless largely because of the considerable control over ASUC activities exercised by the administration. In consequence, student government as a campus political issue has blown hot and cold. The campus administration, while yielding to a degree to the students' desires to interest themselves in activities such as draft counseling, community programs, and student housing, has also insisted that student funds—which are collected by compulsory fees—also be devoted to traditional activities such as band, rally committee, and extracurricular clubs. Relations between the administration and the ASUC have vacillated between harmony and conflict. One of the perennial disputes between the two has to do with the locus of legitimate authority in student government: the administration tends to view it as delegated whereas some students argue that it emanates from the students and belongs to them as a right. The future of student government at Berkeley is uncertain, as it is elsewhere, but there is a distinct possibility that it will become a voluntary association, in which case a looser and more permissive relationship would be likely to develop between it and the campus administration.

THE FUTURE

Because the past eight years at Berkeley have been so fraught with crisis and change, the future of the campus must also be regarded as fluid and unpredictable. On the one hand, if it continues to be harassed on many fronts by the left and sledge-hammered politically and budgetarily from the right, there is no reason to believe that the long-term effects will be anything other than gloom, low morale, and institutional deterioration. On the other hand, significant shifts in a few important political forces could change the picture dramatically. If the student movement should for whatever reasons remain quiescent, if public antagonism toward higher education should subside, if the state's financial situation should reverse itself, if a state administration and legislature openly favorable to higher education should appear in the next few years, and if the Berkeley campus could be protected from intense budgetary competition from other campuses and the other segments of higher education—all big "ifs," to be sure—the campus might well embark on another of its historically famous golden eras characterized by opulence, goodwill, and cultural enrichment. History alone yields some grounds for optimism, for the story of the University of California has been a story of great fluctuations between gloomy crises and golden eras. But the crises of the past eight years have been so deep that one hesitates to rely on history alone as a guide.

THREE

Surprises at Berkeley

Anticipating, Understanding, and Coping with Them (2004)

MIDWAY INTO THIS CHAPTER I describe an unlikely episode that took the Berkeley campus by surprise and created a period of prolonged criticism, defensiveness, and peacemaking on the part of its campus administration. That episode was the SARS (Severe Acute Respiratory Syndrome) "epidemic" of 2002–3. In the wake of that situation some officials in the chancellor's office came up with the idea that the campus ought to be better equipped to anticipate and deal with such episodes. To that end they constituted a group of administrators and seasoned faculty, which they called Project X—later called the Committee on Surprises—which met throughout Spring 2004. The chancellor, Robert Berdahl, was an active member. The charge to the group was to figure out what leads up to and constitutes a surprise for the campus, what the dynamics of surprises are, how they might be most productively contended with, and what surprises might be awaiting the campus in the near term.

I was a member of the Committee on Surprises during that semester. Early in our work it occurred to me that I might be able to produce a document that would systematize its thinking. During my long career at Berkeley I had participated in and become something of a student of dozens of surprise situations that had accumulated from the 1960s to the present. I approached John Cummins, associate chancellor/chief of staff of the campus, with the idea and asked for two research assistants.

Cummins agreed immediately. I completed the essay in May 2004 and the group discussed it at its last meeting. This chapter is the essay as it was originally written. Project X expired in Summer 2004 and was not resuscitated by Berdahl's successor. I believe it might profitably have been brought back, however, because Berkeley has been and will continue to be a surprise-prone institution for all the reasons adduced in the essay.

The objective of this essay is found in its subtitle. I will attempt to define a "surprise" in the context of the contemporary situation of the Berkeley campus. I will then explore the many relevant facets of surprises—the nature of events that constitute them, the contexts that give them their status as surprises, the possible campus roles in creating them, campus reactions to them once they have occurred, and short-term and long-term effects if these are identifiable. The exercise will have a practical, policy aspect as well as an analytic one. The objective is to work toward the result that surprises can be anticipated—at least on a probabilistic basis—and that preparedness for them will make it possible to react to them more as problems than surprises, thus lessening the probability that surprises will become crises.

The empirical sources on which I have relied are three: (a) data and perspectives revealed in the collective discussions of Project X at its meetings; (b) the work of two graduate research assistants—William Hayes and Harold Toro of the Department of Sociology—in the Spring semester of 2004 on selected episodes during the past forty years; and (c) my own intellectual and campus experiences, which have included research on collective behavior, social movements, and organizational responses to conflict, and have involved me as an actor (variously as administrator, faculty member, or advisor) in many campus efforts to deal with crisis situations.

Before considering the character of surprises and their dynamics, it is important to review the larger cultural and social-structural settings in which contemporary universities live.

THE CULTURE OF A UNIVERSITY AND ITS INATTENTION TO SURPRISES

Many organizations are geared to the occurrence of unanticipated events as a routine part of their daily functioning. The most notable of these are

military and police organizations, which are culturally and organization-
ally programmed to respond to violence, crime, protest, and other threats
to the society and community. They are frequently taken by surprise, to
be sure, but the expectation that they have to deal with the ever-present
possibility of surprising situations is part of their culture. A polity, too, is
in the business of dealing with unanticipated conflicts in the community
and has at its disposal many resources to deal with them—channels to
hear about and air citizen concerns, machinery to strike political compromises, and the political authority to make settlements "stick," once made.
Business firms—effective ones, at any rate—also expect as a matter of
routine that unanticipated market conditions will continually appear and
that they should be prepared to adapt to them.

Historically, universities and colleges have lived under a very different
set of cultural expectations. Deriving partly from their monastic origins,
universities have expected to enjoy a peculiar insularity from society and
community, even though they are regarded as a cultural and social
resource for them. The classroom as a microcosm is sealed off from the
daily affairs of administering the organizational side of the university;
scholarship and teaching are protected by academic freedom (which at
bottom is a series of prohibitions against external intervention); and other
devices are insulating, such as the taboo against external funding agencies
managing the research they are supporting. The principle of the faculty
as a "company of equals" is a denial of politics and authority and an
affirmation of the principle of a voluntary and cohesive community,
which carries out its affairs on the basis of collegial influence and consensus. The university is thus regarded as a protected haven for scholars and
teachers and a relatively insulated moratorium for youth before they take
on the occupational, familial, and community responsibilities of adults.
The university culture includes insulation from external politics as well;
the Organic Act of 1868, for example, specified that the University of
California would be shielded from "sectarian, political or partisan
influence."

The flow of history, however, has evidently given the lie to this idealized
cultural image. Totalitarian governments have ravaged universities through
direct political intervention and control. In the United States, where
universities have been relatively protected in comparison with many other
countries, they have nevertheless experienced periodic rage from religious
constituencies for their godlessness, from the right for their radicalism,
and from the left for their establishment ties and loyalties. Efforts to

compromise academic freedom have always been latent and frequently manifest. Legislatures are forever tempted to meddle in the name of citizen and parental outrage and in the name of public accountability. Town-gown tensions are longstanding running sores for many universities. Internally, too, universities develop constituencies of administration, faculty, students, and staff (each often divided into subconstituencies) that may suspect one another and come into periodic conflict.

Despite the historical reality, the idealized image of the university as a community—as opposed to being a polity within a larger polity—persists. The "norm" is the pursuit and transmission of knowledge in relative peace and insulation, and political crises are regarded as rare, ugly events that, once they have occurred, are experienced as abnormal eruptions and disturbances to the community, which is blessed when it is able to return to normality after they occur. The situation is a bit analogous to the public attitude toward earthquakes. They are rare events, not the norm; when they occur they are terrible and frightening, but after a short time people begin to believe they will not happen again and that life can go on. This feature of community culture also probably accounts in part for the fact that the campuses over the years have not built up a full or systematic apparatus of readiness for crises—a structure of roles and responsibilities for anticipating and responding. The image of any kind of garrison state is dissonant with the inherited cultural mentality.

A final relevant point to be made about the culture of universities is their special concentration on individual persons. Faculty members are expected to strive for individual recognition in their careers, and they are rewarded for this recognition. Universities admit individual students, give instruction to and grade them as individuals, graduate individuals, and prepare individuals for and place them in occupational positions. Correspondingly, universities have not been very well equipped to deal with collective conflict and crises, because they, too, are not part of their cultural expectations and normal expected functioning (see chapter 4 for elaboration).

The general implication of these observations about inherited university culture is that, historically, universities as a type of organization are especially prone to surprises (in large part because they would like to believe that they are not part of university life), are ill-equipped to react to them when they arise (in large part for the same reason), and are prone to forget about them in their desire to return to normality once they have happened.

THE INCREASINGLY COMPLEX SOCIAL STRUCTURING
OF UNIVERSITIES AND THEIR DEEPENING EMBEDDEDNESS
IN THE LARGER SOCIETY

Several observations should be ventured about the changing structure of the universities during their historical evolution, all of which are relevant to understanding the kinds of surprises they experience:

· Increasing structural complexity. If we take the University of California as an illustration, we may contrast its simple beginnings as one small campus—with few faculty members and most decisions, however small, being made by the board of regents—with what it has become since. With growth in size has come an increased proliferation of academic departments, schools, colleges, programs, and organized research units—and ultimately in numbers of campuses. It has experienced an equal proliferation in administrative structures—including personnel offices, mailing divisions, administrative deans and assistant deans, and the rest—to manage the increasing size and complexity of the activities and structures that make up the university.

· Increased delegation of authority. As the university has grown in size, complexity, and numbers of campuses, this has been accompanied—irregularly and often with reluctant surrender of powers—by an increasingly complex pattern of decentralization and delegation of authority by the state government to the regents, by the regents to the president, to the Academic Senate, to the chancellors of individual campuses, and to subunits within campuses by their administrative officers. A delicate equilibrium is established by delegation, however, because formal powers, even if delegated, still reside at the center and can be withdrawn or altered. The situation is further complicated by the fact that those parties to whom authority is delegated typically become interested in preserving that delegated authority and anxious not to have it withdrawn.

· Multiplication of structurally based internal constituencies. Structural differentiation typically produces groups corresponding to structural positions. Following this principle, the university has produced identifiable groups. To illustrate such a list: faculty differentiated along lines of disciplinary departmental specialization (physics, math, English, etc., as well as larger groupings such as humanities and sciences) and rank; graduate students (similarly subdivided); under-graduate students and their subtypes; teaching assistants; research assistants; non-faculty research personnel, representatives of programs such as the library, student advising, and athletics; and different levels and kinds of management and staff. Every one of these groups develops interests, and every one of them can become a conflict group if their interests appear to be affected.

· Increasing diversity. The different populations of a university always reflect diversity along many lines, but since the "revolutions" of the 1960s and 1970s, an increased diversity of faculty, students, and staff along social-categorical lines has become especially salient. By *social-categorical* is meant, for example, groups based on ethnicity, race, gender, sexual preference, and status as disabled. Like structurally based groups, every one of these has the potential to be activated as a political constituency, and some stand in readiness if not eagerness to mobilize.

· Increasing salience of "external" constituencies. It is difficult to draw the line between internal and external in many cases, but from the standpoint of the campus, the office of the president, the board of regents, and other campuses of the university can be regarded as external, as can parents of students and alumni and their various subgroups. All of these are clearly interested if not ownership groups. Other longstanding external constituencies are neighborhoods, citizens, and municipal governments. Of more recent significance are "external" (local, national, and state) associations and political constituencies that "mirror" the categorical groups associated with increasing diversity—ethnic and racial communities, gender-based groups, and others. The long-term increase in the activity of federal agencies in the financing of research has made them into external constituencies as well, interested not only in the research programs of universities but also in the general conformity of the university to federal laws and guidelines. Add to these constituencies those that rise from special-interest movements, such as environmental groups, animal rights groups, groups interested in the protection of human subjects, and so on.

· Finally, and most generally, because universities have become much more important in bolstering the increasingly service-based economy and more salient in producing the knowledge relevant for scientific and social policies, they have taken on a generally increased visibility and valence in the society. A corollary is that the more important, consequential, and influential a university, the more it is in the public eye; Berkeley certainly falls in this category.

The reason it is essential to specify these cultural and structural contexts of the university at the outset is because any surprise, to say nothing of its magnification into a crisis, owes its definition, existence, and dynamics to the cultural, structural, and group contexts in which the university is embedded.

WHAT IS A SURPRISE?

At minimum, we think of a surprise as a welcome or unwelcome event or situation that occurs or arises without the hearer or receiver expecting or preparing for it—as with a surprise gift, a surprise party, a surprise attack or raid. The two elements that make up a surprise are (a) the nature of the event or situation and (b) the fact of its being unexpected, that is, that it lies outside that universe of events that are regarded as the "normal" or routine events of life and its rounds.

For purposes of understanding institutional surprises on the Berkeley campus (or at any other comparable institution), this minimal definition will not do. Every day the campus experiences hundreds of unanticipated events—on Sproul Plaza, in the classrooms, in the labs, at department meetings, at athletic events, and in the halls of administration. Yet virtually all these pass without attaining institutional significance. To assume that significance, a surprise must occur *in relation to a definite social context of groups that have explicit or implicit normative expectations about how the university should be conducting itself.* Let me give four concrete examples before elaborating on these abstract elements:

The Filthy Speech Movement

The beginning of the "Filthy Speech Movement" episode in Spring 1965 was the appearance on March 2 of a young man named John Thomson from New York on Sproul Plaza, displaying a sign with the word "Fuck" written on it. It was a surprise—according to the minimal definition—to all parties on campus. That simple event soon exploded into a season of intra-campus conflict, involved many parties outside the university, and led to the threatened resignation of a president and an acting chancellor. What endowed the event with electricity was the convergence of a number of contextual factors, among the most important were (a) the collapse of administrative authority in December, 1964 with the "victory" of the Free Speech Movement and the fall of a chancellor; (b) the shaky authority of an interim administration under acting chancellor Martin Meyerson, especially with regard to enforcing campus rules and taking disciplinary action; (c) the weakening of the Free Speech Movement after its "victory" and its splintering into numerous smaller groups, many of which continued to press the campus for additional reforms and to test the campus administration's authority; (d) the presence of several constituencies, mainly on the political right, that continued to be angry and dismayed about the recent political turmoil on campus; these included some remaining "tough-minded" administrators, a small group of faculty, many alumni groups, many regents, some police, and many state officials; these groups shared an interest in cracking down on protest; the obscenity rallies following Thomson's arrest seemed a natural and legitimate target for disciplinary crackdown; (e) ten days before the Thompson episode campus fraternities had conducted an Ugly Man Context, with ribald conduct and obscene behavior that went unpunished by the administration; some "filthy speech" demonstrators argued that they should have the same rights as the fraternities (see chapter 1 for elaboration).

It does not take a bold mental experiment to suggest that if the Thomson event were to have occurred, say in 1960, it would have been more or less quietly disciplined by either campus officials or police without a public explosion, and if it occurred in 2004 it would perhaps draw a combination of yawns and informal efforts on the part of the campus to remove or insulate the perpetrator from the campus. Real experiments that establish the same point were the "streaker" episodes several years later and the "naked guy" incident of 1992, both of which were "surprises" in the minimal sense and both of which evoked coverage by the press, some campus interest, and ultimately campus and police action. The perpetrators justified both episodes under a vague political rationale (freedom of expression), but neither mobilized any significant political constituencies. They created bemusement and discussion but did not grow into explosions or crises.

The conclusion is that a surprise assumes institutional significance (i.e., becomes a potential or actual crisis) when it activates the interest and expression of demands from real or self-appointed shareholder constituencies that are for salient for the campus.

The "Eldridge Cleaver" Course

In Summer 1968, the Board of Educational Development—a faculty-administrative unit to encourage educational experiments created in 1966 in the aftermath of the campus turmoil of the mid-1960s—approved a course, Social Analysis 139X. The course was entitled "Dehumanization and Regeneration in the American Social Order," and was to feature ten lectures by Eldridge Cleaver, the Black Panther leader, even though it was to be "supervised and taught" by two faculty members in sociology. The ambiguity about whether a qualified faculty or an "outsider" was to teach the course would have created concern on the campus in any event. But larger contextual features almost guaranteed that the announcement of the course (September 11, 1968) would generate immediate heat. Among these were (a) the continuing national emotional and political turmoil arising from the assassinations of Robert F. Kennedy and Martin Luther King, Jr., the previous Spring; (b) the public visibility of Cleaver, who was running for president of the United States for the Peace and Freedom Party; (c) the ongoing trial of Huey Newton; (d) a heavy crackdown on the Black Panther Party by police and FBI, including the shooting incident between police and the party that resulted in the death of Bobby Hutton; (e) the widespread public anxiety (especially on the right) over the violent and "revolutionary" turn of black protest.

Consistent with this heated atmosphere, the announcement of the course immediately provoked an angry denunciation by the conservative superintendent of public instruction, Max Rafferty; a clash the next day between Governor Ronald Reagan and Assemblyman Jesse Unruh (Democratic speaker of the Assembly); a censure of Chancellor Roger Heyns by the California State Senate on September 17; a defiant statement by a sponsoring faculty member that the course would be taught no matter what the regents decided; a regents' decision (September 20) that Cleaver could appear only once; and finally, once the Fall quarter had begun, a prolonged jurisdictional struggle involving faculty, campus administration, and regents over delegation of curricular authority to the faculty and a series of demonstrations and sit-ins.

Once again, context appears to have played an overwhelming role. The board of educational development had approved many courses and educational experiments that had the potential to generate protest, but none had done so during the two years of its operation.

The Kirkpatrick Lectures

On February 15, 1983, a group called SAINTES (Students Against the Intervention in El Salvador) stood up in Wheeler Auditorium and shouted down the speaker, Jeane Kirkpatrick, the U.S. ambassador to the United Nations. She was the Jefferson Lecturer, giving a speech titled "The U.S. Tradition of Human Rights." The disruption was a surprise, in that it was unanticipated, and police and campus administrators were unable to identify most of the disrupting individuals after the room had been cleared and the lecture resumed. (Kirkpatrick subsequently cancelled her second lecture.) The event led to an immediate polarization of both students and faculty on the legitimacy of the protest and heavy politicking in the Academic Senate to gain the passage of a resolution framing the event as "prima facie evidence of a violation of freedom of speech." Subsequently the conservative chair of the board of regents, Glen Campbell, who was close to President Reagan (and Reagan was close to Ambassador Kirkpatrick), demanded that Chancellor Heyman prepare a report on the event, including "an explanation of why this interference with free speech occurred, and what steps are being taken to impose appropriate punishment on the perpetrators of the act." At a subsequent regents' meeting Heyman spoke against Campbell's attempted interference and in effect invited the regents to remove him, not tell him what to do, if they were dissatisfied.

The contextual factors for this blowup were not self-evident. A month before the lecture there had been a massive demonstration against a projected student fee increase, but this seemed not to be relevant to the SAINTES action or the campus reaction to it. Perhaps more important was that students across the nation were then demonstrating against the Solomon Amendment that would deny financial aid to students who did not register for the draft. More generally, most of the faculty and students on the Berkeley campus were opposed to the Reagan administration, including its foreign policies, and for that reason some were prepared to condone strident opposition to them and to excuse incivility in voicing that opposition. The magnitude of the reaction, however, is traceable to the Reagan-Kirkpatrick-Campbell linkage, which assured that the Reagan administration would be an interested if temporary constituency.

The SARS Epidemic

The SARS situation was a clear surprise in that it was unexpected and involved a completely new virus. From its initial outbreak in China in November 2002 and its subsequent global spread through travel, it was readily apparent that any outbreak on the Berkeley campus would not only constitute a health crisis but would also alarm multiple constituencies on the campus and others outside the campus, especially students' parents. The campus undertook planning and preparation for such an outbreak in April 2003, including establishing a SARS task force and initiating various preparatory and precautionary activities thereafter. In this sense the SARS situation was a simple and straightforward surprise—a threat to the health of its campus community. Here, too, however, the situation was magnified by a special contextual feature—the activation of anger on the part of some Asian and Asian-American groups to the perceived "insensitivity" of the campus and the "insult" to Asians by plans to close or postpone programs in which Asian students would be participating. (A important side-bar was that Asian-American alumni had in recent decades become a significant source of donations to the campus.) A great deal of effort on the part of the campus was called forth, both to prepare for the possible outbreak and to deal with the delicate diplomatic situations that emerged.

SOME FURTHER PRINCIPLES INVOLVING THE CONTEXT OF SURPRISES

From the above illustrative cases—and more could be cited—we should conclude that surprises do not simply come out of the blue. They always have a *relational* quality—between an event or situation whose content may or may not seem inherently surprising and relevant and interested constituent groups who come into conflict with one another (often manifested by exerting pressures on the campus administration to act). Beyond this general principle, several more specific observations may be recorded.

The Origins of Surprises

There is no fixed principle here. Some surprises occur outside the campus and mobilize various constituencies. Among these would be (a) the Cambodian incursion followed by the Kent State and Jackson State killings of 1971, which precipitated the "reconstitution movement" on the campus and the temporary closing of the campus by Governor Reagan in that spring; (b) periodic threats by legislators about admissions policies and practices; (c) the possibility that the U.S. government begins to collect information on individuals on campus as part of the Patriot Act. Internal precipitants would be (a) the announcement of Social Analysis 139X (the Eldridge Cleaver course) by the university; (b) the display of the offensive sign that triggered the Filthy Speech episode; (c) the teaching of the controversial course on Palestinian literature on the campus in 2002. Still other cases are mixed. The precipitous administrative ban on certain traditional political activities on the twenty-six-foot strip of land bordering on Bancroft Way at Telegraph Avenue is commonly interpreted as the precipitating event for the Free Speech Movement. Yet those who imposed that ban supposed that there was already some kind of undesirable (if not threatening) political situation that merited the ban. As indicated, however, all surprises express a relationship between an event and interested constituencies. In addition, as will be argued later, this fact creates some ambiguity as to the moment when a surprise actually occurs.

The Origins and Characteristics of Relevant Constituencies

Some of the campus's constituencies are more or less permanent features of the environment. These are the ones that accompany the structural complexity of the institution outlined earlier in the essay—faculty, staff, graduate students, neighboring community, alumni, the regents, the state government, and subdivisions of all of these. They change very slowly, but changes are observable over time; for example, teaching assistants and non-faculty research personnel crystallized as meaningful constituencies and as a byproduct of the vast expansion in the size of the campus and its heavy involvement in federal research in the two decades after World War II.

At the other extreme, some "constituencies" are remote from the university and thus invisible and inactive most of the time but become active when a situation or event excites their interest. The *Wall Street Journal*, normally preoccupied with business, economics, and politics at the national level, has occasionally editorialized about situations at Berkeley. One of these was an outraged statement on May 9, 2002 concerning the course in Palestinian literature; another was an editorial following the regents' action in April, 2004 dissociating itself from Regent John Moores's criticism of admissions on the Berkeley campus, saying he should be receiving a medal rather than a censure. Another "surprise" constituency—though explicable after the fact—was the American Legion, which assaulted Herbert Marcuse and Angela Davis in 1969 when the board of regents became interested in voiding their academic appointments in the university.

On occasion a conflict situation bred by a surprise becomes magnified when relevant authorities are at odds with one another with respect to the substance of a conflict. During the Free Speech Movement, for example, the campus administration was divided with respect to the rights and wrongs of the students' demands and on how civil disobedience should be disciplined. The president and the chancellor of the Berkeley campus were also at odds, and the regents were divided among themselves. During the long period of demonstrations associated with the issue of divestment in South Africa in 1985–86, the campus administration maintained a fairly consistent stance of encouraging peaceful protest but in citing or arresting those who were breaking campus rules or the law. On the issue of divestment itself, however, Chancellor Heyman and President David Gardner held opposing positions, and the regents were initially split. The speaker of the Assembly, Willie Brown, actively intervened in favor of divestment, and on one occasion when the campus administration arrested some demonstrators, the City of Berkeley complained. Ultimately Governor Deukmejian intervened and carried a majority of regents with him in a vote for divestment over the opposition of President Gardner. The general principle is this: when those in authority are divided, this simultaneously gives hope and encouragement to protesting groups and tends to erode the steadiness of the campus administration in its resolve to deal with the crisis situation.

More generally, the activation of constituencies is fostered in periods when national and local political life becomes heated, as the following examples reveal:

· Analysis of the background of the Free Speech Movement and its offshoots, for example, would have to include the lingering idealism of the administration of John F. Kennedy; the salience and successes of the Civil Rights movement (which included both the campus-based civil rights activities of the early 1960s and the "migration" of students from Freedom Summer and related activities to the Berkeley campus in Fall 1964); the presence of a relatively hot political campaign (Johnson versus Goldwater, with the Republican national convention being held in San Francisco that year).

- The national preoccupation with and opposition to the Vietnam War, a major element of which was the military draft, provided an overriding national agenda that made anti-war activity on the campus and in the community the source of many surprises and crises between 1965 and 1971.

- The national (and international) assault on South African apartheid in the mid-1980s found expression in demonstrations for divestment on various campuses of the university.

- Moments of intensive activity on the part of environmental movements and the animal rights movement have resulted in periodic campus protests and demonstrations.

- The preoccupation of Californians with the state's burgeoning immigration population has conditioned the politics of the state and served as the backdrop to numerous conflicts over welfare benefits for immigrants, the board of regents' "rollback" of affirmative action in 1995, and the passage of Proposition 209. This political environment, in addition to counter-pressures to continue affirmative action in one form or another, has set the agenda for much campus activity in the 1990s and into the twenty-first century (see chapter 5).

The external political environment thus provides us with a generalized sensitivity about where action might develop. To be continuously aware of this environment is to increase one's knowledge of the probability of certain types of surprises and conflicts for the campus. Yet the translation of external political preoccupations into predictions of campus action is by no means automatic. The absence of organized protest against the Gulf War of 1991 (except for one "die-in" that passed almost unnoticed) and against the war in Afghanistan in 2001–02 (except for one feeble political rally) are examples of situations that "should" have produced campus action—given the campus's political history—but did not. These negative examples—surprising non-surprises—are worth understanding as well, insofar as mental experiments can produce such understanding. In the two cases mentioned, relevant factors would be the presence of an unambiguous enemy in the form of Saddam Hussein in the one case and the nation's post-9/11 solidarity in the other; the decision of opponents to these wars to centralize protest in major metropolitan areas, which in Berkeley's case "removed" the protest to San Francisco; and perhaps the paralysis of some Jewish leaders of potential protest groups because Israel was such a visible side party in both wars.

A final determinant of constituencies and their disposition is a historical one. Chancellor Heyns once remarked that one of the best predictors of divergent faculty partisanship during the period of the Free Speech Movement and its aftermath was to know where people lined up during the Loyalty Oath crisis of the early 1950s. The latter event created an intense political polarization of the Berkeley faculty that formed, re-aligned, and broke existing collegial and friendship patterns. That cleavage persisted as an earthquake fault line for future conflicts. Heyns's principle is a general one. For example, some academic departments experienced a radical polarization during the years of the Vietnam War, a polarization that dissolved only after contending parties left the scene through resignation or retirement.

A corollary of the principle of carryover of cleavages is that it typically takes a long time to "undo" the internal political effects of a major crisis. One example is the cleavages created in the People's Park episode in 1969—involving the Berkeley campus, the City of Berkeley, south Berkeley residents, and political activists—which have persisted to this day. They flare up periodically. The most notable subsequent episode was the "volleyball riots" of 1991 and their aftermath. The persistence and sensitivities of the interested groups have contributed to the paralysis in working out enduring solutions for that contested parcel of land. Another example is the rumbling that occurred in the 1990s in connection with efforts to memorialize the Free Speech Movement on the campus that excited cleavages solidified as far back as the 1960s. A final example has to do with racial-ethnic cleavages, which are more or less endemic but became concretized in collective memory by the Third World College strike and reactivated as an ingredient of the "thirtieth-anniversary" protests in 1999.

The Dynamics of Escalation

A surprise becomes a crisis through a process of inflammation involving the progressive activation of a widening circle of constituencies, which square off against one another and typically shower the administration with conflicting and urgent demands to act, not to act, or undo an action. In this dynamic the administration is caught in a squeeze situation. By virtue of this principle of escalation, what we are tempted to think of as a "surprise" event is in reality a whole series or layering of surprises, each making the situation more serious and more difficult to manage.

In the Filthy Speech episode, for example, the offensive display by John Thomson was escalated initially by his immediate arrest (the chancellor's office did not learn of the arrest until the evening of the day of the arrest). That arrest gave the event the status of something that was being punished by the administration or police and activated that small group from the residual Free Speech Movement who believed that obscenity was (or could be made into) an issue of free speech. The "obscenity rallies" carried out by this group made the matter inescapably public, and the press reports immediately triggered outrage among some faculty, many regents, and many state officials. Subsequently the battle was fought out at this higher level. The People's Park episode in Spring 1969 was initially a confrontation between campus administration and a large group of activists, but this escalated quickly to include the City of Berkeley, the regents, and the governor's office (Governor Reagan's calling out of the national guard was a kind of culmination of this escalation, though that event itself also served to intensify the conflict). The Jeane Kirkpatrick episode quickly escalated to include contending groups of students and faculty, the regents, and even the president of the United States.

Although the precise constituencies that become activated in a given escalation process cannot be predicted, the process itself appears to be typical. Several features of this process can be identified:

The Role of Ignorance, Imagination, and Attribution   In the 1960s I served in two administrations that were notable in the degree to which they were beleaguered by conflicts and crises—the administrations of Martin Meyerson and Roger Heyns. In connection with both assignments I not only sat in the "cabinet" of the chancellor but also had multiple interactions (mostly as a negotiator) with different protest groups on campus. I discovered on numerous occasion the following principle: each of the contending groups (in this case administration and protesters) believed the other to be intelligent, purposeful, deliberative, and bent on mischief; moreover, each of the groups portrayed itself as confused, divided, and constantly adapting to the moment. Both sides were half-wrong; in reality both were typically stumbling and lurching forward uncertainly and without a grand plan.

The principle is a general one. Different parties (constituencies) in the sorts of conflicts considered in this essay are as a rule *ignorant* of one another, in part because they occupy inimical positions. In the absence of information (and in the desire to achieve closure and direction in an uncertain situation), they typically *imagine* (often with the help of fragmented or stereotyped information) what their antagonists are up to and *attribute* motives, purpose, and design on the basis of this imagining. In extreme form this principle leads to a politics of paranoia. Even in the absence of this extreme, however, the ignorance-imagination-attribution principle leads to rigidities in the orientation of contending groups.

Even when the campus administration is not directly at odds with constituencies but is attempting to navigate among a number of them, imagination also plays a role. One reason the intervention by regents' Chairman John Moores into the admissions process in Spring 2004 was so threatening to the campus is because of the *imagined* reaction of several important constituencies—parents of students, admissions officers and faculty concerned with maintaining responsibility for their delegated authority, and various interested ethnic groups that might be affected— even though these groups had not actually reacted. To say "imagined" is not completely fair, because accumulated history of group reactions gives some guidelines to the interests of groups and how they will react, but it is fair to say that there is inevitably a good deal of guesswork and attribution involved.

The Role of Urgency   In his book on campus conflicts in 1964–65 *(The Spiral of Conflict: Berkeley, 1964)*, Max Heirich (1968) listed a more or less exhaustive series of politically significant incidents in Spring 1965 (for example, police seizure of a microphone from an illegal speaker, the appearance of an obscene magazine, *Spider*, for sale on the campus, and the administration's attempt to have it removed). For each, he identified an element of urgency. This seems to be a general feature of campus crises; in fact it seems to be what justifies applying the word *crisis*. The message is that unless something is done, something worse will happen. The sense may be imposed by the stridency of different groups' demands; by the logic of the calendar (a regents' meeting is upcoming and some result has to be reported); by a sense that a conflict will worsen if nothing is done about it; or by a more general sense that an intolerable situation (such as a sit-in) cannot be allowed to go on indefinitely, or that if the campus administration doesn't do something, someone else—the regents or a state agency, for example—will. As with the disposition of constituencies, a sense of urgency may be imagined in the absence of information about the certainty of a dire outcome if no action is taken. A sense of urgency, moreover, may have its mischievous side if it drives authorities into quick, ill-advised actions that may exacerbate a developing situation.

The Campus as One of the Actors in the Escalating Process   Because of the great emphasis that has been laid on the role of constituencies in surprises and their consequences, it might be tempting to downplay the fact that the campus itself is always one of the actors on the stage. Even if it has done nothing, that inaction may become the object of critical attention and surprise. For example, even though the campus had lived with the graduation requirement for American History and Institutions courses for six decades, that requirement became the object of attack in the 1980s when one group criticized it as educationally meaningless and another group complained that it ignored women and minorities in American society.

With respect to surprises themselves, the fact that a surprise sets up a call for action immediately makes the campus an actor. Whether the campus chooses to ignore the surprise (itself an action), wait for it to pass, consult with relevant constituencies before taking action, or attack the situation immediately and directly, it is nevertheless an actor.

It is possible (usually with the benefit of hindsight) to assess the consequences of the campus's role and, one hopes, extract lessons from them. That it was an inflammatory act for the campus to have imposed a ban on political activities on the Bancroft strip in Fall 1964 is generally conceded, since one recipe for revolution is to revoke an activity that has come to be regarded as an entitlement. The precipitous construction of a fence around People's Park in the middle of the night might be judged similarly, though in that case the campus was running out of options. Hindsight would also advise that measures less formal and public than the arrest of Thomson would have nipped the Filthy Speech episode in the bud.

Sometimes, however, no firm judgments can be made. Confronted with demands for establishing a Third World College in Winter 1968, the Heyns administration simultaneously expressed its support for the demanding groups' aims and referred the matter to the Academic Senate, whose relevant committee was unsympathetic and stalled the process. The administration behaved perfectly properly in this regard but remained in trouble nonetheless. If it had not consulted the senate it would have been in hot water over the issue of shared governance; but sending it to the senate was interpreted and denounced by advocates as irresponsible stalling. Similarly, in the Jeane Kirkpatrick episode, if the campus had done everything that Regent Campbell demanded—identified and disciplined the disrupters forthwith and steeled itself against similar disruptions in the future—the administration would have continued to experience agitation and criticism from those who were convinced on political grounds that the disruption was justified. In other words, critical analysis of the campus's own role in surprises and their consequences cannot settle for simple judgments of "should have done" or "should not have done." As in politics in general, many constituency squeezes turn out to be no-win situations.

BROAD CONTOURS OF THE CAMPUS'S READINESS APPARATUS

As indicated, the particular cultural heritage of Berkeley as a university left it, as of around 1960, without any significant machinery to anticipate or deal with collective crises, even though the campus had experienced some institutional crises, most notably the Loyalty Oath crisis in the McCarthy period. When the "era of surprises" began with the Free Speech Movement, the campus responses were ad hoc decisions by the existing administration—administrative deans, campus disciplinary committees, the police, the vice-chancellor for student affairs, and the chancellor, with occasional but sometimes unwelcome intervention by the president in moments of crisis. Almost of necessity, all efforts to deal with the stream of crises that constituted the Free Speech Movement (October–December, 1964) were of an improvised character, and many of these turned out to be inconsistent and ineffective.

Immediately after his assuming the acting chancellorship in January of 1965, Martin Meyerson appointed a special assistant to the chancellor for student political activity (myself). The position turned out to be one of general political aide and factotum, involving duties as far ranging as coordinating police action in times of heavy disturbance; meeting, negotiating, and occasionally engaging in shouting matches with student and non-student activists; keeping contact with faculty groups; contending with (usually antagonistic) communications from alumni, regents, and politicians; and staying constantly in contact with the acting chancellor on almost all matters—especially daily crises—occurring on campus. In fashioning reactions to different campus situations, Meyerson also involved his own "cabinet," his Council of Deans, and the Emergency Executive Committee of the Berkeley Division (created in the wake of the December 8 faculty resolutions). This machinery, while certainly more adapted to crisis-confrontation than that of the administration of Chancellor Strong, was mainly ad hoc and reactive.

During his conflict-ridded administration, Chancellor Roger Heyns did not renew the exact position of special assistant (though the appointment of John Searle approximated it) but worked intimately on a day-to-day basis with an evolved "command" group consisting of himself, the executive vice-chancellor, and two other aides. He continued to rely on his cabinet, the Council of Deans, and the Policy Committee of the Berkeley Division, which replaced the Emergency Executive Committee as a policy instrument of the Academic Senate that was available for quick consultation with and involvement of the faculty in campus crises.

In 1985 Chancellor Michael Heyman appointed John Cummins as a point person to deal with critical campus situations. He has occupied the position ever since, as it has evolved through the two succeeding chancellorships to its more formal status as associate chancellor/chief of staff. As an adjunct to this position, Cummins generated a more elaborate and systematic structure for crisis management than any that had preceded it. This was a body initially called The Committee, a small group consisting of some central administrative personnel, deans, the chief of police, and a public information officer, among others. Subsequently the group has come to be known as the "operations group," and its membership, while mainly continuous, has changed from time to time and now includes the executive director of the Berkeley Division as a kind of liaison with the faculty.

The operations group meets several times a year, with a "mandatory" meeting in the summer before the Fall semester opens and another before the Spring semester. These meetings have a prospective character, as members share their knowledge and intelligence on what of a sensitive or critical nature might be on the horizon. The group also meets on an as-needed basis at other times when critical situations loom and trouble breaks out. The meetings of the operations group are all open to cognizant vice-chancellors and others who are likely to be involved in surprise situations. The group is clearly a readiness structure, but its members are occupied full time with their own ongoing administrative responsibilities and it has never been used as or pretended to be a policy-making body. Of necessity, too, the intelligence that informs its internal communication and planning is highly selective, dependent on what comes to the attention of its constituent members as they carry out their individual responsibilities.

Very recently—only in the 2003–2004 academic year, and in the wake of the campus crisis associated with the SARS epidemic—the chancellor's office has created on additional body, known as Project X, which adds at least one novel element to campus readiness. This group includes as members the chancellor, executive vice chancellor and provost, associate chancellor/chief of staff, and a couple of additional members of the operations group. The novel element of the project is that it also includes a number of (mainly) faculty members who, by virtue of their own academic research and campus experience, are knowledgeable about situations of conflict and crisis (and organizational responses to them) in general and familiar with Berkeley campus history in particular. Most of the supplementary members do not hold any current positions in campus administration and do not represent partisan positions beyond their general institutional loyalty to the Berkeley campus. Project X is charged in a general way with bringing an analytic approach to the understanding of unanticipated critical events and situations that have faced and might face the campus as one more way of preparing the campus' ability to deal with them efficiently and effectively. The group emphasizes reflective understanding less than moment-to-moment coping with current situations, though the line between the two aspects is easily blurred in any given discussion. It meets for dinner approximately once a month. One part of its agenda has been to imagine the most likely types of surprises that lurk on the horizon in the coming season and to discuss topics such as (a) the constituencies most likely to be affected by a given type of surprise, (b) how and when to communicate with these constituencies (and by whom), (c) what scenarios are most likely to unfold, and how adaptations might be shaped in response to each of these. Different and uniquely qualified "nonmembers" of the group are invited in, according to the character of the envisioned surprise situation. Being new, the mechanism represented by Project X is still in an amateur stage and feeling its way, though it does represent a modest innovation in the evolving art of crisis confrontation. Its brief existence also suggests some ways in which its functions might be extended; these are considered in the final section of this essay.

To complete this sketch of past and present machinery, three supplemental observations are in order:

Almost independently of the different kinds of machinery sketched, there is one observable dynamic of surprise and critical situations that is so typical and striking that it may be a universal feature of organizational crises. I refer to what happens when a crisis reaches a boiling point and a more or less immediate administrative response on behalf of the campus is called for. At such moments urgent meetings are held, often lasting into the late and early hours. These meetings include the officials that must act and bear responsibility, plus an additional number of knowledgeable and involved others (varying from crisis to crisis). These meetings are simultaneously focused and unorganized, as those gathered move rapidly from item to item—imagining what other groups are going to do and what we ought to do, conjuring up other "what if" situations and scenarios, planning and writing public statements and press releases, seeking information, placing phone calls, and engaging alternatively in sessions of self-doubt and self-reassurance. The atmosphere is typically harried, frantic, and beleaguered. These meetings always occur and all appear to display all these features, yet each is so gripped by the drama of the moment that the participants experience them as if no other such meeting has ever occurred. These observations accrue from my own participation in such meetings on the Berkeley campus and the office of the president, as well as accounts of other meetings related to me by others.

One of the by-products of such meetings is the emergence of a consensus—sometimes only loose—as to what the proper action at the coming critical moment ought to be. Such a consensus is, after all, the purpose of the meeting and is dictated by the evident need for closure in understanding and acting in an uncertain and critical situation. The other side of reaching consensus, however, is that for the moment at least other lines of thought and action are ruled out. If the situation changes markedly in subsequent moments, days, or weeks, new understandings, new working through, and new lines of action should be envisioned. It is often difficult to do this, however, if certain options have—however tacitly and unconsciously—been ruled out by earlier decisions and moods of consensus. The unfortunate consequence is that groups in crisis are forever in danger of closing their minds to complexities and perspectives outside the internal drama of the specific crisis.

Insofar as this closed-mindedness comes to persist over a longer time, we encounter what the psychologist Irving Janis came to call "groupthink." This occurs when a group of leaders, usually an inner circle, comes to a certain diagnosis of a situation of conflict or siege and identifies what the situation is all about, who the enemies are, and how they ought to be dealt with. Under conditions of groupthink, outside interpretations come to be ruled out and those who voice alternative or conflicting views tend to be excluded or even punished. It is very difficult to avoid the development of some version of groupthink in conflict situations—again, because of the pressure for cognitive closure to render one's own actions intelligible—but it is nonetheless a mischievous phenomenon that impedes informed and rational responses.

Formal bodies such as cabinets of administrative officers are not especially effective either as preparedness structures or response-shaping bodies. There are several reasons for this: (a) their members are usually engaged full-time or more in campus activities that have little or nothing to do with the developing or occurring crises; for this reason crises constitute nonroutine distractions from very busy lives; (b) their information about any given crisis situation at hand is inadequate and often consists of little more than that imparted to them by those directly managing a crisis; (c) they meet infrequently; (d) they are large and unwieldy as action-taking bodies; and (e) some members of cabinets may themselves be in the eye of the storm—depending on the crisis at hand—and these individuals have understandable biases and interests that influence independent deliberation and diagnosis. There are reasons for keeping such formal bodies advised and on board during periods of crisis for purposes of campus unity and campus morale, but as a rule they cannot be regarded as effective bodies for preparedness and action.

SOME TENTATIVE IDEAS FOR EXTENDING PREPAREDNESS

To conclude the lines of thinking developed in this essay, I offer a couple of suggestions about how to extend and improve the campus's capacity to foresee, recognize, and react constructively to surprises and their escalation. These suggestions are informed by the following general assumptions:

- Significant campus surprises—those that contain the seeds of crisis— become significant because they activate one or more of the campus's complex structures of constituencies who have real or imagined interests in campus policies and practices and whose interests often conflict with interests of other constituencies.

- To maximize knowledge of the disposition of these constituencies and to maintain a cordial and cooperative relationship with them is an essential resource in the containment and management of campus surprises.

- Operational readiness units—those who are assigned front-line responsibility for responding—should be in frequent communication with one another and with policy officials of the university. The import of this is that no significant changes in the operations group should be made, with one minor exception to be noted later.

- There should be a separation between the structure of administrative units—both academic and nonacademic—and the structure of readiness and response, although the communication of information about campus situations to the former is an important feature of maintaining campus unity, commitment, and morale.

- The campus should institutionalize the input of general, dispassionate knowledge about surprises, conflict, and organizational responses at all stages—in advance of, during, and in the aftermath of campus crises.

With these assumptions in mind, the campus might put in place several arrangements:

1. An informal, analytic group such as Project X seems sufficiently useful that it could simply be continued in approximately its same form. A more ambitious variation of it might, however, be envisioned. What is suggested is a group with some core members (perhaps eight to ten) who would engage in regular informal meetings dedicated to analyzing, scanning, forecasting, and working through scenarios. To supplement this core might be a much larger (forty to fifty, say) reservoir or "stable" of campus figures with more specialized knowledge or positions. The larger reservoir would have no name and no official status and would never meet as a whole. A few of its members could periodically and selectively be drawn into meetings of the core, depending on the subject matter being considered. The aim of the meetings would be to develop and consolidate information and intelligence about the campus situation, identify developments in the campus environment, and frame conditional analyses and predictions—all with the aim of continuously attempting to make the

unanticipated more anticipated. Another line of activity of such a group would be to bend its efforts to the difficult task of conceiving various lines of change on the campus that might prevent or mitigate future crises—that is, to attend to the "opportunity" as well as the "crisis-management" side of critical episodes. Perhaps two of the periodic meetings of the core group should be held jointly with the operations group—probably at the beginning of each semester.

This double resource—the core and the reservoir—could be exploited further at moments of impending crisis and during crises themselves. I do not have in mind simply calling more emergency meetings of the group and turning it into an advisory body but calling in a few selected individuals to join the inner circle of administrators and operational groups actually responsible for dealing with the crisis. The aim of this practice would be to assure a continuous input of knowledge and perspectives from a number of individuals who are not only knowledgeable about the background of the crisis (by virtue of their expertise and ongoing activity) but who are also likely to be more "objective" in their assessments and perspectives because they do not live daily on the firing line. After every incident or "crisis" this temporarily assembled group would disband and fade back into the core or reservoir.

It is essential that this loosely structured core-and-reservoir group have no formal administrative status—no FTE, no titles, no ranks, no salary or stipend, no special offices held, no space occupied, no official name, and by virtue of that anonymity no turf to defend and, it is hoped, no vested interests to push as a group. It should be a volunteer corps. With these features of remove from the formal structure of the campus and its own lack of structure, it would be less likely to be perceived as a threat to the formal administrative and academic apparatus of the campus. On the administrative side, the staff, led by the chancellor, should do everything it can to cultivate a culture of openness to ideas and perspectives. A part of this culture should be a matter-of-course readiness to ask which individuals and what perspectives should be brought in during times of impending and actual crisis.

To supplement this advisory body on the administrative side, the chancellor should consider the appointment of a special "eyes and ears" administrative officer whose sole assignment would be to gain knowledge and familiarity with potential surprise and conflict situations and keep the campus administration fully briefed on information garnered. No doubt this function was originally conceived as part of the role of the chief of staff, but that position has become very overburdened with so many other administrative assignments that it does not seem feasible for him or her to take on this role, which ideally should be exclusive to a full-time individual. The "intelligence" official would report primarily to the chief of staff and would dedicate his or her energies to keeping up on local, state, national, and international news that may be foreboding, maintaining contact with members of the core and reservoir groups, interacting on a selective basis with representatives of "sensitive" constituencies and with others familiar with those constituencies, and digesting and systematizing the accumulating information.

2. A further augmentation of readiness could be achieved by putting into place a network of persons in the university who would be responsible for becoming acquainted with and maintaining periodic contact with known representatives of known constituencies of the campus. Some of this is already in place with groups of alumni, donors and donor groups, officials of the City of Berkeley, representatives of student groups, and others. What is envisioned in addition to these contacts is a systematization of knowledge about these constituencies as well as its periodic updating. This network would have no formal administrative structure—it would in no sense be a ministry of foreign affairs—but would be a fluid assignment of university personnel with assigned responsibilities to know about and be in periodic contact with groups. Such a network cannot be established in a mechanical way, largely because of the variation in the constituencies. For example, one of the campus's major constituencies— the board of regents—is largely inaccessible because of the taboo on certain types of communications between campus and regents without going through the office of the president. In addition, the campus has friendly and affable relations with some groups, strained relations with others, and inimical relations with still others. Contacts with this variety of groups necessarily will have to vary accordingly.

The logic behind this suggestion is that in times of looming trouble or actual crisis, the campus will have established a better basis of mutual trust as perhaps the most important resource for preventing the ravages of escalated conflicts. In this context of trust, it is more nearly possible to meet productively with representatives of groups, explain the campus's situation in relation to the issue or conflict at hand, prepare them and explain the reasons for possible disappointments, and do what can be done to secure their cooperation and good will. It is also envisioned that the network would be activated only periodically and selectively, according to the issue and situation at hand. Such activation will not always succeed but has a better chance of doing so than last-minute and ad hoc contacts with groups or simply relying on guesswork and attribution to fathom how they might be disposed or how they might act.

This second suggestion of a group network is advanced more tentatively than the first, because it is a slipperier arrangement and calls for a history of trial, error, failure, and success before a truly appropriate formula for such a network of contacts can be known to be effective.

APPENDIX I. GUIDELINES FOR UNDERSTANDING SURPRISES

Did the event come out of the blue, was it the culmination of a developing situation that went awry, or did it result from some kind of action on the part of the university that created an unanticipated effect?

Can any evidence of "systematic ignorance" (e.g., a limited outlook or point of view, an absence of cognizant person or office in the university) be identified?

Is it possible to identify any special political and contextual factors that magnified the "surprise" and made it into a big or significant event?

What campus agency was initially affected—police, Academic Senate, dean's office, chancellor's office?

Which "shareholders" (students, faculty, off-campus activists, regents, legislature, Berkeley community officials) were affected and/or mobilized? What was the sequence by which they were drawn into the situation created by the "surprise"?

What was the university's immediate response to the surprise? Was this response a unified or uniformly supported one, or was there division or conflict among authorities (faculty, police, campus administration, systemwide administration, regents) about the response?

What was the effect—calming, diverting, mobilizing of new shareholders, aggravating—of the initial university response?

Can any special developmental sequence be traced after the initial surprise-and-response situation, and in what ways did this relieve or deepen the crisis?

Did any new arrangements (rules, addition of responsibilities to a university official, creation of a new office) arise out of the situation?

Can any longer-term effects be identified in terms of creating new groups or cleavages (inside or outside the campus) with which the university had to deal; curricular changes; organizational changes?

APPENDIX 2. EPISODES STUDIED BY RESEARCH ASSISTANTS

The Filthy Speech Episode, 1965

The "Eldridge Cleaver course," Social Analysis 139X, 1968

Third World College Strike, 1969

People's Park episode, 1969

Follow-up episodes to People's Park, for example, the volleyball court episode, 1991

The regents' initiative against appointing Herbert Marcuse and Angela Davis to the University of California faculty, 1969

Disruption of the Jeane Kirkpatrick speech, 1983

The "thirtieth anniversary" episode of ethnic conflict, 1999

The Palestinian Literature course, 2002

REFERENCE

Heirich, Max. 1968. *The Spiral of Conflict: Berkeley, 1964.* New York: Columbia University Press.

PART TWO

Diversity, Affirmative Action, and the Culture Wars

FOUR

The Politics of Ambivalence

Diversity in the Research Universities (1994)

IN 1991 JONATHAN COLE AND Elinor Barber of Columbia University and Stephen Graubard of the American Academy of Arts and Sciences undertook to hold a conference and produce a volume of essays on the issues facing major research universities in the United States. The project was supported by the James S. McDonnell Foundation, the Andrew Mellon Foundation, and the Alfred P. Sloan Foundation. Two planning meetings for the project were held at the academy offices in Cambridge in 1991 and 1992. I participated in the second.

Just after the second planning meeting the organizers invited me to prepare an essay on the mission of the modern research university for the conference and volume. I agreed to do so, though with some reluctance, because I felt that I could only produce an essay on that topic that would be unoriginal if not boring. A couple of months later, before I had begun writing, the organizers called back and invited me to write on a different

Appeared originally in *The Research University in a Time of Discontent*, ed. Jonathan R. Cole, Elinor G. Barber, and Stephen R. Graubard, 37–53 (Baltimore, MD: Johns Hopkins University Press, 1993). Also appeared in the Fall 1993 issue of *Daedalus*, 37–54.

topic, one that encompassed the loosely coupled issues of affirmative action, diversity, and multiculturalism. They were having trouble finding anyone to write that essay. Some prospective authors had declined because it was *too* interesting (i.e., controversial); others had already declared their partisan opinions publicly on those subjects and, it was feared, would simply repeat them. I fell into neither category. Furthermore, I had recently worked out a promising idea: political conflicts in which partisans are ambivalent about their positions yield a special, complex dynamic that cannot be understood without probing the implications of that ambivalence. I decided to develop that theme, and the essay that follows is the result.

Debates over cultural diversity, multiculturalism, and the integrity of the community are perennial in American history. They extend back at least to colonial times, when religious heterogeneity posed major social and political problems for many of the colonies. They became chronic in the nineteenth and early twentieth centuries, as waves of immigrants diversified the population. The movement of the black population northward and later westward, beginning in earnest in the early twentieth century, generated a new heterogeneity, racial tensions, and alarms in the affected communities.

The current debates are thus properly regarded as the latest episode in the long history of the cultural diversification of America. What is new about them is the historically specific confluence of social forces from which they emanate: the Civil Rights movement of the 1950s and 1960s; the campus and antiwar turbulence of the 1960s; the women's movement; the "sexual preference revolution"; the increasing political self-consciousness of many ethnic groups, including "white ethnics"; and the extraordinary increase of immigration—mainly but not exclusively Latin and Asian—during the past several decades.

Episodes involving cultural diversity are not new in American academic circles: the historic flood of children from farm families into teaching via colleges and universities; the entry of Irish Catholic Americans into the professions, notably engineering, through colleges; the struggle over Jewish quotas in the elite private institutions; and the evolution of Eastern private institutions from regional and social elite to national and intellectual elite institutions. All involved issues of cultural diversity in academia. At the same time, the contemporary situation has some novel elements and is grounded in a distinctive cultural setting.

The University Context

The national debates about diversity affect all research universities across the nation. Within research universities these debates are reproduced as a microcosm of the national political arena, with some notable regional differences. The debates occur in the context of the culture of those universities, which imparts a special form and flavor. It is necessary, therefore, to remind ourselves of a few characteristics of that culture.

First, the major research universities in the United States constitute a national *elite* among institutions. This status is evident in all measures—prestige, quality of faculty, quality of students, occupational placement of graduating students, and, not least, cultural voice. They share this elite status with liberal arts colleges on some of these measures. One implication of elevated status for institutions is that the real and symbolic stakes associated with access to them are high. Those who enter as students may secure both status and enhanced life opportunities; those who enter as faculty share in their prestige.

Second, the research universities' cultural traditions give the highest premium to the values of *competitive excellence* and *meritocracy.* They compete aggressively with one another for outstanding faculty and students. They assess both their faculty and their students primarily on meritocratic criteria—that is, universalistic standards of judgment. The successful application of these criteria is, indeed, one of the conditions that sustain the elite status of research universities.

Third, the culture of the research universities is *liberal* in several senses of the term. They, along with the rest of the academy, are the seat and the defenders of that special class of civil liberties known as academic freedom. They are committed, above all, to standards of freedom of inquiry and expression. And in the national political spectrum, both faculty and students at research institutions, although internally diverse, lean in a liberal direction.

Fourth, because of their unique intellectual missions, controversies and debate in universities—perhaps especially in elite universities—take on a special *symbolic intensity.* As institutions, universities do not house much power, but they specialize in and are good at cultural symbolism. Debates in universities tend to take on an intellectualized, back-to-square-one quality. Being shrouded in symbolic discourse, these debates are likely to confound and irritate outsiders.

The Peculiarities of the Current Debates

Viewed simply, the current debates about cultural diversity derive historically from the political pressure that built up in the 1960s and 1970s, as one categorical group after another began expressing a collective claim for increased access to and more equitable recognition in academic institutions. Universities reacted to these demands—and the demands of governmental and other pressures for affirmative action—with varying degrees of responsiveness and effectiveness. Now both the values and procedures for affirmative action are in place, and the increased presence of most of these groups is visible. Recently, the debates have taken a more distinctively *cultural* turn—hence the salience of the terms "cultural diversity" and "multiculturalism."

The debates, as they have built up over the past decades, have generated a historically unique configuration of components:

(1) The challenge has come from an unprecedented number and scope of sources—racial and ethnic minorities, women, and homosexuals—in many cases with the willing and active support of government and other public groups affecting the universities.

(2) The challenge is not only to *gain access* to the dominant culture and opportunities of the university but also to *question the legitimacy* of and perhaps *unseat* that culture—though, interestingly, not so much its associated opportunities. The traditional curriculum is challenged as being Eurocentric. Its language and assumptions are assaulted as being racist or sexist, and the world of heterosexual, older, white males is depicted as a bastion of illegitimate privilege and power.

(3) The challenge is a *collective* one involving the political efforts of identified groups. The logic of affirmative action should not conceal the fact that it is simultaneously an organized effort on the part of traditionally disadvantaged minority and gender groups aimed at the collective upgrading of those groups, as defined on the basis of ascribed *categories*, not simply as individual mobility for selected members of the groups.

(4) Because the identifying (and self-identified) characteristics of the challenging groups are categorical, the challenge has overtones of the *entitlement of groups* to student, faculty, and administrative places in the university and to full citizenship and respect in these places. This feature arises simultaneously from three sources: the character of the demands of the claimants; the efforts of opponents of those demands to label them as illegitimate claims to entitlement; and the tendency of authorities (gov-

ernment officials and administrators) to acknowledge the entitlement aspect by responding to demands as *claims by categorical groups*.

Paradoxes and Vulnerabilities

These special features of the current debates pose a range of institutional dilemmas and anomalies that have not been encountered as such by universities in the past. Not the least of these is the dilemma posed for the dominant culture of the current administrative/faculty "establishment." Historically the elements of liberalism, egalitarianism, and meritocracy have been comfortably fused, as nineteenth-century middle-class liberals challenged the entitlement claims of monarchy, aristocracy, and church in the names of democracy and meritocracy. In the contemporary scene, those components have become strangely dissociated from one another. Liberal academic administrators and faculty generally applaud and welcome "diversity" if it is carried out within the confines of meritocracy and the preservation of the values of the academy. When those values themselves come under attack, however, and when the attacks on them appear to be made in the context of anti-meritocratic demands for entitlement, liberals are cast in an uncomfortable role in which they experience a dissociation of—indeed a conflict between—meritocracy and egalitarianism. Their role now becomes one of a conservative elite, jealously guarding those values of universalism that were invented and best suited to challenge conservative elites.

A closely related feature of the contemporary struggles over diversity is the creation of new, improbable, and unstable combinations of bedfellows. Traditional struggles in academia have involved issues of academic freedom, in which liberal faculty stand up against bastions of power— usually coalitions of business-legal political representatives of the Right— who are alarmed at the liberal/radical ideologies and teachings of academics. (The courts have usually acted as friends to academic freedom, and thus as countervailing forces to the external Right.) In these struggles, academic administrators sometimes have sided with the outside Right, sometimes with the internal faculty Left. Students have tended to be either indifferent or supportive of the faculty Left.

The contemporary political situation has torpedoed those comfortable political alliances and fashioned a new, unfamiliar political quilt. The challenge now comes from a new Left, made up of social representatives of different "minority" claimants—themselves standing in unstable coalition: outside Left political forces, often governmental, who are cognizant of their own dependence on minority constituencies in their political environments; academic administrators who are directly in the line of fire from the external Left; representatives of a generation of radical faculty—perhaps socialized in their student days in the 1960s—and "new" minority members of the faculty and the administration. On the Right are liberal faculty (and sometimes administrators and students), cast in the role of conservatives, evoking universalistic values and meritocracy as a defense rather than a challenge, and eliciting arguments of academic freedom as a conservative defense against "political correctness," laws and rules against "hate speech," and other initiatives emanating from the Left. These liberal faculty are bolstered by their conservative colleagues and by other conservative groups, usually white, in the larger political community, who are alarmed at the challenge from various minority and other Left sources.

If one translates these coalitions into the collective emotions that are typically associated with each, on the one side one finds a fusion of anger, guilt, uncertainty, and anxiety of minorities and liberal and radical white supporters. On the other, one finds the associated anger and guilt of the liberal and conservative forces. Furthermore, *both* of these affective mixes find support in a legitimate ideology—the ideology of egalitarianism, social justice, and past wrongfulness on the one side, and the ideology of universalism, meritocracy, and appeals to the traditional liberal values of freedom on the other. In controversies in which such emotions fuse with ideologies based on such legitimate first principles, the resultant conflict produces high levels of righteousness and vindictiveness and low levels of self-insight on both sides.

The new battle lines are tenuous, however, because every sub-group in both major coalitions has its own particular agenda and its own particular ambivalences, which may surface at any time and occasion a subtle or open realignment. Liberal faculty are torn between their egalitarianism and their commitment to their characteristic academic values of universalism. They are also often uncomfortable with being found in common cause with political conservatives. Asian Americans, like Jews in the past, are torn between the strategies of representing themselves with entitlement-like claims, on the one hand, and "making it" within the context of meritocracy in which they have been effective competitors, on the other. And Hispanic and black minorities, more drawn toward entitlement-like claims, forever wonder whether admission on an entitlement basis does not doom them to second-class citizenship in a world dominated by meritocratic values. All this makes for the greatest political fluidity, and for frustration on the part of observers and analysts who savor the neatness of political division.

To add to the confusion, the polity of the research university is not very well equipped to handle controversies of the sort that have developed. That polity itself is a strange historical mélange, incorporating several different principles of maintaining order and community in the university. It contains historical residues of a *religious calling*, which combines with self-imposed discipline and personal freedom; elements of *collegiality*, a company of equals whose main political cement is civility and mutual influence (within this kind of polity, above all, resides the myth of the university as a unified community); elements of *formal bureaucracy*, superimposed over time by the exigencies of growing size and multifunctionality; and a system of dual governance that is simultaneously *hierarchical* (with administrators retaining final authority) and *democratic* (with administrators delegating widely to academic senates and consulting with faculty, and to a certain extent with staff, students, and alumni). Needless to say, these different principles of polity often stand in tension with one another.

Whatever the mix of these ingredients in any university, it is the case that representatives of that polity are peculiarly ill equipped to handle *collective* struggles among categorical groups. Universities are institutionalized in large part in the name of values of individual achievement and are best equipped to deal with individuals. They admit individuals, give instruction to and grade individuals, discipline individuals, graduate individuals, prepare individuals for and place them in occupational positions. That institutional "tilt" also reveals a shortage of mechanisms to deal with group conflict. That deficit became evident during the turbulence experienced in higher education in the 1960s. Colleges and universities, reasonably able to handle traditional individual academic problems and traditional disciplinary offenses, found themselves ill equipped to deal with group phenomena such as mass demonstrations, protests, and violations of rules. They also discovered that they lacked—and had to invent—machinery to negotiate with such groups.

Two other factors contribute to the vulnerability of universities to group conflict. First, because they are generally liberal and tolerant, if not permissive—as institutions go—some political groups see them as especially inept at playing political hardball when confronted with protest and conflict. As such, universities are magnets for political action. Second, campus conflict is typically dramatized and magnified by the media, which gravitates toward conflict situations in any case, and perhaps takes special glee in publicizing conflict and disruption in institutions that have traditionally presented themselves as seats of collegiality, civility, and community.

Even with several decades of experience with group conflict, universities are still more comfortable in dealing with individuals than with groups. This constitutes a special vulnerability in the current conflict over diversity because so many of the groups involved define themselves in collective, if not primordial, ways—along gender, racial, ethnic, cultural, and life-style lines—and present themselves politically as groups, not as individuals. If one adds to these the "group" challenges from environmental, community action, animal rights, and other groups that impinge on the university's political environment, it becomes apparent that the university stands in a kind of political situation for which its history has not equipped it well.

Results of institutional ineptness in dealing with collective conflict are seen in the kinds of "impossible" political situations in which many universities find themselves. Two examples follow: First, the admission policies of most universities have accepted the "numbers game" logic of admitting a percentage of different claimant groups, either by pointing with pride to achieved results or by vowing to do better in the future. The "impossible" aspect of this definition is that the university is trapped in a zero-sum game. An increase in the percentage of one group means a decrease for another, which in the current atmosphere is politically unacceptable to the losing group. And even an increase does not silence the demands for greater increases. Second, in faculty hiring policies universities have likewise committed themselves to increase the numbers of women and minorities in an absolute sense. Particularly with respect to certain minorities—Native Americans, blacks, and Hispanics—this is currently a collectively impossible goal because of the small pool of doctoral candidates that appear in the market in any given year. The resultant situation is a heady competition for scarce minority candidates who may benefit from the process, but it does not seem to address the general problem of improving access for all minorities.

Prognosis

The upshot of the foregoing assessment is that the contemporary debates over diversity are particularly unclear and intractable. All sides find themselves successfully able to appeal to ideological and cultural arguments that still enjoy legitimacy but which, by a turn of history, have become opposed to one another.

The special character of the present debates also defies those who would write simple scenarios for the future. Rather, it is more advisable to envision a separable set of ideal-type outcomes, all of which are plausible, given the special alignment of social forces at present. The following three scenarios can be imagined:

(1) The program of assimilation of racially, ethnically, and culturally diverse groups to the existing values and roles of higher education. This is the liberal view and envisions continuing traditional patterns of liberal education and occupational and professional training, with students being socialized into these patterns, accommodating to them, and preparing themselves for participation in the institutions of the larger society.

(2) The program of altering the traditional missions of higher liberal education—which, it is agreed, is biased along racial/ethnic, class, and gender lines in any event—to some mission that gives greater recognition to nonmainstream groups. The recent episodes of pressure for curricular change are signs of this tendency, as are recent debates on campus about "political correctness" and the possible threat to principles of academic freedom.

(3) The program of converting campuses into a microcosm of the pluralistic polity, with racial, ethnic, cultural, gender, and other groups competing for the resources as well as the symbolic and real control of the institutional life of the universities. This scenario, too, although not novel in the history of education, would mark a further change in the traditional, liberal mission of educational institutions. And given the frail capacities and universities to manage group conflict, such a "political pluralism" model would prove difficult to stabilize.

Like the future of any complex social institution that is based on multiple values and principles, the future of research universities with respect to diversity will not reveal a clear victory for any of these scenarios. Some aspects of all will continue to be visible. Each one will persist, and each one will have its vicissitudes. With respect to the issue of diversity, then, the future will bring "process" rather than "product" as an outcome, with all involved parties struggling for but never finally gaining new and satisfactory definitions of the situation, institutional advantages, or political domination.

CULTURAL AND PSYCHOLOGICAL DIMENSIONS

Because so much of the contemporary discussion of the diversity debate is externalized into the social and political arenas, reference to psychological dimensions that might be involved in the experiences of those who are "diversifying" and those who are being "diversified" is being neglected. The reason for this neglect is at least in part ideological. If one ventures into the psychological arena, it is often regarded as a means (if not a ploy) to psychologize the issues away as expressions of individual problems and, therefore, not matters for political concern. I do not accept this implication. To explore the psychological dimensions is not to ignore the problem but instead, to probe into ever-present aspects of any process of change in institutional and group life. The remainder of this essay focuses on these aspects.

Old and New Diversification

At the outset it is essential to note that the cultures of universities are *already* heterogeneous and diversified. With regard to the cultures of undergraduate student bodies of these institutions, for example, the following subtypes manifest themselves in varying degrees of visibility, coherence, and self-consciousness:

- A *collegiate* culture, which is highly social, has close links to fraternities, sororities, athletics, and alumni, and manifests a kind of innocent anti-intellectualism

- A *preprofessional* culture of serious, competitive students, who are academic but not always intellectual in orientation

- A culture of *free intellectual spirits* who identify with the faculty and treasure intellectualism and the life of the mind

- A *politically active culture*, typically liberal or radical in political tone and often manifesting a species of anti-intellectualism

- A culture of *expressive protest*, manifested in personal appearance, drug use, sexual liberty, and countercultural values

- Various *niche* cultures, including functionally based groups, such as drama, band, and undergraduate and graduate academic clubs and associations

Similarly, graduate student cultures in research universities have never been homogenous. They vary first of all by disciplinary commitment—field by field in the sciences, social sciences, humanities, and professional schools. Within fields they vary by level of professional commitment and identification with the field of study. They differ in the degree to which they are politically active *within* the university context and the degree to which they give priority to intellectual, political, or moral concerns. Faculty cultures are also diversified within the research university, both by academic fields and by rank and age cohorts. They vary according to the priority they accord to the major sub-missions of the university—for example, excellence and national recognition in research, commitment to undergraduate teaching, and public and professional service. Faculties also differ along the lines of their level of loyalty to or suspicion of academic administrators, their level of commitment to traditional academic values, their derived hierarchies of prestige, and, like graduate students, the salience of intellectual, political, and moral concerns in their outlook.

Formal and informal groups based on particular racial and ethnic backgrounds, gender, and sexual preference have always been a feature of collegiate and university life, but with the increasing heterogeneity of undergraduate student bodies—and to a lesser extent, of graduate students and faculty—these groups have increased in size, visibility, and social and political salience. However, it must be underscored that the new groups enter an arena that is already culturally highly diversified and in which distinct subcultures can be identified.

The Omnipresence of Ambivalence in the Diversifying Process

The preexisting subcultures in a university community *all* constitute opportunities for personal identification for their incoming members. They also extend implicit cultural invitations for any new member so interested or so inclined to join.

To point this out is not to ignore the barriers to participation in all the cultural and life-style opportunities that campuses hold. The most obvious barriers are found in the fraternity and sorority world—a special subculture of the "collegiate" alternative for students—which, even if legally and formally barred from discrimination, certainly continue to be formally segregated along gender lines and informally along class and racial/ethnic lines. In addition, any distinct subculture develops its own mechanisms of closing ranks and of discouraging entry through informal social sanctions of ignoring, snubbing, and making life generally uncomfortable for those regarded as alien to that subculture.

At the same time, the university campus, as a liberal and voluntaristic arena, has a range of freedom of choice. Within some limits, an individual student can choose to be serious or flippant in his or her commitments to academic study, to become "intellectual" or "anti-intellectual," to take a vocational or a liberal route in the curriculum; to adopt a traditional "Joe College" or "coed" role; to become politically active; to become bohemian; to go out for different kinds of activities such as athletics, band, or drama if able and interested; to join clubs; or to go it alone. Similarly, a faculty member has an element of choice as to whether to be a scholarly loner, a conscientious teacher, a participating or nonparticipating citizen in the academic community, a faculty conformist, or a faculty protester.

These choices, moreover, inevitably become invitations to incoming members to become something culturally *different* from what they were before entering that community. This principle is most easily seen in the case of entering undergraduates. They are typically leaving their family and community of residence, whereas graduate students and faculty have presumably already been more fully socialized into the university cultures of their choice. Let us now consider the process from the standpoint of the undergraduate student, with special reference to racial and ethnic diversity.

There are three reasons that the collegiate experience is destined to pull students away from the cultural values and attitudes of their family, their social class, and their community. The first is found in the still viable philosophy embedded in the idea of a liberal education. Such an education is meant to be broadening, indeed *liberating* in its essence. It exposes students to new ranges of factual information, new perspectives, different ways of looking at the world, and, above all, challenges to what they have previously been taught and learned. A liberal education is thus intended to "diversify" the students to make them more universal, more cosmopolitan. Put more dramatically, a liberal education is based on the premise that "the student is always wrong." The sense in which that declaration is true is that the conscientious teacher takes as his or her mission the idea that students' existing knowledge and perspectives are limited; they are meant to be broadened in the educational process. The other corollary of the idea of liberal education is that, in the process, teachers are not supposed to hold out some kind of final, correct worldview, personal philosophy, or set of cultural values to the student, but rather to equip that student better to choose his or her preferred combination of these. Needless to say, this is an ideal representation of a liberal education, which does not always work out according to the ideal; nonetheless, it is still a discernible ingredient of the collegiate experience. The diverse student subcultures—serious youth culture, political activism, and bohemianism—also provide opportunities to experiment and broaden, even though they do not constitute part of the philosophy of liberal education as such.

Second, these ingredients of the collegiate experience promise not only to make the student different from his or her parents, class, and community. They also provide an opportunity for that student to *reject* those origins—to break from them in a process of rebellion that may range from polite to violent. The history of undergraduate education in America is a history of "liberated" sophomores bringing home the "enlightened" perspectives of Darwinism, Freudianism, Marxism, philosophical relativism—and nowadays deconstructionism—during vacations and torturing their stodgy and unenlightened parents with those perspectives. They may also bring home new life-style commitments as well—dissolute carousing, countercultural values, political radicalism, arrest records—and inflict the same torture on parents, even those (or perhaps especially those) who regard themselves as liberal.

Third, the collegiate experience is culturally defined as an avenue for *social mobility.* This cultural ideal is a deeply American one, namely to use higher education as a means to improve one's social standing by advancing occupationally and by gaining status-endowing credentials. Parents themselves usually conspire to assist in this mobility, by saving and paying for college for their children. Sometimes the mobility is not upward but simply "different"—the lawyer's daughter does not become a lawyer, the doctor's son does not become a doctor—and parents may not necessarily approve, but it is mobility all the same.

Liberation, rejection, and mobility invariably have some features in common. They are integral parts of an individual's growth and self-realization. But equally important—and this is where ambivalence makes its entrance—they always involve feelings of guilt. Guilt is always there for the student; it appears *no matter how* he or she resolves the tension between the culture of origin and the cultures that invite one to forsake that culture of origin. If one rejects the invitations of collegiate life, one is guilty for not having seized the opportunities—and perhaps for having disappointed one's parents in the process. If one rejects the cultural values of origin, one is guilty for having rejected them—and for having disappointed one's parents in another way. If one tries to strike some kind of middle ground between the two, one is certain to feel guilty on both counts. With guilt, moreover, comes anger, and that anger is likely to be directed at any and all parties who have conspired to set up the conflict that generated the guilt in the first place.

The developmental ambivalence I have described is more or less universal, no matter what the origin of the student. However, it is particularly salient when the student comes *from* a subculture that regards itself as a distinct, homogeneous, and discriminated against as a minority. Ironically, such students are often incorporated into the middle-class, Anglo, or mainstream American culture. One of the most vivid accounts of this ambivalence was described by William Foote Whyte fifty years ago in *Street Corner Society* (1955), an ethnographic study of life in the Italian community of North Boston. The two protagonists of the study constitute the two facets of the ambivalence—"Doc," the successful local politician who never left the family values, congeniality, and loyalty to friends of the Italian community, and "Chick," the successful businessman who went to a private college and forsook all of those. Both suffered the characteristic regret and guilt associated with the distinctive route he took.

Because of the increasing numbers of racial/ethnic minorities that have entered the college and university scene in recent decades—numbers that promise only to increase in the decades to come—this phenomenon of ambivalence toward culture of origin and culture of invitation is and will be correspondingly more widespread. The core psychological tension is between a real or imagined "home" culture of parents and community who stress continuity, loyalty to group, and perhaps endogamy on the one side and a real or imagined "campus" culture—an amalgam of diverse opportunities that constitute an invitation to leave and reject the home culture and enter some real or imagined larger cosmopolitan and alternative world. The "home" pressure emanates not only from home; any campus with a sizeable group of minority students will have an association of conscious spokespersons for that group who stress cultural identity, loyalty, and demands for respect and participation. The ambivalence is thus real and present and constantly stirs that range of affects—including especially guilt and anger—generated by ambivalence.

As a psychological phenomenon, ambivalence is difficult to deal with and tends to be unstable; it is forever being resolved into simpler alternatives that are easier to live with. The following resolutions are identifiable on university campuses: (1) Accepting—either silently or rebelliously—the invitation to leave the "home" culture and take on one of the available cultural alternatives of the campus; in this case the loyalty to the "home" culture is uneasily repressed or openly rejected. (2) Affirming the "home" culture and repressing or rejecting the real or imagined "establishment" of the university, whether by withdrawing from it or by actively assuming an alienated and critical stance toward it. (3) Striking some compromise between the two sides of the ambivalence and thus trying to have it both ways; the student may be the loyal, conformist child when at home, while simultaneously exploring and adopting other cultural styles when on campus—hiding the two adaptations from one another; the student may be politically active in various degrees on behalf of his or own group but remain in good standing with the academic culture of the university at the same time; or the student may major in something like ethnic studies, which is simultaneously a commitment to an academic path and an affirmation of group identification and loyalty. Some kind of compromise seems the most frequent resolution of cultural ambivalence in contemporary American campus life.

The common tendency of racial and ethnic groups to "ghettoize" on campus is often ignored or regretted. When recognized, it is typically explained by a simple formula like "people being comfortable with their own kind." I believe the phenomenon is more complicated than that and can be interpreted within the framework of the ambivalence that I have noted. Associating informally with one's "kind" is one mode—probably the most typical—of resolving that ambivalence. The campus ghetto is a kind of way station: a means of declaring one's loyalty to a real or imagined home community while participating in and presumably reaping the real or imagined benefits of the alternative cultures that university life has to offer.

The logic of ambivalence also applies to those who are part of the supposed "majority" on diversifying campuses—whether these are referred to as majority, white, Anglo, mainstream, or whatever. This group may, incidentally, include—psychologically—members of minority groups who have opted for the first-noted resolution of their ambivalence. On the one hand, they may experience the feeling that the dominant academic and collegiate cultures are historically "theirs" in some vague sense and that they are therefore being "invaded"; they are likely to interpret their own presence in the community as resulting from their having "made it" on traditional meritocratic grounds while others have not. On the other hand—many being liberal themselves and all being exposed to the traditionally liberal culture of the university—they welcome, or feel the pressure to welcome, historically less-privileged minority and other groups to that culture. This ambivalence of the majority tends to be resolved in a number of ways:

1. Asserting the traditional dominance of "their" historic university, whether this is expressed in the affirmation of meritocratic ideals that others have presumably not met, the conviction that the "diversifying" groups are aliens or less than first-class citizens, or, in some cases, outright racism.

2. Espousing egalitarian causes—liberal admissions policies, affirmative action, and multicultural curricular reform—and identifying with the incoming minority groups, their aspirations, their political positions, their social movements, and perhaps their social life.

3. Striking some compromise between the two sides, and thus having it both ways; perhaps to espouse liberal values but to associate informally with other majority students; periodically to espouse causes, which, however, do not disturb the basic contours of traditional collegiate life. This kind of compromise is also probably the most frequent among majority groups.

These are some of the manifestations of the complex process of personal and social adaptation to ambivalence. Let me end with two final observations. First, the analysis of ambivalence and its implications has been carried out mainly with reference to undergraduate students. The same dynamics and their resolutions, with different weights and in different contexts, apply equally well to graduate student bodies and faculties that are in the process of diversifying. Second, the politics emanating from the adaptations to multiple ambivalences generate an enormously complex mosaic. Not only does one find "minorities" and "majorities" opposed to one another—which is the relationship enunciated most frequently in public rhetoric—but one also finds these groups in common cause with one another, depending on the resolutions of the ambivalences on each side. Moreover, the politics of ambivalence means that many political subdivisions *within* both minorities and majorities emanate from the multiple resolutions of ambivalence. Finally, because these resolutions are superimposed on *other* divisions in the university—divisions among undergraduates, graduate students, faculty, administration, and staff—the possible permutations and combinations of political alliance and political division are even greater. These considerations carry us some distance toward understanding the special fluidity and volatility of politics on the campuses of research universities.

The conclusion to this psychological line of reasoning is similar to the conclusion emanating from the sociopolitical line of reasoning laid out in the first part of the essay. The political divisions that arise from the ambivalences of diversification are profound, multiple and omnipresent, and the bases for these divisions are endemic. These politics show no sign of abating or of yielding any simple social-psychological or political resolution. The political forces of the nation are such that the march of diversification in universities is becoming and will become an established historical fact. However, from the standpoint of the social psychology of diversification and its political manifestations, we must expect continuous process and flux, not a finished product.

REFERENCE

Whyte, William Foote. 1955. *Street Corner Society: The Social Structure of an Italian Slum.* Chicago: University of Chicago Press.

FIVE

Problematics of Affirmative Action
A View from California (1999)

AS PART OF ITS 250TH anniversary celebration in 1996, Princeton University scheduled many cultural and academic events. One of these was a Conference on Higher Education (supported by the Andrew W. Mellon Foundation) held in March of that year and organized by Eugene Y. Lowe, Jr., of Princeton's Department of Religion. A conspicuous theme of that conference was affirmative action.

Lowe invited me to participate in one session on affirmative action but left me free to choose my emphasis. He and others mentioned positively my essay on ambivalence and diversity that appeared in 1993 (chapter 4), and I assumed that that essay had prompted the invitation. In addition, I had written on affirmative action in the academic market in the 1970s, and had been involved with it in my experiences in Berkeley's sociology department, Academic Senate, and administration. In light of that experience, and in light of the fact that affirmative action had boiled up so dramatically in regental and California politics in the late 1990s, I decided to take "a view from California."

Accepting the invitation created a dilemma for me, not unlike that posed by the invitation to write on diversity some years before. Affirmative

Originally appeared in *Promise and Dilemma: Perspectives on Racial Diversity and Higher Education*, ed. Eugene V. Lowe, Jr., 169–92 (Princeton, NJ: Princeton University Press, 1999).

action was and is a highly polarized subject, and one is invited by that polarization to choose one side or another. My own personal views were a mix of a generally favorable disposition to that political project, combined with opposition to some of its rhetoric and to what I regarded as some of its excesses. I decided, however, not to represent my personal views. Instead, I posed a more objective and analytic issue: Following the logic of Max Weber's analysis of charisma, most social reforms originate in a season of conflict and turbulence, but after they are put into place officially, they undergo a process of "routinization" or embedding themselves into society's institutions and becoming more or less standard operating procedures, freer from conflict. Affirmative action apparently did not follow that path. Its decades of "routinization" had resembled more a running sore than a process of adaptation. Why, I wanted to ask, should that have been so? In my contribution to the conference, I attempted to bring every consideration I could think of—cultural, political, social, and psychological—to bear on that question.

As an aside, I should point out that at the time my presentation was not especially welcomed by the other participants and the audience at the Princeton conference, who were almost all unquestioning believers in affirmative action. Nor would it have been welcomed by antagonists on the right, who were equally unquestioning in their commitments. In such polarized circumstances, it is likely that the dispassionate or the moderate becomes an "outcast of the middle" because he or she does not join the polarized debate in its own terms.

AFFIRMATIVE ACTION IN HISTORICAL CONTEXT

From colonial times—and consolidated at the moment of constitutional founding—American society has found its legitimacy in four central cultural values: individual liberty and freedom, democracy, progress manifested in mastery of nature and economic expansion, and equality of opportunity. It is a matter of historical fascination that human slavery, an institution that ran contrary to most of these values, persisted for almost a century after the birth of a republic founded on them. It is also, however, a confirmation of the power of those values that slavery was brought down in their names, and that discriminatory practices established after the Civil War were also curtailed in their names. Yet during World War II Gunner Myrdal could still write of an American dilemma, of a society that simultaneously institutionalized those values (Myrdal focused above all on freedom, democracy, and equality of opportunity) and a system of racial inequality that denied those values.

Affirmative action, born officially about two decades after Myrdal wrote, must be regarded as a continuation of the conversation about that dilemma. But it was not simply an extension of past assaults on inequality. It arose in a new historical context and differed qualitatively from past struggles. What was that context, and what was new about it?

The 1960s witnessed a confluence of three historical circumstances and created the facilitating if not necessary conditions for affirmative action:

- A Civil Rights movement, focused mainly on the South but drawing participation from both black leaders and citizens and liberal whites around the country. This movement was named properly, since it concerned above all civil—or public—society and worked to end traditional denials of rights in that arena. The major battlegrounds were the polity, with voting the focus; public education, with integration the focus; and access to public places, with transportation and businesses such as restaurants the foci. Although economic discrimination became the target of some protest, the main emphasis was civil. Furthermore, the battle for civil rights was about racial injustices affecting black Americans, and did not extend to disadvantaged groups in general.

- Eight years of political domination by the Democratic Party, which, through the leadership of John Kennedy, Robert Kennedy, and Lyndon Johnson, proved to be sympathetic and responsive to the goals of the Civil Rights movement. Moreover, especially under Johnson, the Democrats went beyond civil rights and introduced economic and educational reforms. The war on poverty was couched in general terms, but in practice it encompassed educational programs (such as Head Start) and welfare reforms directed disproportionately toward the poor black population.

- A *generalization* of political protest and alienation, some of it inspired by the goals, methods, and successes of the Civil Rights movement. The new directions included the student movement, targeting the universities and social—including racial—injustices generally; the antiwar movement, which consumed the country from 1965 until the beginning of the 1970s; the mobilization of other disadvantaged racial and ethnic (notably Native American and Hispanic/Latino) groups to protest against injustices specific to them; a mobilization of protest against racial injustice in South Africa; and a revitalization of the feminist movement, with a more explicit emphasis on economic, educational, and other institutional disadvantages than ever before.

These circumstances set the stage for affirmative action. As an institutional invention it combined ingredients from all of them and added a few new ones. In its essence, affirmative action was a set of policies and procedures intended to give disadvantaged groups differential access to economic and educational opportunities and their associated rewards. Like the Civil Rights movement, affirmative action aimed to improve the situation of the disadvantaged. Like Johnson's Great Society, it focused on educational and occupational arenas. It was thus a *synthesis* or *convergence* of themes found in the Civil Rights movement and the programs of the Democratic administrations. It remained conscious of civil and political rights, but it focused more on social and economic rights.

In addition, affirmative action involved a number of extensions beyond the themes of the 1960s:

- It included but moved beyond the removal of obstacles to participation in society's institutions. It actively promoted such participation, in the form of preferential treatment in hiring, contracting, and educational admissions.

- It included the rationale that it would redress past as well as present institutional disadvantages, wrongs, and sufferings. This rationale was explicit in the case of African Americans and Native Americans but came to pervade the entire logic of affirmative action.

- It involved a generalization of concern beyond the Civil Rights movement's focus on race. Affirmative action's initial focus was on American blacks but it soon came to include other racial and ethnic groups—Native Americans, Hispanics/Latinos, Asians, and South Sea Island peoples. It initially included gender as well, and subsequently physically disabled persons. What makes affirmative action sociologically interesting is that it generalized in ascriptive directions. *Ascription* refers to categories that are, by birth or social designation, defined as largely unalterable by personal choice or behavior. Another ascriptive category, age, also entered the picture but not principally as demands for preferred treatment but as demands to end job discrimination against the elderly and the disadvantages imposed by retirement. Finally, sexual preference, a category that lies ambiguously between ascribed and voluntary, also came on the scene, but this, too, involved protest against discrimination rather than active, preferential treatment.

· [Ascription is only an approximate sociological category. In the case of age it is pure, since chronological age, sociologically defined, is unalterable by choice or behavior, even though one might feel or act older or younger than one is. Other areas are less clear. "Passing for white," renouncing ethnic identification, and sex changes give the lie to the adjective "unalterable." At the same time, such changes are regarded as unusual or exceptional, thus confirming the sociological reality of the notion of ascription.]

SOME ADDITIONAL FEATURES OF AFFIRMATIVE ACTION

The Cultural Context

No institutionalized practice exists without explicit or implicit reference to some legitimizing, presumably consensual cultural value that gives meaning and defensibility to that practice. For example, voting procedures, electoral districting, political primaries, and political conventions make sense and gain their institutional desirability by reference to the cultural ideal of representative democracy.

Advocates of affirmative action seek legitimacy in the values of social justice and equality of opportunity. From these values derive the argument that those who have experienced past or experience present disadvantage through some for of oppression have been unjustly treated and deprived of opportunity and merit compensation by preferential treatment. But at the same time, preferential treatment can be regarded as running counter to another connotation of equality of opportunity—namely meritocracy, or the reward of talent and ability without regard to other considerations. University of California Regent Ward Connerly, for example, who spearheaded the movement to repeal existing affirmative action provisions, said, according to the *San Francisco Chronicle* (December 1, 1995), that the initiative was a way to achieve "an inclusive society in which people of all races, religions, and sexual preference have a right to have our talents considered." And in the immediate wake of the passage of the California Civil Rights Initiative in the November 1996 election, the *New York Times* (November 10, 1996) quoted an advocate of the measure as saying "Equal opportunity is what America is all about—not preferences." And in the very next paragraph an opponent of the legislation spoke as follows: "We believe the vote in California in no way reflects the general public's sentiment on the value and viability of affirmative action programs. Most Americans support preservation of equal opportunity, especially in the workplace." Because of this circumstance, the nation has been faced with a situation in which both advocates and opponents of affirmative action policies and practices have legitimized their arguments by referring to the same cultural value, equality of opportunity.

This situation, while not unheard of, is not typical. Debates over welfare policies, for example, often invoke conflicting value perspectives: competitive individualism versus humanitarianism or collective responsibility. Furthermore, the simultaneous reference to the same legitimizing context often gives rise to some interesting formulas. For example, one instruction that appears in affirmative-action manuals is the following: If two applicants for a position are equally qualified, but one falls in a preferential treatment category and the other does not, the position should go to the former. This formula attempts to accommodate, through compromise, the tension involved in the simultaneous appeal to equality of opportunity and preferential treatment: to recognize talent and qualification but to tilt judgments in marginal cases. (It is also true that such a formula creates a difficult if not impossible assignment in practice—how to judge objectively and exactly whether two people are equally qualified when such a judgment inevitably involves multiple criteria, some subjective. But when conflicts over meaning and legitimacy are at hand, the closest attention is not always paid to practical issues of workability.)

In addition, when advocates and opponents of affirmative action appeal simultaneously to the same values, this may create a specter of ambiguity and tension for participants. Those who benefit from preferential attention may experience a sense of vindication for past or present wrongs, but they may also experience a sense that they have not "made it" on the basis of their own abilities and achievements. Those who oppose affirmative action may harbor the same suspicion that those who benefited have not really made it on their own, and, on that basis, may resent or tolerate the "less deserving" in their midst—a particularly subtle and evasive form of racism or sexism. Indeed, the argument that affirmative action "demeans" the beneficiaries by elevating them artificially in a merit-based world was one of the principal claims made by those who wished to dismantle affirmative action policies during the debates before the University of California regents in 1995.

The Political Context

As noted, affirmative action was born in the context of and sustained by a number of social movements—movements by racial and ethnic groups, different wings of the feminist movement, gay and lesbian movements, and more diffuse sentiments against social injustices of all kinds. The project also gave rise to counter or backlash political movements with varying degrees of articulation, energy, and mobilization. This circumstance, if no other, confirms that affirmative action has been a political phenomenon: an institutional crucible in which social movements and counter-movements clash.

The politics of affirmative action are complicated by another political peculiarity. For many social movements, the response of government authorities is to regard them as something "out there," whether they are something to crush, oppose, resist, handle, become divided over, accommodate, or give in to—in other words, to maintain a certain distance from them. Revolutionary political movements, the labor union movement, and the antiwar movement are cases that illustrate this point. In the case of affirmative action, the federal government and some state governments *joined* the movement. For whatever motives, government agencies were often the leaders in promoting affirmative action. Through administrative and judicial pressure the government encouraged if not coerced others to pursue its policies. In higher education, for example, agencies such as the Department of Health, Education, and Welfare and the Department of Labor threatened to withhold research funds from universities unless they instituted and followed affirmative action policies. This government stance not only endowed the relevant social movements for affirmative action with legitimacy, influence, and boldness, but it also gave additional momentum to the affirmative-action project as a whole.

Another political dynamic invited the extension and generalization of the project. Two necessary conditions for a group to derive advantage from affirmative action are for it to (1) identify itself as a tangible group, presumably with a consciousness and identity and (2) make a claim—and make that claim stick—that it is suffering or has suffered disadvantage. The government played a role in establishing these conditions by indicating that it was prepared to respond to claims of ascription and disadvantage. The result was to encourage a special kind of politics, called, variously, the politics of ascription, ethnic politics, or the politics of identity. (It is interesting to note that sociologists and political scientists have recently turned their attention to identity-based social movements and identity politics, thereby acknowledging a social reality that has been created for them.)

As a corollary, there is only limited evidence for the salience of social class as a feature of affirmative action. By and large, advocates of affirmative action do not claim to represent class from an economic point of view, even though they often frame their protests and demands in the language of class oppression. Some might regard this as an oddity, given the significance of class in other eras of American politics—for example, the politics of class in the early history of labor unionism and during the Great Depression. In education, too, class has played a major part in the history of preferential treatment. The preferential admission of children of alumni—long a practice of private and some public institutions—can be seen in some cases as affirmative action in favor of the wealthy. Another example is the preferential treatment of able students from backgrounds too modest to afford a college education, which is class-based preference as well. Preferential admission of athletes, though based in the first instance on athletic talent, is in some cases, such as the recruitment of male football players, class preference in practice. (There is, however, great variation among sports and between the sexes with respect to class origins.)

Identity politics, if we may term it that, may turn against the political authorities who acknowledge them. As we will see, identity-based demands tend to develop into claims to entitlement, because advocates of the identity groups often base their arguments on primordial or quasi-sacred considerations—such as common blood or ancestry—which demand dignity and respect. This imparts an uncompromising character to their claims and demands. This circumstance creates difficulties for politicians, because politicians in democracies engage in compromise if nothing else and, as a rule, are less comfortable with absolute demands than they are with contingent, negotiable ones.

Finally, if demands for entitlement by identity groups come to be translated into quotas for positions, this creates additional difficulties for political resolution. Consider an example from my university, the University of California at Berkeley. That campus has a deserved reputation of being one of the most aggressive in pressing the project of affirmative action. In noting its achievements, the campus makes public annually the percentages of racial, ethnic, and, in some cases, gender groups admitted. In doing this, the campus encourages (no doubt unconsciously) and finds itself in a political numbers game. If the percentage of one group rises, the percentage of another group falls. Some groups voice dissatisfaction if their percentage falls, does not rise, or does not rise fast enough. This creates a permanent presence of complaining groups for campus authorities. It has furthermore resulted in the slow but steady reduction of students from the white population, who (and whose parents) have not been until recently as articulate or mobilized as minority groups.

Points of Ambiguity in Implementing Affirmative Action Programs

Although definite phrases (e.g., Equal Opportunity Employer) characterize affirmative action and manuals and procedures guide implementation, affirmative action has experienced a certain vagueness and ambiguity about both goals and processes. With respect to goals, the following points of uncertainty can be noted:

- Should affirmative action be defined in terms of specific substantive goals or as a general process aimed at ameliorating present and past disadvantages?

- If the former, how should goals be characterized? Should they be regarded as definite quotas or targets? Should they be regarded as aimed at achieving some proportion of a population, or should they be regarded as efforts to move toward "more" or "better" representation of groups, without further specification?

- Which groups qualify for affirmative action? Certain groups, such as African Americans, Latino Americans, and Native Americans come to mind as unambiguous cases, but their recognition has come about at different points in time. Furthermore, different groups within the Latino population have had different salience, with Cuban Americans being the most ambiguous case. Pacific Island peoples are typically listed officially as qualifying minorities but figure only little in practice. Asian Americans constitute another ambiguous case. To take a vivid example at the University of California, Asian-American groups are, de facto, not considered an affirmative-action minority for undergraduate admissions. (Indeed, Asian American groups have argued that they have been discriminated against and would fare better under completely meritocratic standards.) At the same time, some academic departments consider Asian-Americans as de facto minorities meriting special attention in graduate admissions and faculty hiring. The salience of gender as an object of affirmative action has also varied over time. It has been an insignificant issue in undergraduate admissions and has diminished in significance in some other arenas. In the end, the effective qualification of different groups has been largely a function of their capacity to make their case and mobilize politically. In practice, finally, there are great regional and institutional differences in the recognition of different groups as qualifying for affirmative action.

· How are members of groups to be identified as belonging to those groups? Recognition by name is a reasonable but not completely accurate way of identifying Latino groups and women. Recognition of African Americans and Native Americans by name and sometimes by appearance is difficult, sometimes impossible. Asking applicants to identify their group is another measure, but requests of this sort are almost always voluntary and, as a result, incomplete. In 1975—when affirmative action was entering into a high gear—I was chairman of my department at UC Berkeley. I was requested by the administration, in the interests of affirmative action, to specify the racial-ethnic and gender distributions of a pool of candidates for academic appointment but discovered, at the same time, that I was forbidden by administrative rule to request identification from the candidates! The example is extreme but illustrates the ambiguity.

With respect to procedures for implementing affirmative action, a comparable list of uncertainties emerges:

· Is active discrimination in favor of a group permissible? And does this imply active discrimination against another group? One judicial decision, the *Bakke* case in the medical school of the University of California, Davis, suggested that the answer to the former is negative and the answer to the latter is positive, since the ruling was in favor of a white applicant who claimed he was denied admission because places were reserved for minority candidates. However, the ruling has not necessarily controlled informal practices in all situations.

· What constitutes a proper search in alternative-action hiring? Is advertising in a few outlets likely to reach women and minorities sufficient, or should the search be more aggressive? Most institutions have developed definite procedures for searching, but, again, the variation is great.

· What constitutes a proper accounting for affirmative-action efforts? Although formulae have emerged (for example, reporting the character of the search, describing the pool of applicants by race/ethnicity and gender, defending why minority candidates were not hired), these have sometimes produced stock, uninformative answers. Some maintain that to require reporting produces positive results, others complain that reporting has little effect and serves mainly to increase paperwork and costs.

· How and in what detail should affirmative action be policed? Should monitors be satisfied when proper procedures have been carried out or should they be interested in accounting for and influencing results in hiring and admissions?

To summarize up to this point, affirmative ration policies, while conceptually clear in intent and yielding significant results, have been matters of cultural ambivalence, political conflict, and institutional ambiguity. The origins of this, moreover, lie in the uncertain legitimacy that affirmative action enjoys in the context of American values, the political competition that results, and the practical difficulties in implementation—the last derived in part from the first two. These persistent features of ambivalence, conflict, and ambiguity have contributed in part, but only in part, to the potential for reaction and backlash, which appeared in earnest in the 1990s.

Three Interrelated Trends

I have been able to discern three irregular trends in affirmative-action practices during the past quarter-century. When viewed together, they may cast some additional light on why a significant opposition to the program has developed. I confess that I have less than full documentation for these trends and have more confidence in some of the following statements than others:

1. There has been a movement from an emphasis on substantive goals (initiating affirmative-action programs, achieving results in the form of targets) toward an emphasis on procedures. To note this trend is to state the sociologically obvious. It is one aspect of what Max Weber called

routinization. Weber's main illustration was the routinization of charismatic leadership into more stable forms, but the point may be generalized. Any innovation or reform produces an initial period of enthusiasm and vision, but as the innovative becomes the normal, practices come to be regulated by more explicit and stable norms.

This has been, at least in this aspect, the case with affirmative action. Most employers, both public and private, have sooner or later established modes of searching, evaluating, and monitoring affirmative-action policies. Two additional observations can be made about routinization. The first concerns the general ambiguity, noted earlier, in the project of affirmative action. As a general principle, the more ambiguous the project, the greater the urgency to establish understood ways of administering. The objective, seldom explicit, of this adaptation, moreover, is to turn the novel and uncertain into the established and certain.

The second observation has to do with the management of conflict. The substantive goal of affirmative action is to alter practices associated with inequalities in race, ethnic, and gender relations. Such efforts often challenge people's personal beliefs and identities. Resistance to change is invariably strong and conflicts often become bitter and explosive. To focus on the rules of the game—on due process, as it were—often has the effect of diverting conflict away from hot substantive issues and toward more neutral grounds of procedure. In the 1970s, when the University of California and other research universities were under pressure from federal agencies to move forward on affirmative action, UC President Charles Hitch negotiated a kind of truce whereby the agencies would forego insistence on establishing short-term targets if the University would establish procedures designed to further affirmative action. Such a compromise tended to defuse direct conflict and focus attention on the practical.

Under such circumstances, discussion and debate tend to move away from substantive conflict and focus on methodological issues. In the early 1980s, as chair of the Berkeley Division of the UC Academic Senate, I was asked to sit in on visits of representatives of federal agencies to the Berkeley campus to monitor its progress on affirmative action. A fascinating feature of the exchanges in these visits was the focus on methodological points—estimating the size and quality of pools of minorities and women in the academic market, disputing the accuracy of measurements, challenging and defending the university estimates of progress it was making, even arguing about statistical techniques. Some of these discussions became heated. At the same time, they amounted to a way of avoiding confrontations over the substantive rights and wrongs of affirmative action and conflicts between government bureaucrats who were under political pressure to achieve results and the university officials who were pleading for patience and flexibility because of the political exigencies they faced in their respective institutions. The substantive conflicts were hidden in the methodological agenda, but with that agenda discussion could proceed under the tacit—but possibly mistaken—assumption that the parties agreed on the goals and differed only about means. As a result, discussions could proceed with a lower probability of open, bitter, and explosive conflict.

2. Another trend is the movement from preferential treatment to entitlement. The aim of affirmative action was to improve the institutional fortunes of disadvantaged groups. The means were to intervene in labor and markets and contracting policies and in the admissions policies of educational institutions. Over time tangible results began to appear—in different degrees—in government offices, in colleges and universities, and in business and professional firms. With such progress there often develops a subtle but definite shift in expectations among groups that have benefited: that their gains should be consolidated and protected and that further advances should be made. It is only a short step from such expectations to the mentality of entitlement.

Such developments create a difficult political situation. The expectations of all groups simply cannot be met unless positions available in the institutions and organizations involved continue to expand. If those positions expand slowly, remain stable, or decline, then a zero-sum game is at hand. The logic of that game is that if one party gains, the others necessarily lose. This logic conflicts directly with the logic of entitlement to past and future gains. The consequences of that conflict are three: latent or open conflicts among the groups struggling for scarce positions; resistance to further change on the part of those who regard themselves as potential losers; and heightened political pressure on those regarded as responsible for policies—in this case employers, administrators, and government officials. All three consequences have been visible in the history of affirmative action.

3. A final trend is from a focus on economic and institutional justice to a focus on cultural conflict. There is nothing necessary about this trend, but it also expresses a certain logic. Affirmative action promises, above all, improvement for the groups affected—from second-class citizenship to something better. But the process does not stop here. As Alexis de

Tocqueville demonstrated in the cases of the middle classes and the peasantry in eighteenth-century France, advances in one social sphere generated higher levels of dissatisfaction. This is the dynamic of relative deprivation: the wounds of exclusion from spheres not yet improved become all the sorer when advancement is attained in one.

That dynamic is evident in the history of affirmative action. One demand that followed the increased admissions of minorities to colleges and universities in the late 1960s and early 1970s was for programs, departments, and schools of ethnic studies. This demand was for equity in educational institutions in which minorities now had greater numbers. Many such academic units were put in place after a period of faculty resistance and political conflict. Despite some successes, most of these units continue to hold a second-class status in the eyes of older and more established academic enterprises in the colleges and universities.

In the 1980s the demand for academic inclusion and respect took a new turn: a call for the reform of long-established curricula. This involved not only a demand for inclusion but also a cultural attack on traditional college and university curricula and on those believed to be responsible for them. Those who had demanded Third World and ethnic programs were bidding for inclusion as equals. Those who called for ending the traditional "Western Civ" requirement at Stanford and for establishing an "American cultures" requirement at Berkeley were also demanding inclusion, but they combined that with an assault on "Euro-centrism" and a "white male establishment" that exercised its "hegemony" by imposing its Eurocentric views on peoples with different but equally if not more dignified cultures.

The movement for curricular reform in the 1980s—along with related debates on cultural diversity and multiculturalism and the "culture wars"—was a confluence of two major historical forces: first, an escalation of demands on the cultural level by advocates for minority groups and women who still felt disadvantaged on college and university campuses; and second, the postmodern movement, the appearance of which coincided with the collapse of radical Marxism in the 1980s, and which developed, as a barely-beneath-the-surface agenda, a critique and political protest against those who impose power-as-knowledge on disadvantaged groups.

This escalation to the cultural level has not affected the majority of working people in the country, whose main interest is still in the improvement of their economic and institutional position and rewards. The cultural debates have been confined largely to spokespersons for social movements, academics, intellectuals, and the sophisticated press. In those circles, however, that escalation poses a deeper and in some respects more difficult political situation than demands for institutional access. The cultural critique is more aggressive than the institutional one. In addition it excites conflicts over cultural values as well as group interests, thus making the conflicts more fundamental and encompassing.

To summarize this section, I would propose a connection among the three trends mentioned. A combination of increased political conscious-ness of and political pressure by disadvantaged groups and reformers produced a series of economic and educational reforms. The resultant programs and procedures yielded a significant incorporation of previously excluded groups. That success generated increased expectations of two kinds: those based on a sense of entitlement and those stemming from a bid for cultural dignity as well as institutional inclusion. These demands, in turn, created a more aggressive and threatening face, and this increased the likelihood of backlash and counter-movement. This line of analysis may fill in another piece of the puzzle of explaining the backlash of the 1990s. But the story is not yet finished. To complete it I turn to some specifics of the California situation, which reveals some factors not yet considered and helps explain the strength of the backlash in that state.

THE CALIFORNIA AND THE UNIVERSITY OF CALIFORNIA SITUATIONS

In one respect the situation in California has already been addressed. Most of the general aspects and trends discussed previously apply to California, and many illustrations refer to the California scene. That state's situation, however, has been extreme in two senses: Its scene is one of extreme racial and ethnic diversity, and the rollback of affirmative action by the University of California regents and the voters of California are among the most dramatic events in the history of affirmative action.

Affirmative Action in the University of California

As indicated, the main external pressure for affirmative action in the university came from federal research agencies, the government of California, and demands of minority and women's groups. One should not conclude from this, however, that the university itself was completely passive or resistant. Its campuses—most notably Berkeley and Santa

Cruz—have political cultures that welcome reform to improve disadvantaged populations.

Affirmative action affected every sector of the university, but the effects varied by sector. The major variations are as follows:

Administrative Staff Affirmation action policies—expressed mainly in the hiring and advancement of women and minority employees—proceeded earlier and faster with respect to staff. There are several reasons for this. First, the administration, as direct target of political demands, was more sensitive to pressures to institute affirmative-action policies. Second, the administration can effect changes in personnel policies in its own ranks more easily than it can in areas such as graduate-student admissions and faculty recruitment, which are usually delegated to largely autonomous academic departments. Third, administrative staff, in contrast to faculty, requires a diversity of skill levels among its personnel. When applying criteria of competence and quality in hiring decisions, the administration does not have such elaborate machinery as faculty recruitment to assure quality and competitive excellence. Finally, employee turnover is higher for administrative staff than for faculty, thus providing greater opportunity for changes in hiring policy.

Undergraduate Admissions Affirmative action proceeded faster and further in undergraduate admissions than in other academic sectors. Admissions at that level are centralized on the campus and thus more easily affected by central administrative decisions. Furthermore, the characteristics of its recruitment pool—the top one-eighth of graduates from the state's high schools (as required by the California Master Plan for Higher Education)—are well known. Also, a mechanism for preferential treatment of undergraduates was already in place. For years the university had had a "2 percent rule," instituted mainly in the interest of recruiting athletes, which permitted campuses to extend admission beyond the eligible academic pool for 2 percent of is entering class. Subsequently, and in the interest of extending affirmative action, this rule was extended to 4 percent, then to 6 percent. The afforded campuses greater flexibility in recruiting and greater capacity to bring in minority students.

In practice, the experiences of the different campuses of the university were diverse. They varied according to the aggressiveness of individual administrators and according to the size of minority populations in their respective "catchment areas." The large urban campuses of Berkeley and

Los Angeles were more diversified and by the late 1980s had student bodies with a minority of "Anglo" students. The process went less far on less urban campuses such as Davis and Santa Cruz. In the lore of undergraduate applicants in Southern California—a lore that does not mince words—the Irvine campus was known as the "yellow campus," the Los Angeles campus as the "black and brown campus," and the Santa Barbara campus as the "white campus." Regarded as a whole, however, the University of California carried affirmative-action policies in undergraduate admissions very far in comparison with other educational institutions in the country.

Graduate Admissions   Graduate admissions also vary by academic unit and campus, but the general pattern is to evaluate applicants first at the unit level (professional school, academic department), with recommendations going to a central graduate division for approval. The latter very seldom challenges the units' judgments, and when it does it is typically on procedural, not substantive grounds. This decentralization has meant that affirmative action has been pursued variably at the unit level. Some fields, such as engineering and economics, have small pools, and recruitment of qualified women and minorities has been low; others such as education and sociology have larger pools. Furthermore, pools cannot be easily expanded, since strong performance in college is a condition for finding a place in them. In addition, disciplinary "cultures" differ along conservative-liberal-radical lines, and these differences affect the degree to which academic units push or resist affirmative-action goals and procedures. Despite these barriers, many schools and departments in the University of California have significantly altered the racial, ethnic, and gender composition of their graduate student bodies.

Faculty Recruitment   The factors affecting graduate recruitment apply even more to faculty recruitment. Recruitment pools are even more restricted, since a condition for becoming part of them is to have attained a PhD or advanced professional degree. Furthermore, the campuses of the University of California, like those of all major research institutions, are engaged in a constant and rigorous struggle to hire only "the best." This means that many doctoral and professional graduates are not even considered. Finally, the institution of academic tenure restricts the rate at which the goals of affirmative action can be realized. With an annual turnover rate of 3 to 5 percent through retirement and resignation through the 1970s and 1980s (and before the mass exodus of senior faculty via early retirement in the 1990s), the opportunities to hire women and minorities were modest. This combination of factors yielded the smallest quantitative results of affirmative action among faculties, compared to other sectors of the university. Once again, however, the University of California was a national leader in implementing affirmative action at the faculty level.

It was in faculty ranks, however, that the strongest political resistance to affirmative-action programs was found. The bases for this opposition rose mainly from deep commitment to standards of quality and excellence in recruitment and advancement and in its highly developed machinery (multiple reviews of faculty members by departmental faculty, committees on academic personnel, and administrators). Many faculty, themselves politically liberal, shared the belief that hiring and advancement on any standards other than merit was a violation of those standards. Many academic units experienced their bitterest internal conflicts over the hiring of minorities and women. The 1970s and 1980s also witnessed incidents of faculty outrage over administrative reversal of faculty recommendations on minority and women candidates. And on the Berkeley campus, the only really systematic faculty alienation and opposition to I. Michael Heyman, whose tenure as chancellor spanned the 1980s, came from groups of faculty members who believed that he was going "too far, too fast" in pressing affirmative action and compromising standards of academic excellence long embraced on the campus.

Despite the ambivalence, ambiguity, resistance, and conflict associated with affirmative action, by the early 1990s the principles, policies, and procedures of that project were firmly established in the University of California and were legitimate in the minds—if not entirely in the hearts—of most of its constituencies. The most direct evidence of this is that every constituency—the president and his office, the chancellors, the faculty through the Academic Senate, and students through their representative institutions—spoke out officially against the initiative of the board of regents' resolution of July 1995. This polarization between the regents and all other constituencies is a remarkable political fact and will reverberate throughout the university system for a long time.

The Politics of the Regental Action

By the end of 1994 the United States confronted a unique historical situation that set the stage for a popular and governmental backlash against affirmative action, especially the racial and ethnic components. Among the factors contributing to this situation were the following:

- Since 1973 the real wages of Americans had remained virtually stagnant, after a period of steady but variable increase in real wages dating back to World War II. In addition, traditionally secure middle-class positions became less secure as firms and other agencies resorted to downsizing as a competitive strategy. For a country historically committed to material progress and the expectation that the next generation will be better off than the last, this economic fact contributed, perhaps more than all others, to the mood of national sourness about its institutions, including the government.

- The stagnation was aggravated, especially from the early 1980s on, by a regressive movement in the distribution of income, accompanied by social problems such as increases in poverty and homelessness. The causes of the stagnation and regression are complex; they include technological change, international wage competition, a weakening of labor unionism, and the tax and housing policies of the Reagan administration. But whatever the causes, they were a recipe for dissatisfaction among many groups. The significant economic recession of the early 1990s only exaggerated these economic conditions.

- The combination of stagnation and regression often gives rise to protest from the left. Contrary to this expectation, the electoral politics of the country in the last two decades have been dominated by the right and the Republican Party. From the presidency of Richard Nixon to the presidency of Bill Clinton, the country experienced only one episode of Democratic dominance—the unpopular presidency of Jimmy Carter—and the politics of the Reagan and to some extent the first Bush administration emanated from ideologies of the right. Clinton's administration promised a reversal, but most of Clinton's liberal initiatives either failed or stalled, and the election of a Republican Congress in 1994 was interpreted by the winners as a mandate against government in general and governmental involvement in domestic policies in particular.

- One reason difficult economic conditions were expressed in a right-wing mode is that the country experienced, during the same decades, the greatest wave of foreign immigration since the late nineteenth and early twentieth centuries. That fact provided many with an explanation for their economic difficulties: immigrants compete for jobs, are willing to work for less, and increase expenditures on welfare.

- An early initiative of the Republican Congress of 1994 was an aggressive move on the part of influential Republicans to reverse—by radical revision or even abolition—affirmative action as a governmental policy. That initiative put the Clinton administration on the defensive, and while that administration opposed it, it promised a thoroughgoing review of affirmative-action programs with an eye to correcting excesses.

All these long-term and short-term developments constituted a relevant national environment for California; in particular, the national move to weaken or abolish affirmative action was a green light for the state. In addition, some social conditions specific to California intensified those national developments.

- Immigration rates in California were higher than those of the nation. The inflow was mainly from Mexico and Central America, but Asia also contributed. It was repeatedly reported in the media and elsewhere that California was becoming a state of minorities and that by sometime after the year 2000 minority populations would outnumber the Anglo population. Equally common were reports that businesses and wealthier Anglo residents of California were leaving the state and that the overall increase of its population was because of the inflow of immigrants.

- The recession of the early 1990s was more severe in California than it was in the rest of the nation. California's unemployment rates were consistently 2 or 3 percent higher than the national average. California's unhappy economic fortunes were generated in part by reductions in government defense spending, concentrated in Southern California, in the wake of events in Eastern Europe and Russia in 1989–1990.

- California politics have been dominated since 1982 by Republican governors George Deukmejian and Pete Wilson. Wilson built much of his campaign and political program on anti-welfare and anti-immigration issues and threw his weight behind Proposition 187, the 1994 action that would deny the state's educational, medical, and other institutions to illegal immigrants. The constitutional status and impact of that proposition are still unclear, but the political message was clear. On June 1, 1995, Wilson issued an executive order to "End Preferential Treatment and Promote Individual Opportunity Based on Merit." And in Summer 1995, he exploited the themes of anti-welfare, anti-immigration, and anti-affirmative action in his brief, ill-fated bid for the Republican presidential nomination.

· One consequence of the Republican gubernatorial domination was a radical change in the composition of the University of California's board of regents. Regents are appointed by the governor, and those appointed are almost always political supporters of the incumbent governor. Since regental terms are for 12 years, it transpired that every appointment by Democratic Governor Jerry Brown (who preceded Deukmejian as governor) left the regents and no Democrats were appointed to replace them. So as of the mid-1990s, the board of regents was composed entirely of Republican appointments by Deukmejian and Wilson. Many of those regents, moreover, were indebted to Wilson, since appointment to the board is widely considered to be an important political reward and a source of recognition and prestige for those appointed.

· One regental appointment was of crucial significance, that of Ward Connerly, an African American businessman from Sacramento, in 1993. Himself a recipient of contracts under affirmative action provisions for contracting with minority businessmen, Connerly nevertheless had developed a special antagonism toward affirmative action. This attitude was manifested from the beginning of his term, at which time, he recalled, he was "instantly struck by the extent to which group classifications, particularly that of race, were being used in the activities of the university" (Connerly news release, July 5, 1995). He began a campaign of criticism of the university's admission policies, but in the early stages this attracted the open support of only a few regents, though Connerly maintained that many of them "privately shared similar concerns." He complained that the university did not take him seriously (he spoke of his "Lone Ranger" image), so in January of 1995 he decided to increase the issue's public visibility (Connerly news release, July 5, 1995).

Three additional, interrelated contextual features of California politics should be mentioned as background. Those features concern the popular—if not populist—character of its politics. First, dating from its state constitution, California has institutionalized many features of direct democracy, including provisions for initiative, referendum, and the recall of public officials. These features, especially the referendum, have lent a certain cumbersomeness to California politics and, from time to time, timidity on the part of politicians, who pass difficult and explosive political issues on to the voting public. Second, California's political parties, in comparison with states to the east, are weak in structure and in capacity to control and discipline their members. The history of California politics has witnessed many unpredictable elections and many political mavericks, which trace in part to the weakness of parties. Third, and derivative in large part from the first two, many political issues are fought out in the public media rather than negotiated in party caucuses and meetings. The advent of the television age has augmented this tendency and, as a result, California politics are conspicuous for their public free-for-alls. The public airing of political conflict during the debate over affirmative action among the UC regents in Summer 1995 fit this model of public brawls.

The Affirmative Action Debate of 1995

As of early 1995, and as a result of the contextual factors just reviewed, the political climate in California was ripe for an assault on affirmative action. It began in July in the context of the brief campaign on the part of Governor Wilson for the Republican nomination for the United States presidency. This campaign included conservative statements on immigration, welfare, and affirmative action.

Regent Connerly's introduction of the rollback motion on July 5—for consideration at the July 20 regents' meeting—was clearly an instance of "outside" national and state politics coming into the university. Although Connerly had been pressing the issue for some time within the regents and denials of intervention by the governor were issued, the governor's presence was clear. Up to this point there was no significant evidence of initiatives within the university to change the policies and procedures of affirmative action.

Connerly's principal justification for the initiative was that the university, by pursuing its policies, was breaking the law (as manifested in the *Bakke* decision) in its admissions policies. He claimed it was actively discriminating in favor of African Americans, Latinos, and Native

Americans by using race as a criterion for admission (automatically admitting students in those categories on the Davis and Irvine campuses, and giving them special consideration on the Berkeley and Los Angeles campuses). Asian and white students, correspondingly, were being "harmed" because higher standards were being demanded of them. He maintained that the university's standards had been lowered; that the public opinion of California citizens, students, and alumni supported the renunciation of race as an admissions category; that the practices did not promote "racial harmony and integration" but aggravated conflict through practices of racial segregation on the campuses; and that "some of our administrators" were raising the false specter of student protest in opposing his initiative. In the end, Connerly applauded the principle of diversity and argued that his initiative did not mean that the "University is . . . turning its back on affirmative action." He appealed, furthermore, to the principle of equality of opportunity by reminding his audiences that "We need to make clear that there is a difference . . . between providing people with equal opportunity and providing preferences" (Connerly news release, July 5, 1995).

Other parties joined the debate in early July. On the date of Connerly's July 5 news release, the university released a statement by the general counsel stating that the *Bakke* decision permitted colleges and universities to take race and ethnicity into account so long as it is only one factor and so long as "no places are set aside on this basis." At the same time the release promised that "[changes] will be made at UC Berkeley, UCLA, UC Davis, and UC Irvine to assure that the potential qualification and experience of all applicants are reviewed competitively."

Extended releases by the Office of President on July 20 also struck a defensive note. An individual statement by the UC President Jack Peltason, a joint statement by vice-presidents and chancellors, and a resolution by the executive committee of the systemwide Academic Senate all praised affirmative action for furthering diversity and the American egalitarian tradition. Peltason argued that the July initiative was premature, that the decision should wait until the state election initiative of November 1996, and that in the meantime extended review by administrators and faculty should begin. At the same time, he promised investigation and action on the four campuses in question and promised to modify faculty and employee recruiting away from reliance on minority status. The resolution passed by the faculty leadership argued that affirmative action had made the university "a better institution" and called for it to "continue to act affirmatively to increase the participation of individuals from underrepresented groups, evaluating and modifying these programs in order to strengthen them." The resolution did not, however, take an explicit stand on the use of racial and other group membership as criteria for admission, recruitment, and contracting.

The wording of the resolution adopted by the regents on July 20 was strong and decisive in several respects but equivocal in others. On the one hand, it prohibited the university to use "race, religion, sex, color, ethnicity, or national origin as criteria for admission to the university or its programs," either in regular or "exceptional" admissions. It also called for admissions of between 50 and 75 percent of any entering class "on the basis of academic achievement" (the previous policies specified 40 to 60 percent). On the other hand, it gave until 1997 to put these policies in place and called upon the administration to consult with faculty with respect to "supplemental criteria," such as giving special consideration to eligible individuals who have shown "character and determination" despite "having suffered disadvantage economically and in terms of their social environment." Furthermore, it ruled out any policies that might conflict with eligibility for receiving funds from any federal or state agency and did not mention faculty or employee recruitment at all. A final provision contained a statement principle in favor of diversity but against preferential treatment: "Because individual members of all of California's diverse races have the intelligence and capacity to succeed at the University of California, this policy to achieve a UC population that reflects the state's diversity through the preparation and empowerment of all in this state to succeed on their own rather through a system of arbitrary preferences."

[May I digress and point out the general sociological significance of this action? It signaled a shift in the definition of social justice and equality of opportunity—and conflict about these issues—away from race and ethnicity and toward social and economic class, as the reference to "economic disadvantage" suggests. If the regents' actions were to be carried out, this would mark a dramatic shift in the political, legal, and public definition of social inequality and social divisions. We cannot know the precise consequences of such a shift. On the one hand, it could be argued that it would be healthy, because racial and ethnic divisions have such a primordial, enduring, and bitter quality about them and because class and class conflict are more manageable as permanent divisions in American society. On the other hand, at this moment in history class divisions may have an unappreciated volatility in our country, because of the trends toward income stagnation and toward a more regressive income distribution. In all events, however, it is difficult to overestimate the profundity of such a shift.]

Several days after the resolution passed, Peltason issued a statement on it. He, too, reaffirmed the principle of diversity, saying that "it is important to make clear . . . that [the resolutions] have to do with means not with goals." He predicted few changes in contracting and employment programs, because these are constrained by federal and state laws. Noting the January 1997 deadline for action on admissions, he promised to consult with chancellors and faculty on how best to implement admissions policies, "the area in which we expect most change." In the meantime, he promised to set up a multiconstituency task force on improving the preparation of underrepresented minorities and other students for college. He also promised to carry forward on changes in admissions and appointments promised in his July 10 press release. By late October, four intra-university task forces—on contracting, academic and staff employment, undergraduate admissions criteria, and graduate and professional school admissions—had been formed, all with instructions to come back with recommendations for implementing the regents' resolution.

The peace and calm achieved by these actions, however, is only apparent. Virtually every constituency in the University remains in a state of ambivalence and conflict about the summer actions, and as a result very little appears to have been resolved by them. To illustrate:

· *Regents.* Some members of the minority of the regents who opposed the resolutions made an effort, at the January meeting of the board of regents, to reverse the July resolutions. These efforts failed as the regents voted to table the motion. The effort to reverse appears to have little short-run hope, particularly in light of the fact that the voters of the state passed an anti-affirmative-action initiative, the California Civil Rights Initiative, similar in wording to the regents' resolutions, in the election of November 1996. Should that initiative be declared unconstitutional, should California state politics take a turn to the left in the future, and should that reflect itself in an altered composition of the board of regents—a process many years in the making—then a reversal or some other modification of the resolutions of July 1995 might appear on the horizon.

In February 1996, a dramatic confrontation between regents and the president revealed the political salience and volatility of the affirmative action issue. In an administrative act, the new president, Richard Atkinson, delayed the implementation of the regents' resolution on undergraduate admissions from 1997 until 1998. This action prompted a summons to the president to appear in Sacramento for a dressing-down by Governor Wilson, and led Connerly and some other regents to call a special meeting of the board of regents to "review the performance" of Atkinson. (The last time such a meeting was held was in 1967, when Clark Kerr was fired as president of the university.) The meeting was canceled only after a public, written apology by Atkinson. In the wake of that episode several dozen Democratic assemblymen and senators signed a document accusing Regent Connerly of abusing his office and using the incident to stir up support for the California Civil Rights Initiative.

· *Students.* The editorial board of the Berkeley campus student newspaper, *The Daily Californian*, cast a divided vote in favor of the regents' action. To those who have followed the editorial preferences of that publication over the years, that was something like hell freezing over. An equally dramatic thunderbolt occurred in November 1996, when the student newspaper came out in favor of the California Civil Rights Initiative. On the other hand, a modest amount of student activity against the resolutions continued to bubble up on the various campuses. In late February 1996, the student newspaper filed a suit against the board of regents that charged that the July vote was decided in secret and in advance and should be voided because it violated regents' policies calling for public meetings.

· *Faculty.* Most of the faculty "establishment" appeared to wish to accept the summer resolution and work out sensible, informed means of implementing it while working by other means to seek diversity. Another wing of the faculty continued to protest, submitting petitions and seeking faculty expressions of opposition on grounds that the regents violated the principles of university governance by passing the resolutions. The faculty as a whole, however, appeared to be of mixed minds. A poll of faculty conducted by the Roper organization in December 1995 yielded the finding that about half of the faculty favored the renunciation of race and other group criteria (that is, were for the resolution), and half favored their explicit incorporation.

· *Administration.* Although campus administrations have no official choice other than to implement the resolutions, matters are not so simple. A difficult atmosphere persists because of the possibility of unofficial subversion of the official nonrecognition of group criteria in the actual work of admitting and recruiting. Regent Connerly issued statements about undermining the regents' resolutions, and so long as even a small group of regents continue to be in a policing frame of mind, tension and potential conflict between regents and administration remains alive.

· *The state political context.* California politics remained embroiled in affirmative action and other controversies related to the California Civil Rights Initiative. That initiative proposed to end all preferences related to gender, race, national origin, and other related categories. The movement to gain signatures for this met with early difficulties, and late in 1995 Republican supporters of the measure persuaded Connerly to head the campaign to put the measure on the ballot. The movement gained momentum after that time and by the end of February enough signatures had been secured to place the measure on the November 1996 ballot. After a long campaign, which heated as election day approached, the measure passed by 10 percentage points, thereby generalizing the regents' action to employment, educational, and contracting activities and to the state of California as a whole.

The success of the California Civil Rights Initiative is hardly surprising, given the confluence of social and political forces I have outlined. The measure is now bottled up in the courts—with one judge having ordered California to stay its effects, and a panel of three appeals judges declaring it constitutional—and neither proponents nor opponents will accept defeat until it goes to the United States Supreme Court.

Regardless of the ultimate outcome, the measure's passage had one interesting consequence for the University of California. Every constituency in the university, save the board of regents, had gone on record as favoring affirmative action for the university, that is, opposing the initiative. Yet at the same time, its passage at the state level took the university out of the limelight; affirmative action is now at the state and even national political levels (with President Clinton and the Department of Justice weighing in against the referendum). If the measure had been defeated, the regents would have been under enormous pressure to rescind their vote, and the university would have been rocked with internal conflict once again. One can only surmise, therefore, that the university regarded the passage of the Civil Rights Initiative with a distinct ambivalence.

In conclusion, the prospects for affirmative action's future may be put as follows. In California, as in the nation as whole, the advances achieved for both minorities and women have been enormous, and in that respect the affirmative-action project may be considered to have been an *institutional* success. However, it can be claimed only with greater difficulty that it has been a *political* success. Neither its adoption nor its implementation nor the efforts to reverse it seems to have had—or will have—a calming effect on the racial, ethnic, and gender politics of the country. This suggests that the country's main agenda is not really affirmative action; rather the most important underlying agenda concerns the racial, ethnic, and gender struggles themselves. As a result, any institutional contrivance affecting the terms of this struggle, whether affirmative action or something else, will be bound to generate the ambiguity, ambivalence, conflict, and instability that we have witnessed over the past three decades of affirmative action.

PART THREE

Governance and Coordination

SIX

California

A Multisegment System (1993)

THIS ESSAY WAS COMMISSIONED BY Arthur Levine (editor), to be included in a major book on the environment and dynamics of American higher education in the last two decades of the twentieth century. The book was supported by the Andrew W. Mellon Foundation and dedicated to Clark Kerr. The other contributing authors were an all-star cast of scholars and commentators on higher education and included Eric Ashby, Martin Trow, Roger Geiger, Lyman Glenny, Burton Clark, David Riesman, Roger Altbach, Patricia Cross, and Ernest Boyer. I was selected to write about California's three-layered system because, I surmise, my past research on change and conflict in California higher education had been available in published form for almost two decades. The timing of the request to write the essay was fortuitous, since California's system had recently been the subject of attention for a study team of the Organization for Economic Cooperation and Development and had also been recently reviewed by the state of California.

In introducing its 1989 report on California's system of higher education, a team from the Organization for Economic Cooperation and

Appeared originally in *Higher Learning in America 1980–2000*, ed. Arthur Levine, 114–30 (Baltimore, MD: Johns Hopkins University Press, 1993). Used by permission of the Johns Hopkins University Press. A few passages have been modified to minimize duplication of other chapters in this volume.

Development (OECD) described that system as "self-consciously in the vanguard of educational development" (Education Committee 1989: 31). The description brings to mind three features: a degree of self-awareness, pride in leadership, and likely emulation by those not in the vanguard. The history of the system provides ample evidence to substantiate all three connotations.

Self-Awareness   First, California's political and educational leaders have studied its higher education system repeatedly and self-consciously. Major studies prior the 1960 Master Plan for Higher Education appeared in 1934, 1947, 1955, and 1957. Most of these were somewhat defensive in character, seeking ways to stem the competition for status and higher degree-granting authority among California's colleges and to contain the costs associated with that competition (California State Council on Educational Planning and Coordination 1934, Strayer, Deutsch, and Douglass 1948, McConnell, Holy, and Semans 1955, Semans and Holy 1957). The Master Plan Survey Team also conducted a survey before submitted its recommendations for that plan, adopted in 1960. The master plan itself built in the requirement for review by the legislature every decade. A joint legislative committee reviewed the master plan in 1971–1973 (Joint Committee 1973), and both a lay commission and a joint legislative committee studied and reported on it in 1985–88 (Commission for the Review of the Master Plan 1987, Joint Committee 1989). The OECD selected California as a non-European model for study in 1988–89 and, in connection with that investigation, the California Postsecondary Education Commission asked Clive Condren of the University of California to undertake a major study of the California system (Condren 1988).

Pride in Leadership   Second, "self-conscious" has often implied a degree of self-satisfaction. Whereas most of the reviews up to 1960 were conducted in an atmosphere of apprehension of higher education's unmanageability, the reviews since then have endorsed if not celebrated the system. Although both legislative reviews identified problem areas and ways to improve the master plan, neither called for any structural modifications. In 1987 the review commission described California's establishment as a whole as "an extraordinary education system" and the master plan itself as a "unique and timeless foundation" for higher education (Commission for the Review of the Master Plan 1987: 1). Two years later the joint legislative committee called the system "one of the most astonishing educational systems on earth" and spoke of a "postsecondary system of opportunity, quality, and diversity" (Joint Committee 1989: 1).

Likely Emulation Finally, California's system of higher education has been the object of much study and potential emulation from outside. The OECD examiners explained that one of the objectives of their survey of California's system of higher education was "to draw lessons as far as possible for . . . Member countries" (Education Committee 1989: 6). As citizen and scholar of California's system, I have spoken with dozens of individual visitors and scholars and with numerous delegations interested in that system; these visitors came from many other countries (among them Great Britain, Japan, Norway, Indonesia, and the Ivory Coast, as well as the OECD team) and from other American states. Californians tend not to reciprocate by studying other systems, a fact that constitutes further evidence of their general self-confidence.

My objective in this chapter is to examine this evidently remarkable system from the standpoint of its history, its current structure, and its probable preoccupations in the future. I will organize my remarks along three lines: the system's ingenuity as a social invention, its distinctive vulnerabilities, and some predictions of trends and problems in the future derived from our knowledge of the system and our sense of possible social change in California.

THE STRUCTURAL WIZARDRY OF THE MASTER PLAN

A Balance between Structural Rigidity and Structural Flexibility The term "master plan" connotes comprehensiveness of scope and rationality of conception. Although history ultimately may judge it as such, the Master Plan for Higher Education in California was certainly not bred in those conditions. The planners of the late 1950s, as well as the legislature that commissioned them, were faced with a history of restiveness and ungovernability of California's system—ambitions to transform junior colleges into four-year institutions, ambitions to transform four-year colleges into advanced degree-granting institutions, and ambitions to stem this tide on the part of the University of California (Coons 1968: 21–22). It was a situation—to paraphrase Gilbert and Sullivan's dreaded egalitarian utopia in *The Gondoliers*—of "everybody" trying to become (or remain) "somebody." In this context, the imposition of the master plan was an ad hoc act of lid-clamping on this kind of instability. It achieved this in two ways. First, it formalized the principle of differentiation of function, which froze the several categories of institutions of higher education (the university, the state colleges, and the community colleges) into specialized educational missions from which they could not depart or—in the case of the community colleges and state colleges—climb).[1] Second, it built in a principle of differential elitism with respect to admissions, giving the university the top one-eighth of qualified high school graduates, the state colleges the top one-third, and the community colleges open admission of all students eighteen years or older, whether or not they were high school graduates, as long as they could benefit from instruction. The master plan was also a kind of ad hoc political compromise in that it gave—as critics complained—"something for everybody": a monopoly for the university, solid postbaccalaurate status for the state college system, and inclusion in the higher education system for the community colleges (Condren 1988: 30).

Subsequently, however, the situational compromise came to constitute an ingenious combination of structural rigidity on the one hand and capacity for growth and adaptation on the other. By virtue of the structures imposed, ambitions to grow "upward" through change of educational mission were effectively thwarted. At the same time, the system built in the capacity to increase the size of individual colleges and universities and increase the number of institutions within each segment. The examiners from the OECD judged that the master plan "seemed to represent the most advanced effort through state action to organize mass education for a tripling enrollment [between 1960 and 1975]" (Education Committee 1989: 25). In practice, the expansion was mainly "mass" in character (i.e., in the second and especially the third segments). Between 1960 and 1970 the university expanded its student enrollments by approximately 57,000, the state college system by nearly 130,000, and the community college system by nearly 380,000 (Smelser 1973b: 49). It is extraordinary that a system with such a frozen structure can continue to accommodate as rapid and continuous a demographic growth as California's.[2]

A Balance between Excellence and Egalitarianism   It can be argued plausibly that no advanced or aspiring society in the world escapes the dilemma of how to maximize two educational purposes at once: the achievement of the highest quality and the most refined intellectual and cultural expression in its educational system on the one hand, and the provision of a conduit for social mobility, credentialism, and societal participation on the part of the mass of its citizenry on the other. A variety of resolutions of this dilemma are observable in the panoply of the world's educational systems—for example, more or less ignoring mass participation, as in the case of Europe's past elitist arrangements; maximizing participation in the context of low quality, as in some phases of Philippine history; or attempting to stress both quality and participation in a single system, as was done by the City University of New York's experiment in open admissions.

California's master plan marked another distinctive attempt to come to terms with that dilemma involved in stressing both excellence and egalitarianism. Its solution rests on three foundations. The first, already mentioned, is differentiation of function. The campuses of the University of California maintain a virtual monopoly on one aspect of "quality": research and the doctorate. The second, also mentioned, is differential admission, which both "tracks" students into segments on the basis of demonstrated ability and performance (a stress on excellence) and opens the system to all who have reached the age of eighteen and can benefit from instruction (a stress on egalitarianism). The third foundation, which bridges the differentiated aspects (by function and admission), is the transfer function, which permits those who enter community colleges to move subsequently to the other two segments and those who enter the state universities to transfer to the university—if, in both cases, their college academic performance gains them admission. (In practice there are flows in the reverse direction as well, but these are not as critical as the "upward" flows with respect to the fostering of egalitarianism.)

The OECD examiners found the combined effects of these three principles to be striking. Not only is the system able to expand on a mass basis, but it "[maintains] a quality of research and education at the top which [is] unsurpassed anywhere among the OECD countries and probably in the world" (Education Committee 1989: 25). Later we will discover a vulnerability contained in the compromise, but for the moment we underscore its ingenuity as a solution to the excellence-egalitarian dilemma. Summing up, the OECD examiners concluded that the master plan represented "a continuing compromise which is probably more effective than those found in Europe in the search for an optimum combination of equality and excellence" (Education Committee 1989: 29).

The Structuring of Individual and Institutional Mobility   The balances just noted can also be described in terms of their implications for individual social mobility (i.e., the movements of persons or, more precisely, students) on the one hand and institutional social mobility (i.e., the movement of university and college campuses) on the other. With respect individual mobility, a certain sifting-and-blocking process takes place at the termination of secondary education; some students choose not to enter the system of higher education, all can enter the community colleges, one-third (judged by high school performance and test results) can enter a state university, and one-eighth (judged by the same criteria) can enter the University of California.[3] By virtue of the transfer function however, the prospects for upward mobility remain open during the college career—that is to say, students can, if their performance merits it, move "upward" through the system.[4]

With respect to institutional mobility, the principle of the differentiation of functions makes it impossible for college and university campuses to move upward or downward across the three levels—a situation of completely blocked mobility. This contrasts with the situation for individuals, who can move among the segments under some circumstances. However, institutions may compete and move within the segments. It is possible, for example, for a university or a state university campus to improve both its status and its command of resources. The history of the San Diego campus of the University of California since its creation in the early 1960s is a striking example. Moreover, an entire segment can compete with the others and thereby improve its relative position. The state university system has a long history of attempting to achieve parity with the University of California in appellation, salaries, libraries, sabbatical arrangements, and research support.

Described as such, the master plan achieved an ingenious splitting and structuring of opportunities for individual and institutional striving and, in doing that, evolved an unconsciously designed device for segregating and thus diffusing several potential kinds of individual and social conflict.

Governance   To continue the theme of conflict management: one positive aspect of the governance of the system of higher education has to do with the separation of governance by segments. Historically, the governing bodies of the three segments have evolved independently from one another. The board of regents of the University of California is a constitutionally established governing body dating from the beginning. The state university gained its own board of trustees when the master plan was enacted in 1960. But the board was granted only statutory, not constitutional status. The community colleges were governed under the State Board of Education until 1967, when the legislature and governor created a board of governors. In this process of independent evolution, each board has developed a sense of guardianship over its own institutions and a corresponding distaste for either weakening its power through decentralization or surrendering its power to a higher governing authority.

The wisdom of this independent evolution, unplanned and discoverable only by hindsight, is that it has avoided the inclusion of too many contending constituencies under the umbrella of a single governance structure. The importance of this principle is underscored by noticing the brief and unhappy history (1960–74) of the Coordinating Council for Higher Education. This body was created by the master plan to superimpose a kind of voluntary coordination on the higher education system (the coordinating council included the private sector as well). The members of the council were mainly representatives of the segments—in particular their chief executives—and they behaved as representatives in large degree. Much of the history of the council was one of bloc voting and vetoing by the segments, which resulted in its ineffectiveness as a coordinating body. At the time of the 1971–73 review of the master plan, the legislature concluded that the coordinating efforts of the council had been inadequate (Joint Committee 1973: 22). In its place the legislature substituted another coordinating agency, the California Postsecondary Education Commission, which did not incorporate the principle of representation of the segments by staff but rather by members of their governing boards and which had a majority of public representatives rather than segmental representatives. At the same time, the legislature rejected the idea of a super board for all of higher education, largely on grounds that it would bureaucratize the system unduly. It should also be noted that a super board would probably have been plagued by segmental parochialism and jealousies.

THE STRUCTURAL VULNERABILITIES OF THE MASTER PLAN

Governance While benefiting from the diffusion of conflict management, much of the governing structure of the system of higher education has labored under a number of ambiguities. The board of regents, most privileged by independent status, has proved the least problematical and has been subjected to the fewest calls for change. The board of trustees of the state university system has rankled under the fact that its status is statutory. This not only symbolizes its lack of parity with the university but also places the state university system at a disadvantage with respect to budgetary intervention and control by the state. The board of governors of the community college system, superimposed on a large and dispersed body of campuses accustomed to local support and control, proved to be a chronically weak system, and the topic of community college governance occupied most of the attention of the Commission for the Review of the Master Plan in the first phase of its study (Commission for the Review of the Master Plan 1986).

Cost Because the relative costs of (and returns to) different kinds of education defy accurate measurement and calculation, it is difficult to arrive at absolute judgments about the efficiency of various arrangements. In principle, however, it is possible to find several sources of duplication and possible waste in California's higher education system, which greater specialization might reduce.

The first source is that lower division education is sustained in all segments. It is assumed (but not really proved) that lower division education is least expensive at the community college level; considerations of efficiency might lead to the conclusion that these first two years might be removed from the programs of university and state university campuses. Yet scattered efforts to effect this further differentiation of function have engendered strong resistance.

The second source of inefficiency lies in competition within the segments. In the University of California system, for example, the large, general campuses of Berkeley and UCLA are often seen by the newer, smaller campuses as models to be emulated. This drive toward general campus status throughout the system generates pressure to develop very high-cost graduate programs and research facilities. Yet the internal status striving remains both endemic and strong, and the means to curb this impulse are not readily available.

Residual Ambiguities of Mission The mission of each segment can be stated simply, but each retains a certain uncertainty and a resultant uneasiness. The community colleges are restricted to two years of instruction leading to an associate degree and are expected to offer courses in three areas—vocational, transfer (liberal arts), and general instruction. Yet the proper weighting for each of these is unclear and varies over time. In the interests of institutional survival, community colleges are often driven in the direction of expanding their "marketable" vocational programs—marketable, that is, both to students and in the economy.

The state university offers the baccalaureate and selected master's programs and is charged to carry out research related to teaching. Yet the system has proven to be the most restless segment, resembling the middle sibling that it is; it is chronically dissatisfied with the more privileged status of the University of California and strives continuously for parity on one front or another.

The University of California's mission includes those of the other segments plus doctoral training, research, and exclusive jurisdiction over certain kinds of professional training. By virtue of that scope, however, the university campuses might be described as laboring under a certain kind of "functional overloading" of commitments to research, graduate training, professional training, undergraduate education, professional service, and public service (Smelser 1973a, Parsons 1973). Furthermore, given the reward structure of the national and international academic communities, University of California faculty tends to drift toward stressing the spheres of research, publication, graduate training, and national and international participation. In the eyes of critics, this means that they neglect other spheres, especially undergraduate teaching. These ambiguities of mission for each of the segments seem chronic and not easily alterable.

Short-Changing Egalitarianism The Californian compromise between excellence and equality was characterized above as a notable sociological invention. The possibility of transfer among segments, embodying an educational vision of social mobility, is an essential ingredient in this compromise. In practice, however, the transfer function has proved problematic. During the first quarter century of the master plan, the number of community college transfers to the University of California system reached an annual high of just over eight thousand in 1973, a miniscule figure considering the more than one million students enrolled in community colleges. Furthermore, the transfer function has a tendency to atrophy. In the decade after that high point, transfers from community colleges to the University declined steadily to under five thousand in 1985 (Task Force on Lower Division Education 1986: 24).

This apparent "failure" on the egalitarian front generated an extensive debate on the master plan in the late 1980s. The decline was given greater heat by its racial/ethnic overtones. The vast majority of Hispanic and black minority students are in the community college system, and an atrophy of the transfer function implies a sluggishness in the efforts to advance these minority groups. These problems of admission and transfer were at the top of the agenda of both master plan review bodies in 1987–89 (Commission for the Review of the Master Plan 1987: 22–28; Joint Committee 1989: 17–42), and individual university campuses came under pressure to ease the transfer process, increase the numbers of transfer students, and increase the ratio between upper division and lower division students.

The forces determining the educational fate of disadvantaged minority and class groups are complex and multiple. They include the forces of culture, family, poverty, and discrimination, to say nothing of educational discouragement. It seems unrealistic and perhaps unfair to single out the system of higher education as accountable for failures in egalitarianism. Nevertheless, since the master plan was built on the premise that it would be a helpful institution in this regard, it stands to reason that it would also come to attention when blame is being assigned for those failures.

SOME GLIMPSES INTO THE FUTURE

From these reflections we may generate some general predictions about the patterns of challenge, preoccupation, conflict, and accommodation that may be expected in California's higher education system.

The QUEEF Complex: Maximizing Everything

When the Commission for the Review of the Master Plan submitted its final report in 1987, it organized the contents around certain objectives that should guide the missions and policies of the higher education system. These objectives were summarized, in the commission's words, as follows:

· *Unity*, to assure that all elements of the system work together in pursuit of common goals

· *Equity*, to assure that all Californians have unrestricted opportunity to fulfill their educational potential and aspirations

- *Quality*, to assure that excellence characterizes every aspect of the system

- *Efficiency*, to assure the most productive use of finite financial and human resources (1967: 4–5)

(We may alter the order and produce the acronym QUEE—Quality, Unity, Equity, and Efficiency.) Immediately after specifying these four objectives, the commission added a fifth, namely that those aims must be realized through voluntary coordination by the segments, not superimposed by the legislature or governor. This might be termed Freedom, which yields QUEEF as a guiding principle.

Several observations about the list of objectives come to mind. First, the language used to describe them was strong and absolute, containing words such as *all, common, unrestricted, every aspect*, and *most productive*, all of which connote the logic of maximizing. Second, the commission presented each ingredient as though it existed in isolation from the others. Third, the rhetoric and affective tone of the presentation was such that, if asked, almost anyone is put in the position of having to assent to the positive value of each objective. Who can object to quality, unity, equity, efficiency, or freedom?

To represent QUEEF in this way, however, tends to obscure many of the realities of institutional life in higher education. In the first place, it is evident that many of the objectives stand in tension, if not contradiction with one another—and thus cannot be simultaneously maximized. It is difficult to conceive, for example, how the values of unity and freedom can be simultaneously maximized. The goals of quality (excellence) and efficiency (cost control) also tug in different directions under some circumstances. And we noted above that the relations between excellence (quality) and equity pose some kind of dilemma. In the second place, if the state demands and the educational establishment agrees to maximize on all these fronts—which the commission's report asks that it does—this sets up the probability that cycles of over-demand and over-promise, failure to deliver, disappointment, and recrimination will be continuously generated.

QUEEF-like discourse appears frequently in the political and ideological rhetoric about higher education; it is part of the ambivalent give-and-take of pubic support of education and education's plea for that support. (More generally, it is probably part and parcel of the rhetoric that develops when multiple values are embedded in a single institutional complex.) It should the acknowledged, however, that the values of QUEEF constitute a utopian myth about the system of higher education. Such a myth probably gives comfort to many and may be necessary to drive people to higher goals, but at the same time it builds a note of unrealism into the institutional life of higher education and tends to generate episodes of exaggerated feelings of promise, hope, despair, and scapegoating. Since the QUEEF complex is rooted deeply in the cultural values of California (and America in general), I am certain that we will continue to live with that complex and its consequences for decades to come.

Asymmetries in the QUEEF Complex As indicated, appeals of the QUEEF variety tend to generate agreement in principle with the general values invoked. In practice, however, the different objectives of the QUEEF complex are tilted to some degree in the direction of either the state or the educational establishment. Academics and educators tend to like quality and freedom most; representatives of the state tend to like unity and equity most. When academics (at least those in the university) speak of quality, they tend to have in mind quality of research, quality of graduate training, and quality of people in their institutions; when representatives of the state speak of quality, they tend to refer to the quality of undergraduate education.[5] When academics speak of efficiency, they look more to the resources necessary for high-quality output; when representatives of the state speak of efficiency, they usually mean cost containment.

Furthermore, values contained in the QUEEF complex are often arrayed against one another in debate. When representatives of the state invoke arguments based on equity academics counter-invoke arguments based on quality. When representatives of the state invoke arguments based on unity (e.g., standardization), academics counter-invoke arguments based on freedom. Furthermore, these various values are most often invoked rhetorically as general principles and are often accompanied by unverified and possibly unverifiable assertions (e.g., research erodes good teaching; research fosters good teaching). For these reasons, debates within the QUEEF complex tend to be dialogues of the deaf, with both sides remaining unshaken in their commitments and beliefs. Such unprofitable conversations will also no doubt continue as long as the QUEEF complex remains.

Structural Continuity, Expansion, and Difficult Economic Times   It is reasonable to predict that the main structural contours of the master plan—including the principle of differentiation of function, differential admissions, transfer, and separate governance structures—will persist into the next several decades. The reasons for this prediction are, first, that these contours have persisted with notable continuity for three decades and, second, that they will constitute that nice compromise along the dimensions of change/stability and egalitarianism/excellence.

The structure will persist, however, in the context of two ongoing changes. First the population of California will continue to expand. The state's population grew by almost six million in the 1980s, constituting an increase of about 25 percent in the nation's largest state. Although this astonishing rate may ease in the next two decades, the absolute numbers will continue to increase. This will sustain the pressure on higher education to continue its expansion of enrollments and, through them, the size and number of its campuses.

At the same time, it appears that higher education's share of the state economic pie will decrease further during the next decade or so. At present, the university and state university systems command about 10 percent of the state's revenue dollars. This percentage is expected to decrease to about 8 in a decade or so. The basic reason for this decline is competition arising from other state commitments, such as health care and social service. In particular, the schedule of payoff for existing bonds will increase significantly, and expenditures on new prisons and welfare will also rise. These burdens, combined with the continued demand for the expansion and renewal of the infrastructure of state municipal facilities, will squeeze higher education, and it is not clear that sufficient offsetting resources will be found in federal revenues or private largesse.

In one respect this demographic/economic squeeze will encourage continuity in the structure of the master plan. In particular, it will reduce the probability that the State University system will gain significantly in its efforts to secure the doctorate and to build more research into its mission. Both of these are high-cost items, and political leaders will be more reluctant than ever to admit such changes of mission. In another respect, however, the squeeze will push toward a change of mission for the University of California. Under pressure both to expand and to economize, the state may opt to grow in what it sees as the least expensive areas (i.e., in the lower tiers) and to hold back on the building of new campuses for the university. What may have to "give" under these circumstances is the university's commitment to admit the top one-eighth of the high school graduates of California. The past decade has witnessed some pressure on this component of the university's mission, and this will become more severe during the next two decades.

Contending with the Political and Social Effects of Diversity   No assessment of the future of California and its system of higher education begins without reciting the fact that by the year 2000 or so a majority of the state's population will be minority, with Hispanics, Asians, and African Americans constituting main minority groups. Already the community colleges are heavily populated with minority students, as are the state universities (but less so), and within the University of California both Berkeley and UCLA have passed the "majority of minorities" threshold with respect to student population. The future direction is clear, moreover, for all levels: greater racial, ethnic, and cultural diversity of student populations.

The most immediate political effect of student diversification is to increase the pressure to diversify the administrative staff, graduate students, and faculty. (There is continued pressure to diversify with respect to gender as well.) The difficulties in responding to this pressure increase in the order mentioned, in large part because the "PhD pipeline" of African Americans and Hispanics has tended to diminish in the recent past. The fact that expansion of these minorities in graduate student and faculty ranks is difficult in the short run does not have much effect on those pressing to diversify, and the air is filled with a certain amount of ill will and charges of "elitism," "white male supremacy," "declining quality," and other rhetorical assertions. There is no reason to believe that this contradictory situation will not constitute one of the most severe political problems for California's system of higher education in the decades to come.

The other great dimension of diversity is social in character. Institutions of higher education—along with other institutions—have played an important historical role in socialization and in inculcating the values of citizenship, participation, tolerance, and professional commitment and have thus contributed in some degree to the integration of the larger society. That role will continue, and the examining committee of the OECD went so far as to predict that "the burden of incorporation into a pluralistic society has to rest centrally on the integrative capacity of the educational system" (Education Committee 1989: 6).

Yet the vision of "incorporation" is only one possible scenario, given the magnitude of the diversity and the depth of racial, ethnic, and cultural politics. I mention three scenarios, evidence for each of which might be cited:

- The program of assimilation of racially, ethnically, and culturally diverse groups to the existing values and roles of higher education. This is the "liberal view," closest to that voiced by the OECD committee, and envisions continuing traditional patterns of liberal education and occupational and professional training, with students being socialized in these patterns, accommodating to them, and preparing themselves for participation in the institutions of the larger society.

- The program of altering the traditional missions of higher liberal education—which, it is argued, are biased along racial/ethnic, class, and gender lines in any event—to some mission that gives greater recognition to "non-mainstream" groups. The recent episodes of pressure for curricular change are signs of this tendency, as are the recent debates about "political correctness" on campus and its possible threat to principles of academic freedom.

- The program of converting campuses into a microcosm of the pluralistic polity, with racial, ethnic, cultural, gender, and other groups competing for the resources as well as the symbolic and real control of the institutional life of colleges and universities. This scenario, too, although not novel in the history of education, would mark a further change in the traditional liberal mission of educational institutions. And, given the frail capacities of colleges and universities to manage group conflict (see chapter 4) such a "political pluralism" model would prove difficult to stabilize.

Like the future of any complex social institution that is based on multiple values and principles, the future of higher education with respect to diversity will not reveal a clear victory for any of these scenarios. Some aspects of all will continue to be visible. Each one will persist, and each one will have its vicissitudes. With respect to the issue of diversity, then, the future will bring "process" rather than "product" as an outcome, with all involved parties struggling for but never finally gaining advantages, new definitions of the situation and satisfactory accommodations.

NOTES

1. In this essay I refer to institutions according to their names at the time of the reference. The University of California has been called by that name since its inception. The second tier was known originally as *normal schools*, then *teacher's colleges*. When the master plan was put in place in 1960, this tier was called the California State College System; subsequently (1972) it became known as the California State University and College system, and in 1981 it took on the name of the California State University. In the beginning, two-year institutions were known as *junior colleges*; subsequently they were referred to as either *junior colleges* or *community colleges*; now they go almost exclusively by the name of *community colleges*. These name changes reflect the status striving of the second and third segments over the years; the uneasy resistance on the University of California's part to the application of the name university to the second tier reflects the same preoccupation with prestige and status.

2. For a theoretical statement of the structural alternatives to change in the growth process, see Smelser (1973b: 36–38).

3. There are some minor exceptions to these rules, e.g., the "special admissions" procedures in the University of California, by which 6 percent of the entering class can be drawn from the population that does not fall in the top one-eighth as measured at high school graduation. Originally this category was designed to facilitate the admission of athletes, but more recently it has become a means to increase the representation of disadvantaged minorities.

4. There are some strictures on this process as well; for example, it is impossible for students to transfer during their first year at a given college, and universities and colleges require some minimum of residence (e.g., one year) to make a student eligible for graduation from that institution.

5. For example, in the report of the Joint Committee for the Review of the Master Plan, fourteen pages were dedicated to "Undergraduate Education" in the section entitled "Educational Quality." In the same section four pages were dedicated to "Graduate and Professional Education," which was slightly more than the space allocated to "Vocational Education" and slightly less than that allocated to "Adult and Non-Credit Education" (Joint Commission, 1989: 96–123). This kind of allocation of words is surely at variance with the priorities of many academics.

REFERENCES

California State Council on Educational Planning and Coordination. 1934. *Statement of Basic Principles of the Respective Functions and Program of the Junior College, the Teachers College and the University.* Sacramento: California State Council on Educational Planning and Coordination.

Commission for the Review of the Master Plan for Higher Education. 1986. *The Challenge of Change: A Reassessment of the California Community Colleges.* Sacramento, CA: Commission for the Review of the Master Plan for Higher Education.

Commission for the Review of the Master Plan for Higher Education. 1987. *The Master Plan Renewed: Unity, Equity, Quality and Efficiency in California Postsecondary Education.* Sacramento, CA: Commission for the Review of the Master Plan for Higher Education.

Condren, Clive. 1988. *Preparing for the Twenty-first Century: A Report on Higher Education in California.* California Postsecondary Education Commission Report 88(1). Sacramento: California Postsecondary Education Commission.

Coons, Arthur G. 1968. *Crises in California Higher Education.* Los Angeles: Ward Ritchie Press.

Education Committee, Organization for Economic Cooperation and Development. 1989. *Review of Higher Education Policy in California.* Paris: Organization for Economic Cooperation and Development.

Joint Committee on the Master Plan for Higher Education. 1973. *Report of the Joint Committee on the Master Plan for Higher Education.* Sacramento: California Legislature.

Joint Committee for the Review of the Master Plan for Higher Education. 1989. *California Faces . . . California's Future: Education for Citizenship in a Multicultural Democracy.* Sacramento: California Legislature.

Master Plan Survey Team. 1960. *Master Plan for Higher Education in California, 1960 to 1975.* Sacramento: California State Department of Education.

McConnell, T. R., T. C. Holy, and H. H. Semans. 1955. *A Restudy of the Needs of California in Higher Education.* Sacramento: California State Department of Education.

Parsons, Talcott. 1973. "Epilogue: The University Bundle: A Study of the Balance between Differentiation and Integration. In *Public Higher Education in California,* edited by Neil J. Smelser and Gabriel Almond, 275–99. Berkeley: University of California Press.

Semans, H. H. and T. C. Holy. 1957. *A Study of the Needs for Additional Centers of Public Higher Education in California.* Sacramento: California State Department of Education.

Smelser, Neil J. 1973a. "Epilogue: Social-Structural Dimensions of Higher Education. In *The American University*, by Talcott Parsons and Gerald M. Platt, 389–422. Cambridge, MA: Harvard University Press.

Smelser, Neil J. 1973b. "Growth, Structural Change, and Conflict in California Higher education." In Neil J. Smelser and Gabriel Almond (eds.), *Public Higher Education in California*, edited by Neil J. Smelser and Gabriel Almond, 9–143. Berkeley: University of California Press.

Strayer, George D., Monroe E. Deutsch, and Aubrey A. Douglas. 1948. *A Report on a Survey of the Needs of California in Higher Education.* Sacramento: State of California.

Task Force on Lower Division Education. 1986. *Lower Division Education in the University of California.* Berkeley: University of California.

SEVEN

Governing the University of California (1994)

IN SPRING 1993, I received a phone call from Jack Peltason, president of the University of California, inviting me to join the office of the president as an "advisor on long-term planning." He gave no further specifics, but it sounded to me that the assignment was to be more or less "without portfolio." I still have no true idea why he extended the invitation. I did know that the university was in a severe short-term budgetary trough, which, as it turned out, endured until the heady days of the late 1990s. I also knew that the state's demographic and financial outlook raised long-term doubts about the viability of the Master Plan for Higher Education. I had known Peltason in a number of different contexts over the years, and, flattered by the idea that he thought I could be of help, I accepted, and joined his staff for one year beginning in the fall of 1993.

The job turned out to be as shapeless and as enjoyable as I had hoped. I spoke with Peltason and Vice President Walter Massey frequently and on many topics (for example, the nature of authority in a university, year-round academic operations, policy options within the master plan), helped out during a crisis or two, sat in on several systemwide committees, arranged a major conference, and became well acquainted with the people and operations in different branches of the office of the president. As an administrative appointment it was a dream: freedom and influence without responsibility.

Toward the end, perhaps in a mild fit of guilt about the year's experience, I decided, quite on my own, to write a memorandum on what I had learned about governing the University of California. I intended the memo only for Massey and Peltason. It was a kind of goodbye gift. They had asked me to stay on for a second year, but in the meantime I had been offered the directorship of the Center for Advanced Study in the Behavioral Sciences, and had to decline their invitation.

About a year later I send the memo to Richard Atkinson, the new president and also a long-time friend. He read it and encouraged me to publish it. I ignored his advice for a decade, but now I am following it.

This document is about major institutional and organizational issues that should be taken into account by the leadership of the University of California in governing that system. It is written mainly from the system-wide perspective. It expresses information and ideas that have accumulated during my decades of work—at different levels and in different capacities—in the university. It is intended to be general but not completely exhaustive in scope.

QUERIES TO BE ADDRESSED FOR ANY DECISION, POLICY, OR PLAN

The life of an administrator is a continuous round of dealing with concrete decisions, policies, and plans relevant to the administered organization. Most of these come before the administrator not by virtue of his or her initiative, but by virtue of the ticking of the budgetary clock, the initiative of some interested constituency, or the appearance of some "problem" or "crisis." On many occasions the administrative leader is under pressure to decide before being able to think through the major—to say nothing of all—implications of the decision. Nevertheless, in the interest of maximizing the quality of the decision and minimizing the risks associated with it, it is helpful to keep in mind a kind of "checklist" of framing questions to be asked of oneself and others about any decision, policy, or plan. Viewed another way, these are the major bases to be touched when thinking about directing organizational activity.

The first three questions are subcategories of a larger one: "Why is the issue (i.e., decision, policy, or plan) *important* for the University of California?" On some occasions this question is not posed because the answer is self-evident or simply taken for granted; for example, it is important to appoint the most qualified persons to positions of administrative responsibility to assure the most effective running of the university. Seldom, however, does the *prima facie* answer end the matter. Again in the case of a personnel appointment, it may also be important (i.e., politically sensitive) because some special constituency is pressing for the appointment of a particular person or category of persons.

In other cases, an issue is intuitively known to be important, but the reasons for that importance remain tacit. It is helpful to ask, then, about any issue facing the administrator, the following three questions:

1. What *legitimizing* criteria are operative? No decision, policy, or plan arises for an administrator without also activating *value-criteria* that give importance to the issue, and presumably serve as background or general guides to its resolution. To select an obvious example, decisions about admissions policies over the next several years will excite two value considerations: (a) the university's commitment to the value of equality of opportunity (including access to avenues of social mobility) and (b) the university's commitment to maintaining educational quality.

In considering the most important value-criteria affecting the University of California, it is useful to refer to the list developed at the beginning of the report on the long-term planning retreat last Fall:

- Realizing the traditional missions of research, teaching, and service
- Pursuing excellence or quality
- Guaranteeing access to qualified students at all levels
- Observing economy
- Securing the principles of equity and diversity
- Preserving intellectual freedom
- Preserving both autonomy from and accountability to the state and other constituencies that are involved with the university

In a word, if a potential action excites a concern about whether these kinds of values are being realized or violated, then that *action* becomes an *issue*; it is values that give issues their relevance and importance.

2. What *institutional* forces and strictures make the issue problematic? Many of the issues that arise in an organization do so because some change in the institutional environment is observable or appears to lie on the

horizon. Examples of these are demographic changes in the age structure; changing percentages of high school graduates; changing racial-ethnic proportions in the population; upswings and downswings in the economy; constitutional and practical constraints on the state budget; fluctuations in federal research funding policy; new affirmative action legislation; court decisions affecting the university (e.g., confidentiality in tenure cases); the passage or defeat of a bond issue; term limits on California legislators; and dozens of others. As the examples suggest, some of these institutional factors constitute *pressure* of one kind or another on the university: that valued traditions and policies are endangered, that such traditions and policies are not adequate to absorb the envisioned institutional changes, that funding is threatened, and so forth.

3. What *groups* or *constituencies* are interested in pressing the issue, and why? What usually lends heat to an issue is articulated pressure from some group or groups, either acting directly on administrators or indirectly, through other constituencies (regents, legislators) known to be influential. Such groups are the agents for *invoking* the relevant legitimizing values and *representing, interpreting,* and *giving meaning to* the real or supposed institutional forces. It is groups or constituencies who define an issue as a problem or a crisis and try to persuade or force administrators to accept that meaning. It is groups or constituencies that call for or oppose decisions. In a word, it is groups or constituencies that make an issue *political.* The "why" in questions posed at the beginning of this section refers to groups' and constituencies' special sensitivities and interests. These are found, in part, by knowing the ways they represent the value-criteria and institutional forces mentioned earlier. In any event, it is always important to know, as well as possible, where various interest groups are coming from and what social forces and world-views they represent. (A list of these major constituencies—and their special sensitivities—is found in the next section.)

Any decision, policy, or plan can be understood—and must be crafted by administrators—as a complex product that takes into account a mix of legitimizing criteria, institutional strictures and forces, and operative group pressures. To put the matter in terms familiar to economists, the administrator should be regarded not as *maximizing* one particular goal or another, but, rather, as *"satisficing"* (a term coined by Herbert Simon), that is, framing a decision, policy, or plan as a kind of amalgam of the inevitably complex pattern of anticipated gains and losses that arise from the diversity of contextual forces involved.

After all these contexts are identified and weighed, the next question an administrator must address is the *realistic possibilities* that are available for resolving the issue at hand. This ingredient is summarized in the following question:

4. What *options* are available to the administrator? This includes listing alternatives and considering the relative advantages and disadvantages of each. The advantages and disadvantages, in turn, are discovered in the degree to which the option is responsive to the diversity of considerations arising from a scan of the legitimizing value-criteria, institutional forces, and group pressures. It is also important for the administrator to know what options *cannot* be considered, whether because resources are not available, because constituency support is impossible to obtain, or because the options would violate one or more legitimizing criteria. In connection with the available options, one should further ask:

5. What institutional *goals* will be served or otherwise affected by the various options, and what negative consequences will be avoided? The definitive answers to this question can never be certainly known, because of the unanticipated consequences that always characterize institutional life. It seems essential, however, to think as systematically as possible about goals and consequences when considering options for organizational decisions and policy.

Example: In the options for long-term enrollment policy that were presented to the regents in March 1994, each was accompanied by an educated guess about its impact on the Master Plan for Higher Education. That way of thinking was limited, however, because each option was presented in absolute terms, in isolation from the other options. In practice, a policy will usually end up as a compromise that renders precise predictions about its effects more difficult.

The final series of questions for the administrator involves thinking about the *implementation* of a decision, policy, or plan to which a commitment has been made. These questions are three:

6. What are the available *structures* and *mechanisms*—patterns of delegated authority, committees, established procedures, mutual understandings—for implementing the decision, policy, or plan? If such structures do not exist or are inadequate, what kinds must be created? It should be evident, in posing this question, that such structures are potentially both facilitative and obstructive of implementation.

7. Who are the *leaders* or *agents* responsible for carrying out the decision, policy or plan—vice presidents, chancellors, deans, senate

committees, or others? How are their implementing activities to be monitored?

8. What are the major ways that implementation of a decision, policy, or plan is likely to be *diverted* or *undermined* by individuals and groups who do not wish it to be implemented? Such a question seems to smack of paranoia, but that connotation is not intended. We know that a university is an organization that cannot always rely on the direct exercise of authority and that it is a community populated by strong vested interests. It is helpful for an administrator to be aware of precisely where these possibilities lie.

MULTIPLE AUDIENCES, MULTIPLE CONSTITUENCIES

One of the most challenging—and frequently most discouraging and paralyzing—features of the university has to do with the fact that it is nestled into a complex of interested audiences—who, by virtue of their interests, become constituencies. All of these audiences have expectations about the character, performance, and service rendered by the university. (This situation is akin to that described by Henry Rosovsky in his book, *The University: An Owner's Manual*, in which he identified a range of constituencies who fancy they own the university—in his case Harvard, a private institution.)

The most important thing to recognize about these constituencies is that the array of expectations they present, while overlapping, differ from one another and *pull the leaders in different, sometimes contradictory directions.* The challenges to these leaders are to be aware of different constituencies' expectations and priorities; to craft policies that take the diversity of expectations into account when framing and presenting actions, policies, and plans; and actively to define and (it is hoped) to remain in control of the rhetorical contexts that frame these diverse expectations.

The following are the major constituencies to be identified, and the principal preferences and expectations—presented in truncated form—that each brings to the table in considering the university.

Undergraduate Students

Prospective and enrolled students bring the following kinds of expectations to the university:

- The university should maintain its prestige as a credentialing institution, and, as such, an effective launching platform for students into the job world. This preference is often phrased indirectly—"to provide a good education"—but providing credentials and prestige often appears to be more salient than the quality of education as such. (The *ultimate* interest in the value of a university credential, however, does not universally imply that students want to get through college as quickly as possible. Many regard the collegiate experience as a kind of happy moratorium possessing value in itself.)

- The university should keep the costs of education reasonable if not low. Students from wealthier families are most interested in fee levels; students from poorer families are most interested in levels of financial aid.

- The university should facilitate students' lives and experiences but not control them. This principle generates two distinguishable expectations. (1) The university should help students get admitted, register, get into courses, find housing, gain access to libraries and laboratories, secure grants and loans, and graduate. The corresponding resentments are directed against bureaucratic delays, hassling, and frustrations. (Exit polls of students graduating from University of California campuses consistently show high levels of satisfaction with faculty and courses and some dissatisfaction stemming from housing difficulties, administrative frustrations, and poor advising.) (2) The university should respect students' freedom and privacy; few students support an *in loco parentis* role for the university. (It should be noted, however, that both those expectations are fraught with an ambivalence that comes with the developmental stage of many undergraduate students—an ambivalence expressing simultaneously the desire to for independence and the desire to be taken care of. Both sides of the ambivalence appear in students' expressions of dissatisfaction with university life.)

- The university should provide a setting and a culture in which students can liberate themselves from the past constraints of family and community. (Paradoxically, however, activist spokespersons for some cultural groups [for example, ethnic minorities] sometimes insist that universities should recognize, respect, and encourage students' identifications with their communities of origin. This is another source of ambivalence in students' expectations.)

Parents of Undergraduate Students

In some respects the interests of parents are identical to those of their children who are students, but emphases differ, as follows:

- Parents feel, if anything, more strongly than students about the importance of a university's credentialing and prestige-endowing function. Parents are motivated, above all, by the desire *not* to have their children continue as financial and emotional burdens on their lives. (They are, however, happy to have them continue as sources of emotional gratification.) The surest ticket to this end, moreover, is successful job careers for their children, which free the parents and permit the children to be responsible for their own problems. As a close corollary, parents also expect that the university will constitute an avenue of social mobility for their children.

- Parents feel, if anything, more strongly than students about reasonable costs of an undergraduate education, because it is the parents, more often than the students, who absorb those costs. Parents' interest in costs also appears in a derived hope that students will not spend longer than necessary to complete their collegiate education. Time-to-degree concerns thus often reflect the explicit or implicit conflict—an economic conflict in effect—between undergraduate students and their parents.

- Parents feel, if anything, more strongly than students about the need to maintain a safe and secure campus and neighbor-hood environment.

- Parents openly differ with their children-students on several expectations. They do not object as much to—indeed they sometimes favor—*in loco parentis* regulations and policies on the university's part. They are also less interested in—and sometimes aghast at—the university's role in liberating students from their parents and their past loyalties. They do not often relish the prospect of children coming home for visits and assaulting parental values in the name of what they have learned in college. They do not typically relish the prospect of racial, ethnic, religious, or class intermarriage for their children. In a word, the complex of parental expectations boils down to a double hope: that the university will simultaneously prepare their children for a successful future and help keep them out of mischief while they are in college.

Graduate Students

This constituency is neither especially visible nor well organized. By the time students enter graduate school they are well into their career trajectories, and their identifications (and therefore their expectations) lie mainly with their disciplines and departments than with the campus, to say nothing of the university as a whole. Nevertheless, they embody a number of latent interests:

· Graduate students are interested in the prestige of their disciplines on their campus—and nationally—because of the positive impact that that prestige has on the willingness of the administration to favor their discipline (e.g., in the allocation of fellowships and teaching assistantships), on the ability of the discipline to command external research support (and research assistantships), and, most fundamentally, the ability of the department to place doctoral recipients well in the academic and other markets.

· Graduate students have a material interest in fees, as well as levels of remuneration associated with fellowship and grant support, research assistantships, teaching assistantships, and loans. (The area in which this has taken tangible organizational expression is in the unionization of teaching assistants, who represent an ingredient in the "labor-relations" of university life, even though they are not always officially recognized as unions.) Graduate students' material interests are, if anything, keener than undergraduates'. The reason for this is that most graduate students are formally independent of parental support, while most undergraduates still rely on that support. (For this reason, too, graduate students' parents are almost a "nonconstituency" for the university because of their low level of financial interest in their children's lives; however, they, like undergraduates' parents, have an interest in "time-to-degree," as part of their general interest in the economic self-sufficiency of their adult children.)

Faculty

This is probably the most important constituency in the university, as recognized by the frequently stated principle that the university's quality depends above all on the quality of its faculty. This constituency, however, like others, cannot be regarded as a single entity with a single set of expectations. It is helpful, therefore, to identify several major faculty subconstituencies and their associated expectations:

- There is a strong bastion of faculty conservatism embodied in campus academic personnel committees and in the corresponding university-wide committee on academic personnel. The "CAP mentality" associates academic quality with published research and its national and international recognition. This mentality does not necessarily create a general loyalty to the university. Rather, it breeds two further expectations: first, that the campus should provide a supportive infrastructure for the faculty's national or international pursuit of professional accomplishment and recognition; second, the main "job" for the university administration is to persuade the legislature and other interested audiences how important research is and how good the faculty is and should be at it. In most respects the Council of Graduate Deans reflects the same mentality, representing as they do the research and graduate training complex of the University.

- A second important but weaker component of faculty interest is in undergraduate education and reforms. This is embodied in the Universitywide Committee on Educational Policy, in campus educational policy committees, and among deans of Colleges of Letters and Science. It is these groups that have embraced and promoted freshman-sophomore seminars and other reforms. The interest in undergraduate education is often idealistic in character, and those who pursue it consider themselves to be something of a heroic and unappreciated minority.

- Almost all faculty are oriented to protecting the status, material privileges, and freedoms associated with their position. Concretely this orientation expresses itself in committees on faculty welfare, privilege and tenure, and academic freedom. Faculty are sensitive to teaching loads (especially in comparison with other elite institutions around the country), their salary levels (also in comparison with other institutions), and symbols of status. (I remember one occasion when an outraged group of faculty members on the Berkeley campus went as a delegation to the chancellor and objected vehemently to having the same kind of identification card as other "employees.") All this is to say that faculty members, like other constituencies, continuously demand to be reminded, both actually and symbolically, how important they are to the institution.

With respect of faculty's interest in "conditions of work," it is helpful to recall the single time in living memory that the faculty actually took an initiative to organize themselves into a quasi-union. That was in 1970–72, when the faculty association was successfully formed on the Berkeley campus, with chapters emerging later on other campuses, and with the Santa Cruz faculty actually voting that the faculty association should be a collective bargaining unit on that campus. The faculty association still exists as a kind of moribund organization. What is of interest here is that the impulse to collectivize—normally very weak on a campus with the stature and commitment to professionalism of a Berkeley—was precipitated mainly by two events: (1) the legislature's punitive withdrawal of a 5 percent cost-of-living increase after evidence of faculty political involvement in the "reconstitution movement" following the Cambodian incursion and the killings at Kent State and Jackson State; (2) threats on the part of Governor Reagan to cut the budget, in effect increasing the teaching load of the faculty by 20 percent. Although the faculty on the various campuses have been very quiet politically during the four years of hardship since 1990, a movement to mobilize politically would not be surprising if hard times continue.

There is a subgroup of faculty—mostly senior, with long experience in the Academic Senate—who develop a *general* loyalty to their campuses and to some degree to the university system as a whole. By virtue of its institutional loyalties, moreover, this group overlaps with academic administrators in outlook and expectations. Indeed, there is a noticeable flow of personnel between high senate and high administrative positions. Expectations for "shared governance" are strongest in this group, and leaders in the senate are especially sensitive about "being consulted." If active senate members feel comfortably that they are being included as members of the "team"—through full consultation—they are likely to go along with an administration's favored policies, because they share a strong sense of institutional loyalty. If this group gains the impression that they have not been consulted properly, however, they may respond with *substantive* opposition to issues on which they might otherwise have been persuaded to concur.

One final observation on faculty expectations. although faculty appear to have accepted the recent difficult budgetary times stoically, and they have often cooperated in administrative efforts to economize by measures of consolidation and discontinuation of units, my own view is that the majority of faculty genuinely believe that the hard times are temporary, that good times will come again, and when they do, that they can forget all about the tough measures they have experienced and return to the understandings of growth, autonomy, and entrepreneurship. (This belief, moreover, may contribute to the weakness of the faculty's impulse to organize and revitalize a union-like association.) Once before, in the early 1980s, when the university faced a two-year period of budgetary scarcity, President Saxon introduced some provisions for dealing with an era of no growth, even shrinkage. Faculty debated these seriously, but within a matter of months after the economy's turn-around and the return of relatively good budgets, the expansive mentality returned in full force, and it was almost as though this period of hand-wringing and the threat of hard decisions had never happened.

Alumni

Because the university's campuses are large, public institutions, many alumni have moved through them in an instrumental—that is, career-oriented—way and regard their college years as means to an end. These alumni are not likely to have special loyalties or to donate to their campuses. However, each campus has a percentage of graduates who remain attached and loyal. This group is likely to have the following outlooks:

· Unlike many of the university's constituencies, alumni attention is centered mainly on the *individual campuses* they attended. The whole university is seldom the focus of alumni loyalty. That alumni associations and development offices are organized at the campus level reflects this reality. For this reason it is difficult to pinpoint what a universitywide alumni interest and role might be, even though there are some alumni bodies and other institutional arrangements (such as the alumni members of the board of regents) that create a university-wide presence of alumni.

- Loyal alumni focus mainly on two aspects of campus life: the undergraduate experience and campus athletics. Fund-raisers find alumni more willing to give in these areas than others, such as graduate fellowships or capital maintenance, to say nothing of bailing the university out of deficits. The exception to this rule is the alumni of certain professional schools (e.g., law, engineering, business), who form loyalties to their schools, and often give funds directly to them.

- Loyal alumni are likely to be conservative in a specific sense. They want their campus to continue to thrive, and they want it to remain the institution they remember, or imagine they remember. They want to preserve their nostalgia, both for the sake of their own psychic comfort and for the sake of their own children and relatives who may attend in the future. Accordingly, some alumni are likely to resent changes that may seem to alter the collegiate experience as they knew it. For example, some alumni are apprehensive about increased fees because they fear it will change the character of the institution; some harbor a muffled but definite discomfort with ethnic and racial diversification for the same reason.

Staff

"The staff" is not a single constituency either, and it differs according to the level of rank and responsibility in the hierarchy.

- For many intents and purposes, clerical and lower-level service staff can be regarded as generic "employees" with "employee interests" in wage levels and related conditions of work (some are members of an employees' union—AFCSME). However, one sometimes observes among the lower ranks of staff a more-than-usual sense of loyalty to the university as "a good place to work," despite the fact that university salary scales do not measure up to the private sector in many instances.

- Among middle- and higher-level staff (in student services and financial aid, budget offices, libraries, academic units' managing officers, etc.), there is often a strong interest and loyalty to the campus. One derivation from this outlook is a latent, only occasionally expressed resentment of the faculty. Support and managerial staff members may be convinced that they are "really" responsible for running the university but are not given credit for that either from faculty or from their administrative superiors. The faculty may be regarded as a privileged, well paid, and sometimes irresponsible elite that, moreover, does not extend sufficient respect to the service personnel. Many faculty, on their side, reinforce this impression by taking almost no interest of service personnel's contributions when things run smoothly, while being quick to criticize and to try to take matters into their own hands when things go wrong. Because of this outlook, many managerial and support staff members are especially sensitive to symbols of recognition of the role they play in the life of the university.

Other Segments of Public Higher Education

This covers mainly the California State University system and the California Community College System. Two features above all characterize the relations between the university and these segments:

- The several segments are under pressure to cooperate in a context of inevitably competitive striving. The segments compete for state funds, for students, and for institutional status. No amount of rhetoric can deny this. At the same there are legitimate reasons for the segments to cooperate (in curricular coordination, in some academic programs offered in common, in the transfer of students from institution to institution, and so on). The relations among the segments are thus rendered ambivalent and shifting, depending on the relative salience of the competitive and cooperative impulses.

- The non-university public segments are invariably cast in the role of second-class citizens in the state. They do not enjoy the same constitutional autonomy as the university; their faculties are not as well trained, well paid, eminent, or lionized as university faculties; they do not have a research component built into their support from the state; they do not have doctoral programs or professional programs in the prestigious areas of law and medicine; and they are less "elitist" with respect to admissions. Because of this disadvantaged status of the other sectors—and because of the many university faculty and administrators ignore or look down upon them on account of it—the relations between the university and the other segments are fraught with the sensitivities that "second-class citizens" invariably develop.

They react strongly to both real and symbolic rewards and recognition; they are likely to read insults and snobbishness into behavior and words that do not intend to convey them; they (particularly the California State University system) strive constantly for real and symbolic equity. For purposes of maintaining peace and harmony, university administrators and faculty need to be especially careful not to aggravate these sensitivities, and they must practice the delicate art of simultaneously maximizing their institutional position while at the same time expressing support, affirming equity, and giving respect to the other segments.

Board of Regents

Many regents' expectations derive directly from the fiduciary charge assigned to them as a board of trustees. Among these expectations are (a) that the university's financial affairs will be carried out in an honest, reliable, and accountable fashion; (b) that the university's officers will exercise authority responsibly and effectively. When either of these expectations seem to be threatened—for example, when the Berkeley administration collapsed under conditions of student protest in 1964–65, or when the former chancellor of the Santa Barbara campus was involved in financial improprieties in the late 1980s—regents were moved to decisive action.

Beyond these general points, several other observations about regents' expectations are in order:

· Many regents' expectations about the administration of a university are derived from business and legal contexts in which they themselves have pursued their careers. Their understandings about problem-solving and decision-making thus may differ from the academic administrators' understandings. In particular, the regental mentality probably gives a higher priority to decisive action, and does not fully appreciate the time-consuming, consensus-building processes that characterize university decision making.

· The regents take pride in the institutional accomplishments of the university—prizes for its faculty, successes of its students, its leadership role in research, and its imaginative and effective undergraduate programs. Yet the pride in each of these tends to be of an absolute character, that is, without the accompanying realization that the university cannot be equally excellent or effective in all of them.

- As a general rule, the board of regents, like all governing or administrative bodies, does not like to have difficult problems, conflicts, and crises on their agenda. They like to reign over a going, effective institution. The reason is simple: problems that rise up to the regental level usually mean that they have boiled up (or exploded) from the levels at which they *should* have been handled or solved, and, as a result, they become *regents'* problems. There is a second reason as well. The board of regents, as an operating body, is not very well equipped to engage in the day-by-day negotiations and consensus-building that is essential in conflict-management and problem-resolution. The board meets once a month as a rule, and even their (presumably more efficient) subcommittees do not function well on a routine, day-by-day basis. Problems and conflicts are thus doubly disturbing to the regents: first, they demand responsible attention, and second, they do not have the organizational capacity to respond to them effectively.

- Although the board enjoys a constitutional insulation from the give-and-take of the politics of California, it is necessarily a political body for several reasons: (a) its members are appointed by the governor and the appointments are regarded as political plums; the political-party composition of the board is thus always a point of interest; (b) board members, being politically linked, are a ready conduit for political input from both the legislature and the executive; (c) concerned parties—parents, citizens, supporters of special university programs and units, landowners, political lobbies, environmental interests, animal rights interests—show no reluctance to contact individual regents, sometimes in substantial numbers, when they are inclined to promote their interests or are dissatisfied with or threatened by some university decision or policy.

- Regents dislike being "blindsided" by external protest directed at them about some university "mistake" or "scandal" with which they are not yet familiar. This happens from time to time, as controversial situations are reported in the media, and regents first hear about them in the form of political heat. The reason such situations are so troubling is that not knowing about a situation leaves them in a position of not being able to defend the university, and, perhaps more important, subject to implicit criticism that they are not on top of things. In a word, regents do not like to be regarded as failures any more than anyone else does, but such situations make it appear that they have failed. Under these circumstances regents invariably pass blame to university officials who "should" have kept them informed.

The State Legislature

Some aspects of the legislature as "constituency" are well understood and require only brief mention. The legislature is clearly an interested audience because it is responsible for approving the annual university budget, and is therefore the setting for the rough-and-tumble of budgetary politics, in which the university must represent its interests in competition with the other segments of higher education, K–12, as well as the health, welfare, and correctional systems. In addition, the legislature, like the board of regents, is a conduit for political pressure from all varieties of individuals and groups who are interested in the university and, in particular, wish to register their dissatisfactions and complaints against it.

Three observations on the political role of the legislature are in order:

· The legislature reflects a deep tension in California culture: the tension between competitive excellence and egalitarianism. On the one hand, the state's politicians—like the general "public" to be described at the end of this section—want California higher education in general and the University of California in particular to be "the best." That note of competitive excellence appeared in the founding language of the university in 1868, and has been perhaps the single most powerful legitimizing argument for the historically generous dedication of the state's resources to the university. At the same time, being "the best" also means being "on top," that is, occupying a privileged position, and that is where the ambivalence enters. In addition to pride, there exists another impulse—that the university should be open, should have no exclusive sense of its own specialness, and, above all, should not be "elitist." At any give time one can observe both impulses in the legislature—the institutional pride expressed by figures like Nick Petris and Gary Hart, and the institutional suspicion expressed by figures like John Vacsoncellos and Tom Hayden. Both threads constitute political pressures on the university, and together constitute a difficult political element in its environment.

- The university enjoys a status of constitutional autonomy, concretized in its budgetary arrangements: the legislature does not have "line-item" control over the budget. In this way the university possesses an institutional advantage over the California State University system, which has only a statutory status. It should not be inferred from this observation, however, that the legislature does not interfere—sometimes in detailed ways—in university affairs. It cannot do so formally, so it does so informally—through language of "legislative intent," supplementary language, resolutions, recommendations, statements to the press, and informal communications from legislators to regents and university officials. So while not officially accountable, the university often finds itself accountable *de facto*.

- Communications from the public to the legislature about the university are selective in that they emanate from concerned individuals and groups, and, within those, mainly from those who are dissatisfied or disaffected. These parties usually bring some allegedly undesirable situation, some alleged injustice, or some alleged atrocity to the attention of the legislature. This often results in a situation that might be described as "governance by anecdote": a legislator passes on this complaint to some agent in the university and asks for an accounting. Because the point at issue is frequently distorted and almost always negative, the university is cast into a defensive posture, in which it is called up to deny, to explain, to mobilize other facts to correct the ones brought forward. Through these dynamics, the university is continuously called upon to deal with sometimes-unmanageable political complaints.

The Federal Government

This constituency is less omnipresent than the state legislature, because its connections with the university are less comprehensive. The main link is through the support of research—both directly through grants to campuses and indirectly through the support of the national laboratories. In this research role the federal government and the university stand in an interesting symbiosis: they need one another, though they may not always love one another. The government finds itself turning to universities whenever felt research needs—especially those with a supposed link to national goals or national problems—appear in the Congress or the executive; and the university, a main recipient of liberal federal research support for science throughout the Cold War, has come to depend on federal money for its research and graduate-education establishments.

The federal government often serves as a conduit for political pressure emanating from social movements. It is true that individual research projects seldom have political strings attached to them by granting agencies. However, the government (through important granting agencies such as the Departments of Labor, Energy, and Health and Human Services) has taken a direct interest in *internal* university (and laboratory) policies relating mainly to issues such as affirmative action, environmental health and safety, animal rights, and the treatment of human subjects. Although the sanctions available to the federal government are limited, it does possess the ultimate sanction of refusing to grant research funds, as well as all the informal political leverage to be exercised with that ultimate threat in the background.

Corresponding to these two foci of federal relations with the university, two kinds of effort are called for on the part of the latter: (a) to keep an effective presence in Washington, D.C. (in order to influence policies); and (b) to engage in continuous, ungratifying, and frustrating negotiations with federal agencies, whose demands from social causes, social movements, and public concerns forever threaten to compromise the autonomy of the university.

Campuses' Surrounding Communities

The key to understanding the role of these communities also lies in the notion of ambivalence. On the one hand, communities find the presence of a university campus attractive, because a campus brings cultural visibility as well as spending and jobs to them. At the same time the university calls up images to various community constituencies of rowdy and destructive students, acquisition of tax-yielding property, environmental ruination, and noise pollution. In the face of such cross-pressures, a campus is often faced with situations in which, whatever its policy, it stands to alienate one or more community constituencies. Further, the campus community can be an extremely potent force in inhibiting the expansionist efforts of campuses (the community situations in San Francisco, Santa Cruz, and Santa Barbara are vivid cases in point).

An Undifferentiated "Public"

This is a residual category—a kind of general image that springs to mind when one imagines a "typical" viewer of television or reader of the daily press. Needless to say, because this audience is more often than not an imagined entity, many different and sometimes contradictory expectations are projected onto it. Nevertheless, the "public" is a social-psychological construct that is real in its consequences because it is imagined to be real. Because of the fluid, changing quality of "the public," moreover, it is difficult to assign unambiguous, fixed qualities to its "mentality." One persistent theme, however, is that "the public" loves to bask in the glory of the university, and this love is repeatedly manifested in two ways:

· The university, in keeping with the state and regional pride of
  Californians, should be "the best." Any evidence that the university is
  the best or among the best—prizes to faculty, recognition by funding
  agencies, surveys of institutional prestige—helps. This California
  "nationalism" is real, and assures the public that the university, with
  that kind of status, is likely to be secure and successful in its role of
  serving California's citizens effectively, helping California's economy,
  increasing California's influence as a state, and keeping California on
  the map.

· The university is an object of sacred trust and should be held to a
  higher morality than non-public institutions. We should never forget
  that the historical origins of the university are religious and that
  many quasi-religious rituals and representations (such as formal
  commencements, endowment with honors through honorary degrees
  and citations, and inaugurations) survive. "The people" want and like
  this element of sanctity, and correspondingly hold out expectations
  that representatives of the university (both faculty and administrators)
  should be held to some vaguely defined special morality. That kind
  of expectation lends salience and electricity to the issue of high
  salaries and "perks" for administrators and to issues of "dishonesty in
  research" for faculty.

Needless to say, the imputed general expectations of "the public" find their way into the expectations of other interested audiences, such as the regents, students' parents, and legislatures, and are given expression through these groups.

At this moment we shift direction. We now turn to the actual structural arrangements within the University of California, as they have evolved over time, and identify a number of anomalies, ambiguities, and other oddities in that very complex structure. These features do not constitute crises or even ticking bombs by any means, but they are potential sources of problems, inefficiencies of functioning, and possible institutional crises in the future. They are presented in no particular order of importance; some are specific and some are generic. All constitute areas to be regarded as possible foci for institutional reform.

The Relations between the Systemwide Office and the Campuses

It may be that in the interest of institutional flexibility, the respective realms of jurisdiction between the systemwide office and the campuses should remain indefinitely ambiguous and subject to continuously renewed negotiation and intersection—changing, appropriately, from one issue to another as each arises. Nevertheless, it might be a helpful exercise to identify three areas for examination:

· Those areas of unambiguous responsibility of the systemwide administration—for example, legal defense of the university; management of regents' funds; representing the university to the legislature and the governor; and benefits issues such as medical care and retirement.

· Those areas of unambiguous responsibility of the campuses—internal budgetary allocations; the organization of academic departments; the handling of academic, staff, and student discipline; and advancement and promotion of faculty (with exceptions specified in regents' bylaws).

· Those areas of joint responsibility or negotiation—implementation of admissions policies; graduate enrollments; approval of new academic programs and capital planning.

All of these areas should be the subject of continuous questioning and potential alteration. Systemwide and campus responsibilities should not be allowed to drift into fixed, unexamined traditions. Even "sacred" areas of universitywide responsibility such as the legal defense of the university has shown some fluidity as legal advisors have been retained at the campus level, even though formal and legal actions are the responsibility of the office of the general counsel; fee policies might also be a subject of campus responsibility, for example, discretion in fees for professional schools. The best rule of thumb is that the boundaries between campus and system should be regarded as open and fluid as possible.

As part of the same exercise, the often-vexing issue of shared governance or the relations between the administration and Academic Senate—at both the systemwide and campus levels—might be addressed. This issue has two facets:

· *Delegation.* According to the standing orders of the regents, certain items are delegated to the faculty. The clearest of these is authority over the curriculum. There is also a delegation of responsibility for admissions policy, but over time this concern has tended to move under the control of the campus and systemwide administrations because (I would surmise) the issue has become so loaded politically in the face of changing demographics, affirmative action, and activities on the part of pressure groups interested in admissions. In still other areas, such as academic personnel, there has evolved a *de facto* delegation of authority to committees on academic personnel on the several campuses, such that chancellors defy recommendations of these committees infrequently and at their own risk, even though chancellors retain formal authority. As a general rule the existing pattern of formal and informal delegation to the faculty is regarded as legitimate, though certainly not beyond critical evaluation.

· *Consultation.* In the case of academic personnel, some consultation has become so fixed by tradition that it approaches full delegation. In other areas, consultation is less routinized. There exists a general expectation that administrative decisions will not be made unless reviewed and reacted to by appropriate Academic Senate bodies, even though the administration is responsible for final decisions and may not heed senate advice. This pattern of consultation is well established. On any given campus it is standard operating procedure for a chancellor or vice chancellor to send off a proposal to the concerned divisional committees—for example, Educational Policy Committee, Faculty Welfare Committee, Graduate Council—for review. Despite the regularity of this consultation, both the categories of decisions to be reviewed and what constitutes "proper" or "full" senate review remain gray areas, and in any given academic year the chancellor's office or the systemwide office will be accused of not having consulted properly on one issue or another. Existing patterns of consultation are generally felt to be legitimate, but because the senate tends to regard them as an absolute right and because administrators often regard them as a nuisance, consultation is the subject of periodic complaint and contestation. In any event the current pattern of consultation might profitably be reviewed with respect to its efficiency and effectiveness as a device of governance.

A Recurring Tendency: Centralization by Default

There are five kinds of institutional forces that make for a "tilt" toward centralization of responsibility, authority, and governance in the University of California system.

- As the system grows in size and complexity, monitoring mechanisms do not necessarily or automatically become more decentralized. For example, at various times regental policy has required that the regents themselves approve financial and real-estate transactions above a certain dollar amount. When campuses grow larger and increase the number and size of transactions, when inflation progressively lowers the real dollar limit, *and* if the regental policies remain unchanged, the *de facto* consequence is that the system becomes more centralized because activities that become of smaller and smaller significance in reality continue to remain under central monitoring and control.

- The administrative drive for standardization of procedures and economies of scale in procurement and distribution make for more centralized decision making.

- Financial and budgetary crises force decision making toward the center, as control over expenditures becomes a matter of *system* interest in times of scarcity.

- Political crises on individual campuses—conflicts or breakdowns of authority, for example—invite the intervention of the systemwide authorities and board of regents, because such conflicts and breakdowns assume *general* political significance in the university and the state. The recent "Milkin" incident is a case in point: essentially local in significance, the contract, arranged by Milken and the school of management at UCLA, became a "system" issue because both legislators and the media focused attention on the president's office and the board, thus *forcing* the issue to the center. Such conflicts may excite efforts on the part of systemwide administrators and regents to return the issue to the campus level for resolution, but often they cannot succeed in this because the media and other groups and agencies continue to define the issue as a general university issue.

· Many social movements and political pressures—for example environmental groups and environmentally minded government agencies—are directed at the systemwide office because, it is felt, that is where the decisive "action" is. This, too, tends to centralize interest in the issue or policy.

All these pressures tend to involve the center in the decision-making process; further, once the center is involved, it often takes a deliberate act to "uninvolve" it. For this reason it is essential that the systemwide office maintain continuous diligence and undertake periodic cognizance of the ways and degrees in which has become involved in campus affairs "by default"; furthermore the systemwide office should be prepared to intervene in such tendencies when it seems appropriate.

The Structure of the Vice Presidencies

At the present time there are six vice presidents of the university:

Provost and senior vice president—academic affairs

Senior vice president—administration

Vice president—budget and university relations

Vice president—health affairs

Vice president—agriculture and natural resources

Vice president and general counsel

Although these officers are assigned a reasonably clear range of duties and responsibilities, the definition of the offices themselves appear to have emerged mainly from a logic of historical accumulation. For example, the position for agriculture and natural resources originated in the land-grant beginnings of the university, which, though still important, are not as salient in the overall picture of university life as they once were; the title "provost," to go along with the title for senior vice president—academic affairs, emerged in the context of a historically specific reassertion of the importance of academic priorities; and the addition of the title of "vice president" to the general counsel was also the result of a historically specific redefinition of the relations among the general counsel, the office of the president, and the board of regents.

That observation notwithstanding, there is an identifiable institutional logic in the designation of most of the vice presidencies. The distinction between academic affairs and administration is a standard if not universal feature of the structure of universities, and takes into account the special character of the university as an organization. Furthermore, given the fact that the University of California is constitutionally a legal entity, it makes sense that it speak to the state and the law with one, centralized voice, however frustrating as this may appear to individual campuses. This consideration gives institutional sense to the vice presidential status of the general counsel. Similarly, the vice president—budget and university relations makes sense, because of the necessarily centralized basis of budgetary negotiations between the university and the state.

The most evident anomalies are found with the vice president—agriculture and natural resources and the vice president—health affairs. The first gains legitimacy and support from the strength of tradition and by the continuing importance of the agricultural sector of the California economy. The second gains legitimacy and support from the massive institutional presence of the university hospitals and their equally massive share of the university budget. Because these two vice presidents are defined in terms of subject matter rather than function, however, they find themselves dealing with academic affairs, budget, personnel, research policy, and university relations, and for that reason criss-cross in responsibility with the other vice presidents.

There are strong political and symbolic reasons for keeping agriculture and health as separate, visible entities at the highest levels in the system-wide office, and any effort to alter their status would meet with significant opposition. However, organizational rationality suggests a reassignment of their responsibilities along more nearly functional lines, occasioning the elimination of those two vice presidencies and the creation of two new ones: vice president—research (upgrading and replacing the new associate provost for research), and a vice president—professional education and service.

Several arguments can be advanced for such a reform. The new positions would create a certain organizational correspondence with two of the traditional triad of missions of the modern research university— research and service—and each would actualize and symbolize the centrality of those functions. Administrative responsibility for health would be brought under the new administrative umbrella as a branch of professional education. Furthermore, such a reform might constitute the occasion for the decentralization of administrative responsibility for agricultural programs to the several campuses on which they exist—a decentralization that has long been advocated in many quarters. The creation of a vice president—research would also provide an opportunity for bringing policy relating to organized research units—both campus and multicampus—to the top level of systemwide administration. Finally, the creation of a vice president—research would also address a second anomaly, to be considered next.

The Position of the National Laboratories in the University

Under this heading are included the Los Alamos, Livermore, and Lawrence Berkeley laboratories, even though the last does not have the same national security significance as the other two.

Administrative responsibility or the national laboratories has, as a matter of history, rested mainly with the senior ice president—academic affairs. At times this assignment has proved problematical, largely because minding the laboratories has proved to be an exceptionally heavy burden of time, energy, responsibility, and headaches for that vice president.

Three recent changes have addressed that problem directly and indirectly, but in the end only partially:

- The creation of the President's Advisory Council for the National Laboratories, to replace the Scientific and Academic Advisory Committee. That change accomplished several things. First it brought the Lawrence Berkeley Laboratories under the wing of the advisory body; SAAC dealt only with Los Alamos and Livermore. Second, it expanded both the charge and the composition of the advisory body. It is not clear, however, whether the new body has resulted in any administrative relief for the senior vice president— academic affairs.

- The creation of a sizeable staff for administrative coordination of laboratory affairs in the office of the senior vice president—administration. This split the responsibility for dealing with the laboratories between the two senior vice presidents. Some anomalies remain, however. First, the line between policy and administrative oversight is a difficult one to draw, so some potential jurisdictional ambiguities result. Second, the office of the special assistant—laboratory affairs (in the office of the senior vice president—academic affairs) is thinly staffed.

- The creation of the associate provost—research. One impetus for the creation of this office—as it was discussed in the transition team meetings of 1992–93—was that it might constitute an opportunity for the senior vice president—academic affairs—to shed some his direct responsibility for the laboratories. The most extreme suggestion was that the laboratory directors would report to the office of the associate provost. Such a move would certainly relieve the senior vice president but might be regarded as an unacceptable symbolic downgrading by the laboratory directors. As of the moment, the exact division of laboratory responsibilities between provost and senior vice president—academic affairs, on the one hand, and the associate provost—research, on the other, remains uncertain. (Any realignment, of course, would have a bearing on the contract with the Department of Energy; for example, at present the contact calls for the senior vice president on the Joint UC-DOE Issues Resolution Committee.)

In spite of these three recent changes, the relations between the office of the senior vice president—academic affairs and the laboratories remain fluid and possibly anomalous. One opportunity that the creation of a full vice president—research, discussed above, presents is to provide an opportunity for delegation of full responsibility for dealing with the laboratories to that position, and to locate all staff involved with the laboratories under that position. Such a change would accomplish several things: place the laboratories where they properly belong—under the heading of research; coordinate better the different facets of university relations with the laboratories; keep the reporting relationship of the laboratory directions at a vice presidential level; permit the vice president—research to work more intensively with the President's Advisory Council; and provide some relief for the overburdened office of the provost and senior vice president—academic affairs.

The Education Abroad Program and Related Matters

Two separate review committees for the Education Abroad Program (one academic and one administrative) are now at work, and their reports will no doubt address and bring forward recommendations relating to he major issues facing that program. Because I have been closely involved with the EAP over the years, however, I thought it appropriate to venture a few observations of my own.

When the current director of the Education Abroad program (John Marcum) was selected, Vice President Fraser asked the search committee to comment on the issue that was a running sore at that time—should the director report to the chancellor of the Santa Barbara campus (where the headquarters of EAP are located) or the senior vice president—academic affairs? The EAP had solidified its institutional position in its first two decades by forging a close alliance with the Santa Barbara chancellor, Vernon Cheadle, and he had, in turn, assumed a kind of proprietary interest in it. That link with Santa Barbara is still alive, and some people on that campus assume that EAP somehow belongs to Santa Barbara. This constitutes a reporting anomaly for the director of EAP, because EAP is, in every organizational respect, a systemwide program. The current administrative and academic review committees will probably concur in recommending that the EAP director report, for all important purposes, to the provost and senior vice president—academic affairs.

That is a correct recommendation, in my estimation, and should be implemented. There is, however, a second important issue—closely connected to that one—having to do with the context of the reporting relationship to the provost. It is certainly a unit with a primarily academic mission, so it is appropriate that it report to the provost, if to anybody. At the same time, one can raise questions about two aspects of that relationship: (a) should it report *directly* to the provost or to someone else in his or her office? Should the provost, with an enormous range of demanding responsibilities, be directly involved in a unit such as the EAP? (b) should the EAP remain isolated—as it now is—from other international programs and responsibilities of the University of California?

The upshot of both questions is to suggest that, perhaps in the longer run, the office of the president ought to consider the possibility of establishing a position—perhaps an associate provost?—located in the provost's office, with responsibility for international programs and relations.

The reason this possibility comes to mind is that the international involvements of the university are certain to become more pronounced in the decades to come, just as the internationalization of the world as a whole will surely grow. EAP and all other international programs and relations could be linked to such an office. Its creation would also constitute a basis for both growth and coordination of the university's international involvements.

University of California Press

The University of California Press presents few organizational ambiguities. Its mission is relatively clear; it is well directed; its administrative reporting relationships are directly to the provost; it has had its ups and downs but has established a generally satisfactory financial base for operations. There are, however, three enduring points of tension in the press, each of which could come to constitute a problem:

· There is a long-term, low-key struggle between the director of the press and the editorial board on the one side and the Systemwide Academic Senate (especially its committee on committees) on the other. The press is interested in ensuring expertise over the range of subjects that constitute its publication list and advocates for appointments of the best scholars in areas of need; the senate is jealous of its prerogatives of appointment to the editorial board, and also is under some obligation to respond to pressures from campuses on the committee on committees to place their representatives on the editorial board (an appointment to the editorial board is considered a kind of political plum by some members of the faculty). This tension has erupted into open conflict from time to time.

· There is another subterranean tension between the systemwide office of the press (in Berkeley) and the Los Angeles office. It is a matter of regional tension. There is no really consistent regional division of responsibilities between the two offices. UCLA feels that the UC Press offices in Berkeley are regarded as "Berkeley property" and that UCLA, as a major campus, deserves a full university press. There has been a long history of the UCLA administration treating the Los Angeles office of the press rather badly, as if out of resentment that it is not a full press. On the other hand, there is justified apprehension about creating two presses, on grounds that the San Diego campus and ultimately other campuses would agitate for independent presses as well. This regional tension does not constitute a major problem at the moment, but it could in the long run.

· The UC Press, while reasonably stable financially, is under constant pressure not to show deficits or ask for increases in regental subsidization. For the press this creates a constant pressure to publish trade books (which make money) and scholarly books with wider appeal (which sell better than esoteric monographs). Trade and general books also have a kind of glitzy appeal as well, reviewed as they are in places like the *New York Times Book Review* and the *New York Review of Books*. Although the editorial board and the board of control act as a countervailing pressure to this temptation, it is always there, and, if extended, would tend to overshadow the scholarly mission of the press.

The Future Problematic Status of the Organized Research Units

The organized research unit (ORU) is an institutional invention on the part of universities that accompanied the post-World War II era of large-scale foundation and federal government support for research. This statement is true even though a few ORUs predate that era and even though some have been formed independently of programmatic initiatives on the part of foundations and government agencies.

As organizations, ORUs can be regarded as a healthy antidote to departmental tendencies toward academic rigidity and self-isolation (see the section immediately below). The formation of an ORU can be a response to a new, problematical, or exciting research area. (Example: it is probably no accident that the Institute of Industrial Relations on the Berkeley campus was formed immediately after World War II in the middle of a season of postwar strikes and other union activity, apprehension about the stability of labor-management relations, and increased research on industrial relations by economists, political scientists, sociologists, and historians.) In addition, an ORU, being problem-oriented, is more often than not interdisciplinary in its faculty affiliations and research agenda. Despite the fact that ORUs have been one factor in sapping the vitality of academic departments (see below), they have added flexibility and responsiveness to the research activities of universities.

At the same time, ORUs have developed their own types of inflexibility. Although reviews of the typical ORU are scheduled periodically (most commonly, every five years), and these reviews can, in principle, call for phasing-out, the review process has proven to be a weak instrument. The reviews are often routine, and sometimes serve to bolster a director's interests in survival or expansion. Sometimes, however, they serve as a mechanism for encouraging the resignation of an ORU director who has served ineffectively or beyond his or her time. Many ORUs receive state funds to support an infrastructure (director's salary, administrative and clerical support staff, a grant-procuring office, for example). These funds are often targets for budget administrators (they are vulnerable because they do not include faculty full-time equivalent [FTE]); however, they exist as 19900 funds, and seldom vanish at a blow. As a result, ORUs have an inertia that is almost as remarkable as that of academic departments. Taken as an aggregate, the ORUs on a campus are a population of historically precipitated organizations, many of which arose as a response to vital research developments but cannot be weeded out even though the area of research represented by them is no longer vital. (The Institute of Industrial Relations is an illustration of this tendency as well.)

Looking toward the future, one may raise the following questions about ORUs:

- If the era of big science associated with the Cold War—which spilled over into support for research in general—is in the process of coming to a close, is the organized research unit thus called into question as a continuing form?

- How can the same flexibility be assured for eliminating ORUs as has been shown in their creation? Should state funds for ORUs be discontinued and turned to other purposes, so that ORUs are more nearly dependent on the "market" for external research funds? Should funding understandings be changed, so that support for the infrastructures of ORUs is automatically discontinued after a given period (for example, five years)? If the answers to the above questions are positive, this would change ORUs to recurring experiments rather than quasi-permanent installations.

- Should there be some systematic teaching role for the ORUs? At present the Academic Senate maintains prerogatives of control over the teaching role (even though much teaching is, in fact, delegated to graduate student instructors). Many of the researchers in the ORUs have PhDs in their respective fields of expertise, and a case might be made for involving some of the in offering research-related courses by the ORUs.

The Problematic Status of the Academic Department

The following constitutes a number of observations on the status of academic departments in the university. These seem to be in order, because the department is probably the most taken-for-granted, "natural" unit in the institution. It is at the heart of the university's instructional activity—indeed determines that activity—is centrally involved in the recruitment, advancement, and promotion of faculty, and, in principle, is the organizational realization of the academic disciplines for which they are named. Despite this apparent fixity, there are a number of problematic aspects about departmental life. I mention these not out of any special intent to suggest reforms but, rather, as subjects for further reflection.

· Has the academic department lost its intellectual functions? As indicated, the department is at the center of the instructional activity of the university, and in that sense is central to its intellectual life. At the same time, the second half of the twentieth century has witnessed two developments that apparently have eroded much of the intellectual life of the department. (1) There has been a long-term shift of the faculty member's sense of rewards, career advancement, and professional status from the department to the national (and sometimes international) academic discipline. This is a "natural" outcome of the increased premium on research fostered by external funding and the special stress on recognition for published research. Committees on academic personnel, despite efforts at reform, still place the highest premium on published research and national awards and participation (the latter being largely derivative from the former) and less on "local" achievements in teaching and university service. CAPs thus conspire to furthering this trend, which, however valuable on other grounds, tends to erode local campus and department loyalty. (2) The development of organized research units has, in many cases, constituted a centrifugal force in departmental life, as faculty members become administrative officers (directors, associate directors) in them or organize their research through them. (External research funding is typically channeled and gradate students are hired through ORUs, not departments.) This diffuses the faculty's attachment to the department. In practice, the academic department has become a repository for deciding who teaches what and fighting over who gets appointed to the department's faculty. The proper *intellectual* bases for these activities, however, have migrated elsewhere in large part.

· The role of the chair of the department, never strong, is largely without authority. While in principle responsible for assigning teaching, the chair's activity has devolved in many cases—especially in relation to senior, established, distinguished faculty—to cajoling, negotiating, and compromising, rather than exercising formally established authority. While having some discretion in deciding on merit and advancement for faculty, the chair is sometimes reduced to responding to external circumstances (notably offers to colleagues from competing institutions), and simply to forwarding votes and opinions of faculty colleagues to the administration. (It has been said in jest that the role of the chair is to run errands to the administration on behalf of ambitious and disagreeable colleagues.) The chair's authority over departmental staff, while formally intact, is delegated for many intents and purposes to the senior staff official. The chair is one of those many positions around the campus that has considerable responsibility without substantial authority. It is little wonder that one of the main headaches for deans is to persuade unwilling faculty members to chair a department out of a sense of institutional loyalty, which is likely to be diminished in any case.

· Departments are extremely durable, manifesting great continuity over time. There are disciplinary differences in this respect: departments in the biological sciences appear to have been the most receptive to amalgamating into new structures, while the structure of departments in the humanities and social sciences is rigid and resistant to change. This rigidity stands in sharp contrast to the *cultural* or *intellectual* life of the disciplines they represent, which is typically dynamic and ever-changing, as disciplinary research develops in new directions. The reasons for the structural rigidity are found in the budgeting traditions of the university (which allocates FTE budgets to departments) and in the dynamics of organizational self-protection and self-advancement. Whatever the reasons behind it, there persists a kind of contradiction between the structural continuity of academic departments and the discontinuity and flux of the intellectual life of the disciplines that departments represent. The inevitable logic that emerges from this diagnosis is that departmental structures should be made more flexible in order better to reflect the dynamics of the creation of knowledge, however difficult such changes may be to envision.

· Should departments be the agents for organizing undergraduate curricula? Typically they are, as chairs recruit colleagues to give undergraduate courses that bear titles and have contents that are disciplinary in character. Typically, too, department faculty offer lower division courses to "introduce" students to the knowledge of the discipline, and upper-division courses that constitute "preparatory runs" at specialized graduate courses, in that they review the published research in some subfield of the discipline. It can be argued that the academic departments, with their disciplinary commitments and emphases, are among the most formidable enemies of general education, because they succeed in fragmenting knowledge and burying intellectual issues in the way they offer their courses. This reasoning leads to the suggestion that campuses might, in the area of undergraduate education, work toward the determination of instruction by interdisciplinary groups of faculty, committed to organize their course along the lines of ideas and issues, not disciplinary content. This possibility is, of course, closely linked to the issues of changes in the reward and incentive structures of faculty life, which are now linked more or less exclusively to departmental membership and performance.

The Problem of Second-Class Citizenship in the University

In the previous section I discussed two of the university's constituencies that appear to have a preoccupation with their second-class citizenship—managerial staff and the other public segments of higher education [California State University (CSU) and Community College System (CCS)]. The preoccupation of the first arises from explicit and implicit comparisons with faculty, who enjoy first-class citizenship, and the preoccupation of the second arises from the (really and symbolically) subordinated position of CSU and CCS in the master plan. Actually, however, these are only two of the constituencies that are likely to experience a sense of second-class citizenship in the university. A more exhaustive catalogue would include the following:

- Assistant professors, who are ladder-rank and enjoy the prestige of faculty, as well as longer-term contracts, freedom of arranging schedules, and so forth but who labor under the shadow of not yet having received academic tenure and living under chronic anxiety in approaching the tenure decision.

- Temporary faculty (lecturers, instructors) who teach regular courses (sometimes very important ones) but whose terms are generally limited to one or two years (security of employment lecturers are an exception but are still second-class), carry heavier teaching loads, do not have departmental voting rights and often cannot attend department meetings, and do not have senate membership.

- Clinical faculty, many of whom regard such appointments as sources of prestige but who nonetheless hold different titles from "regular" faculty and are compensated on a different basis.

- Non-senate academic personnel who are research personnel, hired by ORUs and on research projects; as a rule they cannot teach, cannot be principal investigators, cannot belong to the Academic Senate, and have a more precarious employment status than faculty—that is, they are dependent on "soft" money.

- Managerial staff, mentioned earlier, many of whom believe that they occupy important roles in "running" the university but who believe they are not properly recognized and that faculty who do not "run" the university receive high, undeserved rewards and prestige.

- Staff involved in ancillary activities, especially student services, who believe they actually serve the students more conscientiously than faculty but feel they do not receive adequate credit or recognition for this.

- Teaching assistants, who are given a high level of responsibility but limited authority in teaching undergraduates; they occupy a chronically ambiguous position that is one-third faculty, one-third student, one-third employee; they frequently believe they are more committed, more conscientious, and better teachers than faculty but are subordinated and not recognized in the area of teaching.

- Undergraduates, many of whom regard themselves as the lowest rung in the academic hierarchy, a viewpoint reflected in the frequent, often unconscious reference to themselves as "just students."

Most of the "second-classness" of these various groups derives from comparisons with the faculty, to whom they feel disadvantaged in some real and symbolic ways. This kind of invidious distinction is inevitable in an organization whose primary functions are organized around faculty values and faculty activities, and whose reward structure is correspondingly structured. To note this is not necessarily to recommend any efforts to alter this kind of stratification system, for doing so would probably entail changes that would be, in effect, quite revolutionary, and would probably have undesirable consequences for the University as an institution. It should be recognized, however, that a myriad of groups that define themselves as less privileged exist in the stratification system of the university. Furthermore, the chronic, low-key dissatisfactions they harbor may be mobilized from time to time into specific protests that constitute political moments for the university.

LOOMING PROBLEMS

This section will contain few if any surprises. It is worthwhile, however, to reflect on the broad situation that promises to confront the University of California in the next decade or two.

Problem Area #1: Serving the Students and Residents of California

This has to be the largest and most persistent problem that faces the university. It has a double face: the increasing *numbers* of potential students through the first decade of the twenty-first century, and the changing *composition* of that flow of students, with respect to ethnicity, race, and social class. The main reason that this problem is so important is that appears that the state will not provide nearly enough resources to accommodate these numbers in the way we have done in the past. Contending with this complex problem will demand more energy, time, and conflict-management—conflict emanating from students, parents' pressure groups, legislators, regents, and faculty—than any other issue. The notes that follow are an attempt to diagnose possibilities for the future.

Looking over the various possibilities for dealing with the problem, three general strategies—each with subvariations—come to mind: reducing the numbers of students admitted; permitting educational quality to decline; and pursuing educational efficiencies. These will be discussed in order. Some remarks on the feasibility and effectiveness of each are included.

Reducing the Numbers of Students Admitted   There are a number of ways
to attain this end; all are unpalatable, and most are politically difficult or
impossible to realize:

1. To break the master plan by simply reducing the level of eligibility
    from the top 12½ percent to some lower percent. For UC to do
    this unilaterally would constitute something like political suicide, as
    the reactions to CSUs unilateral reduction of enrollments for the
    1993–94 year demonstrate. If this strategy is to be viable in any
    way, it will have to be carried out with full concurrence of the
    legislature and governor of the State of California, and very likely
    over the opposition of many groups. Even a carefully orchestrated
    reduction of the percentage of eligibles is politically unlikely for
    two reasons. (a) The egalitarian cultural tradition of California: for
    whatever reasons, California has always regarded the university as a
    most important ingredient of the value it places on social democ-
    racy and social mobility. Every time some action or policy appears
    to threaten that tradition, it becomes politically hot and excites
    strong opposition. (The almost knee-jerk resistance to the imposi-
    tion of tuition and the raising of fees in many quarters is a mani-
    festation of this egalitarian sentiment.) This sentiment is very
    strong and cannot easily be shaken, even by rational argumenta-
    tion. (b) The ambitions of both old and new groups in the state:
    well-established middle-class groups, both "Anglo" and "minority,"
    continue to regard the university as an important instrument in the
    status-preservation of their children. In addition, underrepresented
    and/or ambitious minorities (Asian, Chicano, Latino, African
    American, Native American)—almost all expanding in number—
    regard the university as a key to gaining a more economically and
    politically secure place in the state. Any effort to constrict enroll-
    ments, either by the university or by the state, will meet opposition
    from *all* these groups. If anything, the political pressure will be in
    the opposite direction. It may be that the sentiments that value
    egalitarian and social mobility will turn out to provide the greatest
    long-term help to the university. During the past few years the
    apparent conviction among budget-starved state officials is that the
    university can *both* be slashed budgetarily *and* continue to perform
    its traditional educational role in California. After a certain period
    of time that conviction will become less viable, as declining quality

of undergraduate education, evidence of exodus of faculty to other institutions, and increased difficulty of faculty recruitment excites public sentiment to "turn around" the decline of the institution. Whether this optimistic scenario develops or not, it is still true that reducing traditional percentages eligible for an education at the university will be a very unpopular, probably impossible strategy.

2. To discourage students from enrolling by continuing to raise fees. The discouragement takes two forms: students from wealthier families may desert the university to attend private or public institutions in other states; students from poorer families may desert to CSU and other less expensive campuses, or choose not to continue in higher education at all. We do not know whether these effects of high fees are already evident or, if they are not, when they will begin to be seen. Such knowledge, is however, is rendered somewhat moot by the absolute public opposition—reflected through the legislature—to raising undergraduate fees for California residents. The recent effort by some legislators to limit fee increases to 10 percent (plus the significantly greater hike for professional schools) is an indication that the raising of fees to the point of apparent discouragement of students is already an unviable alternative. In future years it will become only more difficult as a strategy, as it continues to run into renewed public opposition.

3. To discourage students from coming by ratcheting up high-school requirements for admission—for example, math, science, English, history, or social-science requirements. Although an attractive option for some faculty members, this strategy has two distinct disadvantages that probably make it unviable: (a) there is an intrinsic lack of appeal about using pedagogic and educational instrumentalities as *strategies* to erect barriers to numbers or to gain economies; the educational preparation of high school students for college entry should, rather, be assessed *on its own grounds*, not as a means to organizational or economic ends; (b) the strategy may have unwanted implications for access of underrepresented minorities; to elevate requirements would tend to work differentially against less prepared groups in the population; as such it would sooner or later draw the opposition from spokespersons for these groups.

4. To "off-load" some collegiate work on other kinds of educational institutions. This may take various forms: to increase the amount of advanced-placement work available to high-school students (thus making possible a reduction in units and time to graduation in the university); to ship out "remedial" work in languages and other fields to non-university institutions; to make expanded use of university extension so that students may take larger portions of their undergraduate work under that format; to require that increased numbers of students spend their first two years in other institutions (mainly community colleges) with guaranteed or preferred subsequent admission into the university. These probably constitute the politically most viable options, largely because they do not actually reduce ultimate access to the University and because they appear to promise some economies. The objections to all of these seem to boil down to the question of *threats to educational quality*. Many high schools in the state simply do not have the budgetary base, the quality of faculty, or the quality of students to introduce advanced placement courses of adequate quality; hence the expansion of advanced placement offerings might have indirectly "elitist" consequences in that it benefits the smartest, wealthiest, and most motivated students but would leave large numbers of high schools and high school students unaffected. The transfer of undergraduate work to other institutions of higher education also raises questions of quality, especially in the minds of parents who want the full collegiate experience for their children at the university, on the part of university faculty who believe, correctly or not, that educational quality is lower in these other institutions than it is in the university. These threats to perceived educational quality may not prove sufficient to resist such "off-loading," however, because quality is difficult to measure, and because claims of "decline of quality through off-loading" can be written off as unwarranted, academically snobbish attitudes on the part of the university, especially the faculty.

Permitting Educational Quality to Decline This "strategy," if it may be called that, is a particularly insidious one, because it may occur gradually, without giving evidence of itself in any given semester or year (partly because of the problems of measurement and assessment just mentioned). Such a decline in quality may result from direct or indirect causes:

1. If numbers of students continue to flow in but the resources required for faculty, staff, and facilities necessary to educate them do not, then a *direct* deterioration in quality will make itself evident in an increasing student-faculty ratio, larger classes, fewer graduate student assistants, mechanical rather than reflective examination and evaluation, diminished library resources, and possibly a decline in faculty quality through exit to other institutions and difficulty of recruitment.

2. Campuses can respond to increasing numbers of undergraduate students by diverting more faculty effort to accommodate them but only by "cheating" graduate and professional programs. This results in an *indirect* deterioration in quality, in that quality falls in areas other than undergraduate instruction. Although scarcely a deliberate strategy, this effect is a likely one, because the political constituencies representing graduate and professional programs are weaker than those representing California undergraduates, their families, and their membership groups in the community. We have seen how much easier it is to raise out-of-state fees than fees for California residents, and how much easier it is to raise professional (and probably graduate) fees than it is to raise them for California undergraduates. The same logic applies to permitting graduate and professional education to decline; their constituencies (with some exceptions, such as doctors and lawyers) are smaller and more dispersed than the "undergraduate lobby."

Another strategy may, at first glimpse, seem to involve erosion of quality but may not in actuality. That strategy is actively to *discontinue* outright some professional programs (such as teacher training, training of social workers, and preparing some other professionals), many of which have *already* migrated in large part to other, non-UC institutions. To discontinue such professional schools would not affect the Master Plan for Higher Education drastically, because those professional schools (unlike law, medicine, and veterinary medicine) are not granted a monopoly under the master plan, except when they grant the doctorate. Such a strategy has some "downside" aspects, however; for one thing, such programs are among the least expensive of professional programs and discontinuation would not yield enormous budgetary savings; in addition, such discontinuation would mark the desertion, by the premier educational system in the state, of professions that are necessary in the society but which, despite that necessity, suffer chronically from diminished social status among the professions; it would also mean the desertion of large numbers of minority students who regard such professional schools as avenues for advancement.

One other issue arises under the heading of "quality of undergraduate education." As time goes on, more and different groups may take a direct interest in "quality" as their interest in the university becomes more articulated. We have already witnessed the controversies over "cultural diversity" of the curriculum and "political correctness"—both of which reflect the interests of different racial, ethnic, and cultural groups in the quality of education. My own sense is that both the movement for curricular diversification and the "backlash" against it will continue to subside, with occasional eruptions, in the coming years. But other kinds of conflict will develop. More established middle-class groups will probably constitute a pressure group to continue the "liberal-arts" kind of education, because it has served these groups well in the past. "Newer" minorities gaining access to the university will, by contrast, press toward a greater "instrumentalization" or "vocationalization" of the curriculum, on grounds that change in these directions will prepare their children better for the occupational world. This prediction is based on the knowledge that other minority groups in the past have tended to treat their access to institutions of higher education as direct avenues to economic and social mobility, rather than as ways to become "cultured" adults. There is no reason to believe that "new" minority groups seeking a better status for themselves in society will regard higher education any differently.

Pursuing Educational Efficiencies   Late in 1993 the planning staff of the systemwide office prepared a document of potential efficiencies, which came to be known as the Thirteen Commandments. The intent of these was to address the general problem of increased educational demand. They are seen as ways of increasing the "throughput" of students (presumably without diminishing the quality of their education). They address the problem of demographics in that they, as efficiencies, in effect increase the number of places for students by "processing" students already in the university more efficiently. Several of the thirteen efficiencies (expanded use of advance placement credit, expanded use of community colleges, expanded use of extension) have already been discussed. Three of the others (to offer a three-year degree program and give campuses incentives to get students through in four years) are closely related. These are attractive in many ways, but it should be recognized that both of them necessarily have to be regarded as options for selected numbers of students rather than completely general schemes to be applied across the board. It should also be recognized that these two options also will probably attract the richest, the smartest, and the most motivated students—because many less endowed students will have to work part time and many less well-prepared students will not be able to work at a pace necessary to complete their requirements in three or even four years.

Another of the thirteen (year-round operations) appears to have proven itself so ineffective a means in past experiments that it should not be considered seriously. Still another (to charge students the cost of instruction after they exceed the minimum number of units needed to graduate) seems sufficiently "far out" that it will probably not fly as a realistic possibility.

Several other options (to lengthen the instructional day or week, to develop an extended day program) merit implementation because they offer modest efficiencies, will address the problem of unused classroom capacity, and will provide more flexibility in scheduling for some students. One should expect some faculty opposition to these measures, because here is a kind of unwritten but somewhat sacred code among them as to what parts of the day and week should and should not be devoted to teaching (one hears jests about the accepted practice of never-other-than-Tuesday-Thursday-between-ten-and-three). The increased use of summer sessions should also be pursued because it also extends the use of facilities, but this strategy, too, reaches a limit as it (like year-round operations in general) begins to displace regular faculty from offices in the summers and sooner or later exhausts the potential of interested summer-school student customers.

Two final efficiencies should be mentioned. The first is the conversion from the currently mixed calendar system to a uniform semester system. Such a transition involves two ingredients: the development of a common two-term arrangement and the assurance that terms will begin and end on the same day on all campuses. This strategy should be pursued for four reasons: (a) the net balance of academic advantages and disadvantages seems to favor the semester system, except for the San Francisco campus, which is, in effect, on year-round operations already; (b) some modest economies will be gained in the long run (though a study of the magnitude of these economies should precede any changeover); (c) the common calendar would facilitate the development of intercampus collaboration on courses and academic programs; (d) such a conversion would gain public favor for the university as a gesture toward making its own operations more rational and toward cooperating and coordinating with the other public segments. There will be opposition to such a conversion, much of it bred by organizational inertia (mainly on the part of academic vice chancellors and faculty) and by faculty suspicious that the transition to the semester system will be, in effect, a thinly disguised strategy to increase faculty teaching loads.

The last efficiency is the increased use of technology and distance learning. In the eyes of some enthusiasts this is almost a magical solution; in the eyes of others it threatens to depersonalize and thereby damage the educational process more than it already is in our mass institutions. Neither view is merited, in my estimation, and the moral to be drawn from that is that technology and distance learning should be pursued to be sure, but only deliberately and selectively. Every suggested innovation ought to keep in mind the possibilities of technological facilitation and application in the foreground, and these should be implemented where possible. But under no circumstances can technological improvements be regarded as a *general* solution to the problem of student numbers, educational efficiency or cost saving.

Student Numbers and the University's Capacity to Accommodate Them   In contemplating the university's coming decade with respect to undergraduate education, it is possible to envision three levels of reality:

- The extent to which university leaders remain *flexible.* They must continue to develop plans and revise these plans, taking into account *all* the strategies reviewed at all times. They must engage in continuous estimates of the effectiveness of each strategy, scanning for its direct and indirect budgetary and educational consequences, and weighing it in the context of the impact on the university's missions. Planning thus must be regarded as a continuous and continuously revised *process* rather than the production of systematic blueprints that are then implemented.

- The way university spokespersons communicate *with the university's diverse publics.* This overlaps with the internal planning activity, but operates according to a different logic. The university must continuously reassert publicly those themes that have endowed it with legitimacy in the past—that it exists, above all, to serve the people of California; that it strives above all to be a world-class institution, excellent in all its aspects; that it is fully committed to the ideals of social justice and the full incorporation of diverse groups into California's economy, polity, and society. The university also needs to communicate to the larger public that it is, indeed, a public and publicly responsible institution; that it is committed to the pubic good; that it is forever seeking to change in order to improve itself; that it is an economy-minded institution and a responsible recipient of state funds.

- The way history *actually* will unfold. This level is much less neat—or if one prefers, it is messier. It is a battle that is annually renewed and fought out on multiple fronts with multiple strategies: the university will argue for increased funds; it will nudge fees up as it can; it will plead poverty, desertion by faculty, and decline of quality; it will cut programs and costs where it can, recoup other funds where it can; it will engage in some off-loading and some intercampus and intersegmental cooperation; it will pursue some internal reforms; and, above all, it will keep its eye out for new opportunities of support from its supporting constituencies—the federal government, the foundations, and private donors.

In a nutshell, the first level of reality is that of pursuing organizational rationality within the university; the second is that of cultivation of the university's image among its publics; the third is operating within the ongoing actualities of history. The first calls primarily for pubic deliberation in planning; the second calls for responsible communication and the management of rhetoric; the third calls for a deployment of the first two levels, but above all the expediency, pragmatism, and the capacity to adapt continuously to the university's changing environment. It is necessary to remain active on all three levels at all times; and it is important to recognize that they are separate, and not to believe that any one of them is identical to either of the others.

Postscript The preceding discussion is based on the operating assumption that the University of California will remain viable as a state-supported institution, that is, will derive a significant portion of its budgetary support from the State of California. This is probably the most realistic assumption for the foreseeable future. However, if the decline in state resources continues, then the university should be prepared to take the lead in the resolution of what is and will become an increasingly glaring contradiction: between the state's forever *diminishing* financial involvement in the university's affairs, on the one hand, and the university's continuing and possibly *increasing* administrative and political accountability to the state on the other. To paraphrase the "taxation without representation" slogan of the American Revolution, this situation promises to become one of "accountability without support." Such a contradiction is already at hand, and it may intensify in the future. If so, then something more than a series of pragmatic adaptations is called for; what will be needed is a fundamental negotiation and redefinition of the constitutional status of the university. It is not in the interest of the state or its officials to call attention to this contradiction; the university will have to do so and to play an active role in the redefinition of its economic-political-legal environment so that it can live more consistently and comfortably in that environment.

Problem Area #2: The Uncertain Future Environment of Research Funding

About two years ago a meeting of high-level administrators and faculty—mainly but not exclusively in the natural sciences—was held at the American Academy of Arts and Sciences. (It was the planning meeting or what eventuated in the *Daedalus* issue and subsequent book on the future of the major research university—see chapter 4.) The tone of that meeting was one of gloom and doom; everyone spoke as though the end of the Cold War was some kind of disaster, in that it signaled the end of the Vannevar Bush, endless frontier, "big science" era, and that the way of life of the contemporary major research university, derived ultimately from the Cold War, was coming to an end.

That dirge was, of course, exaggerated. My view is that the 1990s will be a very painful transition *from* big science justified almost reflexively by a mentality derived from threats to the nation *to* scientific research justified and supported by a different set of rationales. The country and the world will continue to produce a sufficient number of technological and social problems that merit understanding through research and demand the application of systematically produced knowledge. Furthermore, university based science will remain a solidly institutionalized medium to produce that knowledge. However, at least in this transition period, and perhaps longer into the future, universities—including the University of California—should expect to experience the following effects:

- We will witness an era of flat funding—declining in some areas and rising in others—in contrast to the pattern of growth in support of scientific research that has been experienced, with pulsations, over the past four decades.

- We will also witness a period of fumbling for new justifications—on the part of supporters and supported alike—for governmental funding for scientific research. The current salience of talk about "national needs," "international competitiveness," and "problem-oriented" research is, in part, a reflection of that search for justifications. None of these justifications has yet gained the magical status of the national-defense-in-the-Cold-War logic (including especially the post-Sputnik veneration of science and technology), and some ambivalence continues to tinge all of them.

- As a result of that ambivalence, funding agencies will place stricter and more detailed demands on applicants to justify (and report the results of) funded research. For the same reason, it is difficult to anticipate any return of generous indirect costs on funded research.

- The University of California in particular will cooperate in an ongoing search to justify continuing—or better, not discontinuing—the funding of the national laboratories, and, correspondingly, an ongoing effort to generate formulas that define their missions.

All these efforts will create difficulties for the university—in the first instance because they imply a flat or diminished inflow of resources from federal sources. In addition, however—and less obvious—the changed research environment may intensify a latent but already existing political cleavage between "entrepreneurs" and "conservatives" within the university. The first are administrators and faculty who appreciate the need for opportunism in seeking justifications for research funding, however tortured that search may become—in response to the changing "priorities" generated by political administrations in Washington. The second group are those administrators and faculty who regard the "entrepreneurs" as "sellouts" or "faddists" and insist on the same kind of freedom on the part of investigators to define and pursue scientific research as they had in the (perhaps imaginary) past.

Whatever the vicissitudes of external research funding, we may expect no weakening in the drive of the University of California to continue as a world-class research institution. One reason for this is that all the campuses will continue to be driven by the research-dominated pastern of academic rewards and prestige that became so firmly consolidated during the Cold War era. As indicated earlier, many if not most faculty believe that the budgetary battering of the early 1990s constitutes a difficult phase, a phase to be "toughed out," and that in the near future there will be a return to happier times.

A second reason for this drive for a continued research emphasis is internal to the university. Despite protestations to the contrary, and despite lip-service to the idea of "campus specialization," the motive to compete with and ultimately become like the Berkeley and Los Angeles—and, increasingly, the San Diego—campuses will not lose force, and the faculties and administrations of the other campuses will continue to be motivated by this goal. Furthermore, that motivation will continue to be translated into a demand for campus equity with respect to graduate training programs, graduate enrollments, and research facilities. The smaller campuses will no doubt experience repeated frustrations in their efforts, but this will not diminish their enthusiasm for graduate and research opportunities if the slightest hope for success is perceived.

Problem Area #3: An Evolving Definition of "Service"?

Recall the interesting sequence about the university's service mission that began at the long-term planning retreat in Fall 1993 and continued through this academic year. At that retreat two "service-entrepreneurial" chancellors—Ray Orbach and Karl Pister—and their associates pressed hard for upgrading the service mission in the university's organization and reward system. Reflecting the discussions, the theme of the unity of research-teaching-service was vary salient in the report on the Retreat. Even at the retreat itself some faculty apprehension—mainly in the remarks of Professor Stephen Cox of the San Diego campus—was expressed. The main themes of that apprehension were that such a commitment would compromise the university's independence and make it the servant of external demands (including fads) and that "service" cannot be readily distinguished from political advocacy, which the university should not reward. During the months that followed the retreat the "service" issue proved to be the most controversial in the report of the retreat, drawing hostile and strident faculty reactions from both the San Diego and the Los Angeles campuses, reactions that stressed the same themes.

In reality, the controversy over the place of service in the university is another version of the between the "conservative" and "entrepreneurial" interests mentioned above. It is, furthermore, the identical conflict that appeared after the appearance of the "Pister report" on faculty rewards in 1991. That report called for greater emphasis on teaching *and* service in evaluating faculty for advancement and promotion. It touched off a storm of controversy, and while it has resulted in some formal changes in personnel procedures on various campuses, these have been grudging, and the extent of the actual modifications in the practices of committees on academic personnel is unknown.

The committees on academic personnel are also the bastion of defense against upgrading the mission of service, while its advocates are found among some campus administrators, deans, and faculty in professional schools and some individual faculty who are active in service. The idea of giving salience to "service" thus activates a number of long-standing cleavages in the university—between administrators and faculty, between Arts and Sciences and professional schools, and possibly others.

However, merely because the university came to a standoff over the idea of upgrading service this year does not mean that the issue will go away. As long as the federal government and its granting agencies are thinking in terms of making supported research consistent with "national needs" and as intractable social problems persist, we will witness a periodic emphasis on the service mission, because service from the university is what the larger society demands under those conditions.

We may also witness, in the coming years, a shift in the idea of service in the direction of dealing with *social* problems. In his presidential remarks at the meetings of the National Academy of Sciences in April 1994, Bruce Alberts pointed to a number of visible and pressing "problems" to which he believed "science" and "scientific knowledge" are relevant. His actual list of "problems" contained mainly social problems—crime, health, poverty and inequality, racial and ethnic conflict, for example. While Alberts did not define it as such, he was presenting a new rationale for support of social science. However, he did not make explicit that he might be signaling a shift away from "technological" applications of physical and life science concerns and toward behavioral and social science concerns.

This balance among types of knowledge is, of course, very much up in the air, and will no doubt be a subject and debate within the National Academy of Sciences and on the larger Washington scene for years to come. It will also be part of the University of California's efforts to define its own situation with respect to the its service mission.

Concluding Remark

If a common theme emerges from this discussion of three areas of "looming problems," it is that in the coming years the university is going to be less the master of its own destiny in its major decisions—teaching, research, and service—than in previous decades. This will result from the intensification of interest and involvement of groups external to the university. This is not to predict that the university will become "hostage" to society, but it will have to engage in a prolonged, continuous, and difficult struggle to strike new and ever-changing balances between its own institutional autonomy and self-direction on the one hand, and reacting responsibly to the larger society on the other.

SECURING INSTITUTIONAL FLEXIBILITY

Two contradictory views of the major American research universities— including the University of California—have some currency nowadays:

- The American research universities are flexible, able to adapt their structures and programs to changing historical circumstances. This view is put forward mainly by historians of higher education such as Sheldon Rothblatt, who rests his conclusion largely on an examination of the history of American universities and on a comparison of that history with that of the traditional universities of various European countries.

- The American research universities are barnacled by inertia and incapacity to adapt. That inertia is putatively based on the conservative culture of academics, institutional self-satisfaction bred by occupying a highly esteemed and privileged position in society, and the unresponsiveness of institutions that have become bureaucratized. It was the perception of such inertia that led Chancellor Atkinson to observe—at the retreat on long-term planning in September, 1993— that the main challenge facing the University of California was to be able to "position itself" to adapt to continuously and radically changing circumstances. Moreover, those who stress the university's inertia usually have in mind two points of comparison: (a) the real or perceived sluggishness of the university in responding to urgent needs for dramatic change imposed by a critical budgetary situation and a deteriorating public image; or (b) some dramatic instance of radical change (for example, "downsizing," restructuring management) witnessed in some *other* (usually the corporate) sector.

There is reason to believe that both characterizations may be correct, because the respective points of comparative reference for each are different. Despite this observation it is apparent that the last five years—and probably the next five or more—have drawn more attention to the problem of inertia, largely because of the painful budgetary shortfalls and the equally painful prospect of reducing or removing established and entrenched programs and units. Accordingly, this final section of the memorandum will concentrate on means of increasing institutional flexibility in the university.

Atkinson's characterization of the problem should not suggest that the *whole* institution needs to position itself for change. Much of what is great in the University of California—the conduct of basic research, for example—is so because it does *not* change with every shift in the winds but maintains a sense of self-direction. The points of inertia are selective, and the problem of maintaining flexibility should, accordingly be defined according to specific areas, structures, and procedures. Among these, the following appear to merit closest attention over the coming years:

The Academic Senate

Some commentators on the higher-education scene—notably Clark Kerr—have argued that the faculty is the most conservative of all groups in the university. It is hard to assess the literal truth or falsity of this statement, but it is possible to single out a number of specific reasons—both cultural and structural—that make for nonreceptivity to change on the part of faculty in the University of California:

· The faculty finds itself comfortably situated in an academic world
  that stresses high rewards based mainly (though not exclusively)
  on prestige gained through recognition of published scholarship,
  and either resists or attempts to undermine effort to shift that
  reward system.

- The faculty is jealous of its high status in the university, and resists any change that threatens to diminish or encroach on that status.

- As a rule, the faculty is institutionally defined as "reactive" rather than "proactive" in its governance role. Indeed, the very idea that faculty is to be "consulted" suggests the notion of "reactive." As a result of this general expectation, the faculty comes to define itself as kind of "veto group" or "watchdog" rather than an initiating body. As such, it may easily become a kind of seat of institutionalized distrust of administrators, especially those who want to change things.

- Despite its relative political passivity, the faculty is extremely powerful and can hold a chancellor hostage by the residual, seldom-used, but nonetheless potent threat to express no-confidence. Every chancellor knows that among the greatest threats to his or her administrative existence is to lose the support or incur the active opposition of the campus faculty.

- The Academic Senate is thought to be some kind of conservative "establishment" that does not represent the rank and file of the faculty. This view is most frequently expressed at moments of frustration by administrators—at both the campus and the systemwide levels. Evidence cited for this point of view includes the age of senate officials, their "white male" complexion, and the "undemocratic" process by which they are selected.

- The principles and organization of the Academic Senate are such that sluggishness is built into shared governance. The routine expectation that every decision that affects the faculty should be reviewed by faculty—however important for assuring consensus—constitutes an extra step and delays execution and implementation; faculty bodies that must be consulted meet infrequently, which also occasions delays; the annual turnover of faculty committee members is very high, which means that much faculty and administrative time and effort must be taken up in socializing and familiarizing faculty with the issues at hand and what shared governance entails. Within this general characterization, specific illustrations can be pinpointed—for example, the evidently ineffective functioning of the systemwide Academic Senate committee on committees.

- The coexistence of campus-based divisional and systemwide senate machinery (academic council, academy assembly) makes for further torpor and awkwardness. At a minimum, the systemwide senate reviews constitute extra steps and delay in the consultative process. Perhaps more serious, the systemwide senate interacts simultaneously with its own divisions and with the office of the president and seldom interacts with chancellors and vice chancellors, which helps account for their general suspicion and dislike of the academic council.

This list of obstacles is formidable. Of course, not every one of the assertions may be true as stated; many of them reflect received homilies and are subject to qualification; and not every item is a source of conservatism on every occasion. Taken together, however, these attitudes and structures represent a node of political inflexibility, however valuable they may be from other standpoints—for example, guaranteeing or enhancing the academic quality of decision making.

How can this range of forces making for conservatism and slowness of change be reformed while still maintaining the positive ingredients of shared governance? This question is one of the most difficult of all, for two reasons: (a) some of the forces mentioned are based on strongly held cultural attitudes, which are strongly resistant to change, even when structural arrangements are altered; (b) the faculty—through its governance role in the Academic Senate—has, over time, gained a solid territorial hold on its delegated powers and patterns of consultation; as a result, these have come to have the status of constitutional rights, and any effort to alter them from outside (i.e., by regents or administrators) comes to be defined as an assault on the faculty itself.

In light of these institutional facts, any deliberate reform of senate arrangements is difficult, and unilateral reform by an administration is virtually impossible. My own view is that the best road to reform is for the systemwide administration to challenge—by posing a number of direct, specific questions—the Academic Senate *itself* to undertake a constitutional review of its role in governance, at both the campus and systemwide levels. The actual challenge would best be issued by the academic planning council (if it can persuaded) because it is a joint administration-faculty body that has enjoyed legitimacy in its brief history. It also strikes me that such a challenge could be timed to coincide with the work (perhaps with the report) of the proposed commission on structure and governance in the University of California. Such timing would lend force and credibility to the challenge—the implied reasoning being that if the administration is willing to undertake such a fundamental examination of itself, the faculty should be willing to do so as well.

Establishing and Assuring the Vitality of Mechanisms of Institutional Responsiveness

During the past several positive steps have been taken, each intended to increase the capacity of the University of California to respond to changing circumstances:

- The administration and Academic Senate have cooperated to construct machinery to effect the transfer, consolidation, discontinuation, and disestablishment (called TCDD) of academic programs and units, and some decisions of this kind have been taken, though not without pain. Previously the entire structure and procedures of both administration and senate were oriented only to developing new programs and reviewing ongoing ones.

- On the basis of recommendations by the transition team, the academic planning council has been established, is consolidating its program and procedures, and has undertaken some specific projects related to planning. One of the felicitous decisions made by the APC is that its function is to consider and recommend on general policy issues and *not* to review and approve or disapprove decisions relating to specific programs and units. (Machinery for this is already in existence elsewhere in the senate and the administration, and to have the APC doing it would simply involve it in repetitive, detailed work.)

- One accomplishment of a subcommittee of the APC has been to create a format for simplifying and accelerating (sometimes dramatically) the various procedures for reviewing academic programs and units. If effected, these changes will scarcely create headlines, but they will be a far-reaching and effective set of reforms.

Although the university should be congratulated on these reforms, it is also important, first, to assure that they remain in place and retain their capacities, and, second, to press on to further reforms of the same kind.

With respect to the first requirement, it may be helpful to identify the major ways in which these lines of reform could be undermined:

· The machinery for TCDD could be permitted to atrophy, particularly if the university experiences a season of more ample budgetary support. History provides a lesson in this regard. In the early 1980s, when the university experienced two years of diminished budgetary support, President Saxon issued some policy guidelines relating to TCDD. Being new, these guidelines were hotly debated in both in administrative and senate circles, and the senate entered into a protracted struggle over whether academic tenure applied only to one campus or was a universitywide privilege. (The issue was an offshoot, of particular interest to the faculty, of the "disestablishment" discussion—what happens to faculty members when their units are disestablished.) In any event, when better budgetary times returned the entire subject of TCDD was shelved immediately and more or less forgotten. In the 1990s, with a longer and deeper crisis, the university has actually established machinery for TCDD. But the earlier episode reminds us how easy it is to forget when cloudy skies clear. Forgetting again would in fact be a misfortune, because a truly adaptive institution of higher education should be prepared to transfer, consolidate, discontinue, and disestablish programs in *both* bad and good times, as considerations of academic quality and efficiency so indicate.

· In the brief history of APC we have heard some suggestions that that body should become involved in the review of specific units and programs (for example, the restructuring of professional schools at UCLA, the campus site for administering the Intercampus Arts Program). In both cases the APC considered only the general issues involved and did not undertake standard academic reviews. This is worth mentioning, because the APC stands in constant danger of taking on the role of academic monitoring and academic reviewing (as the academic program and planning review board did and as the universitywide committee on planning and budget does), simply because that role is so comfortable for academics. But if the APC is to remain an effective body, it must continue to focus its attention on general policy and planning issues.

• As indicated, the suggested procedures for streamlining and accelerating reviews of academic units are important reforms. In this area, too, however, there exist bureaucratic tendencies for the reviewing parties involved continuously to seek more information and to review things more thoroughly—if for no other reason than to justify their organizational role—and thus to work toward barnacling the review process once again.

One needs to insist continuously, then, that effective, efficient, and streamlined arrangements remain that way. The paradox involved in stating this principle, of course, is that the first thing that comes to mind is to create some kind of machinery for guaranteeing and monitoring simplicity, a measure which, on its face, creates more complexity and defeats the original organizational intent. Perhaps the best way to achieve the desired effect is to conduct periodic reviews of administrative structures and procedures, without creating standing machinery to do this.

The university should also take a continuing interest in new measures to push effectiveness and efficiency forward. One line comes to mind, a line mentioned by one of the task forces of the transition team: articulating the rhythm of the academic review of academic programs and units with the annual budgetary cycle. (Reviews of academic personnel are certainly so geared, because advancements, promotions, and other actions come into effect once a year, i.e., when the new budgetary year begins.) At present, reviews of academic programs and units are conducted more or less without reference to the budgetary cycle, which makes for difficulty in the timely implementation of reviews. A great deal of imagination may be required to improve on this situation, but if program and review cycles and budgetary cycles are brought into a better relation with one another, this would contribute greatly to the administrative rationality of the university.

Two final points follow; they are raised with a slight tinge of caution on my part, because they are no doubt so obvious. Their obviousness is matched only by their importance, so they are included.

Ensuring the Flow of Business in the Systemwide Administration

The systemwide administration is unmistakably a bureaucracy, and for that reason should be expected to manifest the following *generic* features of a bureaucracy:

- Its division and is people will tend to develop a jurisdictional posture to their spheres of assigned responsibility and competence and will resist intrusion into those spheres on the part of others.

- Issues and projects that are not properly tracked can die a quiet, unnoticed death in the organizational maze.

- Materials may be written and dutifully circulated but their impact on action may be negligible or nonexistent if there is no active follow-up on where responsibility for acting on or implementing them. People in a bureaucracy pursue their careers *within* the bureaucracy and for that reason take an interest in office politics, status-striving, and status-symbolization—processes that on some occasions divert both people and the organization itself from the organization's purposes and activities.

In addition to these generic characteristics, the systemwide administration of the University of California has several peculiarities that also make for sluggishness or paralysis:

- The lines of authority between the systemwide administration and the individual campuses are *in principle* hierarchical (i.e., reporting relations), but these lines are so loosely defined that the *de facto* relations between systemwide and the campuses are a mix of persuasion, negotiation, cooperation, and resistance.

- The total organization of the University of California (one center, nine campuses) is geographically far-flung, so it should expect more problems of communication than organizations that are more concentrated.

- Staff members of the universitywide administration are responsive not only to those to whom they report but also to various other constituencies with whom they routinely deal (campus vice chancellors, provosts, and deans), budgetary officers faculty groups (including senate committees), student groups, and so on. Long-standing relations of mutual understanding, trust, loyalty, and affection are often established between universitywide staff and representatives of these constituencies. This means that the potential for the staff to be caught "between" pressures from different sources is always present.

All these features can make for organizational paralysis. The only thing that can be said about minimizing them—because so many of them seem intrinsic to the university's organizational life—is that vigilance in tracking issues and keeping them alive must remain high. I have noted a healthy tendency among some top administrators frequently to pose the following types of questions: "Where does this go next?" "Where are we now on this issue?" "Who is going to follow up?" These kinds of questions are always essential. And they reflect a preoccupation that should be communicated to those in positions of responsibility at lower levels of the organization.

Thinking Opportunistically

Earlier in the this memorandum, when discussing the core issue of the relationship between access and resources, I indicated that the actualities of institutional life (both past and future) dictate that there is no such thing as definitive long-term planning or long-term solutions to be realized. Dealing with the access-resources problem has had and will continue to have a hit-and-miss character; it will involve year-by-year, month-by-month, perhaps even day-by-day adaptations, re-ordering of strategies, and re-orienting of policies as exigencies and opportunities shift. The moral drawn was that whereas planning is essential as an ongoing enterprise, opportunism has to be the actual name of the game in the survival of the university.

That point can be generalized: if it is true that—as argued above—the history of American higher education manifests a remarkable flexibility and adaptability, those effects have resulted because leaders of higher education have taken advantage of shifting opportunity structure and thus protected or enhanced their institutional positions. (Incidentally, those effects also go a long way in explaining the somewhat jerrybuilt, historically accumulated, complex structures that universities manifest; they "blister" on themselves as opportunities permit.) This, then, is the paradox: the formal, often-voiced ideology of a university is that it deals with the "timeless"—the discovery and generation of knowledge and the transmission of that knowledge to new generations of young people who will be institutional leaders and responsible citizens. In fact, the actual practice is a perpetual, adaptive scramble for resources and other opportunities, a fashioning of temporary compromises with society so that the institution can survive, be supported, and carry on its major missions.

The successful administration of a university thus seems to rest on a creative combination of (a) keeping academic quality always in the forefront; (b) regarding as inviolable the fundamental academic values of the institution such as academic freedom, objective of inquiry, intellectual civility, and formal political neutrality; (c) maintaining a stance of responsiveness to the major clients of the university—students, their parents, and the public spokespersons for them; (d) pursuing continuously new possibilities for resources in the university's shifting environment of opportunities. With respect to the last, it should not be the occasion for embarrassment—indeed, it should be a moment for applause—if the university "structures in" the capacity and the personnel to seek resources aggressively and imaginatively (for example, in the effort better to seek and exploit changing research opportunities nationally, as is part of the charge of the new vice provost for research). In any event, university administrators should be reminded that they should take seriously their long-standing commitment to independence from society. They should be independent, of course, and continue to insist on the sacred and timeless, but it has to be recognized that they are institutions in and supported by society, and must dedicate much of their energy to cultivating that support.

PART FOUR

Marrying Analysis and Action

EIGHT

Report of the Commission on Education (1981)

IN 1980 THE GRADUATE SCHOOL of Education on the Berkeley campus was in a disheveled state. It had experienced several years of alternative neglect and hounding by the campus administration; it had been reviewed harshly several times; it had failed to secure effective leadership; and it was granted marginal status on the campus and nationally. At something of a loss, the campus administration commissioned another major Academic Senate review. As recent chair of the Academic Senate's Committee on Educational Policy, I was asked to chair that commission. This chapter is the text of our report.

The main recommendation of the report—to discontinue the school in its present form but to give renewed priority to the study of education in general on the Berkeley campus—was something of a bombshell. When I met with Chancellor I. Michael Heyman to give a verbal presentation before the report was released, he turned ashen. He explained that it was not politically possible in the State of California to discontinue the only public university graduate school of education in Northern California. Nor did the faculty of the school appreciate the report. For a long time I took care not to frequent the northwest corner of the campus, where the school was housed. (I am still occasionally referred to as the man who wanted to kill the School of Education.) The powerful Committee on Budget and Interdepartmental Relations endorsed the report, and some preliminary inquiries were made about locating the school's faculty members elsewhere on the campus. In the end, however, the main response to the report was to search for and appoint an aggressive dean, who did in fact initiate some important reforms. That dean subsequently informed me that although he was not friendly to the final recommendations of the report, he consulted it frequently as a policy guide.

THE CHARGE TO THE COMMISSION

In the Winter quarter of 1981 the Chancellor's Office of the University of California, Berkeley, appointed this commission, with an open-ended request that we offer a diagnosis of and suggest policies and strategies for the future of the Graduate School of Education on this campus.

Our appointment was precipitated by a dramatic crisis of leadership in the school, a crisis to which we will return from time to time. But by all measures the school has been a troubled academic body for a very long time. We have been unable to discover in living memory a period when the school enjoyed anything other than diminished prestige and second-class citizenship. Nor have we been able to discover any historical periods of really forceful and visionary administrative leadership of the school.

Those unhappy historical circumstances continue to the present, and, if anything, the school's troubles have mounted during the past decade. The most telling symptom of those troubles, moreover, has been the parade of studies and reviews by administrative and faculty committees since 1974. A comprehensive review of all Schools of Education in the University of California system was submitted in 1976 by a subcommittee of the Academic Planning and Program Review Board (chaired by Dean Earl F. Cheit). A short report on the Berkeley School of Education was prepared by a subcommittee of the campus Committee on Academic Planning in 1978. In the same year a very ambitious review was conducted by an ad hoc committee of the Graduate Council (chaired by Professor Stanley Berger). This report received extensive review, comment, and elaboration by the Committee on Budget and Interdepartmental Relations in 1978, by the Graduate Council in 1979, and by the Committee on Educational Policy in 1980. Although the foci of these various reviews differed, they carried a consistently negative tone, describing the school as programmatically fragmented, lacking a coherent intellectual mission, wanting in administrative leadership, checkered if not inadequate with respect to faculty quality, and suffering from neglect on the part of the central campus administration. (A summary of the recommendations of the Cheit committee relating to the Berkeley campus and a summary of the findings and recommendations of the Berger committee are found in appendix 1 and appendix 2.)

Although some efforts have been made in the school to respond positively to a number of specific items in the reviews, its situation in the past decade or so has not been conducive to imaginative or aggressive innovation. Faced with dramatic reductions in enrollment (occasioned mainly by a collapse in the market for teachers) and with a campus administration that refused to authorize replacements for retirements and resignations, the school's faculty declined steadily from a total of 49 FTE in 1967–68 to its current level of approximately 38 (the number of non-ladder teacher supervisors also declined from 33 in 1971 to approximately 12 at the present time). Since the resignation of Dean Merle Borrowman in 1977, the school has had four acting deans (each with a one-year appointment) with the certain prospect of a fifth for 1981–82.

The campus administration's search for a permanent dean in the late 1970s was prolonged and languid. Under instructions to seek leadership outside the school, the search committee turned up a list of six candidates, all of which were deemed unacceptable by the central administration. Subsequently re-instructed to search internally, the committee eventually recommended a member of the committee itself, Professor Robert Karplus of the Department of Physics. The administration's appointment of Professor Karplus was heralded as providing a genuine opportunity for a "turn-around" in leadership for the school. Professor Karplus did in fact submit an ambitious proposal for the future development of the school, but within a matter of weeks before he was to assume official responsibilities as dean (Winter quarter, 1981), he precipitously tendered his resignation-in-advance in a dispute with the campus administration concerning the level of faculty resources to be provided to the school. The resignation immediately reactivated and underscored the school's troubled, drifting state.

This commission's charge, then, arose in a context of short-term crisis superimposed on a whole family of long-term, unsolved difficulties. The actual wording of the charge is as follows:

> The Commission is charged to review the question of how the study of Education, both as a field of scholarship and as an area of professional practice, should be pursued on the Berkeley campus. This will involve

an assessment of the status and potentials of present programs at Berkeley, as well as their priorities and proposed direction. The Commission should not feel constrained by our present campus organization for such studies but should consider a variety of organizational models and their consequences so that we make the best use of our resources, both to advance our knowledge of the educational process and to meet the educational needs of the State of California. To this end, the Commission is encouraged to consult with creative, knowledgeable people in this field.

As indicated, this charge is a very open-ended one. In light of this, the members of the commission felt it essential to determine early what kinds of activity we would *not* undertake:

- We would not constitute ourselves as a full-dress committee of review (on the model of the Berger committee), largely because the school has been amply if not overreviewed in the past six or seven years, and because we lacked both the time and staff resources to complete such a study.

- We would not attempt any systematic appraisal of Berkeley's School of Education in a universitywide context. We realize that altering the programs or status of that school might well carry implications for building, altering, or discontinuing programs in education on other campuses, but to analyze these implications and recommend courses of action to the universitywide administration falls beyond our charge.

- We would not constitute ourselves as a search committee for new leadership in the School or elsewhere on the campus. This is the legitimate responsibility of the campus administration, which has established mechanisms for conducting personnel searches. We will, however, offer some observations on the topic of leadership in general.

- We would not constitute ourselves as a body to evaluate or intervene in current personnel actions (appointment and promotion of faculty, for example) and conflict situations (for example, the grievance of several supervisors against the administration), both of which are the proper responsibilities of other agencies.

On a more positive note, we determined to submit an analysis of the long-term and short-term situation (including both constraints and opportunities) confronting the School of Education, to outline a series of possible options for future policies and strategies, and to submit a reasoned statement of preferences among these options.

In carrying out our charge we have consulted the volumes of study and critical review of the school; specific documents and data supplied by the administration of the school; documents and studies of a number of leading schools of education in other universities; and other miscellaneous publications on education and schools of education. In addition we have interviewed a number of persons knowledgeable about the School of Education and education generally: Professor Geraldine Clifford, acting dean and departmental chairman in the School of Education, and Professor Martin Trow, director for the Center for Studies in Higher Education—both named as special consultants to the commission by the vice chancellor; former dean-designate Robert Karplus; Professor George Strauss, former member of the Committee on Budget and Interdepartmental Relations; former Chancellor Albert Bowker; former President Clark Kerr; Dean Earl F. Cheit of the School of Business Administration; Mr. Harry Judge, director of the Department of Educational Studies in Oxford University, who is undertaking a study of graduate schools of education at Harvard, Stanford, UCLA, Wisconsin, Columbia, and Chicago, all recognized as leading centers of their kind in this country; Dean J. Myron Atkin of the Stanford School of Education; a group of faculty members from the School of Education, most of whom were members of the select committee of that school, appointed on a temporary basis after the resignation of dean-designate Karplus—Lyman Glenny, James Gray, James Guthrie, and William Rohwer; a group of graduate students from the school, each representing one of its divisions— Julia Dickinson (applied social research and humanistic studies), Ira Glick (research and curriculum development), Abbey Heydman (higher education, finance, and school administration), Don Leu (language and reading development), and Virginia Neuhoff (educational psychology); and a few others interested in our activities. All these people gave generously of their time and frankly of their knowledge and viewpoints, and we appreciate their participation in our work. Andrew G. Jameson, assistant to the vice chancellor, provided exceptional staff service to the commission.

Past and current observers of American education have consistently pointed out how important an institution it is in this country, how it has spread more rapidly at all levels than in any other industrial society, and how truly "popular" it is in terms of the masses who have access to it. True as these reflections may be, they do not take account of an abiding ambivalence of American public opinion toward education—an ambivalence that reflects itself in a combination of high hopes extended and low status accorded to that institutional endeavor.

Historically, political leaders and the public have held out the greatest diversity of expectations for formal education: to train citizens in republican virtue; to assure civility and order in society; to help train a disciplined industrial labor force; to keep the idle youth off the streets; to Americanize immigrants; to assure social mobility; to help best the Soviets in the conquest of space; and to help right a multitude of racial, ethnic, and sexual injustices. In a word, education has always been regarded as "a sort of universal solvent for the problems of the polity."[1] However, since problems of the polity are never solved in any complete sense but rather are dealt with sporadically and imperfectly, it is probably in the nature of the case that education has always carried with it a burden of disappointment, frustration, and hostility emanating from those who have endowed it with such hopes.

Possibly because of the recurring "public" missions of education, it has mainly been established as a public institution (notwithstanding the persistence of substantial independent and parochial school sectors in the primary and secondary levels, and a substantial private sector in the postsecondary level). As part and parcel of this public institution, educators as professionals have been traditionally less "free" than other liberal professions such as law, medicine, and engineering with respect to public involvement in and regulation of their affairs. With the exception of professors at the postsecondary level, educators are regarded as less prestigious in the public eye than most other professionals.[2] In keeping with this position in the status hierarchy, educators tend to receive lower salaries and to be recruited from more modest social origins than many other professionals.

As an institution education may be more troubled at the present time than at any moment in its history. The primary, secondary and postsecondary levels—at different times—have faced an overwhelming pressure to grow in order to accommodate enormously expanded cohorts of youth associated with the "baby boom" of the late 1940s and early 1950s, only to face subsequent stagnation if not contraction with subsequent cohorts (and presently to face pressures to expand once again as the children of the baby-boom generation swell the ranks of those marching through the early phases of the life-cycle). Education at all levels, moreover, has faced serious financial constriction for at least fifteen years, associated with increasing demands from other quarters on strained public revenues. At the same time, the schools, particularly at the primary and secondary levels, are faced with a continuing repository of social problems, such as violence, racial and cultural heterogeneity of clientele, desertion of clientele to the private sector (likely to accelerate if voucher arrangements are adopted), and a general decline of public confidence.

We introduce this sketch of societal characteristics and problems of education because they are echoed in important ways in those corresponding institutions in the academy—schools of education—that have been responsible historically for creating and reproducing those cadres of professionals who staff and manage much of the educational establishment.

Historically, the "normal schools" and "state teachers colleges" lived in the shadow of the more prestigious private and state universities; indeed, it was the marginal status of those institutions that, in part, motivated their long struggle to achieve some kind of parity by becoming general "state colleges" and eventually "state universities." Universities that have established schools of education have had different academic pecking orders (for example, the long dominance of the humanities in the Ivy League schools; the strong place of the sciences in many of the land grant institutions), but in all cases schools of education have found themselves on the lower end of that order. Even in those cases where schools of education have lifted themselves to national and international prominence *as education schools* (for example, Harvard, Stanford), they have been unable wholly to shed reputations of low standing on their own campuses, certainly in relation to academic departments in the Arts and Sciences and in relation to most other professional schools. The attitudes and evaluations of society's larger stratification system appear inevitably to be reproduced in microcosm in the university setting.

Berkeley's School of Education is no exception to this general picture, save in one respect: it does not enjoy a very high prestige in comparison with other schools of education. The Ladd-Lipset survey of 1977, based on peer ranking of quality of graduate training, revealed a national ranking of tenth, well below the ranking of most of Berkeley's other schools and academic departments in this and comparable surveys. Furthermore, almost all those who have commented on these surveys have suggested that if the "halo effect" imparted by the general status of the Berkeley campus were corrected for, the actual national ranking might be lower. Be that as it may, the situation of the Berkeley School of Education cannot be regarded as very favorable on any count, and we feel called upon to address a number of historical and contemporary reasons for this state of affairs.

We point first to a fundamental contradiction, not restricted to the Berkeley campus by any means, but one that certainly tends to confuse the mission of many professional schools, including the School of Education, and to aggravate their status and personnel problems. At the risk of oversimplifying by a shorthand formula, we might refer to this as the contradiction between the two principles of "professional service" and "Arts and Sciences." By the former we mean those outlooks and expectations associated with the principle that universities have as a major mission the staffing and servicing of those institutions that society deems important; schools of agriculture, law, business, engineering, and education—all designed to teach, train, and place some kind of professional practitioner—clearly fall under this principle. By the latter we mean those outlooks and expectations associated with the principle that universities have as a major mission the advancement of knowledge through scholarship and scientific research, assessed as more or less original and excellent by academic peers; most academic departments in the Arts and Sciences in leading universities live primarily by this principle.

One of the distinguishing features of American higher education is that—unlike Great Britain, for example—most professional training has been institutionalized *within* the universities and colleges.[3] This means that in any given institution of higher education some kind of marriage between the two principles has had to be fashioned. As might be expected, however, these marriages have varied greatly according to intimacy, dominance, conflict, and stability—both by type of professional school and type of institution of higher education. Different types of professional schools vary in prestige and in level of interaction with their campus environments. Law schools, for example, tend to have high prestige and minimal interaction with the campus community at large. Schools of engineering have relatively high status and more interaction with the rest of the campus, at least with mathematics and the physical sciences. Schools of pharmacy have both low status and minimal campus interaction. Schools of education typically have low status, as noted, but their relations with other schools and disciplines show much variation among universities and colleges.

As a general rule, professional schools in prestigious private institutions tend to be relatively independent from central administration or faculty governing bodies. They generate most if not all of their own funds, make their own admissions policies and decisions, and develop their own training programs. By contrast, professional schools in public institutions are treated like other academic departments. Budgets are allocated by the central administration, admission decisions are made centrally, and governance mechanisms provide significant constraints on their operations. The two exceptions to this picture are schools of law and medicine, where the prestige and resources of these professions have forced many universities to make major concessions and grant them greater independence.

Looking at the Berkeley campus in particular, we find that the place of the professional schools is closer to that found in the typical public university than it is to elite private institutions. Except for the law school—which has been able to establish itself as an "exception" in many respects, even including the academic calendar—courses in professional schools must be approved by a campuswide committee on courses, their graduate admissions must be approved by a central graduate division, their salaries must conform to a campuswide (indeed, universitywide) salary scale, and appointments, promotions and advancements are acted upon by a central budget committee and the central campus administration.

By virtue of these structural arrangements, Berkeley's marriage between the "professional service" and the "Arts and Sciences" principles is both forced and intimate. But in many respects the marriage is also an unequal one. Although the campus originated as a land-grant institution—with a heavy commitment to professional service—and still has schools, colleges, and programs that reflect this principle, its dominant culture is more that of the Arts and Sciences. Berkeley's main reference groups are a number of elite private institutions (Harvard, Yale, Columbia, Chicago, Princeton, and Stanford), as well as a number of other public universities (University of Wisconsin, University of Michigan) that are either dominated by or stress heavily that same culture. Historically, too, Berkeley has been inclined to export (School of Home Economics, to the Davis campus) or discontinue (School of Criminology) professional schools than Arts and

Sciences departments. And finally, despite the fact that other criteria are applied explicitly in matters of appointment, promotion, and advancement, promise and achievement in research have retained a central if not dominant place in relation to those criteria.

This combination of circumstances affecting the professional schools at Berkeley—again, in shorthand, we might refer to it as a closeness to and domination by the Arts and Sciences complex—has made for a kind of unclarity of mission, especially for a professional school like the School of Education with low academic and social prestige. Since practical training activities inevitably become less worthy when the "Arts and Sciences" principle is applied, this creates a situation in which administration and faculty of the school are forever invited *either* to turn their program and activities toward academic scholarship and scientific research (which, ironically, are often foredoomed to consignment to "second-rate" status because they are likely to be less well trained and less accomplished than their judges)[4] *or* to insist that other, more applied criteria ought to be given equal weight and legitimacy (which, ironically, often leads to the judgment that they "can't make it" according to the most important criteria and must therefore fall back on lesser criteria). The same situation tends to generate (at least) two classes of citizens with the school, those who measure up to standards of academic research and those who do not—perhaps because they are involved in the more applied aspects of training. And finally, this situation tends to encourage the school to assume a generally low profile, emerging into view only when absolutely necessary, since visibility is likely to mean that it will be hounded in the name of academic standards or made an exception in relation to those standards.

The state of affairs we have just described is only a part of the whole complex of problem areas that become manifest when the two mentalities we have described are embedded in a single institution. The uneasy and volatile relationship between basic disciplines and applied disciplines on a campus such as our own is one of those manifestations. In fact, the impetus for many types of professional schools has come initially from the discontent of those within a discipline who have primary interests in application. For example, most business schools were formed as "practical" spin-offs from departments of economics. Once having formed, however, those in the more applied enterprises on a university campus are forever looking back over their shoulders at the relevant basic disciplines of interest to them. Links to disciplinary departments are often re-forged, and many of the faculty appointed to those more applied units have received their training in the basic disciplines. Those in the resulting disciplinary subgroups, moreover, tend to be torn between attraction to the basic disciplines housed elsewhere in the university and attraction to the applied emphasis of their home professional school. (Later in the report we shall refer to one type of outcome of this tension— primary identification with the basic discipline on the part of educational psychologists.)

A second series of circumstances has led to a further diffusion if not confusion of mission for the School of Education. For a long period of time, the Berkeley campus enjoyed a position of leadership if not monopoly in respect to certification of those who were destined to become managers and educators of California's educational institutions. With the initiative and growth of both private institutions and state colleges (later state universities), this position of leadership eroded, so that only the privilege of granting the doctorate remains, and this only in relation to the state colleges and universities, not private institutions. In 1975, the entire University of California system (with five teacher-training programs) was training only 8 percent of certified teachers in the state, the state college and university system accounting for 60 percent and private institutions 32 percent.[5] This circumstance, plus the fact that market demand for teachers in general—and applications for teacher training— fell off dramatically in the 1970s and created something of a crisis for preservice teacher-training for Berkeley's School of Education (as well as others). As early as 1968 the proposal was made to reduce "preservice" education and to emphasize mid-career doctoral programs.[6] One result of this shift of emphasis was to move the school a further step away from the professional service emphasis (practical training and certification of teachers) and a step toward emphasis on academic research, as evidenced by the increasing emphasis on the doctorate. Over the years the same shift of emphasis has tended to devalue the EdD in relation to the PhD (because the former is more "practical" and is not meant to measure up to the same academic standards), and to encourage faculty members to apply the same academic standards to the EdD as to the PhD degree, thereby diminishing the difference between the two types of degree in practice.[7]

Another response to the changing academic market conditions of the 1970s was a relative shift in categories of student clientele for the School of Education. Although total enrollment and degrees granted declined on

all fronts, the fall was relatively much greater in preservice teacher education than in other divisions and programs.[8] The school compensated, as
it were, for this relative decline by providing degree programs to a more
diversified range of clienteles. This occurred particularly in the period of
the early 1970s. We will not trace the precise history of this proliferation
but will point out that at present the school has five major divisions[9] and,
within these divisions, approximately 20 separate degree and/or credential
programs (plus two doctoral programs with other departments). Many of
these degree and/or credential programs, moreover, are clearly linked to
specific occupational career-lines in the larger educational establishment.
Within educational psychology, for example, there is a Cal. Re-Ed
program, which offers an M.A. and a "severely handicapped" credential,
as well as a school psychology program (which includes a "pupil personnel
services" credential). The Applied Social Research and Humanistic Studies
Division includes degree programs in adult education and counseling
psychology. These developments have spread the school's efforts much
more widely over the map and complicate—to say the least—any attempt
to give consistent definition to the school's mission.

We cannot complete our analysis of the situation of the School of
Education, however, with this citation of a number essentially environmental conditions. Many other professional schools—and other schools
of education in particular—have experienced the same kinds of contradic-
tions, institutional competition, and demographic and financial vicissitudes that we have mentioned, but many have faced them with more vigor
and imagination, maintaining some coherence of direction, program, and
internal structure. We must cite for Berkeley, then a disturbing lack of
leadership both outside and within the School of Education. To our
knowledge, only one of the past five chancellors—going back to the early
1950s—has given priority to improving the leadership and status of the
School of Education (each conceiving other items on his agenda to be
more important or pressing); and the efforts of the one chancellor who
did try to recruit first-class national leaders were subverted by the unwill-
ingness of excellent candidates to assume the deanship. In recent years the
policy of the provost of professional schools can only be described as one
of punitive starvation, with the accompanying expectation that direction
must come from within the school or from a new dean (who either
could not be found or, when found, was ultimately unwilling to assume
the post).

Little leadership has emerged from within the school either. Eras of both expansion and contraction have been characterized by passive responses to demographic and market conditions. In particular, leadership in the early 1970s consisted of a somewhat shapeless expansion of degree programs to accommodate particular sets of clientele, and the leadership of the late 1970s, consisting of a sequence of one-year acting deans, has scarcely been in a position to initiate major changes of direction. Some modifications of program and some internal administrative changes have been made, often in response to negative criticisms ventured by reviewing bodies, but the fundamental characteristics of the school—including its fundamental problems—remain substantially unchanged.

THE CURRENT SITUATION OF THE SCHOOL OF EDUCATION

Divisional and Program Structure

In many respects these characteristics and problems may be regarded as precipitates of the past we have just reviewed. We refer first to the uncertain mission and priorities arising from the internal fragmentation of the school. Despite some efforts to centralize the governance of the school, and despite the creation of a schoolwide policy committee and some efforts to involve schoolwide participation in the supervision of graduate student research,[10] the autonomy of the divisions has increased in some respects. Each division has developed its own set of core courses, thus limiting the common exposure of students in the school as a whole to certain statistical and methodological work.[11] And in disbanding the much-criticized Teacher Education Division a few years ago, the school called for the association of all credential candidates and their supervisors within a division. (All but a handful of these candidates are now associated with the smaller Division of Language and Reading and Instructional Research and Curriculum Development.) Each division is largely responsible for the entire career of its graduate students. Every student must affiliate with a division upon enrollment, and, in order to change from one division to another, must secure the permission of both divisions. The effective power of the divisions is further revealed in former dean-designate Karplus's statement of plans for the school. A bold and radical document in some respects, the statement nevertheless called for most new directions of expansion to be carried out *within* the divisional structure, with only some modifications of divisional missions.[12]

This crystallization of the divisions into semi-independent fiefdoms has yielded a number of consequences—mostly negative, in our estimation—of which the following are the most important:

- A certain parochialism of divisional interests, with little basis for interaction—and little actual interaction—among faculty members of different divisions. The main reference groups for most of those in educational psychology, for example, is other academic psychologists outside the School of Education; specialists in language and reading have little in common with those who are engaged in training future community college administrators. As a result, the divisions tend to be self-regarding. The school has initiated certain structural arrangements designed to overcome divisional parochialism, but such structures tend to drift toward artificiality, given the lack of underlying common interests.

- A derived parochialism of students along divisional lines. Some isolation of students from one another is to be expected in any event, since such a high proportion of the students are employed full-time (26 percent) or part time (40 percent),[13] since most classes are held in the late afternoons or evenings, and since so many students have competing familial and other interests and obligations. But in addition, the divisional principle aggravates these tendencies. Students' fates are largely in the hands of the divisions' faculties with respect to advising, courses, and research supervision. In some cases—particularly in educational psychology—the requirements for course work in one division have expanded to the point of actually discouraging students from taking work in the other divisions. We also heard some reports of at least covert competition for students among the divisions, though direct evidence for this kind of assertion is understandably difficult to assemble and assess. We did discover that many students from one division know no or few students from other divisions, and the little initiative to overcome this comes from students, not faculty.

- An undermining of *general* interest in the educational process. The school has few schoolwide intellectual activities (colloquia, lectures, etc.). The divisional parochialism may also contribute to the fact that few faculty members maintain contact with individuals and groups in other academic units who are interested in research on and applications to the education process (the aforementioned tendency for the school to maintain a low profile on the campus also contributes to this). Involvement of faculty in such "obvious" places as SESAME, the educational program of the Lawrence Hall of Science, and the Center for Studies in Higher Education is less than might be expected. Few faculty have any systematic involvement in organized research units; the only exception to this statement is the educational psychology faculty, some of whom maintain links with academic psychologists and have ties with the Institute for Human Learning and the Institute of Human Development.

· An anomalous administrative situation. Formally the School of Education is a one-department school, with academic governance being divided between the dean and the chairman of the department. *De facto,* however, the divisions constitute quasi-departments. Each division selects from its numbers a speaker (formerly called chairman), who serves for a period of two years. The position is not a formal administrative appointment however, and the speakers assume their positions without requiring the approval of the dean or the chairman of the department, much less the provost for professional schools. They are, however, given either course relief or the services of a half-time research assistant, and are allocated a certain amount of secretarial support. By and large the divisions design and approve their own curricula, implement their own programs, and advise and evaluate their own students—with few and weak school-wide mechanisms or procedures for monitoring and coordinating these activities.

· Perhaps most important, a tendency to reproduce the various divisions at their proportional strengths and thereby to discourage responsiveness and innovation in the school. When groups of faculty as coherent as the divisions form, they invariably develop into politically significant interest groups, which in turn develop "gentlemen's agreements" with one another and with the school administration to the effect that when a division experiences a loss through retirement or resignation, it has a presumptive "first claim" to replace the loss by an appointment within that division. That many requests to replace have been denied (mainly by the central campus administration) does not weaken this principle, nor does it weaken the academic and structural conservatism that the principle fosters.

With respect to the degree and/or credential programs within the divisions, the school has reduced the number these from thirty-seven to approximately twenty in recent years—in part in response to outside criticisms—but almost one-third of these programs are still administered by only one or two faculty members, suggesting a continuing thinness of spread of faculty, as well as its continuing inability to "cover the waterfront" of programs that proliferated in the first half of the 1970s.

Rank, Age, and Quality of Faculty

Like so many academic units that have experienced a season of growth followed by stagnation or contraction, the school is almost completely "tenured in" and top-heavy with respect to rank. Of the thirty-eight FTE in the school, twenty-eight hold the rank of full professor, eight the rank of associate professor, and two the rank of assistant professor. (There are two senior lecturers with security of employment.) The implication of this rank structure is that the school can expect only the slightest flexibility for redirection of faculty appointments and programs through the mechanism of recapturing the positions of nonpromoted faculty.

With respect to age, the faculty is not so top-heavy. The distribution of ladder faculty is as follows:

61 and over	8
56–60	5
51–55	6
46–50	8
41–45	7
36–40	3
35 or under	1

The schedule of retirements is somewhat variable, some options being extended to each individual. Although we find Professor Karplus's and acting dean Clifford's estimate that the school could expect fourteen retirements over the next five years on the high side,[14] the figure of eight to ten, or 20 to 25 percent of the ladder faculty, seems reasonable, and yields an expectation that even though additional faculty resources may not be allocated to the school in that period, there will be considerable latitude for change in direction of faculty and programs.

Judgments of faculty quality are more difficult to come by, but the relatively low ranking of the school in national prestige surveys suggest that, collectively, the school is wanting on this score. The Berger committee, which conducted the most systematic investigation, reported academic strength in the Division of Educational Psychology and the then-existing Division of Higher Education (since, however, having lost a number of faculty members), but found most other areas academically weak on the counts of research, programs, and instruction (see appendix 2). Our own independent but less thorough review of individual faculty confirms the impression that on the average the faculty in educational psychology is academically strongest (though perhaps least interested in the professional training activities of the school), and that although there are a handful of strong and distinguished faculty members with solid national reputations and important constituencies, the majority manifests scholarly careers of modest to good contributions to traditions of research that are generally weak. Some applied projects are singled out as good to excellent, with most consistent praise given to the Bay Area Writing Project—initiated and carried out, it should be noted, by one non-ladder faculty member. Nowhere, however, even from defenders of the school, did we encounter the assertion that the school comes close to excellence, whether measured by national comparison with like units or in relation to Berkeley's general academic standards.

School Governance

From 1975 to 1977, when Dean Borrowman was partially incapacitated by an accident, and between 1977 and the present, when the deanship has been filled by a series of one-year incumbents, leadership from the Office of the Dean has been understandably weak. We believe that, in part because of this vacuum, the school has tended to "fill in" with other positions near the top. Initially an associate dean with variable duties was appointed, but in time this was changed to a chairman of the department, whose duties are defined as "internal" (recruitment, selection, evaluation of faculty and staff) as contrasted with the dean's "external" role (representing the school to campus administration, local and state constituencies, funding agencies, etc.). Over time, too, the school has established three assistant deanships, one for professional development and applied research,[15] one for student and administrative services, and one for graduate advising. In view of the fact that this structure developed during a period when the size of the faculty was reduced by 15–20 percent and when the numbers of supervisors were approximately halved, and in regarding other campus units of approximately the same size, we conclude that the school is probably now quite top-heavy administratively. Apparently some in the school itself share that view, since the assistant dean for student and administrative services is scheduled to be phased out by July 1981. Whatever other changes are contemplated for the school, then, an independent case can be made for serious review and perhaps consolidation of the formal administration.

With respect to committee structure, the school has moved from an extremely decentralized to a more centralized system, partly in response to outside criticism. Certainly the policy committee and the academic review committee were created in the context of the Berger committee report and pressure from the graduate division. In addition to these two committees, the school has a personnel committee, an affirmative action committee, and a committee on committees. Yet in our assessment, these committees do not move far enough away from the divisional structure of the school. When the formation of the policy committee was initially proposed, some faculty argued for the principle that its members be elected at large; yet after a brisk debate on the subject the divisional principle prevailed, so that the present composition of the committee is the speaker of each division, with two senate faculty elected at large, two non-senate faculty elected by non-senate faculty and two student representatives. That structure is perhaps unduly representational of established interests, providing great opportunity for veto groups to confront one another, and thereby diminishing the probability that the policy committee would focus on some larger vision for the school. The academic review, affirmative action, and personnel committees also incorporate the divisional principle, requiring that one member of each committee be chosen from each division. Only the committee on committees is elected at large, but it is bound by these compositional principles in its appointive work. From the standpoint of committee structure, then, the school is perhaps under- rather than overgoverned, since the committees are formally constructed in large part as crucibles for the representation of divisional interests.

School Morale

Given the analysis we have presented, it would be surprising if morale in the School of Education were anything other than low if not dismal. Morale is intangible, of course, and difficult to measure, but our impressions are overwhelmingly that this is the case. No single group—faculty, supervisors, students—seems satisfied with what the school is or how it operates, though the sources of their dissatisfaction are diverse. Faculty attendance at the infrequent department meetings is low, to the point of their being outnumbered by supervisors and students. Divisions and groups appear to be isolated, defensive, and in some cases distrustful of one another. Some faculty mention their own and others' tendencies to withdraw from the school psychologically and to fashion some new kind of membership circle and professional identity in other places.

OPTIONS FOR THE FUTURE OF THE SCHOOL OF EDUCATION

While our diagnosis of the historical and present situation of the School of Education differs in many respects from past reviews, our assessment of the recurrent or persisting problems is very similar. To summarize, we regard the school as a problematic academic unit on the following counts:

- It is fragmented internally on many dimensions—with respect to general intellectual mission, pedagogic programs, and meaningful intellectual discourse and academic cooperation among faculty members and teacher supervisors in the different divisions and programs.

- It is spread too thin, attempting to cover too many aspects of the educational enterprise than can be expected, given the personnel.

- As a corollary, its involvement in certain important facets of education is inadequate—examples would be science and mathematics education, and the status, role, and problems of parochial and independent schooling.

- Its involvement with other faculty personnel and academic units—including those interested in problems of education— is minimal.

- Although a minority of faculty enjoys outstanding reputations in their fields, the overall academic quality of the faculty is low by Berkeley standards.

- It has suffered from a lack of academic leadership within the school and from either passivity or punitiveness on the part of the central campus administration.

- As a result of all of the above—and other factors—its situation is one of low prestige and less-than-full academic membership on the Berkeley campus.

This list is formidable, and from time to time during our work we experienced a certain sense of hopelessness, based on the observation that the school's problems are so numerous, so enduring, and apparently so intractable that little if not nothing can be done to break into and reverse that family of vicious circles that has entrapped the School in its situation for several decades. In the end, however, and contrary to this posture of despair, we conclude that a concentrated, aggressive, and multipronged effort can lead to a great improvement in the status of teaching and research on education on the Berkeley campus. We stress, however, that this effort must be an exceptional one, and that reliance on routine campus procedures and mechanisms will yield little by way of positive change.

We proceed toward our recommendations by two steps. In this section we will lay out the most nearly complete range of options possible, including both those that others have suggested to us and those that have occurred to us in our own discussions. In listing these options, we will indicate the presumed or hoped-for consequences of each as we present it, but we shall postpone of full statement of reasons for our own recommendations until the final section of the report.

The options we now present fall under three general headings: (1) strategies designed to reduce the isolation of the school from the rest of the campus and to improve its governance; (2) strategies designed to affect the school's level of resources and types of programs, assuming a structural continuity of the school; and (3) strategies designed to discontinue or transfer programs of the school to other campus units, even to the point of discontinuing or transferring the school altogether. We regard these three families of options as standing in an ascending order of comprehensiveness—and radicalness—with respect to preserving the school's traditional structure.

Outcomes to Reduce the Isolation and Improve the Governance of the School

The study of the theory, organization, and practice of education, it could be argued persuasively, is not the preserve of a single academic unit, but is rather the responsibility of the entire campus. At the present time, there is an unfortunate division between that unit explicitly dedicated to that study and other units on the campus, even though there is a great deal of research on, and practical projects dealing with, education at all levels outside the School of Education. Three strategies are available to make for greater interaction between the school and the rest of the campus and thereby to increase greater integration in the study of education on the Berkeley campus.

1. Greater involvement of outside faculty in the School of Education. It might be required that a certain minimum number of outside faculty sit on all appointment and review committees in the school. Professor Karplus's creation of an advisory board composed mainly of outside faculty members is another helpful possibility, particularly if the board met frequently and involved itself in reviewing the school's activities in some detail. The aim of such strategies of ventilation would be to provide mechanisms for strengthening the academic quality of faculty and programs in the School of Education.

2. Greater involvement of the faculty and students of the school in other academic units. Future appointments to the faculty, as a matter of policy, could be arranged as joint, or at least reviewed simultaneously by some other department or school. Second, more systematic work outside the school could be required on the part of graduate students, whatever their divisional specialization. The school could also consider developing a series of undergraduate courses that could be of interest to a wide band of students—a general course in the comparative history of education, for example, or contemporary problems in American higher education. It is difficult to estimate the size or composition of the clientele of such courses, but they would constitute some kind of outreach, as it were, to quarters of the campus with which there is now no contact. It might be possible, finally, to develop some general courses at the graduate level that have interest to some students from other departments and schools.

3. Greater involvement of the faculty in interdisciplinary research. This strategy is a difficult one to legislate, since such involvement must inevitably be voluntary if it is to be workable. The administration might consider, however, discontinuing the research-sponsoring role of the school, thereby encouraging faculty to affiliate in greater numbers with organized research units, in which interaction among faculty and students from different disciplines transpires.

With respect to improving the internal governance of the school, we offer two options—contrasting in character—designed to ameliorate the problems arising from the anomalous divisional structure of the school.

4. Departmentalization of the divisions. This would involve reconstituting the divisions and converting into proper academic departments, along the lines of the School of Engineering or the School of Public Health. One possibility is a two-department school, one with a primarily academic emphasis, including mainly the present faculty of educational psychology, the other with a primarily applied emphasis, including the remainder of the faculty. Other, more complicated forms of organization could be contemplated. In any event, this change would give more definite authority and accountability to the chairs than the present speakers of divisions now have, give more direction to campus and curricular planning for the several units of the school, and regularize and systematize the communication between the heads of the units and the central officers of the school.

5. Discontinuation of the divisions. Alternatively, much might be gained if the divisions themselves were eliminated as quasi-departments to which different faculty members are assigned, with responsibility for programs, curricula, advising, and so forth, becoming a matter of collective school responsibility through schoolwide bodies such as an executive committee, a personnel committee, a curriculum committee, and the like. Programs for degrees and certificates might still be made available for different categories of students, but the administration of these programs would be more collective. Such an administrative change, it is hoped, would make for more responsible interaction among faculty and students in the school, and better coordination of its various programs. It might also provide a vehicle for expanding the core offerings for all students in the fundamentals of education, thereby working against the early compartmentalization into divisions that most students experience.

One final administrative option arises from our earlier observations that the school may be overadministered and that the current division of administrative responsibilities may be too rigid:

6. Increasing the flexibility and effectiveness of administration in the school. The division between external responsibility (assigned to the dean) and internal responsibility (assigned to the department chairman) has struck some as being too rigidly fixed. The corresponding suggestion has been made that the school have a dean and associate dean, with the expectation that the latter will have considerable responsibility delegated to him or her, but that delegation need not be coterminous with the duties of the chairman. The external-internal division might be one principle for delegation, but others might be envisioned as well. This structural change, incidentally, would also provide a new dean of the school with greater discretion and power, which many argue is essential if significant innovations are to be made. In addition, some have suggested that it would be desirable to consolidate the various activities associated with student services and assign them to a single assistant dean, a reform that would make the communication between school administration and students more consistent and effective.

Options Affecting the Resources and Programs of the School

Under this heading we have identified five strategies, ranging from a suggestion to work within the existing structure of resources and programs in the School of Education to a plan for the substantial infusion of both.

7. Maintenance of the status quo. The rationale for this strategy is to acknowledge that the School of Education, as it has evolved over the decades, continues to provide a valuable service to the State of California and to the profession of education by supplying training and certification to a wide range of teachers, managers, and service personnel in the educational establishment. As an institution born of and sustained by the state, it has the obligation to continue this line of service. The implications of the status-quo strategy would be to continue to adjust programs in the interests of new categories of clientele and to recruit faculty and supervisory personnel largely on a replacement basis by division and program.

8. A continuation of selective phase-out and selective highlighting within a context of a steady state of resources. This strategy calls for abandoning the attempt to "cover the waterfront" of the field of education, discontinuing some programs altogether, and moving toward selec-

tive excellence in a few high-priority fields. Administrators might determine, for example, to phase out preservice teacher training altogether, on grounds that this kind of training involves little more than duplication of a wide number of programs to be found in private institutions of higher education and in the state college and university system, as well as other university campuses. To choose another example, the school might decide to discontinue certain lines of research—in higher education perhaps—on grounds that past and anticipated attention of faculty is such that to rebuild the specialization within the school would demand too many new resources, and on grounds that there are substantial resources dedicated to the study of higher education elsewhere on the campus. In any event, whatever its decisions on phasing-out, the freed resources could be dedicated to strengthening or initiating selected programs. For example, the school might determine that placement of doctorates in schools of education ("teaching the teachers of teachers") might be the best form of leadership in the coming decades. Alternatively, it might decide to devote resources to types of education that are acknowledged to be of great importance in the decades to come—for example, science education, educational experiences of bilingual students, technology-assisted education, or the process of moral learning. Or finally, it might decide to concentrate its efforts on the development of demonstration programs for in-service educators, with the Bay Area Writing Project as a kind of model. Whatever the emphases chosen, however, this strategy assumes that programs chosen for phasing-out and programs selected for emphasis will have to be implemented on a gradual basis, since the resources of the school would not be increased and would become available only on the basis of resignations and retirements of current personnel.

9. An immediate infusion of faculty resources to attain the objectives of the strategy just described, but with the anticipation that the School of Education would, through attrition, return to its current size or perhaps even diminish in numbers over time. This strategy is really a minor variant of the strategy immediately preceding, permitting the school not only to determine the pattern of programs to be phased out and highlighted, but providing a supply of additional resources immediately—though in the end, temporarily—to build areas of strength quickly and aggressively. One feature of this strategy is that although it involves an increase in commitment of resources to the school, these would be recaptured for the central administration, perhaps within a decade.

10. Growth in order to strengthen existing coverage and programs. This strategy rests on the assumption that the teaching of and research on education must rest on a comprehensive range of programs, and that the attrition of approximately a dozen faculty FTE and approximately twenty supervisors during the past decade has crippled the School in its efforts to develop and implement those programs. Re-investing those lost resources, and perhaps even more, would permit the school to serve a wide range of constituencies, and develop a broad-gauged program of research on the fundamental psychological and social aspects of the educational process.

11. Growth in order to re-order priorities and develop new programs. This strategy is closest to that submitted by Professor Karplus in anticipation of his assuming the deanship in the School of Education. Stressing the broad areas of education as a lifetime process and the application of new technologies in education—as well as a number of other priorities— Professor Karplus envisioned the appointment of approximately twenty new faculty members (estimated as a net increase of nine FTE) between 1981 and 1986 in a variety of types of appointment to implement those priorities. This argument rests on the premise that really imaginative innovation can be achieved only with an application of new resources, in combination with the maximum possible redirection of existing resources. Under the same premise, of course, various priorities other than those suggested by Professor Karplus could be imagined.

All these options rest on the assumption that the campus administration is able to secure the highest quality of leadership to effect them. We are aware that given the vested interests—both within and outside the school—that have grown up around the current divisions, it is a challenging task to effect *any* changes that will reach far beyond minor modifications of the status quo. We will return to the topic of assuring forceful and imaginative leadership in the final section; but we wish to underscore that, for practically any strategy of change elected for the school, that kind of leadership constitutes the first and most important necessary condition for its implementation and realization.

Options to Transfer or Discontinue School Programs or the School Itself

Some have argued that the structural position of schools of education generally, and the Berkeley school in particular, is so disadvantaged and precarious that no meaningful reform is possible within that kind of professional school. The corresponding recommendations have to do with phasing out or transferring either part or all of the school. We have identified the following variants:

12. Partial redirection. The argument accompanying this strategy is that although there are programs of value in the School of Education they would better be placed in a different environment. For example, it has been argued that since the mission of the Division of Educational Psychology is, in effect, more an academic enterprise than a professional training program, it ought properly to be converted to that form; one suggestion is to transfer the faculty associated with that division to the Department of Psychology, another to establish the faculty as an independent department in the College of Letters and Science. Another possibility would be to "export" the small numbers of faculty associated with higher education to a new, campuswide doctoral program in higher education. Another possibility would be to shift the preservice teacher education program (including the supervisory staff) to another part of the campus, converting it to a special undergraduate program plus additional work necessary for certification. A corollary of this strategy of partial redirection would be a reduction in size of the School of Education, as well as an increasing specialization of its mission, perhaps in an applied direction. It might, for example, concentrate more of its efforts toward reconstituting an explicitly applied EdD for several varieties of educational careers.

13. Gradual phasing-out. This strategy would call for a halt in any appointments to replace retiring or resigning faculty members, while systematically phasing out certain of the school's programs and making an effort to reallocate faculty and supervisory personnel to staff the remaining ones. This strategy would also call for arrangements to assure that students already committed to phased-out programs could finish their certificate or degree program, but to assure that no new students be admitted to those programs. This strategy, in effect, would be to acknowledge that the Berkeley campus should not have a School of Education, but that this decision would be implemented through the attrition of faculty and the carefully monitored discontinuation of programs.

14. Accelerated redirection and discontinuation. This strategy would involve exporting as many programs as possible to other academic units and attempting to locate the residual faculty in other academic units on the Berkeley campus. We stress that the aim of this policy, as well as

the one immediately preceding, is not simply a negative one—that is, to destroy a program or a school—but rather to relocate a range of research and teaching activities in more satisfactory academic environments.

15. Administrative merger of the school. Some have argued that the accumulation of general professional schools in related areas has been an historical but not necessarily a rational process, and that consolidation of these schools would make for greater coherence. One particular suggestion came to us: that the Schools of Public Health, Social Welfare, and Education be reconstituted into a School of Human Resources, with a single dean; such a merger would give greater visibility to the complex of programs carried out in these schools and would permit some initiative and imagination in the consolidation and development of now-overlapping programs in the various schools. Other patterns for partial or complete merger could be envisioned as well, involving other schools with heavy behavioral and social science components.

RECOMMENDATIONS

We begin our recommendations by citing a number of "givens" that have framed our reasoning—"givens" that include a number of fundamental convictions and a number of reality considerations.

1. At this time in the history of the world, the nation, and the state, we can imagine few endeavors that are more urgent and worthy than the improvement of the knowledge of the educational process and the application of that knowledge to that process. Most of the nation's educational establishment—especially the public sector—suffers from a plethora of severe social problems, a paucity of resources to attack them, and dwindling public confidence; and our situation is bright by comparison with that of many other nations. We believe it irresponsible not to acknowledge and affirm this situation.

2. The University of California, Berkeley, should convert this conviction into a major institutional effort on its part during the coming decades. We voice this not only on grounds of the institution's responsibilities but also on grounds that it has the quality of intellectual and other resources to make a difference in this enterprise.

3. More particularly, Berkeley should not abandon that part of the educational mission that involves the training of teachers for the nation's institutions. Its commitment to that mission, however, should not be to

compete, quantitatively and in like manner, with other institutions of higher education in California; rather, it should fashion some distinctive model or models of training that will provide leadership to others.

4. For all the reasons we have adduced in this report, the School of Education as it now exists does not appear to be the optimum medium through which to realize Berkeley's maximum contribution to basic research, applied research, and practical applications to education.

5. This judgment, however, reflects not only a Berkeley problem but also a national problem in higher education. With few exceptions, university-based schools of education have been unable to escape the vicious downward spiral of status, quality, and morale. This has led us to question the viability of traditional schools of education in the university settings.

6. As an entire campus, Berkeley *is* very much in the action with respect to educational research, teacher training, and teaching those outside the campus. If we scan research conducted by faculty members and graduate students in history, political science, sociology, business administration, public policy, and elsewhere, we find activity that is impressive both in quantity and quality. And in a recent survey (March 1981) of campus activities for elementary and secondary school students and teachers on the Berkeley campus, the office of student research located fifty-six separate projects, funded annually at a cost of more than four and one-half million dollars.[16] Only eight of these, however, were sponsored or administered by the School of Education.[17]

7. Berkeley will continue to exist in a universitywide environment. Two aspects of this fundamental fact are relevant to our discussion. First, the campus cannot expect to expand its resources devoted to education or any other enterprise by expanding its student base and thereby increasing its resource base.[18] Second, note must be made that other campuses in the university system have schools or programs of teacher education.[19]

8. Since the campus student base cannot be expanded, it is unrealistic to expect that faculty resources can be more than marginally expanded at best. Implied by this is that faculty resources diverted *to* some unit or program will have to be resources diverted *from* some other unit or program. This situation reduces the degrees of freedom to the campus with respect to the support of educational research and applications.

Within these "givens" we now turn again to the array of options presented. In assessing them we must first record our view that the several forms of "ventilation" (options 1–3) and the internal administrative reforms (options 4–6) do not reach to the heart of the problems of the School of Education we have identified and could well be undermined by the larger forces that have created those problems in the first place. It is not difficult, for example, to envision the systematic subversion of the various efforts to build links to the rest of the campus. Given a prestige structure of the campus that is rooted in a historical process so deep as to be virtually unalterable, a policy of joint appointments would forever be threatened by a tendency to flow "up and out" from the school to other places. Even binding part of the joint appointee's FTE to the school in some contractual way would not necessarily so bind the head and heart. The evident lure of academic psychology and the psychology-oriented ORUs to the full-time, school-bound educational psychologists demonstrates this point. The same prestige structure would likely confound efforts to monitor the quality of the school through external participation in search, review, and advisory committees. This would be a continuing sign of the school's subordinated status, a continuing reminder of the suspicion that the school might descend into academic delinquency unless guarded, and a continuing source of defensiveness on the part of the school. (All these observations apply to option 1.) Developing service courses for schools from other schools and departments (option 2) would be of some value to students not associated with the school and would be likely to provide some opportunity for graduate students in the school to gain experience and employment as teaching assistants, but it would not affect the more fundamental problems the school faces. And finally, discontinuing the school's sponsorship of research (option 3) would not assure that faculty—particularly those with more "applied" interests— would turn to the relevant organized research units for help; in the end such a strategy might simply work toward less overall research support for faculty members in the school.

Nor can we be convinced that the purely administrative reforms that have been suggested will be sufficient. With respect to the departmentalization of the divisions within the school (option 4), for example, such a strategy may breathe a greater measure of administrative responsibility into the divisions, but at the same time might formalize and harden many of those very principles of internal fragmentation that have proved so costly to the school. Dissolution of the divisions (option 5)—a strategy we regard more positively in principle—would weaken those lines of division formally, but as a matter of organizational fact, to abolish them in name would not abolish them in reality. Recent measures designed to weaken the divisions and centralize the governance of the school have ended in reaffirming their salience as the strongest political and resource-allocating principles in the school. Underlying territorial claims have a way of breaking through reorganizational efforts to minimize them. And finally, rationalization and coordination of the central administration of the school (option 6) would yield a gain in economy—cutting back on administrative staff costs—and would probably enhance the flexibility and power of the dean but would do little to uplift the school in its larger campus environment, dissolve the internal divisions, or break through the "quality trap" in which the school has been caged for decades. All these observations reflect our conviction that the realities of low status, diminished quality, and jurisdictional defensiveness are much more powerful than formal administrative efforts to mend them.

We turn next to the options directed toward improving the school through substantial augmentation of its resources, whether those resources are directed toward restoring adequate general coverage of traditional areas (option 10) or toward aggressive building of selected areas of strength (option 11). We recommend neither of these strategies to the campus administration at this time. Our reasons are three. First, this would involve a relative reduction of resources for other units and programs on the campus, given the "zero-sum" assumptions that inform our reasoning; some of these resources would probably have to be shaved from areas having or needing strength. Second, we regard this kind of commitment-in-advance as a very risky investment. Without taking sides on the particulars of the quarrel between former dean-designate Karplus and the campus administration over resources to be allocated, we believe that even if a very strong dean were appointed and a bold, imaginative and promising scheme submitted, that would scarcely guarantee successful returns. We have identified so many vicious circles making for fragmentation, mixed quality, and low status that even spectacular leadership could be ground down by them. Third, and most candidly, we wonder to what such an investment might lead. We can realistically envision a future in which the Berkeley School of Education, under creative leadership, will have climbed to a rank of number one in the prestige ranking of such schools *but still* retain its problematic, diminished standing and effectiveness on its home campus; Stanford and Harvard have already traveled this road and do not provide us with ideal models. These general kinds of considerations also led us to suspect the more modest options of maintaining the status quo (option 7) and redirecting selectively in the context of a stable resource base (options 8–9) would face the same kinds of limitations.

In the end, then, the commission finds itself standing on a razor's edge. Dramatic innovation and sweeping reform in education at Berkeley are required. Can these best be achieved by redirecting some resources and programs toward other places on the campus while retaining a restructured and revitalized School of Education as a unit (option 12), or can these objectives be met only outside that structure, even to the point of ultimate discontinuation of the school as a separate administrative unit (options 11 and 14), or its merger into a larger entity (option 15)?

As critical as this decision may be, the crucial conclusion that we have reached is that the campus administration must embark upon an unprecedented program of *campuswide* change in Berkeley's programs of research and training in education. We advance this recommendation in full knowledge that less sweeping and more cautious programs would meet with less resistance from many quarters; but we have become convinced that more modest measures will not significantly break through the quagmire of problems associated with schools of education in general and Berkeley's school in particular.

Because we are convinced that this effort should be campuswide, we do not recommend the merger of the School of Education with one or more other professional schools (option 15). Although we find some interesting possibilities of recombination of emphases and programs currently in the school with those in other schools, this kind of merger, if more or less wholesale, would not necessarily work to weaken or dissolve the forces of internal fragmentation we have identified. But more important, a merger would still confine the campus' formal commitment to educational research, training, and practice to a single academic unit; we envision a much more ambitious and widespread mobilization of campus resources.

We do not pretend to have invented a complete blueprint for the kind of program we envision. That we believe should be developed in a comprehensive, campuswide planning phase that should be initiated immediately by the administration, a phase involving leading personnel both within and outside the school. Nevertheless, we are prepared to supply a statement of illustrative directions of change we have in mind:

- To relocate the preservice training of teachers more centrally in the life of the campus, to reinvigorate it, and perhaps to expand it as the demand for teachers increases over the next decade. At the present the preservice training in the School of Education is carried out with little participation on the part of the school's faculty and is generally inconspicuous. We envision transforming this effort into a general campus enterprise. A promising format would be to create a broadly gauged faculty group—from several different schools an colleges— responsible for teacher-training reporting directly to a central campus administrative officer. Faculty members could design a series of special programs, which would include a major in a specific school, department, or group (but not a major in education). It could also involve exposure to a few essential core courses (for example, com- parative history of education), opportunities for pursuing special areas of interest (for example, computer-assisted education), and the supervision of teaching necessary for certification. Such a program would reaffirm Berkeley's continuing commitment to teaching education and would give that commitment higher and more central priority than it now enjoys.

- To re-locate those groups and individuals in the School of Education with primarily academic research and doctoral-training interests in academic units congenial to those interests. The most significant move would affect the Division of Educational Psychology, members of which we believe should be incorporated in some way into the Department of Psychology, with which de facto linkages already exist. But it may be the case that other individuals outside that division could also be relocated in various schools and departments (for example, schools of business administration or public policy, or the departments of history, economics, or linguistics), when appro- priate fits of interest can be determined.

- To create a high-quality PhD doctoral program in various areas of education, gathering together groups of faculty from various schools and departments to administer rigorous programs of doctoral training and research. Among other functions these programs would generate degree-holders who would find places as faculty members in the nation's schools of education. One model for such a program would be a doctoral program in higher education, fashioned after the graduate program in demography but with a close linkage with the

Center for Studies in Higher Education. Certainly, given Berkeley's position in the University and State of California, and given the range of faculty interested an active in higher education, this kind emphasis appears to be a natural base for leadership by the Berkeley campus. In time, if areas of academic interest and strength (secondary education, comparative educational systems, for example) develop across disciplines, additional doctoral programs of this kind might be fostered. In any event, such a program or programs would affirm Berkeley's continuing commitment to engage in research and scholarship of the highest quality and to assure academic excellence in doctoral training.

· To centralize and consolidate the public service activities directed toward primary and secondary school pupils and teachers. As indicated, the Berkeley campus is very much involved in the careers of those in the educational establishment other than its enrolled students. These activities, however, appear to have grown somewhat opportunistically—that is, when an entrepreneurial individual or unit has been able to secure resources for a discrete program. Centralization and consolidation of these efforts would identify important gaps in these applied programs and would perhaps equip the administration with a better base for securing financial resources from federal, private, foundation, and intra-university sources.

· To foster a long-overdue expansion in the training of teaching assistants and to evaluate the effects of different teaching strategies in Berkeley's own courses. Although the work of the office of Teaching Innovation and Evaluation Services (TIES) and the Learning Center has initiated some efforts along these lines in recent years, a much more energetic and widespread must be launched and sustained if the training of teaching assistants is to emerge from its region of neglect. The administration should consider re-instituting, on an enlarged scale, a prose improvement program, in which teaching assistants themselves receive instruction in writing skills and exposition, and simultaneously introduce this component into their own teaching of undergraduates. A similar program with respect to the teaching of quantitative materials and skills might be developed. Other mechanisms such as the use of video equipment and critical seminars for teaching assistants could also be instituted. Given the evident and great need to improve literacy and numeracy at all levels of American education, given the continuing need to improve lower division instruction, and given the fact that a large proportion of graduate students at Berkeley will continue on as college teachers themselves, such a program promises to yield returns at many levels.

- To develop continuing education programs and to make more imaginative use of University Extension and other agencies. Although the School of Education has collaborated with and worked through University Extension and to some degree, these efforts have been somewhat limping in recent times. We have in mind re-thinking the relationship between the campus and extension activities in the area of education. One model would be to develop additional practical certification programs through extension. Another model is the special continuing education courses developed and executed, through extension, in the School of Engineering and the School of Business Administration. In some measure these kinds of programs could carry on some of the credentialing functions now housed in the School of Education.

Such are a number of illustrative possibilities for a campus effort to move aggressively forward in the field of educational research and practice. We cannot, however, move to a final conclusion of this report without noting an ambiguity which, when examined, becomes a dilemma. The ambiguity is this: in calling for this kind of campuswide effort we have been silent on one important point: Will this effort entail a redefinition of mission—perhaps along more applied lines—for the School of Education (for example, as envisioned in option 12 for partial redirection)? Or will it entail the ultimate discontinuation of the school (option 14)?

We offer no final recommendation on this important dilemma but we do have some cautionary words. It can be argued that in pursuing the program of reform and development we have outlined, Berkeley is sacrificing an important part of its historical commitment—namely practical professional training. In fact, this kind of training, symbolized by the doctorate, is the monopoly of the University of California among all other state educational institutions. Furthermore, it seems desirable if not essential to train and maintain relations with those who contribute so much to the management of the state and national educational establishments: school superintendents, legislative policy staff, college administrators, consultants, and others. In light of these considerations, does not the campus have a responsibility for advanced professional work at the doctoral level—a degree program aimed not at scholarly activity per se, but at practitioner-oriented education at the highest level?

We would like to believe that the answer to this question could be a positive one, and we would not oppose experimental programs along this line. But we would ask that administrators and others not fall prey to illusions on this score. Berkeley, as a bastion of the Arts and Sciences mentality, is not the most congenial home for professional doctoral programs. This difficulty is nowhere more apparent than in the history of the School of Education. EdD students and EdD degrees have diminished in number, the EdD has been pulled in the direction of the PhD, with the result that the EdD degree is neither applied nor academic, but an unsatisfactory hybrid. Would not the same history unfold if a new effort were made to continue and strengthen a professional doctorate? Indeed, would not that history be all the more probable, given the fact that such a program would in all likelihood have to be developed in a similar, residual school with fewer resources than it now enjoys? In light of these doubts, we believe that a high-quality professional degree program that encompasses a band of leaders and managers in the public sector wider than education would have a higher probability of success than some modification of the EdD.

However this final dilemma is ultimately resolved, we stress that the greatest challenge to the campus administration in implementing any package of innovative developments is to secure the very highest quality of leadership with respect to every separate enterprise we suggest. Searches should be aggressively executed, with the capacity for innovation being the key quality sought; those administrators and other leaders who are appointed should be given the clearest and most open opportunity to achieve full understanding of their charges and the responsibilities they will undertake; resources should be made available in accord with the objectives desired; and the central administration should both support and monitor these educational programs with an attentiveness much greater than has been evident in the past.

We conclude with a statement of our conviction that only through this combination of sweeping structural changes and dynamic individual leadership can the Berkeley campus bring itself to a position of excellence and leadership commensurate with the historical mission of the campus and our obligation to serve the needs of the larger society.

The School of Education can and should assume a leadership role in education both within the university system and in the larger society. That role will require a clarification, and perhaps redefinition, of the school's mission. It will also require an interrelated total program, *one which draws on the strengths to be found among other faculties on the campus.*

Specifically, we recommend that

1. The School of Education cut back the preservice teacher education programs to those which work toward development and testing of new models of teacher education through experimental and research based elements. If none meet these criteria, all should be phased out. Although preservice education is part of the university's mission in the field of education we believe that the Berkeley school has important contributions to make in other areas.

2. The school add to its mission, activities in general undergraduate education.

3. Doctoral education be restricted to strong, research-oriented PhD programs. If the EdD is to be continued, it should be restricted to strong practitioner-oriented programs. The PhD should be offered only in those specializations that can provide a high-quality research apprenticeship.

4. The school's faculty become more aggressive and effective in raising extra-mural funds for research activities in order to help fulfill the school's research mission.

5. The school concentrate its resources in programs where there is existing or potential strength. Such concentration would provide sufficient faculty for each specialization and eliminate the practice of having fragmented, small classes. Specializations that could be provided by other departments on campus or that are offered in the education school at Los Angeles might be phased out.

6. The campus administration play a central role in revitalizing the School of Education. This can be done, in part, by encouraging

joint appointments between the school and other departments or research units on campus.

7. The campus administration encourage more ties between the school and other campus units, such as organized research units and the Lawrence Hall of Science, where such ties do not exist.

8. The campus administration reassign to academic duties, as appropriate, supervisory positions now associated with preservice education. The school be encouraged to use available positions to hire younger faculty who have strong commitments to raising research money, interest in the school's areas of programmatic strength, and new perspectives on the traditional in-service education program. Availability of these positions would also give the school the opportunity to recruit, from within and outside, qualified women and minority applicants for faculty positions.

9. The school and the campus work to re-assign education supervisors to other duties. These might include reappointment to the school in other capacities.

10. The faculty reward system be modified to recognize professional achievement in the field, as well as scholarship. Ties to the field are essential to the mission of the university in education and tend to be underemphasized or ignored by the reward system as it currently operates.

APPENDIX 2. SUMMARY OF FINDINGS AND RECOMMENDATIONS OF THE BERGER COMMITTEE REPORT[21]

The ad hoc Committee of the Graduate Council (chaired by Professor Stanley Berger) held four large open meetings with students and faculty and distributed a five-page questionnaire to all current students and selected alumni. The major bases for its review were the reports of five subcommittees, each of which surveyed one of the divisions of the school.

To sum up the subcommittees' findings (in some cases seconded by the Graduate Council in its memorandum of May 11, 1979):

(a) The *Division of Humanistic and Policy Studies* appeared academically weak. Faculty research, seminar offerings, and dissatisfactions were all judged of insufficient overall quality. Few faculty did research that attracted extramural grants, and almost none of the sort that made available research assistantships. More support funds, it was thought, would enable the division to attract full-time graduate students of higher quality. At present most appear to be mid-career teachers working for doctorates (often PhDs, when the EdD would be more appropriate) in evening seminars, in order to advance their careers. But as it existed, this division seemed too confused and fragmented to warrant continued survival.

(b) The *Division of Curriculum and Instruction* was also criticized for awarding the PhD to candidates whose dissertations were below the standard expected on this campus, and for failing to distinguish clearly between the two doctorates. (As the EdD is regarded as a "second class" degree, most graduate students now opt for the PhD instead, with a resultant degrading of its quality.) Fully half of the graduate students enrolled in this division had full-time jobs; another 19 percent worked more than three-fourths time. Since the school has no undergraduate programs, few teaching assistantships were available. But the outside-job pattern relates less to the availability of support than to the kind of student who applies to the program—typically established Bay Area teachers or administrators seeking to upgrade their positions with a doctorate but unwilling to forego their outside salaries while earning the degree.

The specialized reading and language development program and Mount Diablo District science education program were praised, but other units were thought to be understaffed below viable size and ripe for disbanding. The division was also criticized for its lack of unity, core program, and central organization, and for the inability of students to participate in decision making.

(c) The *Division of Educational Psychology* was generally judged of high quality, perhaps because it comes closer to the Letters and Science norm more familiar to the reviewers. The faculty is almost entirely research-and-theory oriented, sometimes to the detriment of students' professional concerns. It attracts high-GRE students, 99 percent of whom complete the program, and awards only the PhD. Forty-two percent of students are fellowship- or grant-supported; one-third go on to college or university posts. Many students in this division, too, work full-time while enrolled—the median period from entrance to PhD is about five years.

The six programs within the division were individually assessed, generally in terms of the size and quality of faculty involved. "High marks" went to the programs of school psychology (despite some hostility toward this program from others in the school), measurement, and intelligence development; low marks were given to counseling and psychological services. Because of this division's particular strengths and research orientation, there was talk of separating it out from the school—perhaps to integrate it more closely with the Department of Psychology. The ad hoc committee elected not to support this idea.

(d) The faculty teaching in the *Division of Higher Education* was judged of high quality, although it included no national "stars." Much of its earlier reputation came from the Center for Studies in Higher Education, a campus ORU unrelated to the school—whose director since 1977 is, for the first time, *not* a member of the School of Education.

The criticisms of this division were familiar: too many of the PhDs granted should really have been EdDs (4:1 PhD to EdD); the ad hoc committee proposed that a ratio exactly reverse would be more accurate); no TA and few RA posts available because the faculty did little grant-supported research; the students (two-thirds held full-time jobs) couldn't afford to accept anything as low-paying as a research assistantship in any case. To fit the schedules of these working students, many courses met once a week from 4 to 7 P.M., which is scarcely conducive to rich student-faculty interaction, good use of campus resources, or a full integration into university life.

Other problem areas mentioned by this subcommittee included

· The use of the second-class EdD track for less-qualified minor-ity students

· The depressingly "local" as opposed to national placement of gradu-ates (two-thirds in Northern California)

· The paucity of graduate students with any interest in active scholar-ship, as opposed to professional advancement (In this time of degree-inflation and "creeping credentialism," the union card of a doctorate is often essential for higher-level jobs in education.)

The possibility of disbanding the division and forming, in its place, a campuswide "Group in Higher Education," offering its own degrees under the graduate division, was seriously considered.

(e) The *Division of Teacher Education* came in for heaviest attack. It is the most anomalous unit of the school, and unique in the whole UCB graduate division, since it offers primarily three-quarter "credentials" (rather than graduate degrees), the requirements of which are set more by the state than by the university. The numbers involved were reduced from

393 students/33 faculty (supervisors on annual appointment, rather than regular ladder faculty) to 244/23 in seven yeas, and "are likely to decrease further." (The numbers are now 75 and 17.) M.A.T. degrees and advanced credentials for in-service professionals are also awarded. A 2.5 GPA was sufficient for admission to the credential program—another graduate division anomaly.

Credential candidates and the teacher-training program generally seem to be regarded as inferior by the reviewers and by many others in the School. If UCB is to house such a facility, it was argued, it can be justified if it is a *model* of its kind, with a learning center doing active research and selective frontline experimentation in teaching techniques, setting high standards and offering innovative help to other programs and schools—and not just one more "teacher's college" among the many in California.

The ad hoc review committee gave the following recommendations (in some cases seconded by the Graduate Council memoir of May 1979):

(a) Restructure the divisions and programs in something more coherent and workable than the present array of isolated, impotent, and often rival divisions, and the enormous number of programs among them.

(b) Appoint a new dean from outside who can "command the respect of the entire university." Improve the lines of faculty and student consultation with the dean.

(c) Raise the quality of all PhDs to Berkeley levels (the school grants more than 50 PhDs every year), and distinguish more clearly between the EdD and PhD In Fall 1979, 380 doctoral candidates (324 PhD, 56 EdD) were enrolled.

(d) Ensure quality-control by more surveillance by, and cooperation with, people from outside the School of Education: by appointing a *dean* from outside, who will help choose an *advisory committee* of outsiders; commissioning a single outside *expert* to evaluate the school's responses to its "myriad reviews") appointing outside *readers,* with veto power, reporting directly to the graduate division, to all PhD committees—or even require that all

PhDs in education be awarded jointly with academic departments, "as a means of preserving the PhD degree as a certificate of research capabilities."

(e)   Obtain more federal and state support. Stanford's School of Education, rated number one in the United States, is far more research-oriented than ours and can support half its students with grants.

(f)   More fellowships and research assistantships would help break the pattern of narrowly provincial applicants who hold full-time jobs and earn degrees only to win professional advancement.

(g)   Correct the anomalies of the teacher education division—excessive state control of curriculum; the low (2.5) GPA entrance requirement; the relinquishing of admissions decisions to off-campus authorities; total segregation from the rest of the school; low quality of faculty. Dissolving the program, however, was not recommended, as it would involve severe internal and external costs.

(h)   Integrate research and teaching more with demonstrably successful programs in education on campus (e.g., Lawrence Hall of Science, the Science and Math Education Program— "SESAME"—the Bay Area Writing Project), with ORUs, and with the rest of the campus generally. This point was also stressed in the Graduate Council's May 1 memo.

(i)   If new FTE are to be granted, the Graduate Council suggested they only be offered in terms of joint appointments with "academic" departments.

APPENDIX 3. MEMBERS OF THE COMMISSION

Marilyn Christopher, Graduate Student Joint Program of Law and Business Administration

Eugene C. Lee, Professor of Political Science

John T. Wheeler, Professor of Business Administration

Neil J. Smelser, Chair, University Professor of Sociology

1. Joseph Adelson, "What Happened to the Schools?" *Commentary* 71(3) (March 1981): 36.

2. In the best-known national surveys of occupational prestige, conducted by the National Opinion Research Center, in 1947 and 1963, college professors ranked near the top of the prestige scale, along with physicians and lawyers (Justice of the Supreme Court was at the very top), but high school teachers and grade school teachers ranked well below all three. Robert W. Hodge, Paul M. Siegal, and Peter H. Rossi, "Occupational Prestige in the United States, 1925–1963," *American Journal of Sociology,* 70 (November 1964): 386–402.

3. A notable exception is the professional training of psychoanalysts; while their medical and psychiatric training occurs within university-based medical schools, their psychoanalytic training occurs in Institutes of Psychoanalysis, which have few or no formal links with universities.

4. Many if not most of the faculty of professional schools with primarily behavioral and social science emphases (education, social welfare, city and regional planning, public health) are trained in the basic disciplines, not in professional schools of the same genre. Since, however—by virtue of the dominance of the "Arts and Sciences" mentality—those so trained would, by and large, prefer to have academic appointments in the departments of the basic disciplines; those departments have "first choice," as it were, on highly promising or qualified applicants, leaving those kinds of professional schools in a lesser competitive position for talent.

5. Academic Planning and Program Review Board, *The Study of Education: A Review of the Education Programs in the University of California* (Berkeley: Systemwide Administration of the University of California, 1976), 2:10.

6. *Revised Academic Plan, 1969–75.* University of California, Berkeley campus, 1968.

7. Actual enrollments and degrees granted to the two categories indicate that the EdD program has been small in proportion in the PhD program. The enrollment figures are as follows:

	FY72	FY73	FY74	FY75	FY76	FY77	FY78	FY79	FY80
PhD	403	409	359	356	327	301	300	277	280
EDD	84	52	37	45	35	41	39	51	60

Degrees awarded since 1975 show the same dominance of the PhD program:

	PhD	EdD		PhD	EdD
1975–76	59	6	1978–79	50	3
1976–77	68	5	1979–80	44	4
1977–78	37	0			

TABLE I
Number of faculty, students, courses, and degrees, 1980–81

	ASRHS	EP	HEPSA	IRCD	L & R	TOTAL
Faculty	9	12	10	5	4	40
Students						507
Education	96	112	108	40	54	400
Credential	–	–	–	–	–	107
Courses	18	60	37	17	23	145
Degrees (June 1980)						
PhD	5	7	5	2	2	24
EdD	0	0	1	1	0	2
MA/MAT	5	7	6	7	12	37
Credential	0	14	14	76	6	110

8. Enrollments in the PhD and EdD programs fell from a combined total of 487 in 1972 to a combined total of 340 in 1980, a drop of approximately 30 percent; the drop in enrollments in the teaching credential program was from 370 in 1972 to 68 in 1980, a drop of 75 percent.

9. Applied Social Research and Humanistic Studies (ASRHS); Educational Psychology (EP); Higher Education, Finance and School Administration (HEFSA); Language and Reading (L & R); Instructional Research and Curriculum Development (IRCD). Teacher Education is no longer a separate division, but those in preservice training mainly affiliate with either the Language and Reading or the Instructional Research and Curriculum Development program.

The table on this page provides a map of the school in terms of the number of faculty, students, courses offered, and degrees granted as of the academic year 1980–81. (Because miscellaneous categories of students are not listed in this table, the total number of students does not match totals elsewhere in this report.)

As can be seen, the school is dominated on all measures by three divisions— Applied Social Research and Humanistic Studies, Educational Psychology, and Higher Education, Finance and School Administration. However, only a few preservice trainees are assigned to any of these divisions (five students in the Developmental Teacher Education Program in the Division of Educational Psychology).

10. We refer here primarily to the Academic Planning and Program Review Board, a review body that passes judgment on—and sometimes demands revision of—student dissertation proposals. Initiated mainly in response to

pressure from the graduate division after the submission of the Berger committee report, this arrangement has probably resulted in the improvement of some dissertation proposals through critical review and suggestions. It appears also to have been counterproductive in some respects: the review process has sometimes delayed students' progress on dissertations, and on occasion this delay has been damaging to their career chances; it has sometimes exacerbated student-faculty and faculty-faculty tensions; it is regarded as unjust by some students because the composition of the review committees is secret, and the origin of criticisms is unknown; and because the APPRB takes no interest in the dissertation after the proposal stage, its criticism can be subverted with impunity during the actual execution of the dissertation. Still others complain that the APPRB is too lenient in its decisions, permitting slippage of academic quality through perfunctory reviewing, waiving of requirements, and the like. We regard the APPRB more as a symptom than a cure for low quality, and hope that it, and arrangements like it, will be able to pass from the scene in due course.

11. There are three additional "foundations" courses—in the social, psychological, and humanistic foundations of education—that are meant to be taken by all students in the school, but the opportunities for students to "opt out" of these courses by virtue of other work taken is sufficiently widespread that they have lost some of their significance as schoolwide intellectual experiences for the students.

12. The main change was the introduction of a new Division for Science and Mathematics Education, and the phasing out of higher education from Higher Education, Administration, and Policy Analysis.

13. According to the figures supplied by the School of Education, we calculated the following distribution of employment of students in the School, as of March 1981 (see Table 2).

On the whole, then, almost one-third of the enrolled students are employed in some way. Virtually all this employment, moreover, is *outside* the school, since there is no employment for teaching assistants (the school has no undergraduate program, and thus no large service courses for undergraduates), and relatively few research assistants are available in faculty research projects. The figure for full-time employment in the Higher Education, Finance, and School Administration (66 percent) is remarkably high and probably reflects the fact that many if not most of the students are already in school administrative positions and are "credentialing" for career advancement.

14. Geraldine J. Clifford and Robert Karplus, "1981–1984—1985–86 Faculty Targets" (communication to Provost George J. Maslach), August 21, 1980.

15. Designed to coordinate and administer the Media-Telecommunications Laboratory, the Field Applications Laboratory, and the Instructional Research Laboratory.

TABLE 2

Distribution of student employment by division

Division or Program	Full-Time Employment		51–99% Employment		1–50% Employment		Not Employed		Total in Program
	Number of Students	Percentage of Division	Number of Students	Percentage of Division	Number of Students	Percentage of Division	Number of Students	Percentage of Division	
ASRHS	14	14	7	7	42	43	34	35	97
EP	11	9	10	8	53	45	45	38	119
HEFSA	76	60	6	5	19	15	25	20	126
IRCD	20	24	10	12	12	14	42	51	84
L & R	15	27	4	7	21	38	15	27	55
Joint programs	1	2	0	0	20	42	27	56	48
Miscellaneous	11	27	0	0	25	61	5	12	41
TOTALS	148	26	37	6	192	34	193	34	570

16. Office of Student Research, "Director of Campus Activities for Elementary and Secondary School Students and Teachers" (University of California, Berkeley), March 1981. The figure of $4.5 million is conservative, because the level of funding for 11 of the projects was not given in the report.

17. Twenty-five were sponsored or administered by the Lawrence Hall of Science.

18. The Berkeley campus thus differs in circumstance from a campus such as the University of Minnesota, which has no enrollment ceiling.

19. Advanced courses are offered on the Los Angeles, Riverside, Santa Barbara, and Davis campuses, and some preservice teacher education exists on the Irvine, San Diego, and Santa Cruz campuses. Academic Planning and Program Review Board, *The Study of Education: A Review of the Education Programs in the University of California* (Berkeley: Systemwide Administration of the University of California, 1976), pp. III-2-3.

20. Academic Planning and Program Review Board, *The Study of Education,* pp. VII-14, VII-15.

21. Taken from a communication from Neil J. Smelser, chair of the Committee on Educational Policy of the Berkeley Division, to Vice Chancellor I. M. Heyman, January 31, 1980.

NINE

Report of the Task Force on
Lower Division Education (1986)

IN THE MID-1980S THREE MAJOR national reports on the quality of
undergraduate education appeared. They emanated, respectively, from the
National Endowment of the Humanities, the National Institute of
Education, and the Association of American Colleges. These reports were
uniformly negative in their assessment, using terms such as "unhappy
disarray," "loss of integrity," "diminished vision," "majoring in narrow
specialties," and "a vacuum of educational leadership." They were scarcely
uniform in their recommendations, however, the first calling for a revitalization of humanistic learning, the second for mechanisms for involving
students in the learning process, and the third for imparting specific skills
and modes of inquiry. Despite this divergence, the reports, taken together,
constituted a grave indictment of undergraduate education, including
general education, in America, and threw much of the higher education
establishment on the defensive.

In the fall of 1985, the office of the president, and President David
Gardner in particular, responded to this national development by creating
a major task force on the lower division—the first two collegiate years—in
the entire University of California system. These years had long been
regarded as the most problematic of the undergraduate experience. He
asked me to chair the task force. That was a daunting prospect, both
because of the enormous range to be covered, and because of the antici-

pated size and complexity of the multi-campus membership that was necessary. I accepted Gardner's invitation. In retrospect, I perceive that, on account of the scope of the charge and the dimensions of the task force, I took more initiative as leader of this group than in any other like assignment.

The report had an immediate and long-term impact. Two major sessions on the report were held at meetings of the board of regents; some California legislators took an interest in the project; and as chair I traveled to several UC campuses to confer with administrative and faculty leaders about the report. The recommendations concerning teaching assistants were implemented more or less immediately. The report also stimulated reforms in the transfer of students to the UC campuses. It is also fair to claim that in the longer run the report gave the major impetus to the development of freshman and sophomore seminars, now established throughout the UC system. Other proposals, such as the assignment of the most brilliant teachers to large lower division courses and the improvement of teaching evaluation, appeared to have little or no effect.

EXECUTIVE SUMMARY

The Task Force on Lower Division Education was charged to review the university's mission to teach lower division students; the nature and quality of the lower division curriculum; the quality of teaching and learning; and the quality of academic support services. The final report of the task force presents its review against the backdrop of widespread national concern with the quality of undergraduate education and the current legislative review of the Master Plan for Higher Education. It frames its analyses and recommendations in the particular contexts of the contemporary historical situation of the State of California and the University of California. And finally it embeds its analyses and recommendations in a developmental portrait of the lower division student, which requires that curricular and other educational experiences be assessed at least in part according to how well they foster intellectual and personal development in the transitional years from adolescence to adulthood.

Anxious to insure that the recommendations in its report do not fall— as David Hume once complained about one of his philosophical treatises—"still-born from the press," the task force employs three strategies: to limit the number of diagnoses and recommendations to the few considered the most salient; to endeavor to make the diagnoses and recommendations as specific as possible; and to observe the limits of budgetary and institutional realities in generating recommendations.

The report makes clear that lower division education has been from the beginning an essential ingredient in the educational mission of the University of California. Despite this role, the lower division is something of a neglected child in terms of information gathered, attention paid, and critical review given to it. The task force calls for measures to rectify this neglect.

In its review of the quality of teaching and learning, the task force found that teaching in the University of California must be assessed in the context of the other missions of the university and in the context of the resources available for it. The task force examines the roles of the several types of instructional faculty: Academic Senate faculty, non-senate or temporary faculty, and teaching assistants. It also reviews the reasons for what it defines as the three-tiered approach to instruction at the university. A legitimate and positive place for each type of faculty member is noted, but the task force found current arrangements wanting in some respects for each category. In particular, it calls for augmented review of faculty teaching; better review and evaluation and fuller incorporation of temporary faculty into the educational life of the university; and improved recruitment, training, supervision, and evaluation of teaching assistants.

With respect to reforming curricula and programs, the freshman-sophomore seminar is seen as an exceptionally valuable resource in the educational life of the university. Educational experiences in the seminar setting have a positive impact on students' learning, student-faculty relations, advising, the relations between research and teaching, and integrating the lower division student into an environment that can be experienced as confusing or unwelcoming. The task force recommends a significant expansion of freshman-sophomore programs and other, complementary kinds of lower division courses.

The task force also reviewed the problems associated with transferring to the university from community college and state university campuses as they relate to lower division and general education. A significant, but now declining, number of students enrolled in the university experience their lower division years in institutions other than the university, mainly on community college and state university campuses. The transfer of qualified students from these sectors is an essential part of the master plan. In this connection, the task force recommends the following with respect to three facilitative measures: (a) continued discussion and investigation of the California Articulation Numbering System; (b) the development of a general education transfer core curriculum; and (c) the development of reciprocity arrangements among campuses of the university which honor a range of lower division general education courses taken on other campuses. In connection with these three measures, the task force recommends that campuses make special efforts to develop programs of general education at the upper division.

Two of the most profound changes affecting the state and the university are (a) the increasing internationalization of the world—its growing interdependence along economic, political, and cultural lines; California, with its pivotal economic and geographical situation, is in the center of this process; and (b) the increasing diversification of the state's population along racial, ethnic, and cultural lines. The task force recommends that the university respond aggressively and creatively to these two sets of changes in its educational and research programs.

Finally, in a look at the larger picture of knowledge, including the major and lower division education, the task force notes that the late twentieth century has witnessed a spiraling of knowledge that is increasingly technical, specialized, and fragmented. These developments have raised questions if not posed threats to the general mission of the university by tilting it in the direction of vocationalism, specialization, and science at the expense of liberal arts and humanistic learning. The task force identifies some ways of confronting these challenges, and recommends that they occupy a salient place in the University of California's long-term agenda.

A complete list of recommendations, by category follows:

Reforming Curricula and Programs

1. Campuses should institute and expand freshman-sophomore seminars or functionally equivalent educational processes that constitute a chance for lower division students to interact with ladder-rank faculty in a small classroom setting.

2. Campuses should develop and extend general education courses of an integrative or synthetic character in both their lower and upper divisions.

3. Campuses should develop curricular changes and other policies that enhance the international, multicultural, and global learning experiences of students.

Improving the Quality of Teaching

4. Departments of colleges and schools should assign their most brilliant and effective teaching faculty, regardless of title and rank, to large, introductory lower division courses.

5. Faculty evaluation should be improved, making internal peer review more systematic, and including teaching effectiveness on the agendas of external reviewing bodies.

6. Mechanisms should be developed for the more systematic selection, review, and evaluation of temporary faculty, and for their better incorporation into the educational life of the campus.

7. Teaching assistants whose native language is not English should be required to pass the oral Test of English as a Foreign Language (TOEFL).

8. Campuses should review and improve mechanisms for the training, supervision, and evaluation of teaching assistants, especially at the departmental level.

Improving Educational Continuity

9. Colleges and schools should seek more flexible ways of adapting the numbers of courses and sections available at the lower division, so that students will be able to take these during the first two years.

10. The University of California, at appropriate levels of faculty and administrative responsibility, should work toward developing and improving: (a) articulation of specific courses with institutions from other segments, especially on a regional basis; (b) a selective common core of general education courses that, if taken at a specified level of performance in the other segments, would satisfy the general education requirements of the University of California campuses; (c) reciprocity among campuses with respect to curricular requirements that will meet the general education requirements on all campuses.

Improving Information and Quality Control

11. The university and the campuses should secure more extensive and more nearly comparable information on the educational roles of different categories of instructors.

12. Colleges and schools, as well as campus and systemwide adminis-
    trations, should develop mechanisms for periodic and systematic
    review of the quality of lower division education.

Reaffirming the General Mission of the University

13. As a long-term matter, the university and its several campuses
    should continue to observe the changing balance of its educational
    emphases—disciplinary balance, the balance between vocational
    and liberal education emphases, the balance among lower division,
    upper division, and graduate education—in the light of the
    shifting character of knowledge in society.

FINAL REPORT

In carrying out its mission during the past nine months, this task force
has proceeded on the understanding, long established in the university,
that it is valuable—essential, rather—to review periodically all programs
and procedures with an eye to their excellence and their effectiveness.
During the task force's lifetime, however, two developments were pro-
ceeding simultaneously—one national and one at the state level—which
had a direct bearing on our special task.

The first development had to do with the widespread concern in recent
years about the quality of undergraduate education in the nation's colleges
and universities. This concern was expressed early in 1985 with the appearance of three national reports, all critical of current collegiate arrangements. The reports were sponsored by the National Endowment of the
Humanities, the National Institute of Education, and the Association of
American Colleges. The three reports along with several others had a
very large press, and apparently stimulated many reform efforts around
the nation.

The second development was the initiation of a major review of the
Master Plan for Higher Education by the California Legislature. The
master plan has been California's guiding framework for a quarter of a
century. The legislative review is giving great emphasis to lower division
education, the only function shared by all three segments of California's
system of higher education. The members of the task force regard our
own self-examination as in keeping with the purposes of the state's review,
and hope that it will be helpful both to the commission for the Review
of the Master Plan for Higher Education and to the legislature.

In a progress report submitted in February of this year, the task force concentrated on the national reports, reviewing them in the light of recent experiences on the campuses of the university. Each campus and several groups in the systemwide Academic Senate were asked to respond to the reports. By and large, their responses, while acknowledging much of value in those reports, did not share their gloominess. The main reason for this was that every campus of the university had undertaken recent and significant improvement in their undergraduate programs. Many of these improvements, moreover, were along lines called for by the three reports, and nearly all had been initiated before the appearance of the reports. At the same time, the campus responses voiced continuing concern over many aspects of undergraduate education, such as faculty-student relations, the role of temporary faculty and teaching assistants, and substantive inadequacies in areas such as multicultural education.

At the conclusion of its progress report, the task force determined that it would not be profitable to carry on deliberations at the very general level evident in the national reports. Instead, we thought it best to frame our work in the context of the situation of the University of California itself, in the state of California, in the late twentieth century. In that connection we identified a number of contextual features within which we live:

· The University of California is in the state of California, receives its basic support from the people of California, and is committed to serve the people of California.

· The state of California is becoming increasingly heterogeneous in racial and ethnic composition as well as in cultural and political orientations; the University of California is experiencing the same with respect to faculty and student composition.

· The University of California is in a *system* of higher education, with three public segments governed by the master plan.

· The University of California is a multicampus system, with different histories, cultures, community contexts, and graduate-undergraduate and professional-arts and science mixtures.

· The University of California has risen to a position of national and international leadership among universities.

- The University of California has among its missions a heavy involvement in research and graduate training.

- In modern times, knowledge has increased dramatically, and in the process has become more specialized and fragmented.

Everything we have to say about lower division education has to take one or more of these contextual features—or exigencies, if you will—into account, because every one of them affects the lower division work of the university in some way. In some cases these exigencies appear to constitute assets for lower division education; in some cases they appear to constitute diversions from it. In either event they pull the university in different, sometimes conflicting directions, forever threatening to create imbalances; our diagnoses and recommendations are made in relation to these points of tension.

THE MISSION OF THE LOWER DIVISION IN THE UNIVERSITY OF CALIFORNIA

From the beginning the university has included a two-year lower division experience as part of its undergraduate education, meant to bring students into the collegiate world and to preoccupy them from approximately age eighteen to approximately age twenty. Though the mix of missions for these years—and the precise salience of each—has changed continuously, the first two years have been asked over time to accomplish the following sorts of things:

- To develop further certain general skills (writing, language, mathematical, analytic) that are essential for mastery and meaningful discourse in the world of higher learning.

- To provide students with some exposure to a range of traditions of knowledge—that is, with some intellectual breadth—before more specialized studies begin.

- To contribute to the development of critical abilities and critical minds.

- To contribute to a liberal education; to expose students from diverse economic and cultural backgrounds to the great ideas, concepts, and events that have shaped our culture (often stated in terms of the

Western heritage) as preparation for life-long discourse in the company of educated people.

- To contribute to the understanding of the fundamental ideas and concepts on which society is founded, as part of preparation for responsible citizenship; to increase students' tolerance for ambiguity and diversity.

- To provide a common educational experience which serves to define institutional and peer group identification and affiliation.

- To initiate that especially important phase of personal development and attainment of independence associated with the first two years away from the parental home.

In recent decades a new and especially important challenge has risen; this has to do with the increasing racial, ethnic, and cultural heterogeneity of the population of the state of California, including our students and faculty. The challenge for education is: what are the most creative ways to come to terms with and reap advantages from this heterogeneity?

A moment's reflection on this mix of missions reveals that they are not exclusively in the domain of the lower division but are shared in important measure with those educational years that precede and follow it. It is also evident that these missions overlap with those of general education as a whole. Although the task force will be as faithful as possible to adhering to lower division concerns in this report, much of what we say cannot be divorced from concerns with the collegiate experience as a whole or from broader concerns with general education.

THE LOWER DIVISION EXPERIENCE

The Lower Division Years

The first thing to note about the lower division years is that they typically occur with a narrow band of the life span of students—roughly between the ages of seventeen or eighteen and the early twenties.[1] These are years, moreover, that developmental psychologists and others would now describe as falling in that transition between adolescence and young adulthood. And at the risk of some oversimplification, it is possible to identify several issues that confront college-attending students in this age range.

One main theme is coming to terms with the increase in independence, autonomy, choice, and greater freedom from authority that come with moving from the parental home and taking greater responsibility for dealing with one's life. Within the context of this increased freedom, however, is a second, almost contrasting theme of narrowing of life's choices through a process of progressive commitment. In contrast to the adolescent years, where the motif is one of experimentation, of trying on all sorts of clothes, the college years move students toward firmer commitments, of wearing the clothes for a time. There is pressure to think about one career rather than another, pressure to sort out one's political and moral attitudes, and pressure to form affective and sexual ties which may not yet imply full exclusiveness, fidelity, or permanence, but certainly imply a movement in those directions, in contrast to the adolescent pattern. And in each of these commitments, the issue of whether one will succeed or fail is always present.

These themes imply that the post-adolescent years will involve some turbulence, as students work out competitive relations with parents, siblings, and peers in this period of self-realization; as they work through their attitudes toward authority; as they deal with anxiety and guilt resulting from separation from past attachments and the establishment of new ones; as they struggle to sort out and solidify their own identity in a more inclusive context of cultural diversity; as they deal with the combination of exhilaration associated with their new commitments and successes with sadness over foregone opportunities that come with commitment. Above all these years imply a casting about for new ideas, new perspectives, new models to identify with, and new ways to order one's life plans.

It can be agued that an ideally conceived college or university ought to comprise, among other things, an arena which permits if not encourages the most creative possible resolution of the issues just identified. It might also be argued that many arrangements found in the collegiate years are actually geared to that end. The first years of college are typically a period of balance between requirements and choice, giving the student a mixture of constraint and freedom. It is a period that calls for commitment in terms of choice of specialization, preparation for specific kinds of further academic or professional training, or preparation for a specific career path after college, but at the same time leaves the freedom to make those choices in large part to the student. Moreover, the collegiate years provide a multiplicity of voluntary communities—residential, athletic, academic, political, and lifestyle—in which students can find their most comfortable niches.

The structure of academic authority is also relevant from this point of view. In one respect faculty members are definite authorities. They render judgments about students' academic performance and potential that are virtually beyond appeal; and the faculty are the ultimate gate-keepers for students' academic certification. At the same time the faculty role has a benign aspect. Faculty members are removed from disciplining students for behavior outside academic performance; and it is generally expected that the faculty member will be interested in helping students to learn and to grow. (Two images still survive, though in somewhat eroded form: the image of the eccentric professor who is too abstractly removed even to notice students but is nonetheless a person absorbed in the world of knowledge; and the image of Mr. Chips, who so loves the students that he cares only about the cultivation of their minds and their futures.) And faculty members often become powerful role models or mentors who profoundly shape choices that turn students in one direction or another for later life.

Curricular Experiences   In a way, then, the great challenge to the university in the lower division—and, to a degree, in the total collegiate experience—is to make most fruitful the match between students' intellectual and personal development on the one hand and their collegiate experience on the other. This ideal has to be striven for, however, both in the context of the general intellectual missions of the lower division, sketched above, and in the context of the larger exigencies facing the university, also sketched above. In regarding the realities of the lower division experience, then—insofar as we could fathom them—the task force found an unclear picture with respect to realizing the lower division challenge. What do students actually experience during the first two years?

On the curricular side, there is sometimes not much room to maneuver for many students in these years. From the very beginning students on all campuses must think in terms of planning their curriculum to take into account a variety of requirements:

· University requirements. All baccalaureate degrees must comprise a
  total number of quarter or semester units, and students must have

some acquaintance with American history (either a high school course sequence or university course) and a minimum proficiency in English composition (the English A requirement).

- Breadth or general education requirements, which specify courses (which sometimes can be waived by passing an examination) in reading and composition, quantitative reasoning, foreign language, and a spread of work in the natural sciences, life sciences, social sciences, and humanities.

- Departmental major requirements. Many departments require students to take a set of classes emphasizing fundamental skills before beginning the departmental curriculum. Students wishing to major in engineering, environmental design, economics, physics, chemistry, and other sciences must take beginning calculus; a major in a language often must take courses in another language as well; theater arts departments often require a number of prerequisites, and growing numbers of departments have begun to require a computing background.

What kinds of courses do lower division students typically take? The task force found no systematic evidence on this matter, so our initial response to that question is that we really do not know. However, we did obtain a profile of the kinds of courses lower division students on the Berkeley campus take. On that campus there are six hundred lower division courses, which give a great deal of potential choice. But in practice students concentrate their lower division choices on a very limited set of courses. The thirty-four most widely taken courses grant fully half of all student credit hours for freshmen and sophomores, whereas the seventy-nine most popular courses grant fully three-quarters of student credit hours. The seventy-nine courses fall in four general categories: (1) introductory mathematics and physical science courses; (2) reading and composition courses; (3) introductory language courses (French, Spanish, German, Italian); and (4) large survey courses in various disciplines (anthropology, biology, economics, philosophy, and psychology, for example). The last category comprises a diversity of substantive courses, which introduce students to new areas of scholarship by giving an overview of the problems, methods, and findings of each major discipline. These survey courses are often taken to satisfy breadth requirements or to serve as samplers for prospective majors.

The most widely taken courses on all campuses have two general formats. The first is classes or sections of twenty or thirty students, which engage in discussion, drill, and tutorial; these include mainly classes in reading and composition, foreign language, and physical education. The second is large lecture classes—ranging from 200 to 800 students—which are typically supplemented by small discussion groups or laboratories of twenty to thirty students each.

The fact that relatively few courses prove to be heavily populated should not disguise another problem of the lower division. A combination of limited resources supplied to departments and the unavailability of appropriate classroom space conspire to make many important classes unavailable to students when they want to take them. On most campuses many students each year are unable to take Subject A (a remedial basic writing skills course); and in the case of many breadth and prerequisite courses—courses such as introductory English, economics, psychology, political science, biology, statistics, and computer science—literally hundreds of students are routinely denied classes needed to move toward upper division work. Each term is a scramble, with students struggling to get into courses they want or need. This widespread hit-and-miss effect makes it virtually impossible for many lower division students to work even a semblance of intellectual coherence into their academic program. In some underprovided courses, such as introductory English, departments give priority to students who have not been able to take the course earlier—juniors and seniors—but this yields fewer places for freshmen and sophomores, many of whom must wait. This works toward defeating the main purpose of such courses—to develop basic skills and provide introductory surveys *early* in the collegiate years so that students benefit from these in subsequent, more advanced work.

We have mentioned the sparseness of reliable and systematic information on the problems of class size, patterns of courses taken, and course sequencing. We recommend that campuses collect and make available information of this sort, even though such aggregated statistics do not provide direct measures of the quality of instruction. The task force believes, however, that the problem runs deeper than the lack of information. The main reason for the lack is that traditionally universities pay relatively little attention to the lower division experience as an entity, and on our campuses there are few mechanisms in place for systematic review.

As a general rule, faculties make a point of reviewing many parts of their enterprise, under the guiding assumption that reviewing is a fundamental ingredient in quality control and improvement. Faculty members review one another endlessly; special committees external to graduate programs review these programs every several years; colleges and schools assess their undergraduate majors from time to time. The task force finds, however, no similar efforts made at either the systemwide or campus levels to assess the lower division experience as such. These years tend to fall between the departmental cracks, as it were. Yet campuses, colleges, and schools have or can readily create mechanisms such as periodically activated faculty review committees to carry out this function.

Such reviews could raise questions about balance and imbalance of curricular emphases in the lower division years; about who teaches there and how; about what kinds of texts are used; about what kinds of examinations are given; about how much and what kind of writing is assigned; about what courses are demanded but not offered in sufficient numbers for freshmen and sophomores; and about what kind of supervision and evaluation of teaching assistants is done. The recent yearlong effort of the major college divisions on the UCLA campus—sciences, social sciences, and humanities—to assess some of these kinds of questions for review at a May 1986 retreat is an exemplary step, and might serve as a starting point for more general, periodic reviews. In any event the task force recommends this kind of regular surveillance and review, which would serve as an important part of the effort to make the experiences of the University of California's lower division more orderly, and would constitute a needed element in the general effort to maintain and improve those educational years.

We now move to some more focused diagnoses and recommendations. We proceed in an order of ascending generality. First, we will ask about the present state of intellectual resources available for the lower division— who teaches and how? Second, we put forward a recommendation for the lower division years—the idea of the freshman-sophomore seminar—to which we attach major importance. Third, we turn to the relations between general education in the lower division years and general education throughout the collegiate experience. In this connection we will take up two timely topics: (a) the problem of curricular transfer *between* the other segments of California's higher education system and the university; and (b) the problem of reciprocity *among* the campuses of the university with respect to general education and other requirements. Fourth, we identify two major contextual changes affecting California—we call these increasing internationalization and increasing diversification—and make several recommendations about the best educational responses to these changes. And finally we raise a most important issue: intellectual balance in the undergraduate years, including the lower division. This will be a very general discussion, intended to set a long-term agenda for reform rather than generate specific, short-term recommendations.

WHO TEACHES AND HOW?

General Background

The people of California, through their elected representatives, have made the historical choice to provide a university that is mandated to

a. Provide a baccalaureate education for relatively *large* number of young people in the state; this commitment, while involving selection of students on the basis of academic performance or credentials, nevertheless contrasts with the educational philosophy of smaller, extremely selective private institutions (e.g., Oxford, Harvard, Swarthmore)

b. Provide for the *highest quality* undergraduate education for its students, or, in the words of the Master Plan, to "strive for excellence"

c. Provide his education at a *reasonable cost*, a cost which the people of California and the students who benefit from it can be expected to bear

d. Combine this undergraduate education with *additional responsibilities* for graduate education, professional training, and research, and to strive for excellence in those areas as well

If all these requirements are honored, then the university faces a new series of constraints that determine, in large part, simultaneously what it cannot do and what it can do. Given the commitment to numbers the university simply cannot afford the more favorable student-faculty ratios found in the selective private institutions. In fact, the ratio of students to faculty is now funded at 17.61:1 in the University of California. This contrasts, for example, with Stanford's student-faculty ratio of 13.24:1. (If our ratio were brought down to Stanford's, this would mean an additional 2,372 new FTE faculty positions at a cost of $270 million annually[2] to the State of California, not including new offices, laboratories, and other facilities.) These ratios tell us, among other things, that given comparable teaching responsibilities, the size of classes at the university must be larger, on the average, than at institutions like Stanford.

Another feature of the University of California's situation is that if it is to strive for excellence in undergraduate and graduate education and professional training and research on the part of the faculty, then to secure such a faculty involves high costs because in the competitive market in American higher education dozens if not scores of other institutions strive for the same excellence, and will make the best possible bids for talent. This problem is intensified in our state because of high housing costs. This fact of the market—that faculties are expensive if they are to be excellent—also contributes to the difficulty of lowering the university's student-faculty ratio.

Types of Instructional Staff

In part but not entirely because of these exigencies, the University of California has evolved a rather complex, three-tiered teaching system. The first is the Academic Senate itself, which has final responsibility for instruction at the graduate, upper division, and lower division levels, as well as the instruction that takes place in conducting and supervising research. In addition, two special classes of teaching personnel ancillary to the senate faculty have evolved: non-senate instructional staff (also called temporary faculty); and teaching assistants, who are graduate students who serve as supplementary teachers in courses offered by faculty.

In assessing the roles of these several types of instructors the task force found itself repeatedly hobbled by the absence of good information. We found, for example, that few campuses maintain any centralized data on the percentages of courses taught and student credit units offered as between senate and non-senate faculty. Where such data exist, moreover, they are seldom comparable with data—where they exist—on other campuses. The information on the responsibilities of teaching assistants is also incomplete and unsystematic. For this reason, the task force believes that information of the following sorts should be periodically and systematically compiled: the respective roles of ladder and temporary faculty, the status of teaching assistant training and evaluation, and class size by campus as between upper division and lower division. Such information will be helpful, but as we argue below, as such it may not yield direct evidence about the quality of teaching at the lower division and elsewhere.

Despite the deficiencies in data, we can make a few general points about who teaches and why in the University of California. First, who teaches lower division students? The responsibility for lower division education, as with all of undergraduate education, rests with the permanent faculty of the university. However, in any given year, the faculty of the university is composed of approximately 34 percent temporary faculty, some of whom play a role in the lower division curriculum. Contrary to popular belief, however, the largest proportion of our temporary faculty is employed to teach upper division and graduate courses.

Why do we use temporary faculty? First, campuses are required by the office of the president's policy to reserve 10 percent of their total number of available faculty to ensure flexibility to meet new program demands and shifts in enrollments. Campuses actually reserve more, closer to 15 percent. We need temporary faculty to meet these new program demands and enrollment shifts. Second, we need temporary faculty to replace faculty on leave (i.e., sabbaticals or other academics-related leaves) and to fill temporary positions during periods of recruitment for permanent faculty. Approximately 40 percent of our temporary faculty is hired for these two purposes. Third, temporary faculty are hired to teach in those areas of instruction that do not require research expertise (i.e., elementary English composition and elementary foreign language). Fifteen percent of our temporary faculty is employed to teach these kinds of courses. In addition, some 3 percent of temporary faculty teaches remedial courses. It is in these areas of elementary and remedial coursework that lower division students are most likely to be taught by temporary faculty. Fourth, temporary faculty are employed because they have expertise in particular fields; for example, practicing engineers and architects or a violinist from a symphony orchestra. These specialists make up some 26 percent of our pool of temporary faculty. Finally, some 7 percent of the temporary faculty is employed on campuses with no available FTE and the remaining 19 percent are employed for reasons connected with instructional needs that could not be met by ladder faculty.

What role do temporary faculty play in the lower division curriculum? Those temporary faculty who teach lower division students are largely found in a particular subset of courses including elementary courses in reading and composition, foreign language, and math.

In addition to temporary faculty, graduate students employed as teaching assistants play an important role in the lower division curriculum. There are two reasons for employing graduate students as teaching assistants. The first is to provide undergraduates—lower division students in particular—with the small classroom experience, which is the primary learning environment for most lower division students. The second reason is that the experience of serving as a teaching assistant provides important training for the graduate student who is moving toward a college teaching career.

What do graduate students contribute as teaching assistants? For the most part, they teach discussion and recitation sections in lecture courses. In addition, graduate students teach some of the elementary courses such as reading and composition, math, and foreign language. The faculty member has ultimate responsibility for the course; the graduate student may provide some or all the instruction.

The task force is mindful that shifts in the allocation of resources at the lower division are not trivial. The teaching of English composition provides an example. Thirty years ago, baccalaureate education usually included a full year of instruction in composition. In the 1960s composition requirements were generally reduced to a single semester or quarter, and various ways to pass the composition requirement without enrollment were permitted. A calculation for one campus shows that reinstitution of a full-year, mandatory composition course would require approximately sixty full-time equivalent faculty members at a cost of from $1.5 to $1.8 million annually, depending on the level of instructors assigned. Since elementary instruction in composition is not typically assigned to ladder faculty members, the resource base in the non-ladder faculty budget in the college responsible for most lower division instruction in composition. The college has approximately $2.25 million available for non-ladder instruction, of which $180,000 is now committed to instruction in elementary composition. To meet the costs of a year's mandatory instruction would require almost three-fourths of the total budget, leaving very little for instruction in elementary calculus, foreign languages, and other subjects. The moral of this calculation is that even marginal changes at the lower division are likely to have a strong impact on the current distribution of instructional resources.

By and large, the task force finds the general reasons for the mix of Academic Senate faculty, non-senate faculty, and teaching assistants to be both legitimate and necessary. So the main question is not *whether* the university makes use of ancillary teaching personnel; that question would appear to be beyond debate, given the legitimate research functions of the faculty, given the general budgetary limitations on the university, and given the unreality of the idea that enough additional resources might be available so that all teaching could be done by regular faculty.

The Evaluation of Quality in Teaching

The main question, rather, is *how* the university makes use of ancillary personnel. This question deals not so much with the overall numbers or assignments of the three classes of instructors but with their impact on the quality of education in the university. On this question we have virtually no systematic evidence. On the impressionistic side we can report a din of voices giving anecdotal evidence of the most contradictory sort: that temporary faculty are ill-trained and cannot teach effectively; that they are more committed than regular faculty and teach more effectively; that the best teaching assistants are better teachers than most faculty; that teaching assistants are ill-prepared in their subject matter and often cannot communicate in English; that the faculty controls teaching but the others really teach; and so on. In reacting to these assertions, the task force experienced a feeling of frustration and helplessness. Even if we regarded every report as true—or even if every one were true in some unknown measure—we still would not have satisfactory evidence on the issue of quality.

The quality of teaching is difficult to measure. We typically use several measures, all of them indirect or in other ways unsatisfactory. The most common measure is student opinion, reflecting their assessment of the teacher's effectiveness and their level of satisfaction with the teacher and the course. This measure is limited, however, because "satisfaction" may reflect experience of educational growth, pleasure at a good grade, appreciation of a difficult course, appreciation of an easy course, or entertainment—perhaps some mix of all of these. Students' evaluations differ, too, according to whether they are in college, have just graduated, or have been alumni for a number of years. Faculty evaluations of their own and others' teaching are subject to similar ambiguities. There are also various "output" measures, such as retention rates, graduation rates, and subsequent career success rates. These are also imperfect. For an institution not to retain or graduate some students sometimes means that these students have moved on, perhaps, to another institution; and for students who are retained, graduate, or succeed later, it cannot be known how much precollege experiences, collegiate experiences, and general personal maturation during the college years, respectively, figure in these outcomes. We have, finally, various measures of "quality" of a faculty—polls among other faculty, research grants generated by faculty, and so forth—but these usually reflect quality of research rather than teaching.

The task force's conclusion on this count is that any effort to measure educational quality must rest on multiple measures, including repeated, perhaps yearly, self-assessments of students according to their general status and progress in the educational institution, above and beyond their reactions to particular courses and particular administrative situations. Beyond this general point, however, we can venture a few observations about the use, review, and evaluation of quality of senate faculty, non-senate faculty, and teaching assistants.

With respect to senate faculty teaching at the lower division, we believe that campuses will make the greatest gains by assigning their very strongest teachers to large introductory courses. With respect to teaching effectiveness, any campus will have a diversity of talents. Some faculty are brilliant, inspiring, intellectual leaders; some are able but not exceptional; and some seem to find their greatest strengths elsewhere in research and administration. The job for department chairs, deans, and colleges is to identify the very best teachers and entice or direct them into teaching the large introductory courses on as regular a basis as possible. It is not difficult to identify the most effective teachers; most departments and schools can do this on the basis of student evaluations and accumulated reputations. Special consideration for undertaking these lower division assignments should be made in calculating faculty members' other teaching obligations, as well as their general departmental responsibilities, giving recognition to the fact that the effective teaching of large introductory courses—including the effective incorporation of teaching assistants in them—is an especially demanding experience.

We also believe that the evaluation of faculty performance can be better than it is. As indicated, most measures now rest on periodically administered end-of-course questionnaires at the undergraduate level, as well as the testimony of some graduate students. Although efforts to improve this kind of evidence should continue, the task force envisions some additional means of evaluation.

Legend has it that in an earlier age in Harvard's history department, no faculty member could be promoted to tenure until every one of his colleagues had attended at least one of his lectures. It was not a specific lecture, moreover, but one which the colleagues attended at liberty. Colleagues were asked to report to the chairman on the quality of the teacher they observed, and this subject became a matter for collective discussion at the decisive faculty meeting. The task force suspects that this kind of arrangement, in full dress, may not be the exact idea for our time, but some variant would have much to recommend it. For one thing, it would provide evaluative information on teaching that is now virtually lacking; for another, the process would operate as a very powerful form of quality control, encouraging as it would both preparation and organization of course materials; and, not least, it would mean repeated dialogues among colleagues not only about particular teachers but about the ethic and art of teaching, thus helping to bring that subject more self-consciously into the academic culture than it now is.

There is no reason, furthermore, that the criteria of teaching effectiveness should not be raised explicitly in the periodic *external* reviews of departments' introductory and upper division offerings. The question of program effectiveness of the major is frequently brought up in such reviews, but it is usually addressed by looking at prerequisites called for, course sequences, and course coverage. The question of how and how well the faculty teaches the curriculum is not often asked, but the task force sees no reason that it should not be always asked.

With respect to non-senate faculty, we found that although practices vary widely, the evaluation and review of temporary faculty is, by and large, very casual when compared with that of senate faculty members. The decision to hire is often solely that of a departmental chair, with no consultation with colleagues; the supporting materials submitted are often scant; the reviews by deans and personnel committees are often perfunctory; and once in place, the temporary appointee often teaches the course or courses without significant interaction with other faculty.

The task force recommends that the review and evaluation of non-senate faculty be strengthened. We do not have a certain blueprint but recommend the following kinds of measures:

· Campus committees on academic personnel—or perhaps some
  subcommittee—should formulate more systematic guidelines for
  appointment of temporary faculty than now exist; these guidelines
  would include specification of materials to be submitted by department chairs as evidence of teaching effectiveness.

- Campus committees on academic personnel—or, again, perhaps some subcommittee—should themselves develop more thorough and systematic procedures for evaluating temporary personnel.

- At the termination of appointments of one year or less, department chairs should submit to their deans a report evaluating the teaching effectiveness of the temporary appointees. For those holding longer-term appointments, periodic evaluations should be submitted, and these should be reviewed by deans and personnel committees before reappointment or advancement.

Such measures, we believe, would not only yield better evidence of the quality of teaching of temporary personnel but would also provide a mechanism to enhance that quality through more selective recruitment and review.

The task force also notes that the situation of teaching assistants often falls short of fulfilling the official description of their roles. Recent surveys on the Berkeley and Davis campuses have revealed that teaching assistants become fully responsible for teaching as much as 30 percent of lower division courses, mainly in elementary writing and introductory language instruction.[3] This somewhat stark figure raises questions about the selection, training, supervision, and evaluation of teaching assistants.

With respect to selection, the most relevant criteria are that the teaching assistant has adequate command of the subject matter, potential or demonstrated teaching ability, and command of both spoken and written English. Again, although practices vary widely among and within campuses, the surveys show that recruitment and allocation procedures do not assure that these criteria are applied systematically. A primary concern involves those instructors for whom English is a second language. In a 1979 study conducted by the Associated Students Office of Academic Affairs on the Davis campus, 32.6 percent of the undergraduates surveyed agreed that their "TA's lack of fluency in English adversely affected their performance in section."[4] It has been claimed that language problems of teaching assistants constitute the most frequent single complaint among undergraduate students.[5] In many cases the problem of dialect or accent is more nearly at the core of the problem than the teaching assistant's knowledge of the English language itself. The task force recognizes the seriousness of this problem and recommends that graduate divisions on all campuses require, as a precondition for appointment to a teaching assistantship, that all students pass the oral Test of English as a Foreign Language (TOEFL) over and above the written TOEFL required for admission. In some cases this may require that graduate students enroll in one or more courses in English as a Second Language before their classroom teaching begins.

Most University of California campuses conduct campuswide orientation programs for teaching assistants. These programs offer general information on topics such as the roles and responsibilities of a teaching assistant, policies and procedures for employment, campus teaching/learning resources, addressing the needs of special-care students, and conducting the first class meeting. Such programs last two hours to two days and usually are given before classes begin. In addition, department-specific TA programs provide detailed information to TAs about specific courses and about pedagogy. Some of these programs attempt to cover specific teaching skills such as lecturing, leading class discussions, conducting lab sessions, designing examinations, selecting textbooks, and organizing course content.

Information concerning the extent and effectiveness of such programs, however, is not uniformly available because they are sometimes decentralized. The task force is aware that for a number of years resources have been made available for training teaching assistants, and graduate divisions and other units have functioned continuously and well in administering these programs. One problem with such programs, however, is that departmental participation in these programs is usually voluntary, and some departments take no advantage of them and may even develop training programs of their own. In other cases such programs are brief and superficial and lack any follow-up. The task force recommends that graduate divisions and departments take an inventory of graduate teaching assistant training programs and make efforts to institute effective training programs for all graduate students who are appointed to these positions. Campuses should review the degree and quality of departmental TA training on a regular basis. Where structures exist for the purpose, they should be supported, and where they do not, they should be developed.

Supervision and evaluation of teaching assistants are also areas of concern. The surveys show that a significant proportion of teaching assistants are not supervised at all; in other cases the supervision is only perfunctory. The most common form of evaluation is the standard written, end-of-course student survey, which is a useful but incomplete method.

Some departments conduct *in situ* evaluations of teaching assistants; others encourage appraisal through videotape playback, possibly with supervisor consultation. Like supervision, evaluation is also often casual and unsystematic, despite some notable exceptions. In light of this situation, the task force recommends that all faculty who teach courses in which teaching assistants are employed be required to submit a report to the departmental chair at the end of the course evaluating each teaching assistant, indicating the evidence used in this evaluation, and describing how teaching assistants were supervised. These reports should become a regular part of the faculty member's teaching record.

The task force's most general conclusion with respect to both temporary faculty and teaching assistants, then, are that they are a necessary part of the educational system at the University of California for the foreseeable future; that they both constitute bases for augmenting the quality of education; and they ought to be raised from their present status of relative neglect or casualness, given more systematic review and quality control, and thereby integrated better into the university's educational enterprise.

The Idea of the Freshman-Sophomore Seminar

Background One of the recurring apprehensions voiced by those concerned with undergraduate education—particularly at the lower division—is that students are brought together in very large classes and that these do not constitute a very satisfactory setting for learning. The reasons frequently given for this are that students are forced into a passive mode of learning, have only remote one-way contact with the faculty member who lectures, and have little opportunity to sharpen verbal and writing skills and hence many students become cynical and alienated. The task force wishes to make a number of observations on this issue. The first is that the arithmetic of existing student-faculty in a university such as the University of California literally dictates that many classes be large, so they are an inevitable part of the educational scene unless we envision a massive increase in resources. Even institutions with richer student-faculty ratios—Harvard, Stanford, and Yale, for example—have very large lecture courses in which teaching assistants or teaching fellows are employed. The task force does not accept it as a truism, moreover, that large lecture classes are necessarily dull, passive experiences without educational merit. All of us, in reviewing our own college years, can recall really moving, enduring educational experiences for us, even in large lecture settings. In addition, the proper use of teaching assistants—by proper we mean well chosen, well trained, and well coordinated with the lecturer—can add a dimension of intimacy and give-and-take in small discussion settings.

At the same time the task force is aware that if a freshman or sophomore student is enrolled in virtually nothing other than large lecture courses that are not particularly related to one another, this is not conducive to integrating the student into the intellectual life of the campus. One of the core recommendations we make in this connection is that campuses generalize the idea of the freshman-sophomore seminar and strive to assure that at least half of the incoming freshman class is exposed to such an experience.

The Seminar and Its Advantages   The idea of the freshman-sophomore seminar is not new. The Santa Barbara campus initiated a modest program of such seminars in 1974, and a few survive as parts of honors programs. They have been regular parts of the Berkeley curriculum for several years, even though they are limited in number (only about 15 percent of the freshman can take a seminar and sophomores are virtually excluded). On the Los Angeles campus, in addition to the Honors Program, about thirty seminars are offered each year by faculty from the eleven professional schools, and freshmen and sophomores are especially recruited for them. A handful of departmentally sponsored freshman seminars is also offered. In all, about forty-five seminars are now available, and efforts are being made to double that number in the next few years. The Santa Cruz core interdisciplinary program, the lower division honors program on the San Diego campus, and the honors seminar in the humanities program on the Irvine campus are other examples of small-classroom experiences for lower division students. Our recommendation is that these kinds of courses be made more widely available on more campuses.

The kind of course we have in mind involves a small class (of about fifteen) taught by a ladder faculty member, in which the focus is on a central issue in the faculty member's area of research or more general scholarly commitments. Taken together these courses would cover a diverse set of disciplines and subjects. The task force believes such courses have special value in the lower division of the University of California. Among their advantages are the following:

· They provide an opportunity for close, intense intellectual exchange between faculty and students. Reports from faculty who have taught them suggest that their value is as great for faculty as it is for students. Offering these courses revitalizes and dramatically reintroduces many faculty to the intellectual and personal joy of teaching enthusiastic, articulate, and thoughtful young men and women. The gain for the student in these seminars comes from regular and active association and appreciation of what for both scholar and student is an intriguing subject matter.

· They provide an opportunity for similar interchange among students, which is difficult to attain in the large lecture setting and with dispersed residential arrangements. We regard the seminar as an especially valuable setting for students with very diverse economic, ethnic, racial, religious, and educational backgrounds to "mix it up" with one another in common intellectual pursuits in their early undergraduate years. The seminar is also a good setting for the formation of enduring friendships.

· Small seminars, usually requiring significant writing assignments and weekly discussion of core readings, can do far more than large lecture courses to sharpen the writing, verbal, and critical reasoning skills of students. If this happens early in the undergraduate's career, the enhanced basic skills can bring benefits in many other courses and academic settings.

· Small seminars are an effective way of orienting first-year students to what is often a foreign and competitive setting on a university campus. Before settling into the college years many students experience a great deal of anxiety about where they will ultimately swim in the big pond, and the opportunity for participating actively in an intimate education experience is a fruitful way of channeling these feelings and integrating the students into meaningful groups. The factors that affect student retention in the lower division are numerous and not fully understood, but this kind of academic experience would certainly be a positive factor.

· Small seminars provide a setting in which the most effective kind of faculty advising can take place. The task force is cognizant that, particularly in the lower division, much of the detailed advising on courses, requirements, and so forth is best left to a cadre of professional advisors responsible for student services. The kind of advice and support that faculty could provide in these small seminar settings concerns the students' struggles with their larger commitments—their choice of a major, preparation for a career, and so on. Ideally, faculty members who teach a small cadre of students in their freshman and sophomore year could serve as informal advisors to students through their collegiate years.

- The small seminar also serves as a vehicle for the faculty member to link his or her research with teaching. We see great value in having some of the seminars flowing directly from faculty members' research; even relatively specialized research topics can be brought alive if they are pursued in the context of the larger intellectual issues the research raises.

- The kind of give-and-take in the seminar settings encourages what is described as the development of students' citizenship values. The dominant theme of these seminars is cooperative exploration of ideas, with the accompanying development of respect for the ideas of others.

These advantages offer a strong rationale for giving high priority to seminars in the lower division. In recommending their expansion, the task force is mindful that this would not be without cost. To accommodate half of an entering freshman class of 3,000 would require one hundred seminars. The task force envisions some relatively low-cost means that can contribute toward the total resources required to expand these offerings. Large departments with many courses might seek to give some of the less popular courses somewhat less often, thus freeing faculty for seminars. Also, intelligent and productive use of emeriti—for those campuses that have significant numbers of them—can be envisioned. Those emeriti who are still active and engaged, and who would be willing to return to one freshman-sophomore seminar per year, could bring their decades of experience into the lower division classroom. Honoraria should be should be given to participating emeriti. (It should be noted that the certainty of mounting rates of faculty retirement in the 1990s makes the idea of emeriti participation even more feasible.) Ultimately, however, because of the very small size of these classes, offering them on the scale envisioned does raise the question of new faculty resources to support them. Our expectation is that if programs of this sort begin to develop successfully, administrators and legislatures will target them as meriting high priority in making funds available for new programs.

We have developed our thoughts on the freshman-sophomore seminar at some length because such a mechanism appears to have many links with potentially positive features of the lower division experience. At the same time, we do not want to put the idea forth mindlessly or as some sort of monolith. We realize that it is very difficult at present for some campuses—especially those feeling the crunch of recent rapid increases in enrollment—to free any resources to initiate a seminar program. We also realize that there are other, complementary course arrangements that might work toward the same end. One idea to be considered is for campuses to develop one or more interdisciplinary freshman courses, which would be large, to be sure, but if staffed by a number of excellent faculty and a larger than normal cadre of selected teaching assistants would provide a kind of shared civic and intellectual experience for freshmen and serve as a focus for their interest and identification. The most extreme version of this is the "Western Civilization" courses once required for all students on the Columbia and Stanford campuses; we recommend neither that special content nor the feature of requiring such a course of every student—both seem to be out of touch with present times—but point to it as one model. Another model is the former "Social Sciences 2" course in the Harvard postwar general education program, which, although not required, was taken by large numbers, proved intellectually inspiring, and generated a kind of "Soc Sci 2" subculture for many Harvard undergraduates. Still another model would be for campuses to devise one general, interdisciplinary course for the physical sciences, life sciences, social sciences, and humanities, and make that course a prerequisite for majoring in any department in each of those areas.

The alternatives we have brought forward have in common the objective of adding an increment of intellectual intensity, involvement in, and integration into the lower division years while attempting to stay within the bounds of reality with respect to resources required.

THE UNIVERSITY, THE OTHER SECTORS, AND GENERAL EDUCATION

The Background and the Problems

The inclusion of the lower division on the University of California's campuses has always enjoyed a general legitimacy. On only a few occasions in its history have educators and others argued that the lower division should *not* be a part of the university. The subject was raised in 1959 by the Master Plan Survey Team (the group charged with writing the master plan). The team advanced no reasons for eliminating the lower division and gave three reasons for continuing it: (a) as a scholarly institution in which the university has a long tradition of taking students from the freshman level through graduate work; (b) the university cannot build academic majors without lower division offerings; and (c) doctoral students require teaching internships, and lower division teaching is a proper setting for these.

In 1967, the Coordinating Council for Higher Education (the forerunner of the California Postsecondary Education Commission) prepared a report on the subject, responding to a senate concurrent resolution asking for a study of the "desirability and feasibility of eliminating lower division programs at selected campuses of the University of California and the California State Colleges." The report concluded that the elimination of lower division programs was feasible, arguing that instruction in the lower division was comparable in "comprehension and quality" in the community colleges, that transfer to the upper division from community colleges was easily facilitated, and that the cost of lower division education is less in community colleges than in the other segments. The council also saw this elimination as a way of augmenting graduate instruction and research on university campuses, and foresaw a "new and dynamic" type of university that would offer primarily upper division and graduate instruction. The council called upon the university and the California State Colleges to consider such a model in their planning.

In responding, both segments strongly opposed eliminating the lower division. The university in particular argued that all campuses should be general campuses offering programs at all collegiate levels (while also encouraging transfer). It argued further that lower division students derive benefit from their association with advanced students and with faculty members teaching at advances levels. In the end the council adopted the report but recommended no concrete action, and the issue of elimination received no further consideration at that time or subsequently.

While acknowledging this historical stability, we call attention to a special peculiarity of California's system of higher education. It provides for the possibility that many students who receive a collegiate education will experience the lower division years in an institution different from the one from which they experience the upper division years and graduate. We refer of course to the provision of the transfer function—transfer of qualified community college graduates to the other two segments, and transfers between the California State University system and the University of California. This is a key feature of the Master Plan for Higher Education that not only preserves a distinct differentiation of functions among the segments and provides for ascending levels of selectivity in admissions policy among them but also provides an opportunity to move on for those who, for whatever reasons, entered and successfully completed their work in a community college or state university.

In recent years, however, the flow of transfers to the University of California appears to have shrunk considerably. From a record high of 8,193 community college transfers in 1973, the figure dropped to 5,428 in 1980 and to 4,931 in 1985. This phenomenon has caused wide concern among educational and political leaders and has led some to question the viability of the functioning of the master plan. The issue of transfer has been high on the agenda of the Commission for the Review of the Master Plan for Higher Education.

Unraveling the causes of this decline is much more difficult than noticing it. Certainly one factor has been the national trend toward the proliferation of vocational programs in the community colleges, with the consequence that the increasing numbers of students who enter those programs do not elect the kinds of courses that would qualify them to transfer. Among other factors that might be responsible, the Commission for the Review of the Master Plan noted the following: "decreased numbers of high school graduates; increased dropout rates for ethnic minorities; student under-preparation for college-level work; inadequate student financial aid; and the increasing proportion of UC- and CSU-eligible students entering those segments as freshmen."[6]

Whatever the exact mix of factors, some attention has focused on what are perceived as curricular and administrative obstacles to transfer on the part of the University of California. Among these are the uncertainty of what courses taken at the community college level will qualify as general education, prerequisite, or major courses; inadequacy of dissemination of that kind of information when it exists; and imposition of additional lower division requirements on transfer students after they arrive at the university. The task force is uncertain as to the salience of these problems among all other factors affecting transfer, but we certainly encourage steps on the university's part to facilitate the transfer of qualified students.

Suggested Reforms

In connection with that facilitation, three types of arrangements have been initiated or are recommended:

1. The California Articulated Numbering System (CAN), which is composed of written agreements between two or more institutions to accept a completed course on a sending campus to meet a specific course requirement on a receiving campus. An example would be an agreement approved by appropriate faculty members at the Santa Barbara campus to accept Santa Barbara City College's freshman calculus course in lieu of taking freshman calculus. Such agreements, if made on a wide scale and adequately publicized, increase the potential transfer student's ability to plan his or her curriculum and to be assured that fewer curricular surprises and disappointments would be waiting after he or she enters the university.

2. As a more ambitious project, the Commission for the Review of the Master Plan has proposed that the governing boards of the three segments, in consultation with faculty, develop a general transfer core curriculum which, with the courses required for specific majors, would insure "transfer to the University of California or the California State University systems upon successful completion of the appropriate courses and maintenance of the requisite grade point average."[7] The anticipated advantage of such a curriculum would be much the same as those of the CAN system—to publicize the uniform conditions for transfer throughout the segments and in the secondary school system, thereby facilitating preparation for and making the transfer process easier and more certain.

3. With respect to the university itself, it has been suggested that the various campuses honor one another's general education requirements. The most extreme version of this idea would be to assume that any given campus's general education requirements have been met if a student transferring from any other campus of the university has met them there. The advantage of this arrangement would be to facilitate the modest level of transfer from one university campus to another and to assure that a community college or CSU

student who (a) has met the general education requirements of the targeted university campus, (b) fails to be admitted to that campus but, (c) is admitted to another university campus, will not have additional course requirements imposed.

Evaluation of the Reforms

The task force finds merit and promise in all three of these measures but is skeptical about the wholesale adoption of any of them. With respect to the CAN system, the Academic Council of the Systemwide Academic Senate passed a resolution in December 1985, urging "the office of the president to take such actions as are needed appropriate to expand the articulation efforts of the University of California"; it also foresaw continuing faculty involvement in this process. In an accompanying report, however, the council wondered how important the factor of students' confusion over the transferability of courses actually is in the transfer process; noted the complexity of the process because of the diversity of breadth requirements and non-uniformity of requirements for majors between and within campuses; and pointed out the substantial cost and increased workload on faculty and staff entailed in the process. We might add that in order to be effective, articulation contracts cannot be simply one-time-and-forever agreements, but must be periodically reviewed as campuses in all three segments revise their courses continuously.

For these reasons the task force believes that the most productive (and cost-effective) attack on the articulation process is at the regional level and that it would be wasteful to secure all-inclusive articulation agreements. Most transfers occur within distinct regions, and the main "feeder" institutions can be identified easily; only a trickle of students will be found transferring from, say, Columbia Community College, to, say, the Riverside campus. Insofar as these regional articulation systems can be expanded, they will have at least two distinct advantages: to reduce confusion, disappointment, and course repetition, and thereby indeed facilitate transfer; and to afford a university campus input to the quality of community college instruction as courses are reviewed prior to executing or renewing articulation contracts. The task force also recognizes the importance of the systemwide dissemination of articulation agreements to the campuses of the other segments and ultimately to the potential transfer students, and for that reason it encourages the university's efforts to improve communication through programs such as ASSIST, the Articulation System Stimulating Interinstitutional Student Transfer.

The idea of a single common core curriculum is more complex. Responding to that idea in January 1986, the Academic Council concluded that the idea of "identifying lower divisional general education curricula that would be acceptable to four-year segments of higher education" is "a straightforward idea that deserves serious attention." Bt it also warned against attempting too great uniformity across the board.

The task force recognizes that there are several versions of an idea of a common core curriculum and that some are more acceptable or promising than others. The strongest version seems to be that implied by the language of the Commission to Review the Master Plan, which calls for a uniform package containing general education courses as well as courses required for specific majors that would be universally transferable. Such a proposal raises several practical objections and one major objection in principle. It seems a fantasy to believe that such an inclusive common core could be found acceptable by all the departments and faculties of all eight participating university campuses, all nineteen state university campuses, and all 121 community college campuses. Even if that prospect could be envisioned, it would call for an endless, gargantuan, and conflict-ridden effort on the part of faculties to reach that end. More important in our minds, however, is that the effort would work toward an intellectual standardization and rigidity that is out of keeping with the mission of institutions of higher education, which includes the imperative to maximize responsiveness, change, and innovation in the creation and transmission of knowledge.

We do see value, however, in a more modest version of the idea. Instead of being as comprehensive as that of the Commission to Review the Master Plan, a uniform set of UC transfer requirements could be more like a "core of a core," that is, a limited and more easily agreed-upon list. For example, a uniform set of transfer requirements could have as its primary objectives the development of the students' (a) understanding of the principal branches of knowledge, (b) general academic skills, and (c) preparation for upper division study. An illustrative set of transfer general education requirement might involve the following one-year sequences:

English composition

Mathematics

Humanities

Social science

Natural science

Foreign language

Students who complete this set of courses at a specific level of performance would be considered to have satisfied fully the principal lower division education requirements of a University of California school or college. At the same time individual university campuses would maintain the freedom to require additional special courses (e.g., Western Civilization, Contemporary Social Issues, Computer Literacy, etc.) that they regard as especially important. In addition, transfer students would still be held responsible for any lower division major requirements not completed in the community college. Both the additional special lower division courses and the lower division major requirements might, however, be matters of course articulation agreements.

The advantages of this example—and the task force presents it as only an example—is that the requirements are general, straightforward, and easy to understand. They are not dependent on detailed and extensive articulation agreements. They do not restrict the flexibility or creativity of the community colleges to develop other kinds of courses for their students who plan to transfer to the university. They do not imply a complete uniformity of lower division requirements on the part of university campuses. And in terms of breadth of disciplinary study, the illustration compares favorably with lower division general education requirements of most university schools and colleges.

With respect to reciprocity arrangements among campuses, the task force believes that these also merit development. In April 1986, the chair of the Academic Council expressed the collective sentiment when she wrote to the heads of all divisions of the senate, asking them to explain the idea in their committees on educational policy and elsewhere. On June 16, 1986, the Academic Council passed a resolution calling for representatives of campus committees on educational policy and others with expertise to convene to seek common ground for reciprocity among UC campuses with respect to general breadth requirements. In this area of reciprocity, the task force underscores again the notion of a "core of a core" that would constitute the basis for campuses simultaneously honoring one another's general educational requirements and safeguarding the traditions of diversity and uniqueness in mission and perspectives of each campus.

General Education through the Four Collegiate Years

One of the complaints voiced in the national reports was that a very high proportion of courses that constitute "general education" (writing, composition, breadth requirements, interdisciplinary courses) are concentrated in the first two years of college. The task force shares this concern; furthermore, the prospects for developing some kind of common core curriculum and of instituting reciprocity arrangements among campuses with respect to lower division general education simultaneously raise the issue of general education in the upper division years.

Traditionally, much curricular planning and emphasis appears to have rested on a kind of implicit two-stage model of educational development, the stages corresponding roughly with the lower division and the upper division. The first stage, assuming a relatively fresh, uneducated, and uncommitted student, works on these qualities by imparting new information, ensuring a breadth of exposure to many branches of knowledge and learning, and "liberalizing" the student by plumbing new depths of meaning and significance of knowledge heretofore unappreciated. The second stage narrows commitment (to a "major," usually), where the premium is more on mastering an analytic mode: learning the peculiarities of one kind of disciplined thought or another and coming to use it to solve certain problems and generate insights and explanations. Curricular application of this model yields the concentration of the "general" and the "liberal" at the lower division.

The task force appreciates this model but finds it on the brittle side; good education would seem to entail a simultaneous mix among all the elements—acquainting, broadening, and analyzing. Beyond this point, we would also like to posit a kind of third stage, which involves those processes that have been described variously as integration, synthesis, and global learning. Here the stress is on relationships among discrete bits of knowledge and analysis that have not been appreciated before. This kind of thinking, moreover, would seem logically to come late in the educational process, because it rests on an accumulation of a great deal of intellectual experience of the other kinds. In the past some educational institutions have included a capstone course—usually world history or some variant—as a senior experience meant, if not to tie everything together, then to provide the student with a general framework for organizing much of what has been learned. The task force finds much of value in the idea of general, synthetic courses of instruction late in the collegiate years.

In line with this reasoning, the task force recommends that university campuses develop general education courses and programs at their upper divisions. We have already mentioned the value of general, synthetic courses at the lower division as complements to lower division seminars. In addition, campuses should consider developing courses that might serve as capstones for juniors and seniors. We have in mind, for example, courses with international, multicultural, or global themes; interdisciplinary courses centering on intellectual and social problems; and courses synthesizing a number of analytical techniques in logic, mathematics, and computer sciences. Such courses not only have intrinsic educational value in themselves but also are an avenue for each campus, with its own outlooks and strengths, to express its individuality.

The task force recommends, then, selective and deliberate developments along four lines simultaneously: course articulation, a limited core general education curriculum, reciprocity among campuses on general education requirements, and upper division synthesizing or capstone courses. Mechanisms for these developments also suggest themselves. The mechanisms for faculty involvement in course articulation agreements are already in place, and existing ways of making these agreements generally known should be expanded. The development of reciprocity arrangements is a matter for the Academic Senate and its divisions. The development of upper division general education courses is the responsibility of the schools and colleges of the individual campuses. As for a core curriculum, initiative for this might appropriately assigned to the Intersegmental Committee of the Academic Senates, or a similar body made up of representatives from all three segments. The intersegmental committee has already made progress in preparing statements that lay out the competencies expected of secondary school students who intend to go to college. Developing some kind of core transfer curriculum involves a similar task. Final responsibility for any plan for general education requirements, however, would rest with the Academic Senates and administrations of the three segments, in accordance with the ways that curricular authority has been delegated in each.

The Themes of Internationalization and Diversification

Two Lines of Change   The task force is cognizant of and shares the conviction that what might be called the "increasing internationalization of the world" is—in its many facets—the most profound movement affecting civilization in the last half of the twentieth century. We are also convinced that this theme ought to occupy a most salient place in the enterprise of higher education in general, and in the mission of the University of California in particular, in the decades to come.

Internationalization, as the task force understands it, refers to the following kinds of developments: (1) the internationalization of world production, as manifested by the penetration of multinational corporations into the world economy; (2) the internationalization of world finance, as manifested by the increasing importance of quasi-public and private financial institutions in the world economy; (3) the internationalization of labor, as multinational corporations penetrate into host countries' labor forces and as international migration continues; (4) the internationalization of politics, including not only the superpower relations but also the spread of local conflicts throughout the world and the sensitization of almost every part of the world to international tensions; (5) the internationalization of culture, including popular culture, but also involving new languages of interaction that develop when nations deal with one another in ever more complicated terms; (6) the internationalization of scholarship, as manifested by the diffusion of research, international collaboration in research, and exchange programs for faculty and students.

The process of internationalization has been pervasive and profound; it is difficult not to believe, moreover, that a further increase in the interdependency among nations—on all the dimensions noted—will occur in the decades to come. Furthermore, this process itself has posed a deep challenge to our knowledge and understanding of the economic, political, and social world. Most political thinking and most of the relevant academic disciplines have rested on the assumption that the basic unit of social life is the discrete nation, society, or culture. The fact is, however, that the twin phenomena of internationalization and interdependency are rendering this fundamental premise questionable and demand novel ways of thinking, analyzing, and understanding.

To come closer to home, it is evident that the state of California has played and will inevitably play a pivotal role in these developments. As many have pointed out, the state is a major nation in its own right from the standpoint of wealth and trading potential. And it is strategically located from the geographical and cultural points of view. Along with the rest of the United States, California bears a strong relationship to European civilization; but California is also oriented—historically, geographically, economically, and culturally—to the Asian and Latin American worlds in ways that most of the United States is not.

It also seems inevitable that the University of California will play a leading role in this large historical process. It is an institution that has risen to a position of national and international leadership, and those who look forward fully expect it to play a leading role in conducting research on, increasing understanding of, and training those who will be leaders in the new world scene.

Observers of the internationalization process have pointed out the ways in which it works toward the standardization and homogenization of the world, particularly from the cultural point of view. At the local level, however, the process may make for greater diversification and heterogeneity. The state of California is a prime example of this latter effect. A combination of migration and differential birth rates among ethnic groups has produced historical trends that now make California a truly multicultural and multilingual society. These trends, too, are certain to accelerate during the coming decades to the point where those we now designate as minorities will constitute a majority.

This ethnic, racial, and cultural diversity has found its way into the university's student population, by dint of demography and of affirmative action and outreach programs. This process also promises to continue. We may expect an increasing heterogeneity of faculty as well, as more minorities work their way through the higher education system and enter the reservoir of qualified candidates from which faculties are selected. There is no aspect of life in the state—political, economic, cultural, and residential—that is not being affected by these trends toward diversification. Certainly the educational life of the University of California is affected. Our assumptions about the commonality of motivation, outlooks, and commitment of student and faculty grow increasingly unrealistic, and the challenge to provide educational experiences that are simultaneously meaningful, broadening, and integrating is enormous.

University Responses to These Changes   The task force recommends that the University of California give special stress to the twin themes of internationalization and diversification in its educational mission. This effort cannot, however, be conceived of in narrow terms but must be pursued on many fronts. In keeping with our special assignment, we mention curricular responses first.

Both internationalization and diversification make the world more complex and difficult to comprehend; they call for new approaches to understanding the complex forces affecting our society and our lives and for new approaches to understanding heterogeneity. For this reason we recommend that courses offered by interdisciplinary and have a comparative, multicultural, or global dimension. Examples of such courses are the following:

World history

The United States and the world in the twentieth century

Technology and cultural change

Economic development and international inequality

The global economy

World literary traditions

World religious and philosophical traditions

The idea of "system" in international relations

Human and cultural diversity

Cultural heterogeneity and political life

The history and contemporary situation of minorities in American life

The task force does not feel it appropriate to go into detail with respect to where and how such courses ought to be located in students' careers, whether they should be required or optional, and the like. General, interdisciplinary lower division courses on human and cultural diversity or on the international system seem timely and valuable. Certainly the internationalization and diversification themes are appropriate for freshman-sophomore seminars. Other courses of a more comprehensive, synthetic character might be offered later in the undergraduate years. Whatever the pattern that different campuses work out, the task force urges that major efforts of some sort be undertaken with respect to the themes of internationalization and diversification, since these themes are so relevant to the kind of world in which students in this generation will later be living.

Curricular efforts are only one prong of the kind of multipronged response that is called for. The task force envisions a number of other kinds of priorities under the heading of internationalization and diversification:

· To augment research and training in academic areas involving these themes. The new school of international relations on the San Diego campus is one kind of model, but the themes could also be given high priority on the agendas of organized research units (for example, institutes and centers for international studies and the area studies programs on all campuses). Relevant academic departments and professional schools could keep the same themes in mind as substantial numbers of retiring faculty are replaced in the coming decades.

· To develop language instruction in areas that have heretofore been relatively minor, particularly Asian languages, to augment training of language teachers to be placed in secondary schools and community colleges, and to work further toward assuring that those who do not have English as a first language experience only minimal academic suffering from that fact.

· To augment existing programs of international exchange of students and faculty even further, making certain that these programs have an element of reciprocity with other nations.

A precondition for any success of the measures proposed is that the university make every effort to accelerate those efforts and programs that will assure that the composition of all our constituencies—faculty, administration, students, and staff—itself becomes and remains heterogeneous. We have had enough experience with affirmative action programs in the past two decades to be aware of the constant danger of their erosion. The task force has no sure solution in mind on this matter but acknowledges that increased efforts and resources are needed on many fronts: reducing barriers to interest, application, and admissions; establishing relations with schools, parents, and communities; reducing the disadvantages of students once they have arrived; searching effectively in the academic market; and constantly striving to make our educational environment a welcoming one.

The Changing Character of Knowledge

The most fundamental questions to be asked about the character of a collegiate education are these: (1) What is the character of the knowledge to be imparted and capacities to be developed? (2) Through what modes— courses, tutorials, independent study, and so forth—is this achieved?

With respect to the first question, we first take note of a series of trends that have truly revolutionized the state of knowledge in the twentieth century:

- The "knowledge explosion" has continued to accelerate. We have seen dramatic *increases* in the quantity and quality of our knowledge about nature, the organism, the person, society, and culture, as reflected in advances in research in all the disciplines and in interdisciplinary endeavors. We are making simultaneous strides through computerization, sophisticated retrieval systems, and other strategies to make available and master what we know, but such is the pace of change that even these constitute something of a rearguard battle.

- Knowledge has become increasingly *technical*. The development of new knowledge involves new modes of thought, new problems, new types of facts, and new relations between facts. In may cases, words are not available in the vernacular to conceptualize this new knowledge—or when they are, they are not sufficiently precise. New languages—both verbal and mathematical—have to be invented. In addition, unfamiliar paradigms and models have been created, and sophisticated and complicated statistical and computational techniques have been applied. On occasion, the development of neologisms, technical precision, and abstractness gets out of hand, and the resulting jargon obscures rather than facilitates the expression of knowledge. As a result of all these tendencies, new knowledge has become more technical and therefore less accessible to the layperson. To become educated in a field, moreover, a student must master more technical material than ever before. These facts are virtually self-evident in the physical and life sciences—physics, chemistry, genetics, botany, etc. The social sciences have become vastly more technical as well. Economic theory, resting more and more on mathematical expression, is perhaps the obvious example, but the analysis of kinship matrices and linguistic structures by anthropologists and the analysis of intergenerational mobility by sociologists are equally as technical. In history and in many humanities fields—literary criticism and fine arts, for example—analysis still rests mainly on the use of language, but discourse in these areas, too, is frequently abstract and complicated.

· Knowledge has become increasingly *specialized*. As knowledge has advanced, disciplines have tended to develop subdisciplines within themselves (molecular biology, inorganic chemistry, medical sociology, medical anthropology, historical demography). The greater specialization of knowledge is also shown in the proliferation of courses in college catalogues. As a result of this trend, it becomes increasingly difficult for any type of scholar to claim a general knowledge of his or her field. And for the student, acquaintance with—to say nothing of mastery of—any discipline requires more extensive study than ever before.

· As a result, knowledge has become more *fragmented*. As knowledge becomes compartmentalized into disciplines and subdisciplines, it becomes more difficult to relate parts to one another because of noncomparable problems posed, languages and models generated, and explanations given. It also becomes more difficult to synthesize— to relate discrete bodies of knowledge to some larger and more significant dimensions of understanding.

An inevitable consequence of these trends, especially in the sciences and the social sciences, has been the decline of the humanistic impulse as well a the increasing isolation of these disciplines from the "grand ideas" of religion, natural philosophy, and moral and political philosophy from which many of the disciplines were spawned. (By "humanistic impulse" we mean the assessment of knowledge in terms of its meaning for the natural, moral, and spiritual aspects of the human condition.) Consider, for example, the fate of "political theory" in political science. In the not too distant past, political theory dealt with the nature of the state, the proper balance between the duties owed the state by the citizens and the freedoms owed the citizens by the state, the nature of sovereignty, and the like. Over the past several decades, as the scientific impulse swept through political science, this emphasis on political theory was overshadowed by a preoccupation with more technical and more neutral social science theory.

It might be remarked that the overshadowing of the humanistic impulse is not limited to the sciences. Humanism may be on the decline in the humanities as well. Note, for example, how the ascension of formal logic and metaphysics in the twentieth century has eclipsed the ancient philosophical concerns with ethics, aesthetics, the philosophy of religion, and some aspects of political philosophy. Note also the development of highly technical modes of artistic, literary, and musical criticism in the humanities and the tendency of that kind of technical analysis to intrude upon the exploration of the broader human implications of the cultural creations under study.

Turning to the second question, the major modes for imparting and developing knowledge remain the course of instruction offered by academic departments or schools, and clusters of these courses ("the major"), also offered by academic departments. A course occupies approximately one-quarter of a student's academic efforts during a given term. The major is variable, occupying between one-fourth and two-thirds of a student's four-year program. The lower division experience typically involves taking a number of introductory courses in different disciplines to gain "breadth," one of which may introduce the student to his or her ultimate major. The major consists of one or more introductory courses at the lower division (with perhaps some prerequisites from other departments, such as mathematics or statistics) and a cluster of more advanced and specialized courses at the upper division level.

In all these matters the department remains at the center of things. Some campuses have made efforts to undercut that dominance—for example, the effort to give salience to colleges on the Santa Cruz and San Diego campuses, and the interdisciplinary "group" principle in the School of Social Sciences on the Irvine campus. But in all cases the departmental principle emerges, and introductory disciplinary offerings and majors are made available. In the case of special "group majors"—for example, the Political Economy of Industrial Societies on the Berkeley campus—the organizational basis of the major is not by discipline, but virtually every one of the courses that make up the package for the major is offered by discipline-based academic departments.

Educational Consequences and Challenges

Given the changes in the nature of knowledge we have described, and given the dominance of the departmental vehicle, we recognize that at the present time it is difficult to introduce a student to an academic discipline, and it is difficult to fashion a major that gives an undergraduate a comprehensive or integrated grasp of the intellectual substance, style, and method of a field of study. The disciplines themselves are large and specialized, and if the undergraduate elects to touch many facets of a field lightly, he or she may emerge with only a fragmented appreciation of the intellectual core of the field and may be only superficially acquainted with small ranges of its theory and empirical knowledge. In such a case he or she has not received a very valuable "general education," even in the major. If the student elects to probe more deeply into one aspect of the discipline, he or she will emerge preoccupied with the technical issues that are the concern of the subject matter chosen. In this case, too, a nonspecialized education in the major is not attained. Furthermore, because most teachers are likely to have devoted most of their energies to conducting specialized research and to giving specialized courses in the field, the undergraduate is not likely to receive much assistance from them in any attempt he or she might make to gain some general sense of—much less to synthesize—the major.

Years ago Joseph Tussman vividly characterized this tension between the specialized pursuit of knowledge and the search for synthesis and integration as a "conflict between the university and the college":

> The university is a collection of highly trained specialists who work with skill, persistence and devotion. Its success is beyond question, but it pays the price of its success. The price is specialization, and it supports two unsympathetic jibes: the individual specialized scholar may find that with Oedipus, the pursuit of knowledge leads to impairment of vision, and the community of scholars, speaking its special tongues, has suffered the fate of Babel.
>
> [Those] who are the university are also, however, [those] who are the college. But the liberal arts college is a different enterprise. It does not assault or extend the frontiers of knowledge. It has a different mission. It cultivates human understanding. The mind of the person, not the body of knowledge, is its central concern. . . . The university for multiplicity and knowledge, the college for unity and understanding.
>
> The college is everywhere in retreat, fighting a dispirited rearguard action against the triumphant university. The upper-division, dominated

by departmental cognitive interests, has become, in spirit, a preparatory run at the graduate school, increasingly professional. Only the lower division remains outside the departmental fold.[8]

Even the last assertion is not really correct, for most of the introductory work in the lower division is given by departments.

One fundamental kind of "tilt" now institutionalized in the university, then, is that toward specialization at the expense of synthetic knowledge. A related tilt, seen in places though not everywhere, is that toward specialization at the expense of breadth. Faculty who design and teach a major are keenly aware of how little of their disciplines can be covered within the span of a major. The corresponding tendency is for some majors to expand, and this is at the expense of breadth. Perhaps the most extreme case of this is the undergraduate professional schools, of which engineering is the most frequently cited illustration. Unlike many subjects that involve many years of postgraduate study, engineering education is organized in such a way that students enter professional ranks immediately after receiving the bachelor's degree. There is great pressure to include sufficient mathematics and physical sciences and to cover a range of engineering courses—often in fields in which recent technological progress and advances in knowledge are enormous. A survey of catalogues for the University of California campuses has shown that "engineering majors tend to have fewer breadth requirements."[9]

One proposal for undergraduate professional programs is that they be extended beyond the four collegiate years to permit two full years of liberal education.[10] (In a 1984 survey, more than one-third of a sample of electrical engineers expressed the opinion that four years was not adequate for training electrical engineers.)[11] The task force does not recommend this solution unilaterally. We are aware of the significant cost considerations involved in adding a fifth year to the collegiate experience for many students; and we are aware that some attempted five-year programs have failed because students continued to choose other available four-year options. Nevertheless, we regard the "breadth problem" for undergraduate professional schools to be severe; and we urge campus faculties and engineers to seek ways to improve the liberal education components of those programs without sacrificing their professional quality.

We cannot conclude this discussion of intellectual balance without pointing to a final "tilt"—that toward the physical and life sciences and away from the humanities and to some degree, the social sciences. The sources of this tilt are to be found, in the long run, in the great faith that Americans have placed in science and its applications, and their long-standing skepticism toward "impractical" subjects such as the arts and humanities.[12] In recent years this emphasis has risen to greater salience, as the United States has experienced extreme economic competition from other nations and as science and technology have been singled out as major weapons in this struggle. Whatever the sources, the pressure has resulted in an uneven flow of resources into the scientific side of the university: scientists receive differentially higher salaries than others; they have much greater access to external research funds, which means, among other things, salary supplements and less teaching; high-tech bonds float among voters, although bonds for art museums, auditoriums, and libraries do not. The point of this observation is not to question the importance of scientific endeavor, but to point out that a chronic drift in this direction threatens to skew the historic mission of the university as a comprehensive seat of research, teaching, and learning in all fields.

This discussion of balance raises fundamental questions about the structure of our system of collegiate education—including the lower division. The problems identified, moreover, do not lend themselves to incremental, short-term tinkering with the system. Mindful of this, the task force expresses its conviction that these issues are among the most salient facing the university in the late twentieth century and that they should constitute major items in its long-term agenda. Among the general lines of change that might be contemplated in relation to the issue of balance are the following:

· Academic departments should not be the only agencies to introduce students to their fields in the lower division; such courses could also be offered by interdisciplinary teams, in order to increase the probability that the general implications of specialized knowledge be stressed.

· Courses should be problem-oriented as well as discipline-oriented, and focus on topics such as bureaucracy and freedom, the fate of democracy in large industrial societies, and the political implications of ethnic and cultural heterogeneity.

· Selected undergraduate professional programs should be transformed into five-year baccalaureate programs or into master's degree programs.

- Some righting of a major imbalance should be attempted by infusing new resources into teaching and research in the humanities and social sciences.

- Traditional "colleges of arts and sciences" should be further decentralized, so that clusters of departments are made responsible for synthetic lower and upper division offerings that are more appropriate for undergraduates than are the quasi-postgraduate courses that now constitute many undergraduate majors.

- Serious questions should be raised as to whether the traditional "liberal arts" emphasis should continue to be the basic model for undergraduate education; as the dynamics of knowledge change make this model increasingly difficult to realize, new models might be sought.

We trust that the faculties and administration of our university will not lose sight of this larger picture—even of its somewhat revolutionary implications—as they continue to strive for excellence in the face of continuing and bewildering changes in their historical situation.

APPENDIX I. MEMBERS OF THE TASK FORCE

Neil J. Smelser, Chair, University Professor of Sociology, Berkeley

Thomas Bond, Provost, Revelle College, Professor, Department of Chemistry, San Diego

Walter Capps, Professor, Department of Religious Studies, Santa Barbara

Katherine Clark, Visiting Lecturer, Department of English, Irvine

Bruce Cooperstein, Provost, College Eight, Associate Professor, Department of Mathematics, Santa Cruz

Carlos Cortes, Professor and Chair, Department of History, Riverside

Patricia Fitchen, Visiting Lecturer, Department of French, Santa Cruz

Dean Florez, Student, Undergraduate Student Affairs, Los Angeles

Julie Gordon, Principal Policy Analyst, Academic Affairs, office of the president

Evelyn Hu, Professor, Department of Electrical and Computer Engineering, Santa Barbara

Kenneth Jowitt, Dean, Freshman and Sophomore Studies, Professor, Department of Political Science, Berkeley

Leon Mayhew, Dean, Letters and Science, Davis

Calvin Moore, Associate Vice President—Academic Affairs, office of the president

Gary Nash, Professor, Department of History, Los Angeles

Carol Newton, Director, Honors Program, Department of Biomathematics, Los Angeles

June O'Connor, Associate Professor, Department of Religious Studies, Riverside

Lisa Ray, Director of Basic Courses, Visiting Lecturer, Department of Rhetoric, Davis

Eric Rentschler, Director, Film Studies, Associate Professor, Department of German, Irvine

Joseph Watson, Vice Chancellor, Undergraduate Affairs, San Diego

Suzanne Weil, Graduate Student, Department of English, Berkeley

APPENDIX 2. CHARGE TO THE TASK FORCE

The task force is to undertake a broad review of lower division education in the University of California, including the university's mission to teach lower division students, the nature of the lower division curriculum, the types of courses offered, enrollments in these courses, staffing patterns, academic support services, and such other issues as the task force considers important in assessing the overall quality of lower division education. As part of this review, the task force will consider the findings of reports prepared by the campuses in response to three recent reports on undergraduate education.

In the course of its deliberations, the task force should consider the following issues and make recommendations where appropriate:

1. The nature of the university's mission in lower division education

   - What is the importance of lower division education to the university's teaching mission?

   - Are the resources devoted to lower division education appropriate?

2. The nature and quality of the lower division curriculum

   - Are the campuses' current general education requirements adequate? Should there be a common lower division curriculum for the university as a whole? For each campus?

   - What should be the balance between courses taken to fulfill general education requirements and those taken as prerequisites for the major?

   - Are current procedures for periodic review of the curriculum adequate?

3. The quality of teaching and learning

   - Are courses needed for general education requirements and prerequisites for the major available to all freshmen and sophomore students in the proper sequence? How do campuses respond to changes in student demand?

   - What is the optimum balance among types of courses—that is, seminars, lectures—for the student's first two years in the university? Is an appropriate balance of courses available to all students?

   - Who teaches lower division courses? What is the appropriate balance between full-time/part-time, tenure-track/non-tenure-track?

   - What is the appropriate role for teaching assistants. Are TAs adequately trained and supervised?

   - Should lower division students have greater opportunities to work with senior faculty? If so, how might this be accomplished?

   - How should learning be assessed?

   - How can high-quality teaching be recognized and rewarded? Are current practices sufficient?

4. Academic support services (academic advising and learning skills programs)

   · Should there be universitywide objectives for advising lower division students?

   · How is academic advising handled on the campuses? What is the faculty's role? Is the advising system effective?

   · What is the role of learning skills program, such as tutoring, in educating lower division students? Are these programs effective?

The task force is expected to submit a preliminary report to Vice President Frazer in February 1986 and a final report, including recommendations, in June 1986.

NOTES

1. This statement is less nearly true than it once was. In recent times, a higher rate of "stopping out" before college and entering or reentering college after working, attending to family obligations, serving in the military, etc., for a period has resulted in greater dispersion of age levels among college students.

2. This figure obtained from the University of California, office of the president, includes faculty salaries and benefits plus instructional support (salaries of administrative, clerical, and technical personnel and office and instructional supplies and equipment).

3. *Survey of TA's at UCD, 1982 Results—First Summary*, prepared by the Teaching Resources Center, UC Davis; *Report on TA training at UC Davis, 1980–81*, prepared by the Teaching Resources Center, UC Davis. *Teaching at Berkeley*, University of California, Berkeley, Fall, 1985.

4. *Report on TA Training at UC Davis, 1980–81*, p. 8.

5. See "Let's Talk It Over," *Newsweek* (December 1985), pp. 43–44.

6. Commission for the Review of the Master Plan for Higher Education, *The Challenge of Change* (Sacramento, March 1986), p. 8.

7. *The Challenge of Change*, p. 8.

8. Joseph Tussman, *Experiment at Berkeley* (New York: Oxford University Press, 1969), pp. xii–xiv.

9. Academic Senate, "General Education in the University of California," July 1984.

10. National Institute of Education, *Involvement in Learning: Realizing the Potential of Higher Education* (Mortimer Report). National Institute of Education, 1984.

11. Harris poll, reported in *IEE Spectrum* (June 1984), pp. 128–32.

12. Henry Nash Smith, "The Humanities in the University," in *Public Higher Education in California*, edited by Neil J. Smelser and Gabriel Almond, pp. 209–20 (Berkeley: University of California Press, 1974).

TEN

Intercollegiate Athletics at Berkeley

A Report of the Chancellor's Blue Ribbon Commission on Intercollegiate Athletics (1991)

AS OF 1990, the Berkeley campus occupied a neither-here-nor-there position in major intercollegiate sports. It competed in the Pac 10, and had some good years, but usually ended up around the middle or slightly below in the standings. In minor sports it competed across the board, and in a few of them had compiled outstanding national records. In addition, the organization of athletic activities on the campus revealed some anomalies, for example its failure to merge men's and women's athletic programs in keeping with the national trend.

The arrival of Chang-lin Tien as chancellor of the Berkeley campus in 1990 brought a notable change. A bubbling, energetic man, he was an avid fan and enthusiast for intercollegiate competition. He was noted for the spirited "Go Bears" finale to his speeches, and for rushing into the end zone and giving high-fives to football players after a Cal touchdown. (Wags remarked that this didn't detract unduly from his other chancellorial duties, because Cal didn't score very often.) Early in his administration he appointed a special blue ribbon committee on intercollegiate athletics. Predictably, the committee was composed of a mix of administrators, faculty, students, and alumni. The chancellor asked me to chair it, probably because by that time I was known as a veteran chair of major committees. From the standpoint of athletics, I was a Cal fan, but not a very public one. Contrary to what some on the campus suspected, the chancellor made no effort to influence the work of the committee.

From a personal point of view I found that chairing this committee was more demanding than any other like assignment I had experienced. The different academic sports and programs on campus were vested, self-protective, and vocal. Alumni individuals and groups were interested, partisan (sometimes almost religious in fervor) and also vocal; every one of them seemed to know exactly when and where Cal athletics had gone right or wrong (mostly wrong), but there was little agreement among them on this score. I entertained a record number of unsolicited delegations of interested parties during the months of the committee's life. Despite all this, the committee worked cooperatively and achieved consensus on the report and its recommendations.

SUMMARY OF RECOMMENDATIONS

General Mission

The Berkeley campus should maximize the opportunities and facilities for all of the athletically interested members to participate in their chosen activities.

The chancellor and athletic director should affirm that Cal's intercollegiate athletic mission is to compete, yearly and across the board, at the top levels of the Pacific Ten Conference and in post-season and national championship play.

Organization of Athletics

The Intercollegiate athletic program and recreational sports should be amalgamated into a single structure under a single athletic director; the activities programs of the Department of Physical Education should also be brought into this structure.

The athletic director should have access to the chancellor—and the chancellor should be involved—on policy and programmatic issues; on operational matters the athletic director should report to one of the vice chancellors.

The faculty athletic representative to the NCAA should report directly to the chancellor.

Student-Athletes

The athletic director and the faculty athletic representative should conduct a review of the impact of demands for "athletically related" activities on student-athletes' academic opportunities.

The office of the registrar and academic departments should review and revise policies and procedures that create difficulties of access to classes and to majors that affect student-athletes.

The office of admissions should work to coordinate better its communications about admissions with recruiting efforts in the athletic program.

The campus should make every effort to augment the academic resources available to student-athletes (such as the Athletic Study Center).

Faculty and Athletes

The Academic Senate should provide guidelines for resolving conflicts arising from student-athletes' competing obligations to athletics and to academics.

The Academic Senate should rejuvenate the faculty associates program; faculty and athletic-department representatives should device specific mechanisms for increasing their contact and improving their relations.

Budgeting and Financing

The campus should avoid across-the-board cutting and eliminating specific sports as short-run strategies to meet deficits; athletics should be carried forward at (at least) their present level of support through achieving administrative economies and providing other funds.

In the years ahead the campus should seek substantial levels of donations for the athletic program in three areas: supporting the Athletic Study Center; endowing those sports that are endowable; and providing athletic facilities, such as a new multi-purpose arena and a grass practice field.

INTRODUCTION

Several decades ago, C. P. Snow, the don at Cambridge University, wrote of "two cultures" of the university—the "scientific" and the "humanistic"—which stressed different outlooks and values and were pitted against one another in ways that were ultimately damaging to the academy. Snow's formula set off the usual flurry of spilled ink, seminar dialogues, and talk in the corridors and at parties. The distinction had enough truth and struck enough nerves to merit that debate. In the end, however, the dichotomy proved to be overdrawn if not stereotyped. For one thing, there are multiple outlooks and values *among* scientists and humanists—to say nothing of social scientists and others left out by Snow. For another, his dichotomy seriously downplayed the overriding *common* commitment in academia to the intellectual mission of the university in society, to standards of scholarly research, and to the goal of educating society's coming generations. As the decades have passed, Snow's daunting portrait has turned out to be one of those creative oversimplifications that come to fray around the edges, lose their force, and gradually become vaguer by virtue of their assimilation into the complexities of the real world.

The committee takes a similar view of another widely held stereotype about two other "cultures" that are found in most American colleges and universities: the "athletic" culture and the "academic" culture. In the minds of many, these cultures are regarded as antagonistic to one another in a variety of ways:

- Cultivation of physical strength and dexterity versus the cultivation of the mind

- Stress on competition and winning versus the cooperative exploration of ideas

- Commercial entertainment versus commitment to the life of the intellect

- Academic study as a necessary but unwelcome diversion from the competition and *camaraderie* of sports versus academic study as the primary value of college life

- Authority versus collegiality as the way to guide group activity

- Decisive action by a leader versus committee work and reflection

In the concrete these contrasts make for lack of understanding and sometimes lack of affection between coaches, athletic directors, and alumni enthusiasts on the one side, and some faculty and students on the other. To carry the logic of the stereotypes further, it is commonly believed that some athletes are mediocre and indifferent students while others suffer the fate of all who are involved in two opposing cultures—overburdening of time, personal conflicts, and constant exposure to the danger of giving too much to one and too little to the other.

The committee appreciates the fact that these stereotypes are real because they are believed in many quarters, and that they have real consequences. In particular, we will have some observations on this score with respect to the life of student-athletes. On most counts, however, we find the "two cultures" view to be wanting in accuracy, oversimplified, and often mischievous. There is a mental dimension in physical coordination, and vice versa. Most intercollegiate sports are primarily participatory in character, and are neither spectator sports nor commercially rewarding enterprises. Further, the academic as well as the athletic side of university life is fraught with competitiveness—among students, among faculty, and between students and faculty. There is a mix of both collegiality and authority in managing a team and in directing an academic department or a classroom. Finally, on the subject of athlete as student, the committee has found that most of the evidence on motivation, academic performance, and graduation rates underscores the similarities rather than the differences between athletes and other students.

The committee also sees a special kind of link between athletic and academic activities on the Berkeley campus. If the traditions and culture of Berkeley are noted for any single theme, it is for the value we place on excellence. That value of competitive excellence pervades—and should pervade—all dimensions of campus life, including academic work and athletic participation. We note, too, that intercollegiate athletic competition fosters qualities such as discipline, persistence, and cooperation in its individual participants. It also develops solidarity, spirit, and continuity between generations in a campus community that historically has not been a leader on those counts. And finally, we stress that athletic participation is closely related to values of health and personal development that are an important part of the Berkeley campus culture. Thus, while the committee affirms the primacy of the University of California's commitment to education, academic values, and scholarly pursuits, we also stress that excellence in competitive athletics can coexist without compromising that commitment. We see athletics and academics as complementary, not contradictory.

In carrying out its work, the committee spoke to scores of individuals from numerous constituencies. We encountered one conviction almost unanimously voiced: the Berkeley campus stands in need of a firm, decisive, and positive statement from the chancellor on a mission for its intercollegiate athletic programs. Most stressed the positive effects that would flow from such a statement; some also stressed that as matters now stand—that is, absent that statement—they suffer ambiguity and frustration with respect to their goals and their work.

The committee shares this conviction. We believe further that a definitive mission statement would go far in breaking through the attitude of ambivalence that the Berkeley campus has traditionally expressed toward its athletic programs. Accordingly, we now present for the chancellor's consideration our recommendations on the essential ingredients of such a statement.

The mission statement should take as its starting point six postulates about *athletics in general:*

- Participation in athletics of all kinds is beneficial to the health and development of students, faculty, and staff, and is thus an essential part of university life.

- The campus should maximize the opportunities for all its athletically interested members to participate in their chosen activities.

- Accordingly, the campus should strive to develop athletic programs, activities, and facilities on a campuswide basis. Concretely this means greater attention to women's athletic activities, where the existing levels of facilities and student involvement are lower.

- Consistent with its general institutional mission, the campus should cultivate excellence of performance in all campus activities.

- All athletic activities should be organized and pursued in a way that is consistent with—and does not in any way undermine—the university's primary commitment to academic excellence.

- The academic expectations—including those concerning graduation rates—for student-athletes should not differ from those for students in general.

Implicit in the six postulates is a seventh, linking *intercollegiate* athletics to them: the mission of intercollegiate athletics should be regarded as consistent with—and an integral part of—these principles. Specifically, Berkeley's intercollegiate athletics should be organized and conducted in ways that ensure academic integrity and maximize the educational opportunities for participants.

Within this general context, the committee believes that the most important single issue with regard to intercollegiate athletics is to determine at what level the campus should compete and remain faithful to those postulates. To telegraph our conclusion, we believe that that level should be at the top in all competitive sports.

In considering a statement on that main issue, the committee observed—at the risk of simplifying things—a number of paths that universities and colleges have taken with respect to intercollegiate competition:

1. Full commitment to national standing in the very top ranks, usually in one or a few selected sports—the models of Notre Dame, Miami University (Florida), and the University of Nevada at Las Vegas

2. Full commitment to national standing in highly selected, often "minor" sports—the models of Johns Hopkins University in lacrosse and the University of Maine in hockey

3. Commitment to excellence and top conference (and sometimes national) ranking across a broad range of sports—the models of Stanford and UCLA, though the latter has recently moved in the direction of selective elimination of some teams

4. Commitment to remaining in top competitive conferences but sustaining only average performance—the model of Northwestern University

5. Commitment to a deemphasis and regionalization of most sports—the models of most Ivy League universities, with notable exceptions such as Princeton University in basketball

6. Elimination of intercollegiate teams, including major sports—the model of the University of Chicago with respect to football

In the past few decades Berkeley has uneasily occupied a kind of no-man's land between paths 3 and 4, competing and sometimes winning in top national competitions in selected sports, such as water polo, but sustaining only an average and sometimes a below-average standing regionally and nationally in the major revenue supports of football and men's basketball. As a result of this "neither-here-nor-there" status of Berkeley's intercollegiate programs, dissatisfactions have been frequently heard, with some voices calling for an all-out commitment to path 1 and others stressing the virtues of path 5 for an institution like Berkeley.

The committee is also uneasy with the campus's historically ambivalent investment in its intercollegiate programs, and recommends that the chancellor lead the campus to a clear and augmented commitment to a position of leadership in national intercollegiate athletics. This commitment calls for the following:

- A resolve to compete across the board at the top levels of the Pacific Ten Conference; this implies frequent appearances in postseason play and national championship events.

- Within this general resolve, an acknowledgment of the special place of the major revenue and potential revenue sports; the general intercollegiate mission cannot prevail unless Cal excels and wins in football, men's basketball, and women's basketball.

- An acknowledgment that "across the board" applies a strong commitment to the entire range of field, court, aquatic, and other sports, including especially the Olympic sports. Many of these sports have competed at the top—winning some national titles—in the past two decades. The competitive level of those sports should be sustained, and that of the others elevated.

These are the goals we recommend to the chancellor. The committee believes further that unless an endorsement of those goals is accompanied by a statement of what is needed to implement them, the result is likely to be resolve without action, promise without delivery. Accordingly, the chancellor should, in his mission statement, specify the following:

- The quality of personnel (athletic directors, coaches, staff, athletes) required

- The organizational structure required to launch and support the activities necessary to excel on the intercollegiate scene (for example, recruitment, promotion) and to minimize counter-productive competition among the athletic programs

- The financial and budgetary commitments (and limits) that are necessary (and advisable) to attain the goal of excellence in athletic competition

- The means by which the financial and budgetary commitments can be assured

In the remainder of this report the committee offers options with respect to each of these lines of implementation. In most cases we endorse specific options as recommendations to the chancellor.

ADMINISTRATIVE STRUCTURES

The Organization of the Athletic Program

The Committee recommends, with uniform and complete consensus, that the intercollegiate programs—as well as the recreational sports program and the activities programs of the Department of Physical Education—be unified under a single athletic director. We find this consensus echoed among almost all of the individuals and groups with whom we have communicated—though we also find the tone of that consensus ranging from enthusiasm at the one extreme, through general acceptance in the middle, to resignation accompanied by some apprehension at the other extreme. Given the increased responsibilities of the athletic director that this consolidation implies, the committee also believes that the new position should be raised to the executive program level from the management and professional level, where it now resides.

We recommend further that under this athletic director, and reporting directly to him or her, should be a number of top staff members, organized along two lines.

- Associate or assistant directors responsible for given teams or clusters of teams. For teams with special popularity and visibility and actual or potential revenue-generating capacity (we have in mind football, men's basketball, and women's basketball, as the sports world is currently organized), the coaches should report directly to the athletic director. Other directors would be responsible for groups of teams, clustered when possible by some affinity—for example, field sports, aquatic sports, other Olympic sports. The committee recommends further that, in this scheme of organization-by-clusters could, and should, when feasible, include both men's and women's sports, for example, one cluster might cover men's and women's track and field as well as men's and women's gymnastics. By this cross-cutting principle, too, coaches of both men's and women's teams would report to some directors who are men and some who are women.

· Associate and assistant directors organized along lines of functional responsibility. We have in mind directors of media and promotion, student services, facilities coordination, planning, fund-raising and development, and special programs (e.g., club sports, intramural sports, summer camps, instructional activity in physical education, programs for the disabled).

These recommendations call for major structural revisions of existing arrangements for virtually all athletic programs on the Berkeley campus. We now specify the nature of these revisions. We acknowledge throughout, however, that the organizational principles and arrangements we propose are general ones, and are subject to modification in light of the experience and preferences of the incoming athletic director.

First, the recommendations increase the organizational *unity* of intercollegiate athletic programs. Instead of three athletic directors—men's, women's and recreational sports—reporting to (and competing for the attention of) one campus administrator, we envision a single director speaking for all the athletic programs under his or her direction. The committee regards the proposed arrangement as mitigating if not dissolving one of the major fault lines of conflict in the present program—conflict among separate athletic directors. Also under this heading of unity, we point to a final advantage: a single athletic director would represent intercollegiate athletics as a single unit to the diverse constituencies with which he or she must work; at the present time intercollegiate athletics speaks to both the campus and the outside community with many voices.

Second, the recommendations improve the organizational *inclusiveness* and *coherence* of the athletic programs. With respect to *inclusiveness*, we mention three specific points: (1) Club sports, previously under the aegis of the recreational sports program, would not be conjoined in the same organization, with other men's and women's intercollegiate sports. (2)

Activity courses in physical education would be moved from the Department of Physical Education to the general campus athletic program. The committee also sees this as a positive step. In any event, the position and importance of the activity course supervisor in physical education programs and courses has tended to atrophy over time, though graduate students in the Department continue to play a vital role. We believe that to incorporate these courses into the general athletic program would provide a better linkage between them and intercollegiate sports. We also suggest that some coaches of intercollegiate sports—along with teaching assistants in the department—offer some of these physical education classes; this would both build on that linkage and provide supplementary income for those coaches. (3) Intramural sports could also be incorporated into the single, larger athletic programs. With respect to *coherence*, we believe that organizing the associate and assistant directors according to sports clusters and according to functional specialization is more rational and systematic than the present, historically (and to some degree accidentally) accumulated divisions along the lines of men-women, intercollegiate-recreational and intercollegiate-physical education.

Third, the proposed arrangements promise some improvement along the lines of *efficiency* and *economy*. We envision, for example, that the allocation and management of *all* athletic facilities for *all* programs would be a responsibility to be carried out within the proposed unified department; this would surely not eliminate competition for facilities—which are scarce and overdemanded in any case—but it should, in large part, substitute the mechanism of coordination for the mechanism of struggle in allocating those facilities. In addition, the organization of departments along the functional lines of media relations, ticket sales, student services, and so forth, for all programs should achieve some economies of scale in relation to current arrangements, which subdivide these according to the separate classes of programs. The committee does not hold out any grand illusions about massive savings to be realized through amalgamation and rationalization; almost all such efforts prove less yielding in practice than they promise in the abstract. Nevertheless, some budgetary savings should be gained through the consolidation of activities on a program-wide basis.

Fourth, our recommendations reduce significantly the principle of subdividing athletics along *men-women* lines. No set of arrangements can eliminate this principle completely, of course, because many types of athletic competition are irreducibly organized according to men's teams and women's teams. However, we believe that three of our suggestions diminish this principle: (a) eliminating the positions of men's athletic director and women's athletic director, (b) organizing-by-cluster, and (c) cross-cutting of men-women lines in reporting relationships. One advantage of these arrangements is to reduce the long-standing competition and conflict along gender lines in the athletic programs. Another advantage is to work further toward minimizing differential treatment of men and women and thus equalizing the treatment of athletes regardless of gender.

In specifying this advantage, however, the committee underscores vigorously one additional point. In effecting such a reorganization, the Berkeley campus should guard against reducing the status, support, or visibility of women's athletic programs. Those of our informants who were opposed to or cautious about the unification of men's and women's programs explicitly feared such an effect, and it may have accompanied similar efforts at unification at other universities. In addition, care should be taken to assure that women have responsible positions and are involved in the decision-making apparatus of the reorganized athletic program. In short, the changes we propose should be implemented in a manner that is thoroughly consistent with the regulations and policies of the NCAA and the Berkeley campus philosophy, regulations, and procedures relating to gender equality.

In closing this section, the committee notes three additional safeguards that should be observed in implementing the amalgamation we propose.

1. It is essential to guarantee the continuation of existing instructional standards and academic credit for physical education activity courses. The committee finds one option attractive: to administer activity courses through the Department of Athletics, to supervise their quality in appropriate college and Academic Senate channels, and to staff them with a mix of intercollegiate coaches and graduate teaching assistants in physical education.

2. Our recommendation calls for a greater degree of structural separation of organization of coaches and teams on the one hand and the functional specialization of activities such as ticket sales, promotion, and so on. Special care should be taken to assure smooth communication and coordination among these various branches.

3. We envision one possibly counterproductive scenario if teams at different levels of competition—Division I and club sports, to be specific—are integrated too closely in a reporting relationship to an associate director. That scenario is that claims to equity will be excited by organizational proximity, and this may lead to runaway costs associated with one team continuously demanding what a more favored team has by way of facilities and support.

In this connection, the committee wishes to make clear that we do not endorse the idea that all sports are equal and should be supported at equal levels. More specifically, we recognize a fundamental distinction between intercollegiate and club sports teams and athletes in terms of recruitment, time demands, and commitment of resources. We do not recommend any blurring of this distinction. Nor should constant, open competition for equity of support be permitted. Two ways of muting this kind of competition are available. The first is the "Stanford principle" of explicitly layering sports into tiers—with understood and different support levels for each—but leaving the boundaries between tiers fluid so that individual sports can move from tier to tier over time as their performance level, economic support, and other circumstances dictate. The second is simply to retain a sharp administrative and reporting separation—which we now have—between club or recreation sports and other levels of inter-collegiate competition. The committee favors as much integration of different levels of sports as is feasible administratively, but also calls attention to the persistent problem of inter-sport competition and the desirability of not "structuring" such competition into the administrative apparatus.

Reporting Relations of the Athletic Director

Five types of reporting possibilities for the athletic director have come to the committee's attention:

· To the chancellor proper; most major campuses have instituted some form of direct reporting to the chief executive officer

· To the vice chancellor—business and administrative services

· To the vice chancellor—undergraduate affairs

· To the vice chancellor—development

- To have a vice chancellor solely responsible for the organization, management, and development of intercollegiate athletics; in this case the athletic director would, in effect, be a vice chancellor, and different categories of associate and assistant directors of programs and activities would report to him or her; this vice chancellor would, as is usual, report directly to the chancellor.

The Berkeley campus has tried the second, third, and fourth forms—in that sequence—over the past decade or so. Our own recommendation is a mix of these and proceeds according to the following logic.

Consistent with his strong commitment to intercollegiate athletics, the chancellor must be directly involved in the athletic program and must deal directly with the athletic director. Moreover, there are some matters connected with intercollegiate activities that should come directly to the chancellor, because they have large budgetary implications, because they are politically sensitive, or because they are items for which the chancellor may be held responsible in the last accounting (for example, possible recruiting violations, possible misuse of funds). At the same time, it is apparent that the chancellor has an enormous range of commitments and responsibilities to the state of California, the board of regents, the office of the president, and the Berkeley faculty, students, staff, alumni, and community; because of these commitments he cannot be expected to monitor any program in a detailed, day-by-day way.

Taking these considerations into account, we present a double recommendation.

a. With respect to the especially important, comprehensive, or volatile issues mentioned, the athletic director must have direct and immediate access to the chancellor, who in turn must become involved. However, to avoid the possibility that such issues (and other, less urgent concerns) become a matter of daily personal telephone calls, the chancellor should assign to one of his key staff—perhaps an assistant chancellor—the responsibility for screening, sifting, and passing on such communications directed toward the chancellor. Such an arrangement would guarantee that the line from the athletic director to the chancellor's office will never be sealed off, thus occasioning the frustration that comes from isolation, inaccessibility, and lack of support.

b. With respect to matters of operational responsibility, the athletic director should report to the chancellor through one of the vice chancellors to whom the chancellor has delegated appropriate authority. Issues that cannot be resolved internally to the athletic program should be brought to the attention of that vice chancellor.

As for the various vice chancellorial possibilities mentioned for operational reporting, it is possible to cite the advantages and disadvantages of each:

- To report to the vice chancellor—development would make for a happy relationship between intercollegiate athletics and alumni and other supporters; but by the same token it might foster temptations that arise in the marriage among alumni, money and sports.

- To report to the vice chancellor—business and administrative services would put the athletic director directly into the budgetary operations of the campus and would probably facilitate decision-making on budgetary matters, but at the same time it would tend to remove the athletic programs too much from the academic heart of the campus.

- To report to the vice chancellor—undergraduate affairs probably makes the most intrinsic sense, since that officer is directly concerned with admissions and other aspects of campus life that affect athletics most directly; at the same time many issues brought to that office fall outside its normal range of responsibilities, and decisions might be delayed as further consultation is required.

- To merge the athletic directorship with a vice chancellorship would certainly give the position greater visibility and create a direct line to the chancellor; yet that option would accomplish no more by way of administrative unity than we have suggested, and to place athletics formally at such an elevated administrative level would generate an unwanted asymmetry.

When the last word is spoken, the committee finds no completely compelling reason for preferring any one of these options. We recommend that the athletic director should report on operational matters to *one* of the vice chancellors, but the actual choice should depend not so much on questions of intrinsic logic as on considerations of mutual interest and comfort of the actual persons involved.

While the chancellor did not charge the committee specifically to examine the situation of student-athletes, we include this topic because we believe it to be central to intercollegiate athletics. Members of the committee interviewed some three dozen men and women student-athletes from a variety of teams and discussed the emerging issues among ourselves. We offer the following report and recommendations.

The main problems faced by student-athletes at Berkeley stem from the fact that they have a kind of dual career—often, in effect, two full-time jobs. Their academic environment is as demanding and competitive as it is for all students; at the same time they compete in athletics at the highest level, where success demands great commitments of motivation, time, and energy. To do well in both is a formidable task, and it is striking that many manage to succeed in both.

One part of the mission of intercollegiate athletics is to provide a context in which student-athletes can effectively pursue academic interests and participate in student life. Yet our interviews reveal that this goal is not very well realized at the present time. Like many with dual careers, some athletes feel caught in the middle. They sense on the one hand that some faculty, staff, and students regard them as somewhat exotic, over-privileged outsiders, and on the other hand that some coaches—particularly those new to the campus—can be insensitive to the academic demands placed on students at Berkeley.

Academic marginality does not square, incidentally, with the understanding that many athletes had before enrolling and still have about Berkeley. Most recruited student-athletes chose Cal in part because of its academic reputation and educational opportunities. Many whom we interviewed had scholarships offered from other institutions with successful athletic programs yet chose Berkeley on academic grounds. Most still believe that it is possible to succeed both academically and athletically, and that athletic participation fosters academic performance by imposing discipline, providing social support, and engendering confidence. Not one interviewee complained about Berkeley's academic requirements. On the contrary, most expressed a sense of pride that they could succeed in a demanding academic environment, and a belief that Cal should use its academic strengths as an asset in recruiting.

At the same time, our interviews revealed that many student-athletes face obstacles in taking advantage of those educational opportunities. We first list these reported obstacles, then present some recommendations.

Time demands. The NCAA has legislated strict limits on mandating "athletically-related" activities for student-athletes. Some of our interviewees objected to such rules, saying that individuals should be able to practice freely as long as they remain in good standing. Even these students, however, acknowledged great pressure on their time occasioned by practice, travel, and competitive play. Other student-athletes confirmed the results of national surveys and agreed that demands from coaches for intense, year-long dedication take a psychological toll, have doubtful athletic value, and are detrimental to academic effort. Yet the pressures to comply with the demands of an intense athletic program are great. The problems for "red-shirted" players deserve special mention on this score. These students are prohibited from playing for one (usually their freshman) year, and thus gain little from their status, but they, too, are subjected to demands to participate in athletically related activities.

Summer school. Many student-athletes attend summer school to take classes not available to them during the academic year or to satisfy the NCAA's "satisfactory progress" requirement for continuous eligibility. If this attendance is consistent with student-athletes' academic interests, it can be a valuable supplement. If, however, it is mainly a kind of compensatory effort to "survive" academically because of excessive demands placed on student-athletes during the academic year, then the necessity to attend summer school becomes part and parcel of the hardships engendered by athletic demands.

Access to classes. Because travel and practice schedules constrain the number and kinds of courses athletes can take, the campus has given them limited priority in class enrollment. Imperfections in the enrollment system—including its computerized aspects—remain, however, and should be corrected to ensure that athletes can enroll in courses that are not simply available but are educationally appropriate.

Access to majors. Student-athletes are among those who suffer from inability to enter certain "impacted" majors. These majors typically limit entry by requiring a minimum grade point average or many prerequisites or both. Student-athletes often suffer in this competition in part because of the time demands and scheduling difficulties noted.

Examination conflicts. A recurrent problem is rescheduling midterm and final examinations to accommodate competitive schedules that are beyond student-athletes' or even the campus' control. The annual spring conflict between the NCAA and conference championships and Berkeley's final examinations are an example. Some faculty members and departments accommodate by alternative scheduling and other devices, but others are adamant.

Academic advising and tutoring. The Athletic Study Center has contributed much to the academic development and graduation of many student-athletics who entered Berkeley with gaps in their academic preparation or who find it difficult to deal with the heavy demands placed on their time. The center provides programs to strengthen students' academic skills and use of time, organizes a nightly study table, and cooperates with the office of the faculty athletic representative in monitoring progress toward graduation. Although the center is understandably and justifiably a popular institution in the eyes of student-athletes, its effectiveness should be extended further by additional staff and improved logistics.

Faculty involvement. Many student-athletes express disappointment about their lack of contact with faculty. Only a few spoke of incidents of overt hostility, but the more common belief is that faculty do not care about the experiences and problems of student-athletes.

Student services. Many student-athletes experience anomalies and frustrations in the registration process, and in the provision of student services such as housing and parking, health services, and financial aid.

Student input on athletic department policy. Student-athletes have valuable information and opinions on topics such as coaching philosophy, training, and academic advising. The Women's Athletic Council provides a context for providing student opinion about department policy, but no such mechanism exists for men.

The committee does not pretend that all the items on this checklist apply only to student athletes. Students with jobs also have examination conflicts and heavy demands on their time, and students of all descriptions experience problems of access to majors and courses, remoteness of faculty and advisors, and inadequate student services. In this respect our interviews with student-athletes uncovered generic campus problems that have appeared in other, broader surveys.[1] For this reason we would echo the recommendations of these surveys relating to the improvement of academic and social life on the Berkeley campus.

A number of problems we uncovered, however, relate to student-athletes in particular, and in connection with those, we offer the following set of interrelated recommendations:

- The athletic director and the faculty athletic representative should undertake a comprehensive review of possible academic harm that may arise from demands for "athletically related" activities.
- Such a review should focus on off-season demands and on the requirements imposed on freshman redshirts.
- The office of the registrar should review scheduling policies as they relate to both athletes and other students with constrained schedules, with an eye to promoting greater flexibility of classes.
- Academic departments and schools should consider a policy of "special admissions" to their majors—that is, access on the part of a limited number of students who do not formally meet their GPA and other requirements—to parallel the policies that now govern admissions to the campus as a whole.
- The campus should make a special effort to augment the level of academic support resources available to student-athletes (such as the Athletic Study Center).
- The office of admissions should work to coordinate better its communications about admissions with recruiting efforts in the athletic program.

Two additional recommendations on faculty and student-athletes appear in the next section.

One final issue emerged from our interviews with student-athletes and coaches. That concerns the continuing differences among some intercollegiate sports with respect to travel, practice conditions, and equipment. These stem largely from different levels of funding. The committee regards the enhancement of these conditions for disadvantaged sports as a matter of priority.

Faculty and Athletics

One part of the "two cultures" view of athletics and academics poses an opposition of interest between faculty and athletics: the faculty members are hostile to sports as frivolous if not menacing to academic values; the faculty member versus the indifferent athlete; the anxious coach pleading favors for their players from reluctant faculty; and the faculty committee as moral watchdog over the unholy, anti-intellectual alliance among athletes, coaches, alumni, and administrators bent on winning at all costs. Our committee found these stereotypes to be vastly overdrawn—largely because there is such variation in attitudes among both faculty and among those involved in athletics—and largely irrelevant to the Berkeley campus. Nevertheless, the mutual isolation of faculty from campus athletics (and vice versa) is remarkable. Even interested and supportive faculty members are limited in their contact with athletics to watching and cheering at games, and coaches and other athletic department officials seldom communicate with faculty. We direct most of our remarks and recommendations to the issue of improving these relations.

Faculty Athletic Representative   The faculty athletic representative to the NCAA has a distinct responsibility to ensure the academic integrity of the intercollegiate athletic program and to monitor its compliance with all NCAA regulations. In the absence of the chancellor, the representative casts the institution's vote at conference and NCAA meetings. In so far as the representative speaks to the chancellor, his or her role is to offer independent advice on sensitive policy and compliance issues and to safeguard the academic interests of student-athletes. To perform this role, the representative needs direct access to the chancellor. The new situation we recommend for the Berkeley campus—a single athletic department and a direct link between the chancellor and the athletic director on policy matters—makes an easier and more direct interaction between the chancellor and the representative especially appropriate now. That kind of interaction is standard practice in all Pac-10 institutions, and should be put in place on this campus as well.

Chancellor's Advisory Committee on Intercollegiate Athletics   This committee is a natural adjunct to the faculty athletic representative. In recent years it has provided valuable advice to the chancellor on campus policies relating to the place of student-athletes on campus, and should be continued.

Examination and Related Conflicts   Up to now the Academic Senate has generated no explicit guidelines for resolving conflicts between scheduled athletic events on the one hand and examination dates and due-dates for term papers on the other. Existing policy is to treat these conflicts as matters for request and negotiation between student-athletes and faculty members on a case-by-case basis. As indicated, faculty members vary greatly in their flexibility on this issue, and, as a result, the level of difficulty for student-athletes with conflicting obligations also varies greatly. The committee asks that the Academic Senate develop some general guidelines for resolving academic-athletic scheduling conflicts in equitable ways. We believe that the general principle should be that if both sets of obligations can be met without loss, flexible arrangements to accommodate both should be developed.

Improved Relations   About six years ago the Academic Senate initiated a faculty associates program for athletics. In this program, completely voluntary in character, individual faculty members would "associate" with a team of their choice—go to practices and games, become acquainted with students and coaches, and sometimes develop informal advisory relations with athletes. Faculty participation in this program was considerable, and reports on it were generally positive. Recently the program has atrophied because there has been little organizational effort to renew it on a year-to-year basis. We recommend that it be revitalized, and mechanisms to assure the continuity from year to year be put in place.

In addition to the faculty associates program, which creates positive links among faculty, coaches, and players, we envision a number of other voluntary mechanisms, some already in place, that would work toward the same end:

- A pool of faculty members, built up by volunteering, could meet individually with potential recruits; it would be especially helpful if a faculty member from a given department could represent the student-athlete's intended major.

- The popular "honorary coach" program—in which a faculty member joins a coach and team for practice, meals, and an intercollegiate game—could be expanded.

- Groups of coaches could invite faculty members to lunch and other meetings (and vice versa) to exchange information about athletic and academic programs.

- Coaches and other athletic department personnel could, as guests or observers, sit in on appropriate committee meetings of academic departments and the Academic Senate.

- Sessions for department chairs and faculty on aspects of athletics (such as the nature of the Athletic Study Center) could be arranged.

These kinds of arrangements—others could be imagined—are directed toward increasing traffic on the two-way road between academic and athletic life on the campus.

SPORTS AND FINANCES

The sustained ambiguity of sports finances over the years—the failure *either* to support sports adequately *or* to decide not to do so—has let to an unfortunate kind of "beggar-thy-neighbor" competition in the athletic programs. Gains for men's or women's sports, and for individual teams within those programs, are typically regarded as losses for others.

This ambiguity of support has also led to a cumulative set of dissatisfactions. Decisions to drop sports in the face of budgetary stringency have been avoided, but decisions to fund them adequately have not been forthcoming. Each year individual teams are faced with uncertainty, and engage in endless skirmishes among themselves and with the chancellor's office about what they have done and not done and what they have received and not received in previous years. We believe that, with the presence of a new chancellor and with some new administrative and funding arrangements, a new spirit can be engendered. The campus is now in a position to follow General Marshall's advice—"don't fight it, decide it"—and build a more effective athletic program, including healthier and more mutually supportive attitudes within it.

We divide our discussion of financial support into short-term and long-term aspects, recognizing, however, that the two aspects are intertwined. The lack of long-term financial prospects leads to yearly crises, with the resultant uncertainty, mutual accusations, and diminished morale. Such crises, moreover, dampen hopes for long-term security. Conversely, adequate long-term prospects for support ease short-term anxieties.

Short-Term Financing

The current problem s that the combined athletic programs show a deficit of between $350,000 and $400,000 for 1990–91, and anticipate at least a doubling of that sum for 1991–92 because of student fee and housing cost increases as well as budget cuts. The main short-term problem is how to deal with the deficit; the long-term problem is to prevent its regular recurrence. Blaming one department or sport or taking money from one to support another is not a real solution and may be counterproductive. The campus must point toward integrative solutions that will maximize excellence in performance and extend participation in sports. We put forward the following main alternatives for the chancellor to consider:

1. To impose cuts on existing sports activities across the board, thus spreading the burden and not damaging any one or few sports excessively.

2. To drop several sports as a way of "covering" the deficit.

3. To address the problem by short-term deficit financing. A feasible means would be to secure offsetting dollars from the chancellor's discretionary funds in order to increase income in the future.

4. To divert discretionary funds to cover the deficit fully. This would entail diverting some $1-plus million per year to the new athletic department over a six-year period. This would go far in carrying the deficit, covering increased student fees and housing costs, increasing grants-in-aid to athletes, and marginally improving other aspects of the athletic program, including fund-raising. During the six-year period a major fund-raising drive could be undertaken to endow the athletic programs on a permanent basis.

Each strategy would bring a varying mix of consequences to the athletic programs and a varying mix of savings and costs to the campus.

The committee recommends *against* either of the first two options. Across-the-board cutting would leave Cal without excellence in any sport, and would demoralize many because it ignores consideration of merit, performance, and leadership. The committee has heard evidence of demoralization over the current round of cuts. We fear that this strategy would likely lead ultimately to the suggestion that Cal drop Division I sports altogether. To eliminate some sports does have the virtue of being selective and protecting other sports but several disadvantages outweigh this. For one thing, elimination reduces participation. For another, it would suggests that Cal is abandoning the one thing for which it should be well known—achieving excellence over a wide range.

In the best of all possible worlds, the committee recommends the fourth option—full financing from discretionary and ultimately from endowment funds—as the surest way to send out a clear signal to all concerned about the chancellor's commitment to intercollegiate athletics and to push Cal's athletic program to a new plateau of excellence. The campus should retain that option as an ideal.

The committee also realizes that the world will not be the best in the next several years—that budgetary hardship will be likely to recur, and that other, equally worthy causes will compete for scarce endowment resources. Nevertheless, we recommend that the chancellor avoid the first two options, and pursue a creative financing policy that will draw from several sources: (a) to realize modest savings from cuts that are truly limited to removing nonessential elements of athletic programs; (b) to realize hopefully significant administrative savings that result from our suggested unification of the current athletic programs under a single athletic director; (c) to "carry forward" some portion of deficits when it appears that cutting would adversely affect quality and competitive performance—for example, by reducing grants-in-aid to athletes; and (d) to give athletic teams and facilities a significant claim on resources emanating from donations or gifts. The committee regards it as necessary *not* to damage the athletic programs through one or another form of budgetary starving; we regard it as desirable to sustain at least and improve at best those programs by providing ample resources and facilities.

Long-Term Financing

The committee sees three discrete long-term financing targets for athletics at Cal: a program to endow the Athletic Study Center; an endowment program for the "endowable sports"; and efforts to provide new athletic facilities such as a new multi-purpose arena principally for basketball. These targets are discrete in large part—that is, do not complete for the same donors. Supporting the Study Center would appeal to many donors whose interests are primarily academic and an arena offers a once-in-a-lifetime naming opportunity for a major donor (as in the case of Pauley Pavilion at UCLA and the Haas building for Business Administration at Berkeley).

The Athletic Study Center

The committee singles out this center as one of the sports program's most valuable assets. It contributes to sports by helping athletes to augment their academic performance. Among our informants, many coaches and others referred to this program as a kind of "life blood" for some intercollegiate programs, aiding immeasurably in recruitment, sustaining eligibility, increasing retention and graduation rates, and—most important—preparing that vast majority of athletes who will not find places in professional sports to prepare for their future careers outside the athletic world.

The Athletic Study Center is a "natural" target for support through endowment. The Berkeley campus enjoys traditions of insisting on high academic standards and refusing to compromise them; the center helps sustain these traditions for athletes. It is an obvious link between the academic and athletic sides of university life. A program to endow this unique resource would appeal to a range of potential donors who are supportive of Cal athletics and are especially interested in the circumstances of student athletes.

Endowing the Endowable Sports

The committee understands that the idea of an "endowed sport" means that its entire annual operating budget (including grants-in-aid to athletes) is completely financed from endowment into the indefinite future. Calculating at the conventional 5 percent yield, this means that an endowment of approximately twenty times the annual operating budget is required to cover that budget and to hedge against inflation in subsequent years.

Using that yield and taking the 1990–91 operating budgets into account, the committee calculates that an endowment of some $15 million would be required to maintain Cal's men's and women's sports at their current levels. To increase the competitive level (by supporting grants-in-aid comparable to most Pac-10 members) would require an additional $10–15 million in endowment. These figures should probably be expanded in light of increasing costs in future years. Nevertheless, we feel that the grand total of $25–30 million is a realistic one for bringing Cal up to the level of funding and competitive strength of comparable institutions such as UCLA.

Certain components within the operating budget of a given sport are more endowable than others. Specifically, grants-in-aid to athletes and definite capital projects are easier to "sell" to prospective donors than are sports equipment and travel expenses—to say nothing of making up for accumulated past deficits. The evident strategy is to gear fund-raising efforts first to those ingredients of the sports program's budget that are most attractive to donors. Similarly, some sports appear to be more "endowable" than others, for a combination of reasons—because it has intrinsic appeal as a sport, because it has a long history at Cal, or because it has people of means among its potential alumni and other donors.

The idea of endowing sports is not new. The Men's Bear Backers group made a concerted effort to endow sports a decade ago through the Cal Sports 80s Campaign. This program has enjoyed considerable success with respect to rugby, crew, swimming, and water polo, but little success for baseball, gymnastics, soccer, and track. Within the past several months the Bear Backers have proposed a program to endow football grants-in-aid, asking different regions to support a specific position (for example, center) on the football team.

At the present there is limited endowment support for women's sports at Cal, even though several sport-specific scholarships have been established. Efforts targeted at parents and grandparents of women athletes and at the growing number of former athletes among our alumnae are well advised, particularly as time goes on.

The committee recommends that the campus analyze each men's and women's Division I intercollegiate sport, that specific targets be set, and that endowment campaigns be established and pursued vigorously through the development office.

Athletic Facilities

The committee shares the widely expressed belief that Harmon Gymnasium is antiquated and that a superior facility is necessary to take Cal basketball "to the next level" of leadership in the Pac 10 and regular invitation to postseason tournament play. In addition, a larger arena can generate significant additional revenues from a men's (and possibly, over time, women's) basketball if funding for the arena is through a gift or gifts so that debt service is not a major cost. Not least, such an arena would do much to relieve the chronic shortages of facilities for recreational sports.

Estimates of the cost for an arena vary widely, depending on the number of seats envisioned and the variety of additional functional features it might include. The committee believes that a figure of $30–35 million, exclusive of land and future maintenance, is a reasonable estimate. Opportunities for using university land should be explored first. Another possibility is a joint venture with the city of Berkeley in which the city would be responsible for all or most of the land.

Those fund-raising officials we interviewed from the development office and from Bear Backers were both optimistic about fund-raising for an arena. The realistic possibilities include a single, very large "naming" contribution or several sizeable simultaneous gifts to launch the project. In any event, the committee believes that the selection of a definite site and a strong statement from the chancellor about the future of Cal athletics and its priorities are necessary conditions for soliciting major gifts.

Among the highest priorities for the development of fields and facilities is a grass practice field for football (at the present time practice is conducted on the artificial turf in Memorial Stadium and the overused grass field of Strawberry Canyon). Cal is the only Pac-10 school without such a facility. A grass field is desirable for reasons of health and safety of the athletes and for improving the competitive play of the team. The various athletic programs have other facilities needs as well, and we trust that the newly appointed committee on athletic courts and fields will develop a comprehensive statement on needs and priorities for facilities.

CONCLUSION

The most adequate summary of our report is found in the summary of recommendations at its beginning. We conclude by affirming several principles that have guided us throughout. First, athletics on campus should be brought up to the top levels of achievement on the Berkeley campus. Second, this goal should be pursued in ways consistent with Berkeley's enduring commitments to academic values and scholarly pursuits. Third, the committee regards the goal as attainable through a combination of effective leadership and a sufficient input of resources over the years.

APPENDIX I. CHANCELLOR'S CHARGE TO THE COMMITTEE, DECEMBER 1990

Within the context of Berkeley continuing to field a competitive athletic program in the Pacific 10 conference and enhancing the academic experience of student-athletes, there are three broad areas I would like to committee to address and make recommendations on:

1. What is the institutional mission of intercollegiate and recreational sports at Berkeley, taking account of the concerns of all elements of

the campus community, including alumni? How can this mission be met in an era of budgetary constraints?

2. How should these programs be managed and organized? Should the current arrangements be maintained or should these programs have one overall director? To whom should that director(s) report?

3. Included within the first two points but meriting special attention is the budget for these programs. The intercollegiate athletics program in particular warrant attention because of current or potential deficits. Please provide specific budgetary recommendations for the coming three years.

Embedded within these three broad areas are a host of questions, which are bound to be of interest to the Committee. Among these are the relations between men's and women's intercollegiate athletics programs; the breadth of our sports programs; adequacy of and competition for facilities; maintenance of facilities.

APPENDIX 2. MEMBERS OF THE COMMITTEE

Neil J. Smelser (Chair of the Committee), University Professor of Sociology

Harry Agler, former Chair, Bear Backers

Jack Citrin, Professor of Political Science and NCAA Faculty Athletic Representative

John F. Cummins, Assistant Chancellor

Barbara Gross Davis, Dean of Educational Development

W. Russell Ellis, Vice Chancellor—Undergraduate Affairs

Preston Hotchkis, President, UC-Berkeley Foundation

Bonaparte Liu, President, Associated Students of the University of California

Lynn Koll Martin, Board Member, Bear Boosters

David Osborne, former President, UC-Berkeley Foundation

Martin Sanchez-Jankowski, Professor of Sociology

Carl Stoney, President-elect, California Alumni Association

Bud Travers, Assistant to the Vice Chancellor—Development

Aaron Wildavsky, Professor of Political Science

APPENDIX 3. WORK OF THE COMMITTEE

During the course of the committee's work, we held interviews—either before the whole Committee, before subcommittees or singly—with the following persons or groups:

- Chancellor Chang-lin Tien
- Vice Chancellor John Heilbron
- Vice Chancellor—Undergraduate Affairs W. Russell Ellis
- Vice Chancellor—Business and Administrative Services Daniel Boggan
- Former Vice Chancellor—Development Watson M. Laetsch
- The Divisional Council of the Berkeley Division of the Academic Senate
- The major athletic directors—David Maggard, Lue Lilly, and William Manning and the acting athletic director, Rick Greenspan
- The football coach (Bruce Snyder) and the men's basketball coach (Lou Campanelli)
- Coaches of all other intercollegiate and club sports (two group meetings with the entire committee)
- Staff members of the Men's Athletic Department and the Women's Athletic Department
- The chair of the Department of Physical Education, Roberta Park
- Director of the Athletic Study Center Jerrold Takahashi
- Officers and other representatives from the Berkeley Foundation, California Alumni Association, Bear Backers and Bear Boosters

- Approximately thirty-six student-athletes from football, men's basketball, women's basketball, and a variety of other sports

- Selected representatives from athletic programs on other university campuses

In addition, the committee received dozens of written and oral communications from persons interested in the athletic programs at Berkeley. The committee expresses its appreciation to those on whom we called and who called on us for their interest and cooperation.

In addition to interviewing, the committee consulted many written documents on Berkeley's and other campus's athletic programs. We met together as a committee approximately ten times to plan, digest information, discuss and decide on issues, and review drafts of this report.

NOTE

1. Report of the Task Force on Lower Division Education in the University of California (Smelser report), 1986; Report of the Commission on Response to a Changing Student Body (Maslach report), 1990.

ELEVEN

Thanksgiving Dinner Report (1977)

FROM 1977 TO 1979 I was director of the Education Abroad Program of the University of California for the United Kingdom and Ireland. This meant supervising the academic study and being a benevolent uncle for some 135 students each of those two years. While the students were scattered over more than a dozen campuses, I was stationed at the administrative office on Strutton Ground near Westminster Abbey, and my family and I lived in Highgate in North London.

At that time the prevailing practice was for the director and associate director to host as many of the students as could attend at a dinner in our homes on the Saturday after Thanksgiving Day. (The practice was subsequently watered down to a hosted dinner in a London hotel restaurant.) The dinner was an important and meaningful occasion for the students at that time of year and a massive operation for the directors, almost military in its demands for coordination.

After my first Thanksgiving Dinner in 1977 I was possessed to write a satirical director's report on the occasion to Bill Allaway, the director of the Education Abroad Program on the Santa Barbara campus. When Bill had interviewed me for the job in late 1976, he invited my wife, Sharin, to the interview, and among other questions he asked her about preparing a dinner for almost 100 students at Thanksgiving. She must have given the right answers; I won the job.

The following report is based on only slightly distorted truths. I wrote it mainly for therapeutic reasons, to unburden myself of the chaotic experience of hosting the event, but I took the occasion to poke fun at the academic-bureaucratic mentality of university life. I present it as a light contrast to the other sober, straight-faced reports in this section. In doing so I hope to contribute modestly to what Alan Dundes, the famous folklorist, referred to as "the paperwork empire" of urban and bureaucratic humor (Dundes and Pagter, 1975).

Highgate, December 1, 1977

Dr. William Allaway
Director
Education Abroad Program
Santa Barbara, CA

Dear Bill:

This communication constitutes an extraordinary report from the United Kingdom/Ireland, University of California, Education Abroad Program office. I know there is nothing mandatory about submitting a Thanksgiving Dinner Report to Santa Barbara. In fact, I have re-read the director's manual in the past few days, and could find no written reference to such a report. I suppose, too, that I could have waited until June and included this report as a subreport of the larger Director's Annual Report. But I choose to submit it now. Why, you might be asking, have I come to the decision to submit the Thanksgiving Dinner Report to the Santa Barbara office, when it is not part of the director's normal duties?

The reason is that I know you personally *care* about Thanksgiving dinner, and will be both gratified and relieved at receiving this report. You have never actually confessed your concern, but I definitely discerned it at our very first meeting, at which you closely questioned my wife, Sharin, on the precise quality of her feelings about the prospect of preparing such a dinner. So intense was your interest on that occasion that I know that you must have spent much of Saturday, November 26—the actual day of the dinner—brooding over whether it was a success or failure. I imagine that you are still curious and anxious. For these reasons I feel it important to submit you a direct report without further delay.

Planning for the event began early. I cannot overemphasize the importance of early planning. Future directors and their spouses should know this. An important part of the early planning was to place a telephone call to Ruth Eigner, who played a key role in the Thanksgiving dinners of 1975 and 1976. This phone call proved enormously helpful with respect to what, how much, and where to buy. Perhaps her most important piece of advice concerned the issue of green peas. She warned, "avoid serving green peas." Upon being pressed for reasons she said that green peas have a way of falling off plates, and that they fall between things. The main things they fall between, moreover, are students' shoes and the carpet. This suggestion made good sense to all of us, except Alan Nelson [associate director], whose house has a carpet that is pea-green in color. He forcefully presented the argument that it was in *his* house that the green peas were going to be served, and if crushed they would not show on his carpet. He actually went so far as to suggest that crushed green peas might be of some organic value to the carpet, and might even extend its life. After weighing the arguments, I ruled against green peas. As a matter of fact, I was sufficiently impressed with Ruth Eigner's advice that I submitted to staff the idea of imposing a *general* size limitation on things served, thinking, perhaps, that no single item should be smaller than an American-size golf ball. This idea proved overdrawn, largely because it was too restrictive. It would, for instance, have ruled out carrot sticks and sliced cucumbers, which proved to be a refreshing change from the diet of overcooked vegetables that our students had been eating in various universities' dining halls.

One reason for the importance of advance planning is that you have to leave enough time for the plan to fail in a variety of ways. The first way it fails is that you cannot buy what you want where you want. The British have a long-standing and unchallenged tradition of assuring that if you have a long list of items to buy, no more than one, and sometimes none, will be purchasable in the same store or shop. We discovered that for every hundred different kinds of items you might wish to buy, approximately forty-three of these have just been sold out, and another thirty-seven were "on order." The pumpkin problem illustrates this principle nicely. First, of course, we had the issue of fresh versus tinned pumpkin. One of the difficult problems concerning fresh pumpkin is that nobody could be quite sure if what the British call a pumpkin constitutes a genuine American Thanksgiving-type pumpkin.

Assuming we could have solved that issue, we had next to face the prospect of grinding and mashing about 50 pounds of pumpkin. Pumpkin meat is tough, and that would have been a major endeavor, no matter what means we used. Besides, in the end the issue of too-much-work-grinding-pumpkin was overwhelmed by the issue of the Mouli food mill, to which I will refer presently. With respect to tinned pumpkin, the question was one of availability. Shop after shop indicated either that they didn't know what it was, that it didn't exist, or that we were mad to be searching for tinned pumpkin. We did locate one special American store in the Bayswater area, but its phone was disconnected. As a last act of desperation, Sharin telephoned Harrods, which for some reason had stocked up on thirty or forty cases of tinned Canadian pumpkin. Since the day was looming, we jumped on the chance and bought twenty-four tins.

I mentioned the Mouli food mill. You probably know that it is a French product, a grinder of food. The original motive for wanting a Mouli mill was for mashing thirty pounds of potatoes for the dinner (my pet scheme and only real contribution). We had trouble finding a Mouli. Actually, that statement is not quite accurate; we had trouble finding a normal-size Mouli. Most places didn't have any Mouli's but a few shops had a Mouli that appeared to have a holding capacity of about a half-cup. I do not know what such a Mouli is meant to grind or mash, but a quick calculation on my part indicated that it would take between 115 and 120 millfulls to complete the potatoes. (At the same moment I decided in favor of tinned pumpkin.) Sharin found one shop where they knew what a big Mouli was, and the owner promised to put in an order for one to arrive on Wednesday before the Saturday dinner. It didn't come in on Wednesday, nor on Thursday. In a panic, Sharin started canvassing one shop after another, and finally located, in an out-of-the-way kitchen store, London's only large Mouli food mill, in the nick of time. It was our next-to-last purchase, the last being a deep plastic garbage pail that was needed to keep fresh (by submerging in water) several hundred carrot-sticks that the Nelsons had prepared.

You should also be aware of the paper plate problem. I do not want to appear critical of the British paper manufacturing industry, but I have to say that paper plates are not their *forte*. Ruth Eigner testified to that. She had used the standard British paper plates the year before, and within a matter of minutes after receiving a portion of moist turkey, the plate would wilt over one's hand like a three-day-old piece of lettuce, making it difficult to keep green peas and other types of food from falling off.

Judy Nelson suggested one attack on the problem, namely to use two paper plates per person, one on top of the other. It was a constructive thought, but a direct experiment revealed that the main difference was that after five minutes the plates resembled two rather than one piece of wilted lettuce. We were in deep trouble. By Thursday we had been able to find nothing but the vulnerable paper plates, and not a single solid, plastic-covered, partitioned, American-type paper plate could be found in London. We were all frantic and desperate. I considered the most radical of solutions, telephoning you long-distance, asking you to go to Safeway to buy 170 small and 85 large plastic covered paper plates, and to air mail them by special delivery to us. Indeed, I was even ready to expend director's contingency funds to finance that request. At the eleventh hour, however—and this has to be the high moment of the pre-Thanksgiving day searches—Sharin found some sturdy, plastic-covered partitioned plates at the John Lewis store, which had failed us on almost all other items. They worked well, and cut the spillage rate way down. We tried to wash them and save them, but this didn't work for those that had knife-cuts through the plastic coating; those plates got as soggy as the ordinary ones would have.

Actually, working on the paper plate problem served to deepen my thinking on the issue of green peas. After considering the matter carefully, I have decided that it is not completely fair to claim that green peas, *as such,* constitute the problem. To think that way is to penetrate the issue only superficially. Rather, it is when you begin to think of green peas *in combination with* soggy paper plates that you advance toward grasping its essence. In fact, I would put the primary onus on the plates rather than the peas; almost *anything* would fall off those plates. When you move beyond thinking about green peas alone, in short, the green-pea issue itself becomes much less significant and pressing. I thought I would pass this insight on to you, so that you might share it in future with directors-elect and their spouses.

On the basis of our experience, I venture a recommendation. Even though we solved the paper plate problem this year, that is no guarantee that it will be solved in future years. In fact, I think we depleted John Lewis's inventory of plastic-coated, partitioned plates and even an advance order might not produce more. I suggest that you require of all incoming directors and their spouses that they personally bring in a supply of Safeway paper plates for a dinner for eighty to a hundred students. This should be made a regular part of the director's responsibilities and it should be communicated to the interviewees in advance of actually offering them the position, so they will be aware of the exact conditions of appointment. You might even think of raising the removal allowance from $600 to $610 to cover the additional responsibility. It would prove a useful policy, I am certain. For one thing, it would provide another nice American touch. Also, it would make for one less frantic search in November. And, to be frank, I know of no measure short of this that would contain the green-pea problem so effectively and so permanently.

So much for planning. I should also give you a brief account of the dinner itself. Though there had been weeks of time-consuming preparatory activities, things heated up during the 24 hours leading up to the dinner. The Nelsons, responsible for the vegetables (except for actually cooking and mashing the potatoes) brought in several of our Westfield College students—on pain of academic punishment, I believe—to spend Friday afternoon peeling. I went over to the Nelsons' house that day and discovered them knee-deep in peelings and with hands glued to the peeling devices. All the vegetables were in ample supply, but something had gone wrong on the carrot front. I think somebody was working on the formula that the students would be so starved for fresh vegetables that we should calculate a half-pound of carrots per student. As I mentioned, that was when Judy was forced to purchase the plastic garbage can. In keeping with the spirit of feasting and generosity that pervaded the holiday, I retrieved fifteen pounds of carrot and cucumber peelings—being certain to separate the potato peelings from them—put them into plastic bags, and presented them to our landlady, who keeps two rabbits in her garden.

Saturday morning was nothing short of chaotic. Sharin was frantically attempting to bake the pumpkin pies while attending to our nine-year-old son, Joseph, who had selected that morning to come down with a strep throat. I was not at the Nelsons, but it was reported that they spent much of the morning borrowing plates from neighbors so they could have something to put the excess supply of carrot sticks on. I had saved the operation of cooking and running the potatoes through the Mouli until Saturday morning, so they would be fresh and hopefully hot. It proved a bigger task than I had anticipated, and I soon fell behind schedule. I will not burden you with a detailed account of that morning, but I will point out that asking a person to send thirty pounds of steaming potatoes through a Mouli on a Saturday morning is a certain way to convince him of the limits of human capacity. The only really bad moment came when a boiling potato toppled over the rim of the Mouli and fell into my shoe-top, causing minor skin burns. It was at this moment of physical pain that I had my only second thoughts about the whole enterprise. I was able to step back, as it were, and look at myself, a pathetic little creature on hands and knees on the kitchen floor, moving my arm repetitiously in an idiotic circular fashion, forcing whole boiled potatoes into potato paste. It was only at this moment that I permitted myself to ask the hitherto-unasked question, "Is this the sort of thing that a director of an Education Abroad program of the University of California ought to be doing?" It was only a fleeting query, however. I pressed it from my mind and attacked the Mouli and the potatoes with renewed energy.

The dinner itself was a great success, if the amounts consumed and the raves of the students are any measure. I attribute the success largely to the quality of the food and its preparation, but I also think we can claim with some pride that we were able to pull off the event without major disaster. Actually, we evolved, without plan, a crude division of labor during the event that served well. Alan hauled large containers of food around, retrieved them when they were empty; Judy provided supplies of carrot sticks and other raw vegetables and took charge of mixing the green salad (I contributed $1\frac{1}{2}$ quarts of my special salad dressing). Sharin was in charge of the pumpkin pie (which drew most compliments); and Bernie [my secretary] grandly entertained students, occasionally pausing to pour me a glass of white wine, which was essential to keep me going while carving the two thirty-five-pound turkeys. There were only two notes that were other than positive. First, in carving the birds, I wrecked those muscles in the right arm that are activated when one carves; that in itself wouldn't have been so bad, but if you add those wrecked muscles to those that were wrecked in rotat-ing the Mouli, the arm was virtually gone by late afternoon. Second, in the confusion, I had neglected to respond to a request by Judy that I bring two very large wooden salad-mixing forks we own, and she had to mix the salad in a huge washbasin on the kitchen floor with two teaspoons as implements. I should assure you, however that this was virtually the only instance of inelegance at the party.

That constitutes my report. Please feel free to show it to all members of your Santa Barbara staff, as well as to our superiors, including your new chancellor [Robert Huttenback] (who likes almost everything associated with food and feasting) and even to the governor [Jerry Brown] (who dislikes elitist professors who shun students; I can tell you that I felt very un-elitish and dedicated to students when I was mashing the potatoes on the kitchen floor).

Respectfully submitted,
Neil J. Smelser, Director

REFERENCE

Dundes, Alan, and Carl R. Pagter. 1975. *Urban Folklore from the Paperwork Empire.* Austin, TX: American Folklore Society.

INDEX

academic freedom, 25, 62, 69, 78, 79, 111, 182, 230; "political correctness" as threat to, 115, 169

Academic Planning and Program Review Board, 234

academic planning council (APC), 225–26

Academic Senate, Berkeley Division, 13, 15, 27, 51, 61, 102; academic freedom supported by, 62; and affirmative action, 124, 135; Committee on Educational Policy, 56, 69, 95, 233, 234; Divisional Council of, 358; educational reforms proposed to, 42; Emergency Executive Committee, 21–23, 28, 37, 42, 53, 95; faculty code of conduct adopted by, 70; and intercollegiate athletics, 332, 341, 349–50; and Kirkpatrick lectures, 85; during obscenity crisis, 36, 38; "puff-in" at, 32; Representative Assembly created by, 70; Third World College proposal referred to, 93; undergraduate participation in, 73

Academic Senate, systemwide, 2, 80, 183, 194, 207, 222–25; Academic Council of, 310–12; affirmative action supported by, 141, 146; Intersegmental Committee of, 314; and lower division education, 281, 285, 294, 296, 314; teaching role of organized research units controlled by, 203; UC Press and, 201

advising, academic, 328; for student-athletes, 347

affirmative action, 110, 124–51, 176, 191, 194, 250, 316, 318; in administrative staff hiring and advancement, 139; ambiguity in implementation of, 132–34; cultural context of, 128–30; in faculty recruitment, 140–41; in graduate admissions, 140; historical context of, 125–28; political context of, 130–32; regental action on, 89, 144–51; trends in practices of, 134–38; in undergraduate admissions, 139–40

Afghanistan War, 89

African Americans, 112, 126, 132, 133, 168, 209; and *Bakke* decision, 145; in community college system, 164; and faculty hiring practices, 114; redress of injustices against, 127; regental appointment of, 144

Agler, Harry, 357

Alberts, Bruce, 220

Allaway, William, 360–67

Allgood, Fred, 14

Alpha Epsilon Pi, 31

Altbach, Roger, 155

alumni, 83, 94, 101, 113, 116, 146, 184–85, 269, 297; Asian-American, 86; constituency of, 64, 81, 87; and intercollegiate athletics, 330, 331, 333–34, 343, 344, 349, 355, 357; preferential admission of children of, 131

American Academy of Arts and Sciences, 53, 107, 217

American Council of Education, 72

American Federation of State, County and Municipal Employees (AFSCME), 185

American Federation of Teachers, 50, 69

American History and Institution courses, 93

American Legion, 88

American Sociological Association, 11; Council of, 10

American Sociological Review, 11, 55

antiwar movement, 25, 30, 43–49, 58, 66, 89, 90, 108, 130

Aptheker, Bettina, 41, 45

Articulation System Stimulating Interinstitutional Student Transfer (ASSIST), 310

Arts and Sciences, 220, 239–42, 267, 274n4

ascription, 110, 127–28, 130–31

Ashby, Eric, 155

Asians, 112, 146, 168, 209; affirmative action and, 127, 132–33; immigration of, 108; and SARS epidemic, 86

assistant professors, 207

Associated Students of the University of California (ASUC), 29–30, 36, 39, 73–74, 357; Office of Academic Affairs, 300

Association of American Colleges, 279, 284

athletic programs. *See* intercollegiate athletics

Atkin, J. Myron, 237

Atkinson, Richard, 149, 174, 221–22

attribution, role in crisis escalation of, 91–92

authority: by default, 49–51; delegation of, 80, 194

Bakke case, 133, 145, 146

Baldwin, James, 20

Barber, Elinor, 107

Bay Area Writing Project, 249, 256, 273

Bear Backers, 355–58

Bear Boosters, 358

Berdahl, Robert, 76, 77

Berger, Stanley, 234–36, 249, 250; Committee Report, 269–73, 276n10

Berkeley, University of California at: Academic Planning Committee, 234; Academic Planning and Program Review Board (APPRB), 275–76n10; Academic Senate (*see* Academic Senate, Berkeley Division); antiwar protests at, 43–49; Athletic Study Center, 332, 347, 348, 351, 353–54, 358; Athletics Department, 341, 358; authority by default at, 49–51; Budget and Interdepartmental Relations Committee, 233, 234, 237; Center for Studies in Higher Education, 2, 237, 247, 265, 271; Chancellor's Advisory Committee on Intercollegiate Athletics, 349; Chancellor's Office, 234 *(see also specific chancellors);* College of Letters and Science, 258; Courses Committee, 50; crisis and change at, 56–75; Educational Policy Committee, 234; embeddedness in larger society of, 81–82; English Department, 42, 326; Ethnic Studies Department, 67, 71; German Department, 62; Graduate Council, 194, 234, 269, 272, 273;

Institute for Human Learning, 247;
Institute of Human Development,
247; Institute of Industrial Relations,
2, 202; intercollegiate athletics at,
330–59; lower division courses at,
290, 300, 303; obscenity crisis at, 25,
30–40; Office of Dean of Students,
33, 53; Physical Education Depart-
ment, 331, 338, 340, 358; Physics
Department, 37, 235; Pieces of Paper
Committee, 52–53; Political
Economy of Industrial Societies
group major, 321; Political Science
Department, 326; Psychology
Department, 258, 264, 271; Religious
Studies Program, 67; School of Busi-
ness Administration, 237, 266;
School of Education (*see* Education,
Graduate School of, Berkeley);
School of Engineering, 34, 254, 266;
School of Human Resources, 259;
School of Journalism, 67; School of
Public Affairs, 67; School of Public
Health, 1, 254, 259; School of Social
Welfare, 259; sit-ins at, 11, 20–25, 50;
Sociology Department, 77; structural
complexity of, 80; Student Judicial
Committee, 29; student political
activity at, 9–55 (*see also* Free Speech
Movement); Student Union, 25, 27,
31, 46, 50; student-oriented educa-
tional reform at, 24–25, 41–43; sur-
prises at, 76–77, 82–97; Women's
Athletic Council, 347
Berkeley Daily Gazette, 39
Berkeley University Teachers' Union,
44
Berlin, Free University of, 57
Black Panther Party, 84
blacks. *See* African Americans
Boalt Law School (Berkeley), 21, 52
Board of Educational Development
(BED) 43, 70–71, 84–85
board of regents, 51–53, 80, 94, 102, 103,
160–61, 343; alumni members of, 184;
and affirmative action, 89, 129, 138,
144–51; as constituency, 81, 83, 87,
88, 101; and dynamics of escalation,

91–92; and "Eldridge Cleaver"
course, 84; expectations of, 187–89;
governance and, 176, 177, 184,
187–90, 192–97, 208, 224; and Kirk-
patrick lectures, 85; and lower divi-
sion eduction, 280; response to crisis
of, 63–66, 68–69; and student politi-
cal activities, 16, 20, 23, 24, 28–30,
32, 34–38, 41
Boggan, Daniel, 358
Bond, Thomas, 325
Borrowman, Merle, 235, 249
Bowker, Albert, 237
Boyer, Ernest, 155
Brown, Edmund "Pat," 35
Brown, Jerry, 144, 367
Brown, Willie, 88
Bruce, Lenny, 31–32
Bundy, McGeorge, 46
Burdick, Eugene, 46
bureaucracy, generic characteristics of,
227–28
Burnstein, Malcolm, 21–23
Bush, George H. W., 142

Caen, Herb, 38
Cal Camp, 30
California, University of, 174–78 (*see also
specific campuses);* academic departments in, 204–6; centralization of,
195–96; constituencies of, 178–92;
Education Abroad Program of, 200–
201; institutional flexibility of,
221–30; national laboratories in,
198–99; organized research units in,
202–4; press of, 201–2; problems
facing, 208–21; relations between systemwide office and campuses of,
193–95; second-class citizenship
in, 206–8; vice presidencies of,
196–98
California Alumni Association, 358
California Articulation Numbering
System (CAN), 282, 309, 310
California Civil Rights Initiative, 128–29,
148–51
California Legislature, 189–90, 284;
Assembly, 88; Senate, 84

California Postsecondary Education Commission, 156, 158, 307
California State Board of Education, 161
California State University (CSU) system, 170n1, 186–87, 190, 206, 209–10, 308, 309
Cal Sports 80s Campaign, 355
Cambodia, American incursion into, 57, 73, 86, 183
Cambridge University, 42, 332–33
Campanelli, Lou, 358
Campbell, Glen, 85, 94
Campus Women for Peace, 44
capital punishment, protests against, 58
Capps, Walter, 325
Carnegie Commission on Higher Education, 56; Project on Undergraduate Education, 56; Technical Advisory Committee (TAC), 56
Carter, Edwin, 35
Carter, Jimmy, 142
Central Intelligence Agency (CIA), 66
centralization, 195–96
Chamberlain, Keith, 50
Cheadle, Vernon, 200
Cheit, Earl F., 27, 235, 237; Committee Report, 268–69
Chessman, Caryl, 58
Chicago, University of, 237, 241, 336
Chicago Seven trial, 45
Chicanos, 209
Christopher, Marilyn, 273
Citrin, Jack, 357
Civil Rights movement, 58, 88, 108, 126, 127
Clark, Burton, 155
Clark, Katherine, 325
Cleaver, Eldridge, 57, 65, 72, 84, 87, 103
Clifford, Geraldine, 237, 248
clinical faculty, 207
Clinton, Bill, 142, 143, 151
Cold War, 203, 217–19
Cole, Jonathan, 107
College Eight, 325
Colleges of Letters and Science, 182
Columbia Community College, 310
Columbia University, 107, 237, 241, 306; political turmoil at, 57

Colvig, Ray, 13, 54
Commission on Education, Report of, 233–78
Committee, The, 95
Committee for Non-Violent Action, 44
committees on academic personnel (CAPs), 182, 204
Communist Party, 62
communities, relations between campuses and, 191
Community College System (CCS), 186, 206
Computer Literacy courses, 312
Condren, Clive, 156
Coney, Donald, 50
Conference on Higher Education (Princeton, 1996), 124–25
Congress, U.S., 142, 143, 191
Connerly, Ward, 128, 144, 146, 149, 150
Constance, Lincoln, 47
constituencies, 62–65, 69, 78–79, 86–87, 96, 257; and affirmative action, 141, 148; complex structure of, 80–81, 98; "external," 81; of faculty members, 249; governance and, 161, 174–78, 181–85, 189–91, 206, 212, 216, 228; heterogeneous composition of, 318; and intercollegiate athletics, 335, 339; minority, 112; origins and characteristics of, 87–90; relationship with, 99; role in crisis escalation of, 91–92
consultation, 194–95
Contemporary Social Issues courses, 312
Cooperstein, Bruce, 325
Coordinating Council for Higher Education, 161, 307
Cortes, Carlos, 325
Council for an Academic Community, 69
Council of Deans, 95
Council of Graduate Deans, 182
Cowell Hospital (Berkeley), 2, 18, 19
Cox, Stephen, 219
Crittenden, Rupert, 20, 21
Cromwell, Oliver, 53
Cross, Patricia, 155
Cuban-Americans, 132
Cummins, John F., 76–77, 95, 357

Cunningham, Thomas J., 23
curricular reform: affirmative action and,
137; in lower division education, 281,
282, 289–93, 327; student-oriented,
24–25, 41–43

Daily Californian, The, 16, 36, 39, 44, 46,
149
Darwinism, 119
Davis, Angela, 68, 88, 103
Davis, Barbara Gross, 357
Davis, University of California at, 2,
278n19, 326; affirmative action at,
133, 140, 144, 149; lower division
courses at, 300; Rhetoric Department, 326; School of Home Economics, 241
deconstructionism, 119
delegation, 80, 194
Democratic Party, 84, 126, 127, 142, 144,
149; 1968 National Convention
(Chicago), 45
Deukmejian, George, 88, 143
Dickinson, Julia, 237
diversity, 81, 107–23, 316–18 (*see also* affirmative action); ambivalence towards,
117–22; components of debate over,
110–11; in context of elite institutions, 109; political and social effects
of, 168–70; vulnerability to group
conflict over, 111–14
Dow Chemical, 66
Dundes, Alan, 361

Education, Graduate School of, Berkeley,
3, 233–78; Applied Social Research
and Humanistic Studies (ASRHS)
Division, 244, 275n9; California
Re-Ed program, 244; Curriculum
and Instruction Division, 270; Educational Psychology Division, 249,
258, 264, 270, 275n9; Field Applications Laboratory, 276n15; Higher
Education, Finance and School
Administration (HEFSA) Division,
249, 271, 275n9, 276n12, n13;
Humanistic and Policy Studies Division, 269; Instructional Research

Curriculum Development (IRCD)
Division, 245, 275n9; Instructional
Research Laboratory, 276n15; Language and Reading (L & R) Division, 245, 275n9; Learning Center,
265; Media-Telecommunications
Laboratory, 276n15; Office of Teaching Innovation and Evaluation Services (TIES), 265; Office of the
Dean, 249; Science and Mathematics
Education Division, 276n12; Teacher
Education Division, 245, 271–72,
275n9
Education Abroad Program, 200 (EAP);
for the United Kingdom and Ireland,
2, 360–67
Educational Policy Committee, 194
Education at Berkeley (Muscatine committee report), 70
egalitarianism: balance between excellence
and, 158–59, 163; short-changing of,
163–64
Eigner, Ruth, 362, 363
Eisenhower, Dwight D., 58
Ellis, W. Russell, 357
endowments, athletic, 354–55
Energy, U.S. Department of, 189, 199
English as a Second Language courses,
301
entitlement, 110–12, 131, 136, 138
escalation, dynamics of, 90–94
ethnic studies, 57, 67, 71, 121, 137
excellence: balance between egalitarianism
and, 158–59, 163; competitive, 109

faculty: affirmative action and, 133,
140–41, 149–50; athletics and, 332,
347–51; delegation of authority to,
194; expectations of, 182, 182–84;
hierarchy of, 207; impact of crisis
and change on, 60–73; for lower
division courses, 281, 283, 293–302,
327; and student political activities,
20, 24–28, 32–34, 36–45, 51–53
Faculty Committee on Academic
Freedom, 73
Faculty Committee on Student Policy
Activity, 27, 34, 37, 39

Faculty Committee on Student Political
   Activity, 34
Faculty Welfare Committee, 194
Farmer, James, 20
Federal Bureau of Investigation (FBI),
   84
feminism. *See* women's movement
Ferlinghetti, Lawrence, 20
Filthy Speech Movement, 30, 56, 82–84,
   87, 91, 93, 103
Fitchen, Patricia, 325
flexibility, institutional, 221–30
Foote Commission, 70
Franck, Peter, 37
Frazer, William R., 200, 328
Freedom Summer, 88
Free Speech Movement (FSM), 9–13,
   15–22, 57, 64, 66, 70, 72, 88, 94;
   administration restrictions triggering,
   10–11, 63, 87; Associated Students of
   the University of California and, 73;
   collapse of, 43; December 1964
   Sproul Hall sit-in of, 11, 20, 69, 83;
   divergent faculty partnership during,
   90; educational reform advocated
   by, 42; Graduate Coordinating
   Committee of, 26, 50; during
   obscenity crisis, 34, 36–38, 91; rules
   on student political activity in
   aftermath of, 25–26, 28, 30; Searle
   and, 17–18; social-psychological
   complexities of, 19; Steering Committee of, 13, 17, 21, 26, 33, 36, 38,
   40–41, 54
Free Student Union (FSU), 41, 43, 50
Free University, 30
Freudianism, 119
full-time equivalent (FTE), 203, 205, 235,
   248, 257, 261, 273, 295

Gardner, David, 2, 88, 279–80
Geiger, Roger, 155
general education, 43, 279, 290, 292,
   308–14; majors and, 322, 327; mission
   of, 287; models for, 42, 306; transferring, 281–83
Glenny, Lyman, 155, 237
Glick, Ira, 237

Goffman, Erving, 10
Goldberg, Art, 38, 54
Goldberg, Suzanne, 21, 26, 34, 37, 47
Goldwater, Barry, 89
Gondoliers, The (Gilbert and Sullivan),
   157
Goodman, Paul, 20
Gordon, Julie, 325
graduate students (*see also* teaching assis-
   tants); affirmative action in admis-
   sions of, 133, 140; expectations of,
   181; in education (*see* Education,
   Graduate School of, Berkeley)
Graubard, Stephen, 107
Gray, James, 237
Great Britain: education abroad program
   in, 2, 360–67; higher education in,
   240. *See also* Cambridge University;
   Oxford University
Great Depression, 131
Great Society, 127
Greenspan, Rick, 358
Gulf War, 89
Guthrie, James, 237

Hafner, Richard, 13, 27, 54
Hart, Gary, 189
Harvard University, 1, 13, 241; constituen-
   cies at, 178; Graduate School of Edu-
   cation, 237, 239, 262; lower division
   courses at, 293, 298, 302, 306; politi-
   cal turmoil at, 57
hate speech, laws against, 112
Hayden, Tom, 189
Hayes, William, 77
Head Start, 126
Health and Human Services, U.S.
   Department of, 191
Health, Education, and Welfare, U.S.
   Department of, 130
Heilbron, John, 358
Heirich, Max, 11, 92
Heydman, Abbey, 237
Heyman, I. Michael, 85, 88, 95, 141,
   233
Heyns, Roger, 9, 17, 29, 64, 68, 90, 95;
   and antiwar activism, 45, 49; bunker
   mentality in administration of, 52;

California State Senate censure of,
84; Third World College supported
by, 93
Hirsch, Morris, 45
Hispanics. *See* Latinos/Hispanics
Hitch, Charles J., 72, 135
Hoffman, Abbie, 45
Hoffman, Alex, 21, 32
Hotchkis, Preston, 357
House Un-American Activities Commit-
tee, 58
Hu, Evelyn, 326
Hume, David, 280
Hurwitt, Robert, 31
Hussein, Saddam, 89
Huttenback, Robert, 367
Hutton, Bobby, 84

identity politics, 131
ignorance, role in crisis escalation of,
91–92
imagination, role in crisis escalation of,
91–92
immigration, 89, 108, 143–45, 348
Institutes of Psychoanalysis, 274n3
institutional flexibility, 221–30
Intercampus Arts Program, 226
intercollegiate athletics, 330–59; facilities
for, 355–56; faculty and, 332, 348–51;
financing of, 332, 351–55; mission of,
331; organization of program, 331,
338–42; reporting relations of athletic
director, 342–44; students in, 332,
345–48
Interfaith Workers, 50
internationalization, 282, 315–18
Irish Catholics, 108
Irvine, University of California at, 2,
278n19; affirmative action at, 140,
146; English Department, 325;
German Department, 326; School of
Social Sciences, 321
Italian Americans, 120

Jackson State University, 85–86, 183
Jameson, Andrew G., 237
Janis, Irving, 97
Jellen, Mayra, 26

Jews, 108, 112
Johns Hopkins University, 336
Johnson, Lyndon Baines, 44, 46, 89, 126,
127
Joint UC-DOE Issues Resolution Com-
mittee, 199
Jorgenson, Dale, 52
Jowitt, Kenneth, 326
Judge, Harry, 237
Justice Department, U.S., 151

Karplus, Robert, 235, 237, 245, 248, 253,
257, 262
Katz, Eli, 62
Kennedy, John F., 88, 126
Kennedy, Robert F., 84, 126
Kent State University, 85–86, 183
Kerr, Clark, 2, 12, 62, 65, 155, 222, 237;
background as labor-management
negotiator of, 17; firing of, 56, 68,
149; and Lenny Bruce's proposed
campus appearance, 32; Meyerson
and, 51; and obscenity crisis,
34–36
King, Martin Luther, Jr., 84
Kirkpatrick, Jeane, 85, 91, 94, 103
knowledge, changing character of, 319–21;
educational consequences of,
322–25
Kornhauser, William, 32
Kurzweil, Jack, 45

Labor, U.S. Department of, 130, 191
labor unions, 41, 130, 131, 142, 202, 315;
negotiations between management
and, 17; teaching assistants in, 181
Ladd-Lipset survey, 239
Lady Chatterley's Lover (Lawrence), 33
Laetsch, Watson M., 358
Latinos/Hispanics, 112, 126, 127, 132, 133,
168, 209; and *Bakke* decision, 145; in
community college system, 164; and
faculty hiring practices, 114; immigration of, 108
Lawrence, D. H., 33
Lawrence, John, 16
Lawrence Berkeley National Laboratory,
3, 198

multiculturalism, 108, 110, 122, 137, 282, 314, 317
Mundell, N. M., 51
Mura, Laura, 31
Muscatine, Charles, 42, 43, 70
Myrdal, Gunnar, 125–26

Nash, Gary, 326
Nation, The, 17
National Academy of Sciences, 220–21
National Collegiate Athletic Association (NCAA), 331, 341, 346, 347, 349, 357
National Endowment for the Humanities, 279, 284
National Institute of Education, 279, 284
national laboratories, 2–3, 198–99
National Opinion Research Center, 274n2
Native Americans, 126, 132, 133, 209; and *Bakke* decision, 145; and faculty hiring practices, 114; redress of injustices against, 127
Navy table incident, 57, 66
Nelson, Alan, 362, 363, 365, 366
Nelson, Judy, 363–66
Neuhoff, Virginia, 237
Nevada, University of, at Las Vegas, 336
New York, City College of, 58
New York, City University of, 159
New York, State University of, Buffalo, 53
New York Review of Books, 202
New York Times, The, 129; *Book Review,* 202
Newton, Carol, 326
Newton, Huey, 84
Nixon, Richard, 142
Northwestern University, 336
Notre Dame University, 336

Oakland Army Terminal, 45, 56
Oakland Induction Center, 57, 66
Oakland Tribune, 35, 39
obscenity, conflicts over, 25, 30–40, 82–84
O'Connor, June, 326

Olympic sports, 337, 339
O'Neill, Robert, 52
operational readiness units, 99
Orbach, Ray, 219
Organic Act (1868), 78
Organization for Economic Cooperation and Development (OECD), 155–59, 169
organized research units (ORUs), 202–4, 207, 261, 269, 271, 273
Osborne, David, 357
Oxford University, 42, 293; Department of Educational Studies, 237

Pacific Island peoples, 127, 132
Pacific Ten Conference (Pac-10), 330, 337, 349, 354–56
Palestinian Literature course, 87, 103
Parents Defense Committee for Berkeley Students, 20
Park, Roberta, 358
Participant Education, Committee on, 71
Patriot Act (2001), 87
Peace and Freedom Party, 84
Peltason, Jack, 2, 146, 148, 173–74
Pennsylvania, University of, 53
People's Park, 57, 65, 66, 69, 90, 91, 93, 103
Petris, Nick, 189
Pister, Karl, 219, 220
pluralism, 73, 115, 169
"political correctness," 112, 115, 169
Pope, Saxon, 18, 184
Powelson, David H., 19
preferential treatment, 127–29, 136, 139, 144
President's Advisory Council for the National Laboratories, 198
Princeton University, 124–25, 241, 336
Project X, 76–77, 96, 99
Proposition 187, 144
Proposition 209, 89
Provisional Committee to Protect Student Rights, 37
psychoanalysis, 18, 19

QUEEF Complex, 164–66

Text:	11.25/13.5 Adobe Garamond
Display:	Adobe Garamond
Compositor:	Toppan Best-set Premedia Limited
Indexer:	Ruth Elwell
Printer and Binder:	Sheridan Books, Inc.